Problem Sol

MW01223581

Problem Solving with C

Second Edition

M.T. SOMASHEKARA
Department of Computer Science and Applications
Bangalore University, Bengaluru

D.S. GURU
Department of Studies in Computer Science
University of Mysore, Mysuru

K.S. MANJUNATHA
Department of Computer Science
Maharani's Science College for Women, Mysuru

PHI Learning Private Limited
Delhi-110092
2019

₹ 595.00

PROBLEM SOLVING WITH C, Second Edition
M.T. Somashekara, D.S. Guru and K.S. Manjunatha

ISBN-978-93-87472-22-8 (Print Book)
978-93-87472-21-1 (eBook)

The export rights of this book are vested solely with the publisher.

Fifth Printing (Second Edition)   ...   ...   **June, 2019**

Published by Asoke K. Ghosh, PHI Learning Private Limited, Rimjhim House, 111, Patparganj Industrial Estate, Delhi-110092 and Printed by Rajkamal Electric Press, Plot No. 2, Phase IV, HSIDC, Kundli-131028, Sonepat, Haryana.

To

*All our **school teachers***
who provided us with the right foundation

Contents

Foreword..*xvii*

Preface ....*xix*

Acknowledgements ....*xxi*

1. PROBLEM SOLVING USING COMPUTERS..**1–16**

    1.1   Introduction   1
            1.1.1   Steps Involved in Problem Solving Using Computers   1
    1.2   Algorithms   3
            1.2.1   Characteristics of Algorithms   3
            1.2.2   Examples of Algorithms   3
            1.2.3   Advantages and Disadvantages of Algorithms   6
    1.3   Flow Charts   6
            1.3.1   Symbols Used in Flow Charts   6
            1.3.2   Examples of Flow Charts   7
            1.3.3   Advantages and Disadvantages of Flow Charts   10
    1.4   Pseudocode   10
            1.4.1   Sequence, Selection and Iteration   10
            1.4.2   Examples of Pseudocodes   12
            1.4.3   Advantages and Disadvantages of Pseudocode   14
    Summary   15
    Review Questions   15
    Problem Solving Exercises   15
    Interview Questions   16

2. **EVOLUTION OF PROGRAMMING LANGUAGES**...17–24

2.1   Introduction   17
2.2   Classification of Programming Languages   17
       2.2.1   Machine Level Languages (MLLs)   18
       2.2.2   Assembly Level Languages (ALLs)   19
       2.2.3   Higher Level Languages (HLLs)   20
       2.2.4   Fourth Generation Languages   21
2.3   Language Translator   22
Review Questions   23
Interview Questions   23

3. **OVERVIEW OF C LANGUAGE** 25–48

3.1   Introduction   25
3.2   Characteristics of C Language   26
3.3   Drawbacks of C Language   27
3.4   Components of a C Program   27
3.5   Input and Output in C   29
3.6   Execution of a C Program   30
       3.6.1   Under MS-DOS Environment   31
       3.6.2   Turbo C++/ Borland C++ Integrated Development Environment   31
       3.6.3   Under Unix Environment   31
3.7   Errors   32
3.8   C Language Primitives   33
3.9   Keywords and Identifiers   34
3.10   Constants   35
       3.10.1   Numeric Constants   35
       3.10.2   Character Constants   38
3.11   Variables   39
3.12   Data Types   39
       3.12.1   Character   39
       3.12.2   Integer   40
       3.12.3   Real Type   41
Summary   43
Review Questions   44
Interview Questions   46

4. **INPUT–OUTPUT OPERATIONS** 49–64

4.1   Introduction   49
4.2   The getchar() and putchar() Functions   50
4.3   The scanf() and printf() Functions   51
4.4   Formatting of Outputs   56
       4.4.1   Formatting of Integers   56
       4.4.2   Formatting of Floating Point Values   57

4.4.3   Formatting of Characters   59
4.4.4   Displaying Data in Tabular Form   60
Summary   61
Review Questions   62
Programming Exercises   62
Interview Questions   62

5.   OPERATORS AND EXPRESSIONS 65–98

5.1   Introduction   65
5.2   Assignment Operator [=]   66
5.3   Arithmetic Operators [unary +, unary -, +, -, *, /, %]   67
        5.3.1   Types of Arithmetic Expressions   69
        5.3.2   Precedence of Arithmetic Operators and Associativity   70
5.4   Relational Operators [<, <=, >, >=, ==, !=]   73
5.5   Logical Operators [&&, ||, !]   75
5.6   Shorthand Arithmetic Assignment Operators [+=, -=, *=, /=, %=]   78
5.7   Increment/Decrement Operators [++, --]   79
5.8   Conditional Operator [?:]   81
        5.8.1   Nesting of Conditional Operators   82
5.9   The sizeof() Operator   84
5.10   The Comma Operator [,]   85
5.11   Type Conversion   86
        5.11.1   Forcible Conversion or Type Casting   87
5.12   Precedence Levels and Associativity Among All the Operators   89
Summary   90
Review Questions   91
Programming Exercises   92
Interview Questions   93

6.   DECISION–MAKING AND BRANCHING (SELECTION) 99–135

6.1   Introduction   99
6.2   The simple-if Statement   100
6.3   The if-else Statement   104
6.4   The Nested if-else Statement   108
6.5   The else-if Ladder   111
6.6   The switch Statement   119
        6.6.1   Nested switch Statement   127
6.7   The goto Statement   128
Summary   129
Review Questions   130
Programming Exercises   131
Interview Questions   134

7.   LOOPING STATEMENTS IN C 136–172

7.1   Introduction   136
7.2   The while Loop   138
7.3   The for Loop   145
       7.3.1   Variations of for Loop   148
7.4   The do-while Loop   150
7.5   Which Loop to Use When   154
7.6   Jumps in Loops   155
7.7   Nesting of Loops   158
       7.7.1   Jumps in Nested Loops   162
Summary   166
Review Questions   166
Programming Exercises   168
Interview Questions   170

8.   FUNCTIONS 173–212

8.1   Introduction   173
8.2   Advantages of Functions   173
8.3   Classification of Functions   174
8.4   Functions with no Arguments and no Return Value   175
8.5   Functions with Arguments and no Return Value   177
8.6   Functions with Arguments and Return Value   181
8.7   Functions with no Arguments but with Return Value   185
8.8   Functions Returning a Non-integer Value   186
8.9   Nesting of Functions   188
8.10   Return Statement vs. Exit()   189
8.11   Recursion   191
8.12   Storage Classes   199
       8.12.1   Automatic Storage Class   200
       8.12.2   Static Storage Class   201
       8.12.3   Register Storage Class   201
       8.12.4   Extern Storage Class   202
8.13   Multifile Programs   204
Summary   205
Review Questions   206
Programming Exercises   209
Interview Questions   210

9.   ARRAYS 213–267

9.1   Introduction   213
9.2   Definition of an Array   214
9.3   One-dimensional Arrays   214

9.4   Multidimensional Arrays   223
        9.4.1   Two-dimensional Arrays (2-D arrays)   223
        9.4.2   Three-dimensional Arrays   241
9.5   Arrays and Functions   246
        9.5.1   Passing Three-dimensional Arrays to Functions as Arguments   257
Summary   259
Review Questions   260
Programming Exercises   262
Interview Questions   264

10. STRINGS **268–309**

10.1   Introduction   268
10.2   String I/O   269
        10.2.1   The `scanf()` and `printf()` Functions   269
        10.2.2   The `getchar()` and `putchar()` Functions   271
        10.2.3   The `gets()` and `puts()` Functions   272
        10.2.4   The `sprintf()` and `sscanf()` Functions   273
10.3   Initialization of Arrays of `char` Type   274
10.4   Arithmetic and Relational Operations on Characters   276
10.5   String Manipulations   282
10.6   Two-dimensional Array of `char` Type   294
        10.6.1   Initialization of a 2-D Array of `char` Type   296
10.7   Strings and Functions   302
        10.7.1   Passing 1-D Arrays of `char` Type as Arguments to Functions   302
        10.7.2   Passing 2-D Arrays of `char` to Functions   303
Summary   304
Review Questions   305
Programming Exercises   306
Interview Questions   308

11. STRUCTURES AND UNIONS **310–357**

11.1   Introduction   310
11.2   Definition of Structure Template   311
11.3   Declaration of Structure Variables   311
11.4   Initialization of Structure Variables   313
11.5   Operations on Structures   315
11.6   Arrays and Structures   317
        11.6.1   Array of Structures   317
        11.6.2   Arrays within Structures   325
11.7   Structure within Structure   328
11.8   Structures and Functions   332
        11.8.1   Passing Structures to Functions as Arguments   332
        11.8.2   Returning a Structure from a Function   338

11.9   Union   340
    11.9.1   Unions within Structures   342
    11.9.2   Structures within Unions   345
    11.9.3   Arrays within Unions   345
11.10 Enumerated Data Type   345
11.11 `typedef`   349
Summary   351
Review Questions   352
Programming Exercises   354
Interview Questions   355

12.   POINTERS **358–410**

12.1   Introduction   358
12.2   Pointer Operators &, *   360
12.3   Pointer Arithmetic   361
    12.3.1 . Pointer Expressions   363
12.4   Pointers and Arrays   364
    12.4.1   Pointers and One-dimensional Arrays   364
    12.4.2   Pointers and Two-dimensional Arrays   368
12.5   Pointers and Strings   373
    12.5.1   Array of Pointers to Strings   375
12.6   Pointers and Structures   377
    12.6.1   Pointers to Structures   377
    12.6.2   Structures Containing Pointers   379
12.7   Pointers and Unions   380
    12.7.1   Pointers to Unions   380
    12.7.2   Pointers as Members of Unions   381
12.8   Pointers and Functions   381
    12.8.1   Passing Pointers as Arguments to Functions   381
    12.8.2   Returning a Pointer from a Function   387
    12.8.3   Pointers, Strings and Functions   388
    12.8.4   Pointers to Functions   393
    12.8.5   Passing One Function as an Argument to Another Function   395
12.9   Pointers to Pointers   397
12.10 Dynamic Memory Allocation   398
    12.10.1 Built-in Functions Supporting Dynamic Memory Allocation   399
Summary   404
Review Questions   405
Programming Exercises   407
Interview Questions   408

13. FILE HANDLING IN C **411–443**

13.1 Introduction 411
13.2 Operations on Files 411
13.3 Opening and Closing of Files 412
13.4 File I/O Functions 413
    13.4.1 Character Oriented Functions–fputc(), fgetc() 413
    13.4.2 String Oriented Functions–fputs(), fgets() 415
    13.4.3 Mixed Data Oriented Functions–fprintf(), fscanf() 418
    13.4.4 Unformatted Record I/O Functions–fwrite(), fread() 420
13.5 Random Accessing of Files–fseek(), ftell(), rewind() 427
13.6 Error Handling During File I/O Operations 435
13.7 Command Line Arguments 438
Summary 439
Review Questions 440
Programming Exercises 441
Interview Questions 442

14. THE C PREPROCESSOR **444–467**

14.1 Introduction 444
14.2 Files Inclusion Directive – [#include] 445
    14.2.1 The #include Directive 445
14.3 Macros Definition Directives [#define, #indef] 445
    14.3.1 Macros with Arguments 448
    14.3.2 Nesting of Macros 453
    14.3.3 Macros vs. Functions 455
    14.3.4 Advantages of Macros 457
14.4 Conditional Compilation Directives
    [#ifdef, ifndef, #endif, #if, #else] 458
    14.4.1 #ifdef – #endif Directives 458
    14.4.2 #ifdef – #else – #endif Directives 458
    14.4.3 #ifdef – #elif – #else – #endif Directives 459
14.5 ANSI Additions 462
    14.5.1 The Stringizing Operator # 462
    14.5.2 The Token Pasting Operator ## 462
    14.5.3 The #error Directive 463
    14.5.4 The #pragma Directive 464
Summary 464
Review Questions 465
Programming Exercises 466
Interview Questions 467

15. PROGRAMMING AT BIT LEVEL **468–482**

15.1 Introduction   468
15.2 Bitwise Operators [&, |, ^, ~, <<, >>]   468
    15.2.1 Applications of Bitwise Operators   473
15.3 Bit-Fields   477
Summary   480
Review Questions   480
Programming Exercises   481
Interview Questions   482

16. GRAPHICS USING C **483–524**

16.1 Introduction   483
16.2 Initialize the Graphics Mode   483
    16.2.1 graphdriver   484
    16.2.2 graphmode   484
    16.2.3 pathtodriver   485
16.3 Resetting the Graphics Mode   485
16.4 Displaying Text   486
    16.4.1 outtextxy()   486
    16.4.2 outtext()   486
    16.4.3 settextstyle()   486
16.5 Determining the Resolution of a Display Device   488
16.6 Drawing Different Shapes   489
    16.6.1 Drawing Line   489
    16.6.2 Drawing Circle   492
    16.6.3 Drawing Polygon   493
    16.6.4 Drawing Rectangle   495
    16.6.5 Drawing Ellipse   499
    16.6.6 Pieslice ():   501
    16.6.7 Drawing Bars   502
    16.6.8 Some Simple Applications Using Graphics Functions   504
16.7 Line and Circle Drawing Algorithms   510
    16.7.1 Bresenham's Line Algorithm   510
    16.7.2 DDA Line Drawing Algorithm   512
    16.7.3 Bresenham's Circle Drawing Algorithm   514
16.8 Two-dimensional Transformation   517
    16.8.1 Translation   517
    16.8.2 Scaling   517
    16.8.3 Rotation   518
Summary   523
Review Questions   523
Programming Exercises   524
Interview Questions   524

17. SEARCHING AND SORTING 525–562

    17.1   Introduction   525
    17.2   Searching   525
            17.2.1   Linear Search   525
            17.2.2   Binary Search   528
    17.3   Sorting   532
            17.3.1   Exchange Sort   532
            17.3.2   Selection Sort   536
            17.3.3   Bubble Sort   541
            17.3.4   Insertion Sort   545
            17.3.5   Quick Sort   550
            17.3.6   Merge Sort   555
    Summary   560
    Review Questions   561
    Programming Exercises   561
    Interview Questions   562

18. MISCELLANEOUS TOPICS 563–579

    18.1   Creation of a Two-dimensional Array Dynamically   563
    18.2   Creation of a Three-dimensional Array Dynamically   567
    18.3   Variable Length Arguments to Functions   569
    18.4   Const and Volatile   571
    18.5   Generic Pointers   571
    18.6   Self-Referential Structures   572
    18.7   Trigraph Sequences   575
    18.8   How to Measure Time Taken by a Function in C?   576
    Summary   577
    Review Questions   578
    Interview Questions   579

Appendix A   *Mathematical Functions* 581–582

Appendix B   *Character Test Functions* 583–584

Appendix C   *String Manipulation Functions* 585–586

Appendix D   *File Manipulation Functions* 587–590

Appendix E   *Utility Functions* 591–592

Multiple Choice Questions 593–610

Solution to Interview Questions 611–628

Glossary 629–631

Index 633–638

Foreword

It gives me great pleasure to write foreword for the book entitled *Problem Solving with C* (Second Edition) by Dr. M.T. Somashekara, Dr. D.S. Guru and Dr. K.S. Manjunatha. C is a structured programming language which is portable, flexible and yet very powerful. It is extremely useful for both application programming and system programming as it encompasses important features of high level languages along with elements of the assemblers. I compliment the authors, who have long experience in teaching and research, for taking up this useful project of writing the book on *Problem Solving Using C*, the most widely used general purpose programming language.

The significant feature of this book is that each chapter begins with an introduction of the topic under consideration which gives a proper perspective of that which comes in the sequel. Each chapter ends with summary, review questions, programming exercises and interview questions which will be very useful for students and job seekers alike. This book is written keeping the undergraduate students and prospective programmers in mind. Even those who lack past knowledge and experience in programming will find this book a very good companion along the road leading to excellence in C programming. The style is simple and the approach is easy to understand and progress in programming and the coverage is complete in all respects. I am sure this book will be a boon for those who aspire to master problem solving using the C language, in general, and for the undergraduate students of Computer Science, Computer Applications, and Computer Science and Engineering, in particular. May this book go through many more editions in future and continue to benefit the community of learners of programming using the C language.

Chidanandagowdak

Dr. K. Chidananda Gowda
Former Vice-Chancellor, Kuvempu University, Shimoga
Former Principal and Professor of Computer Science and Engineering
Sri Jayachamarajendra College of Engineering (SJCE), Mysore

Preface

The C language is a general purpose, higher level language developed by Dennis Ritchie at AT&T Bell Laboratories in the early 1970s when there was a dire need for a powerful language required to support the development of both application software and system software. The C language stood up to this need. It supports structured programming methodology. Embodying a very rich set of operators and data types, it enables the programmers to write efficient and compact programs. It is also called middle level language since it provides the features of both machine level languages and higher level languages.

The book, now in its Second Edition, is an extension of Dr. M.T. Somashekara's previous book titled as *Programming in C*. This thoroughly revised and updated text is divided into well-organized 18 chapters with a very useful examples, programs, review questions, programming exercises, true/false questions and interview questions at the end of each chapter.

The first chapter consists of a general introduction to problem solving using computers, and problem solving tools comprising algorithms, flow charts and pseudocodes. The second chapter gives a brief, but neat description of the evolution of programming languages comprising Machine Level Languages, Assembly Level Languages, Higher Level Languages, and Fourth Generation Languages. An overview of C language is given in Chapter 3, which covers characteristics of C language, constants, variables, and data types. Input-output operations are covered in Chapter 4, which covers input and output functions and also the formatting of outputs. The fifth chapter deals with the arithmetic, relational, logical operators and other operators in detail. Chapter 6 covers decision-making and branching statements covering various types of 'if', 'switch' and 'goto' statements. Looping statements used in C language are covered in Chapter 7. Chapter 8 details different types of functions, their classification, and the advantages of using functions in good programming. Single dimensional arrays, multi-dimensional arrays, and arrays and functions are described beautifully in Chapter 9. Chapter 10 covers strings, their I/O operations, string manipulations and strings of functions. A very good and detailed delineation of structures, structures within structure, combination of structures and arrays as well as structures and functions along with unions is provided in Chapter 11. 'Pointers' is a powerful concept in C and a mastery over pointers is pointer itself to the expertise and accomplishment of a good programmer. The use of pointers under different circumstances as well as pointers to pointers is considered in detail in Chapter 12. A file is defined as a collection of related data stored in secondary storage devices like disk. Chapter 13 extensively covers file handling in C. The preprocessor, a distinctive feature of C plays a very important role in enhancing readability, modifiability, and portability of C programs. All the important details of the preprocessor are delineated in Chapter 14. Chapter 15 gives details of programming at bit level using bitwise operators. Graphics using C is delineated in Chapter 16 which consists of displaying text, drawing different shapes along with a few algorithms at the end of the chapter. Chapter 17 deals with searching and sorting algorithms and their implementation in C. Chapter 18 is the last chapter which covers eight miscellaneous topics. Five appendices, glossary, multiple choice questions with answers and solutions to interview questions are placed at the end.

We sincerely hope that the students will enjoy learning C and problem solving through C with this well-written book. It even caters to the needs of those who are new to programming as no prior knowledge of programming is required to read this book.

Constructive criticism and suggestions for improving the contents of the book will be thankfully acknowledged and all such communications may reach us at phi@phindia.com; somashekar_mt@hotmail.com; dsguruji@yahoo.com or kowshik.manjunath@gmail.com.

M.T. Somashekara
D.S. Guru
K.S. Manjunatha

Acknowledgements

Bringing out a book is a herculean task. It requires lot of hard work, patience, dedication and determination. Apart from these, the support and encouragement from the well-wishers play a vital role as they are motivating and also they act as catalysts to focus on the work with the right spirit. We take this opportunity for expressing our gratitude to all of them.

We profusely thank Prof. K. Chidananda Gowda, former Vice-Chancellor, Kuvempu University, Shimoga for having penned foreword for the book in spite of his busy schedule. In fact, we are privileged to have his foreword. We are highly indebted to Prof. S. Sadagopan, the Director, IIIT, Bengaluru; Prof. V. Rajaraman, Honorary Professor, IISc, Bengaluru; Dr. P.G. Siddheshwar, Professor, Department of Mathematics, Bangalore University, Bengaluru; Dr. P. Nagabhushan, Professor, Department of Studies in Computer Science, University of Mysore, Mysuru; and Dr. P.S. Hiremath, Professor, Department of Computer Science (MCA), KLE Technological University, Hubli, Karnataka, for their constant support and inspiration.

We also express our heartfelt thanks to Dr. G. Hemanth Kumar, Professor, Department of Studies in Computer Science, University of Mysore, Mysuru; Dr. B.V. Dhandra, Professor, Department of Computer Science, Gulbarga University, Gulbarga; Dr. Kurup G. Raju, Professor, Department of Computer Science, Kannur University, Kannur, Kerala; and Dr. Satyanarayana, Professor, Department of Computer Science, SK University, Ananthapur, Andhra Pradesh, for their encouragement and support.

Our sincere thanks are also due to all our contemporary colleagues and friends in the Department of Computer Science of Bangalore University, Bengaluru; University of Mysore, Mysuru; Mangalore University, Mangalore; Gulbarga University, Gulbarga; Karnatak University, Dharwad; Kuvempu University, Shimoga; Karnataka State Women's University, Bijapur, for their encouragement and motivating words.

We also express our gratitude to Dr. J.T. Devaraju, Professor, Department of Electronics Science, Bangalore University, Bengaluru; Dr. Shanmukhappa S. Angadi, Professor, P.G. Department of Computer Science and Engineering, VTU, Karnataka; Dr. Bhagyavana Mudhigoudar, Head, Department of Computer Science, Maharani's Science College, Bengaluru; Prof. Mukhundappa B.L., Department of Computer Science and Prof. Manjunatha D., Department of Electronics, Tumkur University, Tumkur; and Prof. Joy Paulose, Department of Computer Science, Christ University, Bengaluru, for their support and inspiration.

Special thanks to Mr. Shylesh K., a close companion of ours and a software developer, who has always been with us being supportive. We also thank the publisher PHI Learning and its editorial and production teams for their meticulous work to bring out the text in the present pleasing book form.

Last but not the least, we thankfully acknowledge the unconditional support extended by our family members, without whose support we could have not completed this book.

M.T. Somashekara
D.S. Guru
K.S. Manjunatha

1

Problem Solving Using Computers

1.1 INTRODUCTION

Considering the enormous amount of power and capability of computers in terms of speed with which they work, accuracy they provide and the wide variety of operations they perform, it is not difficult for us to associate them with problem solving. Today, in almost all spheres of our life, computers have found their place and many complex things have become easier to accomplish with the aid of the computers, which otherwise would have been extremely difficult. The major areas where computers are put to use include banking, defence, manufacturing, education, medicine, gaming and the list goes on. Fundamental to all these areas and many others are the kind of problems that are to be automated. In order to automate the activities in all these areas, the anatomy of the activities needs to be understood and they have to be transformed into the form, which is amenable to the computers. This is where the need for problem solving tools to simulate or capture the behaviour of the activities comes into picture. The problem solving tools include algorithms, flow charts and pseudocodes. Once the problem solving tool(s) are arrived at, the next step is to implement the procedure in a programming language. We learn the C programming language in the chapters to follow and use it to solve a number of problems. In this chapter, we throw light on the problem solving tools with suitable illustrations in order to get the required aptitude to solve problems with the aid of computers.

1.1.1 Steps Involved in Problem Solving Using Computers

The following is the sequence of steps involved in solving a problem using computers.

Problem definition

Includes stating the problem clearly and unambiguously, and clearly understanding of what is required for its solution.

1

Problem analysis

Involves the identification of (a) inputs, i.e. the data that are to be manipulated, (b) outputs, i.e. the expected results and (c) other additional requirements or constraints, if any, on the solution.

Algorithm design

Involves the design of the procedural solution for the problem, i.e. step-by-step procedure to arrive at the expected outputs by giving the available inputs in the problem domain.

If the given problem is complex, we can adopt **top-down design** approach. The basic idea behind the approach is that the given problem is broken down repeatedly into smaller, easily understandable and manageable sub problems. The procedural solutions for each sub problem are then arrived at. The process of breaking down a given problem into sub problems is also called **stepwise refinement**. All the procedural solutions are then integrated together to get the solution to the given complex problem. The top-down design or stepwise refinement is the hallmark of structured design paradigm, which the C language is known to support very well through its flexibility to define sub programs or functions. It becomes evident later as we progress into the later chapters dealing with C programming. For now, we deal with algorithms and the other forms of problem solving tools like flow charts and pseudocode, which are used to represent the procedural solutions, in detail in the section to follow.

Coding

Here the algorithm designed is converted into a program using a programming language. Each step in the algorithm is realized by means of one or more statements in the programming language. In this book, the C language is used as the coding tool.

Testing and debugging

Testing involves verification of the correctness of the program created. Testing is normally done by running the program with all types of sample data and then observing the output.

Debugging is the process of detection and correction of errors in the program code like syntax errors, runtime errors and logical errors. We will get to know more about these types of errors later.

Documentation

Documentation includes recording the general description of the program's behaviour under different situations and its special features. There are two types of documentation namely technical documentation and user documentation. Technical documentation involves the technical details of the program which are of use for its further maintenance by the programmers and user documentation involves instructions about the usage of the program.

Maintenance

Maintenance of programs is another vital step. Due to the fact that the user requirements keep changing, the programs also need to be changed to meet the changing requirements. Proper documentation of the programs would be of immense help to programmers in charge of maintenance.

1.2 ALGORITHMS

An algorithm is defined to be a step-by-step procedure to solve a given problem. It is a procedural solution to the problem on hand.

1.2.1 Characteristics of Algorithms

1. Each instruction in an algorithm should be precise and unambiguous.
2. Each instruction should be executed in a finite amount of time.
3. The algorithm should work on all legitimate inputs.
4. The required output should be obtained after the algorithm ends.

1.2.2 Examples of Algorithms

To find the area of a rectangle

The area of a rectangle is given by the product of its length and its breadth. Mathematically, we can express it as Area = Length * Breadth. Hence, in order to find the area of a rectangle, its length and breadth are required to be known.

Inputs: length and breadth
Output: area

Algorithm 1.1

```
1. read length
2. read breadth
3. area = length * breadth
4. display area
5. stop
```

To find the simple interest

The simple interest is obtained with the formula S.I. = $p*t*r/100$, where p stands for principal amount, t stands for time period and r stands for rate of interest. Hence, to calculate the simple interest, principal amount, time period and rate of interest are required.

Inputs: principal, rate, time
Output: simple interest

Algorithm 1.2

```
1. read principal
2. read time
3. read rate
4. simple interest = principal * time * rate/100
5. display simple interest
6. stop
```

To find the larger of the two numbers

Inputs: two numbers a and b
Output: largest of a and b

Algorithm 1.3

```
 1. read a
 2. read b
 3. if a > b then goto step 7
 4. if b > a then goto step 9
 5. display a and b are equal
 6. stop
 7. display a is greater than b
 8. stop
 9. display b is greater than a
10. stop
```

To find whether a number is even or odd

Input: a number a
Output: whether a is even or odd

Algorithm 1.4

```
 1. read a
 2. rem = a mod 2
 3. if rem = 0 then goto step 6
 4. display a is odd
 5. stop
 6. display a is even
 7. stop
```

To find the largest of three numbers

Inputs: three numbers a, b and c
Output: largest of a, b and c

Algorithm 1.5

```
 1. read a
 2. read b
 3. read c
 4. if (a > b) and (a > c) then goto step 8
 5. if (b > a) and (b > c) then goto step 10
 6. display c is the largest
 7. stop
 8. display a is the largest
 9. stop
10.display b is the largest
11.stop
```

To find the sum of the first *n* natural numbers

Input: a number n
Output: sum up to n

```
1. read n
2. sum = 0
3. i = 1
4. i = i + 1
5. s = s + i
6. if (i <= n ) then goto step 4
7. display sum
8. stop
```

To find the sum of the digits of a number

To find the sum of the digits of a number, we use a variable **sum** to collect the sum and it is initialized to zero. We extract each digit in the number and add it to **sum.** Extraction of each digit is done by dividing the number by 10 and collecting the remainder. The remainder happens to be the least significant digit that is extracted. By repeating this with the remaining part of the number until the number becomes zero, we extract all the digits.

Input: number n
Output: sum of the digits in n

Algorithm 1.6

```
1. read n
2. sum = 0
3. r = n mod 10
4. sum = sum + r
5. n = int(n / 10)
6. if (n > 0) then goto step 3
7. display sum
8. stop
```

To display only the prime numbers in a given range of integers

In order to display only the prime numbers in a given range of integers, we need to provide the lower limit and upper limit of the range. The procedure for finding whether a number is prime or not should be repeated for each number in the given range. As a result, this problem calls for repetition of execution of some steps.

Inputs: the lower limit (l) and the upper limit (u) of the range of integers
Output: only the prime numbers within l and u

Algorithm 1.7

```
1. read l
2. read u
3. i = l
4. flag = 1
5. k = 2
6. r = i mod k
7. if r = 0 then flag = 0
```

```
 8. k = k + 1
 9. if k <= i/2 then goto step 6
10. if flag = 1 then display i
11. i = i + 1
12. if i <= u then goto step 4
13. stop
```

1.2.3   Advantages and Disadvantages of Algorithms

Advantages

1. As an algorithm is a step-by-step procedure stated in plain English, it is easy to understand the logic involved.
2. Algorithms are independent of any programming language.
3. Algorithms make the creation of programs in a programming languages easy.

Disadvantages

1. There are no standard rules governing the construction of algorithms.
2. Writing algorithms does consume considerable amount of time.

1.3   FLOW CHARTS

A flow chart is a pictorial representation of an algorithm. The step-by-step procedure for solving a problem is elegantly represented by graphical means and it increases the degree of comprehensibility of the procedure.

1.3.1   Symbols Used in Flow Charts

Flow charts comprise a number of graphical symbols, each symbol representing a different purpose. The following are the commonly used symbols.

The parallelogram symbol is used to represent input/outut operation.

The rectangle symbol is used to represent computation operation.

The rhombus symbol is used to represent decision-making.

The circle symbol is used to represent a connector.

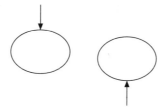

The flowlines are used to denote the flow control.

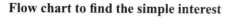

1.3.2 Examples of Flow Charts

Flow chart to find the area of a rectangle

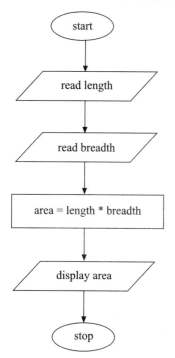

Flow chart to find the simple interest

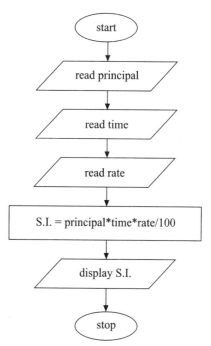

Flow chart to calculate net salary of an employee

Flow chart to compare two numbers

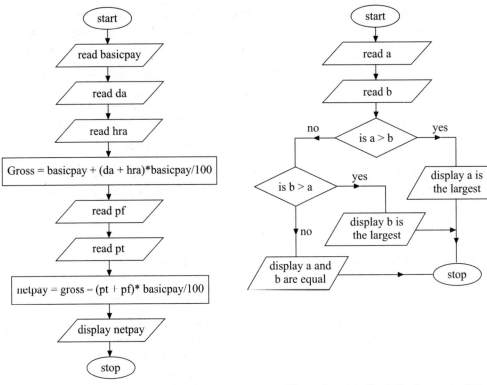

Flow chart to find whether a number is even or odd

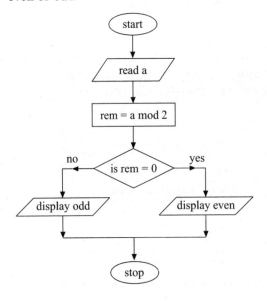

Flow chart to find the largest of the three numbers

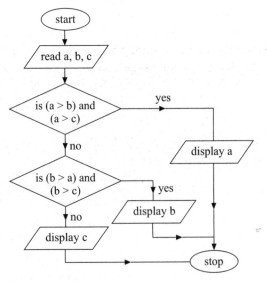

Flow chart to find the sum of the first n natural numbers

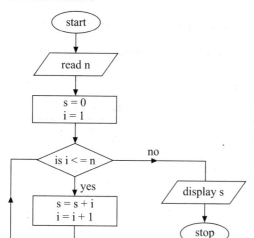

Flow chart to find the sum of the digits of a number

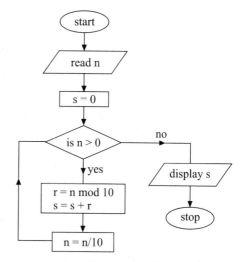

Flow chart to generate prime numbers beween two numbers

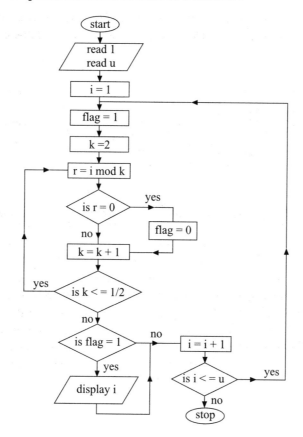

1.3.3 Advantages and Disadvantages of Flow Charts

Advantages

The following are the advantages offered by flow charts.

1. *Better communication:* Flow charts being pictorial representations of algorithms, elegantly denote the flow of control and hence make more comprehensible.
2. *Proper documentation:* Flow charts conveniently provide a way of documenting the procedure or the business logic involved in a problem.
3. *Makes coding easier:* Once a flow chart is ready, programmers find it very easy to write the corresponding program.
4. *Facilitates debugging:* Debugging is the process of detection and removal of errors in the logic of a program. Flow charts in the initial stage itself help the programmer in debugging.

Disadvantages

1. Flow charts are time consuming and laborious to draw with proper symbols. Even though for small problems it is easy to draw flow charts, it becomes tedious when it comes to drawing flow charts for complex problems.
2. Many a time a flow chart and its corresponding program do not match as the programmers modify the program without bothering to redraw the flow chart, as it is a tedious job.
3. There are no standards pertaining to the details that should be included in a flow chart.

1.4 PSEUDOCODE

Pseudocode is another way of representing an algorithm. As the name itself indicates, pseudocode comprises plain English statements and higher level language constructs to express conditional execution and repeated execution. Thereby pseudocode is influenced by some higher level language. We use pseudocodes in the later chapters to present the procedural solutions to a number of problems prior to developing the C program code.

1.4.1 Sequence, Selection and Iteration

Structured programming approach is based around three fundamental constructs. They are sequence, selection and iteration. As C is designed to support structured programming, it also provides these basic language constructs. **Sequence** refers to serial execution of instructions, i.e. one instruction after another from the first instruction to the last instruction without fail. **Selection** refers to conditional execution of instructions, i.e. Execution of instructions is subject to some condition. **Iteration** refers to repeated execution of instructions as long as some condition is true. Any programming situation can be realized with the help of these three constructs.

Sequence: As already mentioned, Sequence refers to serial execution of instructions, i.e. one instruction after another from the first instruction to the last instruction without fail. Look at the following two examples, which reflect sequence construct.

Example 1.1

To find the area of a triangle

```
read base
read height
area = 0.5 * base * height
display area
```

Example 1.2

To find simple interest

```
read principle
read time-period
read rate-of-interest
si = p*t*r/100
display si
```

As can be seen, in both the examples all the instructions get executed serially from the first instruction to the last without fail.

Selection: As already mentioned, selection refers to conditional execution of instructions, i.e. Execution of instructions is subject to some condition. Selection is implemented with the help of **if** statement and its various forms.

Example 1.3

```
if (a > b) then
    display "a is greater than b"
end if
```

Here, the instruction display "a is greater than b" gets executed only when the condition (a > b) is true.

Selection construct can be used to select one block of instructions out of two blocks

Example 1.4

```
if (a > b) then
    display "a is greater than b"
else
    display "a is less than or equal to b"
end if
```

The instruction display "a is greater than b" gets executed if the condition (a > b) is true. Otherwise display "a is less than or equal to b" gets executed.

Selection construct can be used to select one block of instructions out of many blocks also as shown by the following example.

Example 1.5

```
if (a < b) then
    display "a is less than b"
else if (a > b) then
    display "a is greater than b"
```

```
else
    display "a is equal to b"
end if
```

Iteration: As already mentioned earlier, Iteration refers to repeated execution of instructions as long as some condition is true. Iteration is also called looping. Iteration is implemented with the help of **while** loop construct, **repeat-until** and **for** loop constructs.

Example 1.6

```
i = 1
while(i <= 10)
Begin
    display i
    i = i + 1
end while
```

The **while** loop displays integers from 1 to 10. Note that the instructions display i and i = i + 1 get executed repeatedly as long as the condition i <= 10 is true.

Example 1.7

```
i = 1
repeat
Begin
    display i
    i = i + 1
until (i >= 10);
```

The **repeat-until** loop is to once again display integers from 1 to 10. Note that the instruction display i and i = i + 1 gets executed repeatedly for each value of i ranging from 1 to 10.

Example 1.8

```
for i = 1 to 10 do
begin
    display i
endfor
```

The **for** loop is to once again display integers from 1 to 10. Note that the instruction display i gets executed repeatedly for each value of i ranging from 1 to 10.

1.4.2 Examples of Pseudocodes

Pseudocode to find the area of a rectangle

```
Read length
Read breadth
area = length * breadth
display area
```

Pseudocode to find the simple interest

```
read principle
read time
```

```
read rate
simple-interest = principle * time * rate/100
display simple-interest
```

Pseudocode to calculate the net salary of an employee

```
read basicpay
read hra
read da
gross = basicpay + (hra + da) * basicpay/100
read pt
read pf
netpay = gross - (pt + pf * basicpay/100)
display netpay
```

Pseudocode to compare two numbers

```
read a
read b
if (a > b) then
    display a is the largest
else if (b > a) then
    display b is the largest
else
    display a and b are equal
end if
```

Pseudocode to find whether a number is even or odd

```
read a
rem = a mod 2
if rem = 0 then
    display a is even
else
    display a is odd
end if
```

Pseudocode to find the largest of three numbers

```
read a
read b
read c
if (a > b) and (a > c) then
    display a is the largest
else if (b > a) and (b > c) then
    display b is the largest
else
    display c is the largest
end if
```

Pseudocode to find the sum of the first n natural numbers

```
read n
sum = 0
```

```
i = 1
while (i <= n) do
      s = s + i
      i = i + 1
end while
display sum
```

Pseudocode to find the sum of the digits of a number

```
read n
sum = 0
while (n > 0) do
      r = n mod 10
      sum = sum + r
      n = int(n / 10)
end while
display sum
```

Pseudocode to generate prime numbers between two numbers

```
Read l
Read u
i = l
while (i <- u) do
      flag = 1
      k = 2
      while (k <= i/2) do
            r = i mod k
            if (r = 0) then
                  flag = 0
      endif
      k = k + 1
end while
if (flag = 1)
      display i
i = i + 1
end while
```

1.4.3   Advantages and Disadvantages of Pseudocode

Advantages

1. Conversion of a pseudocode into a program in a higher level programming language is straightforward.
2. Pseudocodes are easy to modify when compared to algorithms and flow charts.
3. As there are no specific rules to follow, pseudocodes are easy to write also. Any programming situation can be provided with a pseudocode in a fairly easier way with the use of simple logic structures, namely sequence and selection and iteration.

Disadvantages

1. Graphical representation of the step-by-step procedure is not available.

2. Similar to algorithms and flow charts, pseudocodes also lack standardization. As a result, pseudocodes created by different programmers will look different, making the communication a little difficult.

SUMMARY

- A problem is a problem which remains as a problem as long as it is not solved.
- Computer is an indispensible device for solving problems through computing with high accuracy and with high speed.
- An algorithm is a step-by-step procedure to solve a problem. The procedure is expected to be made of unambiguous instructions and produce the expected results within a finite amount of time.
- An algorithm is expected to work on all legitimate inputs.
- A flow chart is a pictorial representation of an algorithm. It offers higher degree of readability.
- A pseudocode is another tool for expressing the procedural solution to a problem. Conversion from a pseudocode to a program in a programming language is easy.

REVIEW QUESTIONS

1.1 What is a computer?

1.2 What are the features of computers?

1.3 Mention some areas where computers have played a dominant role.

1.4 What is the need for problem solving tools?

1.5 What is an algorithm? What are the essential properties of an algorithm?

1.6 What are the advantages and disadvantages of algorithms?

1.7 What is a flow chart? What are the different symbols used in a flow chart?

1.8 What are the advantages and disadvantages of flow charts?

1.9 What is a pseudocode? Wat are its advantages?

PROBLEM SOLVING EXERCISES

Write the algorithm, flow chart and pseudocode for the following problems.

1.1 To find the area and circumference of a circle

Area = 3.14 * r^2 Circumference = 2 *3.14 * r

where r is the radius of the circle.

1.2 To find the area of a triangle

Area = 0.5 * b * h

where b is the breadth and h is the height of the triangle.

1.3 To find the type of a triangle when its three sides are given

If a, b and c are the sides of the triangle, then

If all sides are equal, it is equilateral triangle

If any two sides are equal, it is isosceles triangle

If all the sides are different, it is acute triangle.

1.4 To find the type of a triangle when its three angles are given

If a, b and c are the angles of the triangle, then

If all angles are equal, it is equilateral triangle

If any two angles are equal, it is isosceles triangle

If all the angles are different, it is acute triangle.

1.5 To validate a given date.

1.6 To find the difference between two dates

The difference between two dates is the number of days between them.

1.7 To convert from decimal to binary number.

1.8 To convert from binary number to decimal number.

1.9 To reverse a number.

1.10 To accept marks in five subjects and grade a student

If percentage is between 35 and 49   —Just pass

If percentage is between 50 and 59   —Second class

If percentage is between 60 and 79   —First class

If percentage is above 79   —Distinction

1.11 To generate the multiplication table of a number.

1.12 To accept a point in an XY-plane and display whether it is in the first, second, third or the fourth quadrant.

INTERVIEW QUESTIONS

1. What are the characteristics of an algorithm?

2. What features characterize structured Programming methodology?

3. Devise pseudocode to find the largest and the second largest of three integers

4. Devise pseudocode to find whether an integer is an Armstrong number or not (An integer is said to be an Armstrong number if the sum of the cubes of the individual digits is equal to the integer itself. Example: $153 = 13 + 53 + 33$)

5. Devise pseudocode to find whether a decimal integer is a palindrome or not.

2

Evolution of Programming Languages

2.1 INTRODUCTION

A language is a means of communication. We interact with each other in various languages like English, Kannada, Tamil, etc. Just try to stretch your imagination for a moment about our life without these communication languages. Unimaginable! Isn't it? Our languages act as vehicles of communication. It is with the help of these, we express our feelings to others and get the required work done. We accomplish many things through communication.

Considering the enviable and enormous power and capabilities of computers in terms of wide variety of operations they perform, in terms of speed with which they operate, the accuracy which they guarantee, it is not difficult for us to associate computers with problem solving. We often refer to computers as problem solvers. A computer can do variety of tasks provided the problem is expressed clearly in a suitable language. Given problem has to be expressed in the form of well-defined set of instructions by means of a suitable language.

Each family of computers is designed to support its own set of instructions. The term **Instruction set** is often used to collectively denote the set of all the instructions supported by a family of computers. If a problem is given to be solved by a computer, the problem has to be first broken down into a sequence of logical steps known as **algorithm**. Then, the algorithm has to be converted into an appropriate sequence of instructions of the computer. The set of instructions thus constructed is referred to as a **program.** This is where the concept of programming languages comes into picture. The programming languages act as vehicles of communication between computers and us by enabling us to write programs for computers to solve problems.

2.2 CLASSIFICATION OF PROGRAMMING LANGUAGES

In the evolution of programming languages, thus far, four phases are identified. Accordingly, the programming languages are classified into the following four levels.

1. Machine Level Languages
2. Assembly Level Languages
3. Higher Level Languages
4. Fourth Generation Languages.

2.2.1 Machine Level Languages (MLLs)

The machine level languages came into existence soon after the advent of computers. These languages are often called first generation languages. The alphabet of the machine level languages included only two symbols 0 and 1. All electronic components which make up a computer are bistable in nature. They can be either in ON state or in OFF state. The ON state of an electronic component is denoted by 1 and the OFF state is denoted by 0. Since 0 and 1 belong to the binary number system, the MLLs are also known as binary languages.

In the MLL programs, all the instructions and data had to be represented by means of possible combinations of 0s and 1s only. The general format of the low level instructions is as follows:

`opcode operands`

where `opcode` specifies the operation to be performed over one or more `operands`. For example, the low level instruction to add two numbers a and b could be:

`10001 1100 1001`

where `10001` denotes the addition operation and the bit patterns `1100` and `1001` denote the operands a and b respectively. Even though programs could be written using these languages, the process of writing was a laborious job.

Some of the advantages and disadvantages of machine level language are as follows:

Advantage

1. **Fast execution:**   Program written in a machine level language executes fast as it is already in a machine understandable form and hence no need for any translation.

Disadvantages

1. **Difficulty faced by programmers:**   The programmer was expected to be aware of the details of the internal architecture of computers like memory size, word length, etc. In addition to these, the numeric codes for all the instructions should have to be remembered.
2. **Lack of readability:**   The programs written using machine level languages lacked readability. This is because of the fact that all the data and instructions had to be expressed in terms of possible combinations of 0s and 1s only. Because of the lack of readability, modification of programs also became tedious.
3. **Machine dependence:**   Since computers vary in their architectural details, different computers will have different machine level languages. If M1 and M2 are two computers belonging to two different families, then they will have two different machine level languages L1 and L2, respectively. In order to interact with M1, instructions should be written using L1 only and similarly, to interact with M2, instructions should be written using L2 only. Machine dependency throws the burden of learning the machine level languages on the programmers for each machine with which they would like to communicate. It is highly impossible to learn the machine language for all the machines available in the world.

2.2.2 Assembly Level Languages (ALLs)

The ALLs are an improvement over the MLLs. These languages are often called **Second Generation Languages**. In ALLs, symbolic words, also known as **mnemonics**, are used in place of numeric opcodes. Examples of mnemonics include ADD, which indicates addition operation; SUB, which indicates subtraction operation, etc. Symbolic names are used to denote data items. Examples of symbolic names: NUM1, NUM2, etc.

Example of an ALL instruction

ADD NUM1, NUM2—To add the values of NUM1 and NUM2

The usage of symbolic words and symbolic names greatly contributed to increased degree of readability of programs. Even though there is an increase in the degree of readability of programs, the other limitation of machine dependency still persisted. Each computer family has its own assembly level language. In order to interact with a particular computer, the corresponding ALL has to be learnt and used to write instructions. Similar to the case of MLLs, here also, the programmer is required to be aware of the architectural details of computers while writing programs.

The instructions written in ALLs are not directly understandable by computers. This is because computers understand only 0s and 1s. They do not understand the meaning of symbolic words and symbolic names. So the programs written in ALLs should be converted into their MLL equivalent programs. This is where the concept of assembler comes into picture. **Assembler** is a system software, which converts assembly level language programs into the equivalent MLL programs. During the translation process, each assembly instruction is converted into its equivalent machine instruction. So, there is one-to-one correspondence between assembly instructions and MLL instructions.

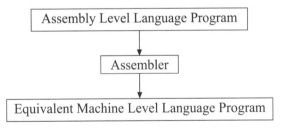

The assembler, before it proceeds to convert assembly program into its equivalent machine instructions, it checks for the syntactic correctness of the assembly program. The syntax of assembly programs refers to the grammatical rules governing the construction of the statements. If the assembler finds that the program is syntactically correct, then it produces the equivalent machine code. Otherwise, it reports the error messages, which are to be corrected, before the program is assembled again.

Some of the advantages and disadvantages of assembly level languages are as follows:

Advantage

Easy to remember mnemonic codes compared to machine code and hence writing assembly language program is easy for the programmer. Assembly language programs are more readable than machine language programs.

Disadvantages

1. Computer cannot understand assembly language directly and hence the program need to be translated into machine language using a translator namely assembler.
2. Similar to machine language, even assembly language is also machine dependent where the mnemonic codes which specifies a particular operation vary from one machine to another.

2.2.3 Higher Level Languages (HLLs)

The higher level languages came into existence in the third phase of development of languages and hence these are often called Third Generation Languages. These languages eliminated the limitations encountered by both the MLLs and ALLs. There is a further increase in the degree of readability of programs. The statements written in these languages are just English like sentences and hence more comprehensible. The programmers are relieved of the burden of being required to be aware of the architectural details and the languages are made more problem centric. The programmers only need to worry about the method of solving their problems rather than worrying about the internal details of computers, which affect programming. More importantly, HLLs are made machine independent. That is, programs written in some higher level language for one computer can be run on the other computers with little or no modification at all in the programs. The HLLs include BASIC, FORTRAN, COBOL, PASCAL, C, etc. So C, is one such HLL.

As we noted, the HLLs offered advantages like: Higher degree of readability, machine independence and the program writing task is more problem centric than machine centric. But the statements written in the programs of higher level languages cannot be understood by computers since computers can understand only 0s and 1s. The programs of HLLs should be converted into their MLL equivalent code. This is where the concept of compiler/interpreter comes into picture. **Compiler/Interpreter** is defined to be a system program, which converts a HLL program into its MLL equivalent. A program written in a HLL is called a **Source Program** and the machine code obtained after conversion is called **Object Program**. Each statement in a program of the HLL is converted into a number of machine level instructions. So, there is one-to-many correspondence between higher level language program statements and MLL instructions. For instance, the statement display(a, b); is compiled into a sequence of machine instructions for pushing the values of **a** and **b** onto the memory stack, saving the return address in the stack, saving the CPU registers, calling the funcion `display()`, etc.

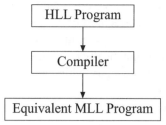

Each HLL has it own compiler, similar to assembler. The compiler before it proceeds to convert a HLL program into its equivalent machine instructions, checks for the syntactic correctness of the HLL program. The syntax of a HLL refers to the grammatical rules governing the construction of the statements in it. If the compiler finds that the program is syntactically correct, then it produces the equivalent machine code. Otherwise, it reports the error messages, which are to be corrected, before the program is compiled again.

Some of the major advantages and disadvantages of high level languages are as follows:

Advantages

1. **Ease of writing:** Easy to write a program in high level language as it relives the programmer the burden of remembering either the machine code or the mnemonic codes. This characteristic makes them highly readable. Here the entire program is written using English like statements and mathematical operators.
2. **Machine independent:** High level language programs are independent of the particular machine. This feature makes them highly portable that means programs written in a particular high level language for one machine can be used on other machines also with slight modifications.

Disadvantages

1. High level language programs cannot be understood by the machine directly as the machine can understand only machine language programs. Hence the programs written in a particular high level language should be translated into machine language using suitable translator like compiler or interpreter.
2. Takes more time for execution as it involves the translation of every instruction in the program to machine language.

2.2.4   Fourth Generation Languages

We now know that higher level languages score over both the MLLs and ALLs on two accounts.

1. HLL programs are more readable and thus easy to understand and modify if need be.
2. They are machine independent, means they are portable.

But writing programs in HLL requires some degree of proficiency in programming skills, techniques of programming and data structures, etc. and the programs written in HLL are procedural in nature.

Later, a need was felt to develop languages which are non-procedural in nature and thus which could be used by even non-technical users. The need led to the development of fourth generation languages. Examples of the fourth generation languages include DBase, FoxPro, Structured Query Language, which are normally referred to as database languages and graphics packages, report generators, etc. The programs written in these languages also should be compiled by the corresponding language compiler to get the low level instructions, which are uderstandable by computers.

Some of the advantages and disadvantages of fourth generation languages are as follows:

Advantages

1. Programming is easy and hence can be used by even non-technical users without much programming skill.
2. User can specify the format of the output they want in somewhat a natural language.

Disadvantage

Less efficient compared to high level languages.

2.3 LANGUAGE TRANSLATOR

We know that a computer can understand only two binary digits 0 and 1. This requires writing all the instructions in the program by using only these two specific symbols. Even though the programmer writes the program by means of mnemonics like ADD, SUB, MULT, etc. in an assembly level language and in almost English like statements and mathematical operators in high level language, a computer cannot directly understand the program written in these two languages. The programs must be translated into machine language by means of a suitable translator.

A program written in assembly level language is translated into machine instruction by means of a language translator known as **assembler**. Sometimes the assembler produces the machine code for the same machine in which the assembler runs, it is called as **resident assembler**. But if an assembler runs on one machine and produces the machine code for another machine, it is called **cross-assembler**. Similarly, the program written in high level language can be translated into machine language by means of translators like compiler and interpreter. Even though the compiler and interpreter do the same task, they do it in a different way. Following are the fundamental difference between a compiler and an interpreter.

Compiler	Interpreter
A compiler reads the whole source program and then finally generates the machine code	An interpreter reads only one line at a time from the source program, converts it into some intermediate form and then executes the converted line
Translation and execution work in two different phases	Translation and execution work side by side
Once the program is compiled into machine code, no need for translation each time for execution	Need to be translated for every execution
Fast	Slow
Debugging is difficult	Debugging is easy
Takes more space	Takes less space
In the case of compiler for errors in the entire source file, the compiler will generate an error report	Interpreter generates the error in any line and it stops.

Similar to cross-assemblers, we have cross-compilers also. A cross-compiler is one which runs on one machine and produces low level code for another machine.

REVIEW QUESTIONS

2.1 What is an algorithm?

2.2 What is a program?

2.3 Define instruction set.

2.4 What is the need for programming languages?

2.5 Mention the classifications of programming languages.

2.6 Binary number system is very much associated with computers. Why?

2.7 Mention the limitations of MLL.

2.8 How do ALL score over MLL?

2.9 What is meant by mnemonics?

2.10 What is an assembler?

2.11 There exists one-to-one mapping between ALL statements and MLL instructions. True/False.

2.12 What do you mean by syntax of a language?

2.13 What is meant by machine independence?

2.14 Write down the advantages offered by HLLs.

2.15 List out some HLLs.

2.16 What is a compiler?

2.17 What are the functions of a compiler?

2.18 Define source program and object program.

2.19 There is a one-to-many mapping between HLL statements and machine level instructions. True/False.

2.20 Why were the fourth generation languages necessary?

2.21 List out some of the fourth generation languages.

INTERVIEW QUESTIONS

2.1 What are the advantages of Machine level language?

2.2 What is the significance of a compiler?

2.3 How do you detect syntax and logical errors in a program?

2.4 In what way does an algorithm differ from a program?

2.5 Distinguish between compiler and interpreter.

2.6 What is a cross-compiler?

2.7 What are the advantages of a compiler over an interpreter?

2.8 Name some compiler-based high level languages.

2.9 What are the advantages of an interpreter over a compiler?

2.10 Name some interpreter based languages.

2.11 Can we create and execute the machine codes in different machines?

2.12 Which is more difficult to detect whether syntax error or logical error?

2.13 Mention some of the popular 4th generation languages.

2.14 What is the difference between a natural language and a computer language?

3

Overview of C Language

3.1 INTRODUCTION

The evolution of programming languages is dynamic in nature with the introduction of new concepts, new programming methodologies and better ways of handling the complexity of problems. One of the main challenges faced by the computer scientists is to develop a programming language which is more general rather than suitable for specific applications. The programming languages that existed before the advent of C language like BASIC, COBOL, etc. were suitable for developing application softwares. An **application software** is one which is written for the purpose of accomplishing some user-defined job. Examples of application softwares include library management software, payroll software, etc. These languages were found to be inadequate for developing system softwares. A **system software** is one which is aware of the architectural details of the hardware components and can directly interact with the hardware components of computer systems. Examples of system softwares includes language compilers, operating systems, etc.

There was a need for developing a language which would support both the application software and the system software development. Keeping this in mind, many computer scientists started working on the project. Initially, a language by name **Basic Combined Programming Language** abbreviated as (**BCPL**) was developed by Martin Richards, Cambridge University. This language was found to have some limitations. Next, Ken Thomson at AT&T Bell Labs developed a language and named it **B**, the first letter in the abbreviation BCPL. Even the B Language was found to have some shortcomings to support development of both business applications and system softwares. Later, Dennis Ritchie in 1972 developed a new language by inheriting the features of both BCPL and B and adding additional features. He named the language as just **C**, the next letter in the abbreviation BCPL after B. This is how the C language came into existence.

In the initial days, the usage of the language C was confined to only academic circles. Once Unix operating system, which widely used applications developed using C language, gained widespread popularity even in the business circles, C started gaining importance. Many C compilers entered into the market for commercial purposes. The American National Standard Institute (ANSI) has standardized the language and set some standard guidelines to be followed by all the C compiler writers. The standardized version is referred to as ANSI C.

3.2   CHARACTERISTICS OF C LANGUAGE

In spite of availability of a number of high level languages for programming purpose, C language has an edge over other languages due to its following salient features:

1. **C is called a middle level language:**   C combines the features of both Assembly Level Languages (Low Level Languages) and Higher Level Languages. For this reason, C is referred to as a Middle Level Language. The feature of low level language is that of enabling us to develop system level programs through the manipulation of data at bit level. In addition, it leads to the program compiled version of the code being efficient and compact. The features of HLLs are those of higher degree of readability and machine independence. Due to this capability, C is found to be a suitable language for writing system programs such as language compilers, operating system and database systems.

2. **C supports structured design approach:**   Structured design is a technique of programming. The basic idea behind this technique is to divide a big program into number of relatively small programs so that managing the program becomes fairly easy. In addition, it enables the programmer to write highly complicated and large programs easily. Structured approach reduces the development and testing time considerably which in turn enhances the programming productivity.

3. **C is extensible:**   C compilers come with what is called a standard library, which includes the low level code for the standard functions. We can also define our own functions, add them to the library and make it available to other programmers. The library can thus be extended by including our own functions.

4. **C is rich in data types and operators:**   C provides rich set of data types, both built-in as well as user-defined data types. And it also provides rich set of operators, many of which are not available in other higher level languages. These help in writing compact and efficient programs. We will discuss in detail about the data types and operators provided by C later.

5. **C is portable:**   The popularity of C language is, to some extent, attributed to its portability feature. C programs written for one computer can be run on other computers also with little or no modifications to the programs. C language is not restricted to any one particular operating system and hence can be executed on almost all available operating systems without any modification.

6. **Predefined functions:**   One of the real strengths of the C language is the availability of extensive library of predefined functions which makes programming much easier and also allow the programmer to write large and complicated programs easily with minimum effort. For many of the simple tasks like finding the square root of a number, calculating the sine and cosine value of an angle, the programmer need not write a program instead he can utilize these functions which are available in the C library.

7. **Strong association with UNIX:** The C language has close association with UNIX operating system, which is one of the most powerful operating systems especially for multi-user systems. The reason being UNIX operating system was written entirely in C. Even though C language was originally implemented on UNIX, it can be used on other operating systems also.

3.3 DRAWBACKS OF C LANGUAGE

Even though the C language is preferred over languages like BASIC, COBOL, FORTRAN due to its salient features mentioned above, it still suffers from the following drawbacks:

1. **Non-availability of operators for composite objects:** C language does not provide any operators to deal with composite objects like array, strings, and structures directly.
2. **No operators for input and output manipulation:** Unlike most of the other high level languages which support operators for input and output operations, C does not have any operators for input and output. In C, all the input and output operations are done with the help of standard library functions.

3.4 COMPONENTS OF A C PROGRAM

C program is basically a collection of functions and variables. Each function is nothing but a subprogram which has its own input and output and it can transform data from one form to another. These functions are integrated suitably to solve a given problem. A function itself is a collection of many statements. A C program consists of the following components in addition to a set of functions.

Comments: Comments lines are the set of lines written by the programmer for his reference to indicate program title, author name and other relevant details related to the program. Appropriate and meaningful comment lines can be embedded anywhere in the body of a program, not necessarily in the beginning itself. Judicious usage of comments while coding is a good programming practice since it increases the degree of readability and understandability of programs and helps during maintenance stage of larger programs. In C, any segment of text enclosed within the pairs of characters /* and */ is taken as a comment. The compiler just ignores the comments. Usage of comment lines will not have any effect on the execution time of the program.

Example 3.1

```
/* Program to find the area of a circle */
```

Header files: Functions in a C program may be either user defined functions or library functions. Library functions are predefined functions which are available as part of the C language. C compilers are provided with what is called a standard library and it consists of definitions of a large number of commonly used built-in functions. Since these functions are readily available, we do not need to rewrite them if we want to use the functionalities of the functions. They can simply be utilized by our programs. In order to use them, we need to include some files as part of our program. These files are generally called **header files** since they are included in the beginning of the program itself. Examples of header files include `stdio.h, conio.h, string.h`, etc.

For example, the header file stdio.h contains declarations of functions and other definitions, which are required for Input–Output operations. Examples of functions declared in the file are: getchar(), putchar(), gets(), puts, fscanf(), fprintf(), etc. The header file conio.h contains declarations of functions and other definitions, which are required for console I/O operations. Examples of functions declared in the file are: clrscr(), getch(), putch(), etc. Similarly, the header file string.h contains declarations of functions and other definitions, which are required for string manipulations. Examples of functions declared in the file are: strlen(). strcpy(), strcmp(), strcat(), etc. The preprocessor directive #include is used for this purpose.

Example 3.2

#include <stdio.h>

In response to the above directive, the contents of the file stdio.h are added to the source program by the preprocessor. Note that the file stdio.h is surrounded by pointed brackets. This is to indicate to the compiler to search for the file in the include directory.

Symbolic constants: Sometimes a program may require certain data which will not change during the execution of the program. These constants are referenced with some symbolic names. All the symbolic names should be defined before they are referenced in the program. All the symbolic constants are defined by means of preprocessor directive #define as follows:

Example 3.3

#define PI 3.14

assigns the symbolic name PI to the constant value 3.14.

Global variables: In many situation, certain data are required to be accessed by many functions. Instead of declaring them inside each and every functions, we can declare such variables before the main() function. Such variables are known as **global variables** and they are declared as follows:

```
int a, b;
float b;
int main(void)
{

    Return 0;
}
```

main() function: Even though a C program consists of several functions, the execution of the program begins at a unique function called main(). Every C program will have one and only one main() function. This is where the execution of a program starts from and ends with. The main() function in turn calls other functions at appropriate place. These functions may be either user defined or library functions. Opening brace { of the main() marks the logical beginning of a program and the closing brace } marks the logical end of the program. The statements enclosed within the opening brace and the closing brace form the body of the main(). It consists of two parts: 1. Local variables declaration, where all the variables, which are accessed only by the main () are declared, and 2. Statements, which include the executable statements. The executable statements can be calls to different functions. General syntax of a main function in C is

```
main()
{
        Local Variables Declaration

        Executable statements
}
```

```
Eg:   main()
      {
              int a, b, c;

              a = 10;
              b = 20;
              c = a + b;
      }
```

In the above example the statement int a, b, c; is called a declaration statement which tells the name of the variables and the type of value those variables can store to the compiler. The statements a = 10; b = 20; c = a + b; constitutes executable statements. These three statements constitute the body of the main () function.

User-defined functions: Writing a large program with only main () is not effective. Programmer needs to write a number of functions with each one being capable of doing some useful task. These functions can be written either before or after the main (). These functions are called user-defined functions and they are called at appropriate place in the main () function. We will discuss user-defined functions at length later.

3.5 INPUT AND OUTPUT IN C

The main objective of any program is to manipulate some input and to get the desired output. Data is manipulated as per the instructions in the program. Unlike most of the other high level languages, in C, input and output operations are accomplished using standard functions. C is rich in its collection of input–output functions. One of the most general input functions in C is scanf () and it allows the user to input values to variables using standard input device namely, the keyboard. Similarly, the most general output function in C is printf () and it is used to display the output values on the standard output device namely, the monitor.

The following program illustrate this.

```
/* Program to illustrate input and output functions */
#include <stdio.h>
main()
{
```

```
        int a, b, c;
        printf("Enter two numbers \n");
        scanf("%d %d", &a, &b);
        c = a + b;
        printf("%d", c);
}
```

In the above program, the statement #include <stdio.h> is essential as it contains the declarations of functions and other definitions, which are required for input–output operations. The declaration statement int a, b, c; declares three variables a, b, c of integer type. The next statement printf ("Enter two numbers \n"); displays the message "Enter two numbers on the standard output device namely monitor". In C, any sequence of characters enclosed within "and" is considered as string constant. The character '\n' is called new line character and it causes the output of next printf() to start from the next line. The statement scanf("%d %d", &a, &b) is an input statement which allows the user to enter two integer data and will be assigned to the variables a and b respectively. The statement c = a + b is called an **assignment statement** which assigns the value of the expression a + b to the variable c. The last line printf("%d", c) displays the value of the variable c on the output device. Statements contained within the braces { and } constitute the body of the main() function.

Output of the above program will be

Enter two numbers

10

20

30

In addition to scanf() and printf(), C language supports a number of other functions for input and output operations which we will discuss later.

3.6 EXECUTION OF A C PROGRAM

The following are the four general steps involved in the execution of a program written in C irrespective of the operating system being used:

1. **Creating the source program:** Creation of the source program is done with the help of a text editor. A text editor enables us to create a new text file, modify the contents of an existing file, etc. The source program is typed into a file say, demo.c. Note that the C program files end with the extension .c

2. **Compiling the source program:** Once the source program is ready in a text file, next, the file is submitted to the C compiler. The C compiler processes the source program and if the program is syntactically correct, produces the object code.

3. **Linking the program with the functions in the standard library:** Once the object code of the program is obtained after successful compilation, the linker links the object code with the functions in the standard library referred to by the program. After successful linking, the linker will then produce the final executable code.

4. **Executing the program to get the expected outputs:** The executable code produced by the linker is then run. This involves providing suitable input to get the required output.

3.6.1 Under MS-DOS Environment

The following sequence of commands are used to create and execute a C program in MS-DOS environment (at the command prompt).

1. Creating the source program
   Edit `demo.c`
   The utility program edit has been used to create the source file `demo.c`
2. Compiling the source program
   `tc demo.c`
   `tc` is the Turbo C compiler, on successful compilation, it produces the object program file `demo.obj`
3. Linking the program with the functions in the standard library
   Link `demo.obj`
4. Executing the program to get the expected outputs
   `demo`

3.6.2 Turbo C++/ Borland C++ Integrated Development Environment

(The sequence of commands)
To create a source file
Select file option
Select new option
Type the program code in the edit window
Press F2 to Save the file
To compile the program
Select compile option
Click on compile menu item
Or
Press alt + f9 (+ indicates that both alt and f9 keys should be pressed simultaneously)
To run the program
Select Run option or press ctrl + f9
To see the result
Press alt + f5

3.6.3 Under Unix Environment

The following sequence of commands are used to create and execute a C program in Unix Environment.

1. Creating the source program

   `ed demo.c`

   or

   `vi demo.c`

   `ed` and `vi` are the editor programs in Unix environment.

2. Compiling and linking

    `cc demo.c`

    In Unix environment, both compiling and linking take place together and, on success, they produce the executable object code stored in the file `a.out`

3. Executing the program to get the expected outputs

    `a.out`

    The final executable object code can be collected by a file other than the default file `a.out`

    The general syntax of this variation is as follows:

    `cc -o objectfile sourcefile`

    where `sourcefile` is the file containing the C program code and `objectfile` is the file which collects the final executable code.

    `cc -o demo.out demo.c`

    Here, the final executable object code is stored in the file `demo.out`. It can be run by just specifying it at the shell prompt as:

    `$ demo.out`

    We can even combine several source files and produce a single executable object code if need be, The general syntax of the compilation command for combining n source files is as follows:

    `cc filename1.c, filename2.c, ...,filenamen.c`

Example 3.4

To combine three source files `demo1.c`, `demo2.c` and `demo3.c` and produce a single executable object file, the command is

`cc demo1.c, demo2.c, demo3.c`

After successful compilation and linking, the final executable object code is collected by the default file `a.out`. It can be run by typing it at the shell prompt.

The command `cc -o demo.out demo1.c, demo2.c, demo3.c` on successful compilation and linking, produces the executable code and stores it in the file `demo.out`.

3.7 ERRORS

Programming without errors is quite a difficult task. We do come across different types of errors while executing a program. The following is the classification of errors depending on the order of timing they crop up.

- Compile-Time Errors
- Linker Errors
- Runtime Errors
- Logical Errors

All these errors should be dealt with. Only then we get the expected behaviour and the expected results from the program.

The **Compile-time Errors** occur if the programs do not conform to the grammatical rules of the language being used. Thus, the compile-time errors are also called **Syntactical Errors**. They are caught during compilation itself. We correct the syntactical errors and recompile the programs until the compiler is satisfied with the syntactical correctness of the programs and produces the equivalent object code.

The **Linker Errors** occur during the linking process when the external symbols referred to by the program are not resolved. For example, if we call a function which is not defined, the linker figures out and reports the appropriate error. The linker errors (if any) occur after the successful compilation of the program.

The **Runtime Errors** occur while a program is being run and hence the name. They occur due to both program internal and external factors. Examples of runtime errors due to internal factors include "Division by zero", and "stack overflow". Examples of Runtime Errors due to external factors include "Running out of memory", "Printer out of paper", etc. We need to exercise extra care to handle these errors. We should identify the potential segment of code where these errors are anticipated and take corrective steps when they occur thereby avoiding abnormal termination of a program. The Runtime Errors (if any) occur after the successful compilation and linking of the program.

The **Logical Errors** occur if the solution procedure for the given problem itself is wrong. In this case, the outputs produced by the programs would be incorrect. Correcting the solution procedure itself by better understanding of the problem eliminates these errors. The Logical Errors (if any) are to be figured out by ourselves by verifying the output that are produced by the program.

3.8   C LANGUAGE PRIMITIVES

Each language will have its own set of permissible characters, the characters form the most basic building blocks of the language. By using only these characters, the language constructs are formed. For instance, if we consider our natural language, English, it consists of 52 (26 Lower case 26 Upper case) permissible symbols. English words are constructed using appropriate combination of only these characters, so the 52 characters form the **Character set** of English. Character set of a language is also called **Alphabet**.

Computer programming languages are not exceptions in this regard. They also will have their own set of permissible characters, which are used to form their program elements. So is C, the Character set of C includes:

Letters of English alphabet (Both upper case and lower case):
A.......Z   a......z

All symbols of the decimal number system:
0.......9

Special symbols:

.	Dot	?	Question mark
,	Comma	'	Single quote
;	Semicolon	"	Double quote
:	Colon	!	Exclamation symbol

|	Vertical bar	+	Plus sign
/	Right slash	<	Opening pointed bracket
\\	Back slash	>	Closing pointed bracket
~	Tilde symbol	(	Opening parenthesis
_	Underscore	)	Closing parenthesis
$	Dollar sign	[	Opening square bracket
%	Percent symbol	]	Closing square bracket
&	Ampersand symbol	{	Opening brace
^	Caret	}	Closing brace
*	Asterisk	#	Number sign
–	Minus sign	=	Equal symbol

The class of characters, which are not printed, but instead, cause some action are commonly referred to as the **control characters or white spaces**. They are represented by a backslash followed by another character. They are treated as single character by the compiler. Following are the control characters.

Backspace	\b
Horizontal tab	\t
Vertical tab	\v
Carriage return	\r
New line	\n
Form feed	\f
Alert character	\a

A combination of characters from the alphabet of C is called a **C word**.

3.9   KEYWORDS AND IDENTIFIERS

Keywords are those words of C which have predefined meaning assigned by the C language. They form a part of the database required by the C compiler itself. They should not be used for any other purpose other than the purpose for which they are meant. The keywords are also called **reserved words**. They are equivalent to dictionary words of natural languages like English. There are 32 keywords supported by ANSI C. Following are the list of keywords.

auto	double	int	struct
break	else	long	switch
case	enum	register	typedef
char	extern	return	union
const	float	short	unsigned
continue	for	signed	void
default	goto	sizeof	volatile
do	if	static	while

An **identifier** is one which is used to designate program elements like variables, constants, array names, function names, etc. There are a couple of rules governing the construction of valid identifiers. They are:

1. An identifier can have maximum 31 characters (ANSI C standard)
2. The permissible characters in an identifier include letters, digits and an optional underscore symbol.
3. It should start with a letter.
4. Special characters other than underscore are not permitted.
5. It should not be a keyword.

Example of valid identifiers:

number
A1
A_1
A1b

Invalid identifiers: Reason

1a	starts with a digit
a 1	space in between is not allowed
a,b	, is not allowed

3.10   CONSTANTS

A **constant** is one, the value of which does not change during the execution of a program. A constant also gets stored in a memory location and the contents of such location do not change during the execution of program and also the address of the location is not accessible to the programmer. Depending on the types of data, constants are broadly classified into two classes, i.e. numeric constants and character constants.

3.10.1   Numeric Constants

Numeric constants, as the name itself reveals, are those which consist of numerals, an optional sign and an optional period . They are further classified into two types, i.e. integer constants and real constants.

Integer Constants

Integer constants are whole numbers (i.e. without fractional part). These are further classified into three types depending on the number systems they belong to. They are:

(i)   Decimal integer constants
(ii) Octal integer constants
(iii) Hexadecimal integer constants

Decimal integer constants

A decimal integer constant is characterized by the following properties

(a) It is a sequence of one or more digits [0…9, the symbols of decimal number system].

(b) It may have an optional + or – sign. In the absence of sign, the constant is assumed to be positive.

(c) It should not have a period as part of it.

(d) Commas and blank spaces are not permitted.

Valid Decimal Integer constants

345
–987

Invalid Decimal Integer Constants

3.45   Decimal point is not permissible
3,34   Commas are not permitted

Octal integer constants

An octal integer constant is characterized by the following properties:

(a) It is a sequence of one or more digits [0…7, symbols of octal number system].

(b) It may have an optional + or – sign. In the absence of sign, the constant is assumed to be positive.

(c) It should start with the digit 0.

(d) It should not have a period as part of it.

(e) Commas and blank spaces are not permitted.

Valid Octal Integer constants

0345
–054
+023

Invalid Octal Integer Constants

03.45   Decimal point is not permissible
03,34   Commas are not permitted
x45   x is not a permissible symbol
678   8 is not a permissible symbol

Hexadecimal integer constant

An hexadecimal integer constant is characterized by the following properties:

(a) It is a sequence of one or more symbols [(0…9), (A…Z), (a…z), the symbols of hexadecimal number system].

(b) It may have an optional + or – sign. In the absence of sign, the constant is assumed to be positive.

(c) It should start with the symbols 0X or 0x.

(d) It should not have a period as part of it.

(e) Commas and blank spaces are not permitted.

Valid Hexadecimal Integer Constants

0x345
–0x987
0x34A
0XA23

Invalid Hexadecimal Integer Constants

0X3.45   Decimal point is not permissible
0X3,34   Commas are not permitted

Real Constants

The real constants also known as floating point constants are written in two forms, i.e. fractional form and exponential form.

(i) Fractional Notation

The real constants in fractional form are characterized by the following characteristics:

(a) They must have at least one digit and a decimal point.

(b) An optional sign (+ or –) can precede a real constant. In the absence of any sign, the real constant is assumed to be positive.

(c) Commas or blank spaces are not permitted as part of a real constant.

Examples of valid Real constants

345.67
–987.87

Invalid Real Constants

3 45   Blank spaces are not permitted
3,34   Commas are not permitted
123   Decimal point missing

(ii) Exponential Notation

The exponential form offers a convenient way for writing vary large and small real constants.
For example:

- 23000000.00, which can be written as $23 * 10^8$ is written as **0.23E8** or **0.23e8** in exponential form.
- 0.000000123. which can be written as $0.123 * 10^{-6}$ is written as **0.123E-6** or **0.123e-6** in exponential form.

The letter E or e stand for exponential form.

A real constant expressed in exponential form has two parts: (a) Mantissa, (b) Exponent.

Mantissa is the part of the real constant to the left of E or e and the exponent of a real constant is to the right of E or e. Mantissa and exponent of the above two numbers are shown as follows.

Mantissa	Exponent
0.23 E8	0.123 E–6

In the above examples, 0.23 and 0.123 are the mantissa parts of the first and second numbers respectively. and, 8 and –6 are the exponent parts of the first and second number respectively.

The real constants in exponential form are characterized by the following characteristics:

(a) The mantissa must have at least one digit.

(b) The mantissa is followed by the letter E or e and the exponent.

(c) The exponent must have at least one digit and must be an integer.

(d) A sign for the exponent is optional.

Valid real constants in exponential form:

1E3

12e–5

0.12E5

Invalid real constants in exponential form

12E	No digit specified for exponent
12e3.4	Exponent should not be a fraction
12,3e4	Commas are not allowed
234 * e9	* not allowed

3.10.2 Character Constants

Character constants, as the name itself indicates, are those which consist of one or more characters of the alphabet of C.

Depending on the number of characters present, character constants are further classified into two types:

(i) Single character constant

(ii) String constant

A **single character constant** consists of only one character and it is enclosed within a pair of single quotes.

For example: 'a' is a single character constant

'9' is a single character constant

A **string constant** consists of one or more characters and it is enclosed within a pair of double quotes.

For example:

"abc" is a string constant

"12bn" is a string constant

Note that "123" and "1" are also string constants.

3.11   VARIABLES

A **variable** is a named memory location, the value of which can change during the execution of the program containing it. The name of a variable should be a valid C identifier. In addition to the rules for forming identifiers, the general convention followed while naming variables is that the name selected for a variable reflects the purpose of the variable. However, this is not the compiler requirement but only to increase the readability of the variables.

In C, all variables should be declared before they are used. The syntax of declaring a variable is as follows:

```
data-type variable;
```

Note that the declaration ends with a semicolon.

Example 3.5

```
int a;
```

To declare more than one variable of same type, the variables are separated by commas as shown below.

```
data-type variable1, variable2, variable3,…..,variablen;
```

Example 3.6

```
int a, b, c;
```

3.12   DATA TYPES

Data types refer to the classes of data that can be manipulated by C programs. The three fundamental data types supported by C are character, integer and real type.

3.12.1   Character

char

All single characters used in programs belong to character type. The keyword **char** is used to denote character type. The size of a variable of **char** type is one byte. The range of values that can be stored in a variable of char type is -128 to 127. That is, $(-2^7$ to $2^7-1)$. When a character is assigned to a variable of type **char**, what is stored in the variable is the ASCII value of the character.

```
char c;
```
c is declared to be a variable of type **char**.

c = 'a'; assigns the character 'a' to the variable **c**.

printf("%c", c); would display the character **c** on the screen. Whereas, printf("%d", c); would display the ASCII value of the character 'a', 97.

We can even assign an integer value in the permissible range to the variable **c**.

Example 3.7

c = 65 is a valid statement.

Now, printf ("%d", c); would display the value 65 and the statement printf ("%c", c); would display the character 'A'. Note that 65 is the ASCII value of 'A'.

unsigned char

The unsigned char is a variation of char type. The size of a variable of unsigned char type is also one byte. As the name itself indicates, the range of values that can be stored in a variable of type unsigned char is 0 to 255 (0 to 2^8-1).

3.12.2 Integer

int

All numeric data items with no fractional part belong to integer type. The keyword **int** is used to represent integer type. Normally, the size of a variable of type **int** is the word size of the computer system being used. We will consider 16-bit machine. In the case of 16-bit machines, it is 2 bytes. The range of values that can be stored in an **int** variable –32768 to 32767 (i.e. -2^{15} to $2^{15}-1$).

int type provides three more modifiers: unsigned int, short int, long int. These variations are to have control over the range of values which can be stored.

unsigned int

The size of a variable of unsigned int is also 2 bytes (16-bit machine). It can store only positive range of values. The range of values that can be stored in a variable of unsigned int is 0 to 65535 (0 to $2^{16}-1$).

unsigned int ui;

ui is declared to be a variable of unsigned int type.

short int

The size of a variable of short int is also 2 bytes. It is similar to **int** type in the case of 16-bit machine.

short int s;

s is declared to be a variable of short int type.

long int

The size of a variable of long int type is 4 bytes. The range of values that can be stored in a variable of this type is –2147483648 to 2147483647. Note that there is a substantial increase in the range of values.

long int l;

l is declared to be a variable of long int type.

The combinations unsigned short int and unsigned long int are also permissible. unsigned short int is similar to unsigned int in 16-bit machine. But the range of values that can be stored in a variable of unsigned long int is 0 to $2^{32}-1$.

In all of the modifiers of int type, the keyword int is optional and can be skipped while declaring variables of their type.

Example 3.8

```
unsigned ui;
short s;
long l;
unsigned short us;
unsigned long ul;
```

are all valid declarations.

3.12.3 Real Type

float

All numeric data items with fractional part belong to real type. The keyword **float** is used to declare variables of float type. A variable of float type requires 4 bytes and the range of values that can be stored in it is 3.4e–38 to 3.4e + 38. It stores floating point numbers with 6 digits of precision. The floating point numbers stored in a float variables are called **single-precision numbers**.

```
float f;
```

f is declared to be a variable of **float** type.

Modifiers of **float** type include long float (double) and long double. The modifiers facilitate storage of higher range of floating point numbers and they provide increased accuracy.

Double

A variable of double type requires 8 bytes of memory space and the range of values that can be stored in it is 1.7e–308 to 1.7e + 308. It stores floating point numbers with 14 digits of precision. The degree of accuracy provided by double type is more than that provided by float type.

```
double d;
```

d is declared to be a variable of double type.

Long double

A variable of long double type requires 10 bytes of memory space and the range of values that can be stored in it is 3.4e–4932 to 1.1e + 4932. It stores floating point numbers with more than 14 digits of precision. The degree of accuracy provided by long double type is even more than that provided by double type.

```
long double f2;
```

f2 is declared to be a variable of long double type.

Void

The void data type is the ANSI addition to C. It is used in two situations.

  (i) To indicate that a function does not require any parameters or the function does not return any value.

(ii) To create generic pointers.

The usage of the data type becomes clear when we learn the concept of functions and pointers, which are covered later.

Size and range of values of different data types on a 16-bit machine

Data type	Size (in bytes)	Range of values
char	1	−128 to 127
unsigned char	1	0 to 255
int	2	−32,768 to 32,767
unsigned int	2	0 to 65,535
short int	2	−32,768 to 32,767
unsigned short int	2	0 to 65,535
long int	4	−2,147,483,648 to 2,147,483,647
unsigned long int	4	0 to 4,294,967,295
float	4	3.4E − 38 to 3.4E + 38
double	8	1.7E − 308 to 1.7E + 308
long double	10	3.4E − 4932 to 1.1E + 4932

Size and range of values of different data types on a 32-bit machine

Data type	Size (in bytes)	Range of values
char	1	−128 to 127
unsigned char	1	0 to 255
int	4	−2,147,483,648 to 2,147,483,647
unsigned int	4	0 to 4,294,967,295
short int	2	−32,768 to 32,767
unsigned short int	2	0 to 65,535
long int	4	−2,147,483,648 to 2,147,483,647
unsigned long int	4	0 to 4,294,967,295
float	4	3.4E − 38 to 3.4E + 38
double	8	1.7E − 308 to 1.7E + 308
long double	10	3.4E − 4932 to 1.1E + 4932

Program to illustrate data of different types in C

```c
#include <stdio.h>

int main(void)
{
    int a;
```

```
float b;
char c;

printf("Enter an integer number \n");
scanf("%d", &a);

printf("The Integer Number is  %d\n", a);

printf("Enter an real number \n");
scanf("%f", &b);
printf("Real Number is %f\n", b);

flush(stdin);
printf("Enter an character \n");
scanf("%c", &c);

printf("The Character is %c\n", c);
return 0;

}
```

Explanation: In the above program, we have declared three variables a, b, c of int, float and char type respectively. This program allows the user to enter three different data using scanf() function and the data input will be displayed on the monitor using output function namely printf(). This program is an illustration of how scanf() and printf() functions can be used to input and output data of different types.

SUMMARY

- Application software is one which is written for the purpose of accomplishing some user-defined job
- System software is one which is aware of the architectural details of the hardware components and can directly interact with the hardware components of computer systems.
- Dennis Ritchie invented the C language in 1972 at AT and T Bell laboratories
- C is called a Middle Level Language
- C supports Structured Design approach
- C is Extensible
- C is rich in data types and operators
- C is portable
- One of the real strengths of the C language is the availability of extensive library of predefined functions
- The C language has close association with UNIX operating system
- Header files are those that are included in the beginning of a program itself.
- All the symbolic constants are defined by means of preprocessor directive #define

- Local variables are those that are declared within a function and accessible only within the function
- Global variables are those which are seen by more than one function
- The Compile-time Errors occur if the programs do not conform to the grammatical rules of the language being used
- The Linker Errors occur during the linking process when the external symbols referred to by the program are not resolved
- The Runtime Errors occur while a program is being run and hence the name. They occur due to both program internal factors and external factors
- The Logical Errors occur if the solution procedure for the given problem itself is wrong
- Character set of a language is also called Alphabet.
- Keywords are those words of C which have predefined meaning assigned by the C language.
- An identifier is one which is used to designate program elements like variables, constants, array names, function names etc
- A constant is one the value of which does not change during the execution of a program
- A variable is a named memory location, the value of which can change during the execution of the program containing it
- Basic data types supported by C include char, int and float and their variations

REVIEW QUESTIONS

3.1 What are the advantages of higher level languages?

3.2 What is an application software?

3.3 What is a system software?

3.4 Write the differences between application software and system software.

3.5 C is called a middle level language. Why?

3.6 Who invented BCPL language?

3.7 Who invented B language?

3.8 Mention the limitations of B language?

3.9 Who invented C language?

3.10 What are the salient features of C language?

3.11 In what way C is superior to traditional languages like BASIC, COBOL, etc.?

3.12 Explain the structure of a C program.

3.13 What are local variables?

3.14 What are global variables?

3.15 How do we define a constant?

3.16 What are the steps involved in executing a C program?

3.17 How do you compile multiple source programs in the Unix Environment?

3.18 What are the different types of errors?

3.19 What are syntactical errors? Give examples.

3.20 What are linker errors? Give examples.

3.21 What are runtime errors? Give examples.

3.22 When do we get logical errors?

3.23 What do you mean by the alphabet of a language?

3.24 What is a C word?

3.25 What is a keyword?

3.26 Mention any five keywords of C.

3.27 What is an identifier? Mention the rules to be followed while forming identifiers.

3.28 Identify whether the following are valid or invalid identifiers.

(a) al   (b) a b   (c) rollno   (d) _count   (e) ISPRIME

3.29 Define a constant. Give an account of classifications of constants.

3.30 What are the rules for integer constants?

3.31 What are the rules for real constants?

3.32 Differentiate between a single character constant and a string constant.

3.33 What is a variable? Write the syntax of declaration of variables.

3.34 C is rich in data types. Justify.

3.35 What are the modifiers of `int` data type and mention their significance.

3.36 Distinguish between `char` and `unsigned char`.

3.37 Why a variable is to be declared?

3.38 In what way variable declaration differs from constant definition?

3.39 Distinguish between `float` and `double data` types.

3.40 What are the modifiers of `float` type? Mention their significance.

3.41 What is the range of values which can be stored in a variable of type `int`?

3.42 What is the size of a variable of type `double`?

3.43 What is the number of digits of precision provided in the case of `float` type?

State whether the following are true or false

3.1 Float is a keyword.

3.2 A keyword can even be used as an identifier.

3.3 No_of_ Students is a valid identifier.

3.4 The size of a variable of type `long double` is 10 bytes.

3.5 Exponential form of real numbers can be used to represent both vary large and very small real numbers.

3.6 There is no difference between a `char` constant and a `string` constant.

3.7 The number of digits of precision provided by both `float` and `double` types are same.

3.8 The range of values that can be represented by a variable of type `char` is 0 to 255.

3.9 We can assign an integer value to a variable of type `char`.

3.10 `void` is a data type provided by C.

3.11 Format specifier for printing short `int` variable is `%ld`

3.12 By default a real number is treated as float.

INTERVIEW QUESTIONS

3.1 Why C has close association with UNIX operating system?

3.2 Is C a general purpose language? If so why?

3.3 Can we execute a C program without the source program after compilation?

3.4 What features of C make it middle level language?

3.5 List the characteristics of a structured program. In what way C is a structured programming language?

3.6 How is the declaration `int a = 5` represented in the memory?

3.7 What do you mean by low order and high order bytes?

3.8 What happens when a `double` variable is assigned to `float` variable?

3.9 What happens when a `long int` variable is assigned to `int` variable?

3.10 How do you display an integer number in octal and hexadecimal systems?

3.11 What happens when a variable is redeclared in a program given below?

```
#include<stidio.h>
int main(void)
{
    int a = 26;
    int a = 42;
    printf("value of a = %d\n", a);
    return 0;
}
```

3.12 Identify the wrong variable name.

(a) Int   (b) FLOAT   (c) double   (d) long_Double

3.13 What is the output of the following programs

(a)
```
#include<stdio.h>
int main(void)
{
    int a = 020;
    printf("%dd", a, a);
    return 0;
}
```

(b)
```
#include<stdio.h>
int main(void)
{
    char t='a';
    printf("%d%c", t, t);
}
```
(c)
```
#include<stdio.h>
int main(void)
{
    char t='a';
    t++;
    printf("%d%c", t, t);
    return 0;
}
```
(d)
```
#include<stdio.h>
int main(void)
{
    int a=48;
    a++;
    printf("%d%c", t, t);
    return 0;
}
```
3.14 What is the output of `printf("%d", "printf");`?

3.15 What is wrong in the following programs

(a)
```
#include<stdio.h>
int main(void)
{
    const int a;
    a=10;
    a++;
    printf("%d", a);
    return 0;
}
```
(b)
```
#include<stdio.h>
int main(void)
{
    const int a = 10;
    a++;
```

```
        printf("%d", a);
        return 0;
    }
```

3.16 Identify the syntax errors (if any) in the following C program:

```
#include<stdio_h>
int main {void}
{
    printf('Compiler can detect Syntax Errors only')
    printf('Logical errors are difficult to detect")
    return 0;
}
```

3.17 Identify the syntax error (if any) in the following program:

```
#include<stdio.h>
int main(void)
{
    printf("Programming in C is fun"); printf("C is a case
sensitive Language"); return 0;}
```

3.18 How do you print an integer number declared as short int?

4

Input–Output Operations

4.1 INTRODUCTION

The main objective of any program is to process data according to a set of instructions given in a program to produce the desired output. This operation of processing the data to produce the output is known as **data processing**. A computer is basically a tool for processing the data according to the given program to produce the desired output. Hence, a computer is referred to as a data processor. Each program revolves round some data. Of course, data are the reasons for the existence of programs. Programs require some inputs to be given; they will then process the inputs to produce the expected outputs. Accepting inputs, processing the inputs to produce the expected outputs and presenting the outputs to the outside world are the three fundamental functions of programs. Accepting the required inputs from input devices and displaying the produced results on output devices are referred to as **Input–Output operations**. All the earlier higher level programming languages provided their own statements for the purpose of input–output operations.

C language deviates from this fact even though C programs are not an exception as far as the Input–Output operations are concerned. Dennis Ritchie, the inventor of C, purposefully did not include I/O statements as part of the definition of C language. The reason behind this is to make the language a portable one. That is, to make the C programs run in different environments without or with little modifications. The inventor of C language left the task of dealing with the I/O operations to the designer of C compilers.

We know that operating systems provide the facility for I/O operations. Different operating systems deal with I/O operations in different ways. For instance, the way DOS accepts inputs from the input devices and displays output on the output devices is different from the way Unix deals with them. But in both the environments the functions `scanf()` and `printf()` only are used to accept inputs and to display outputs respectively. Here, the `scanf()` and `printf()` for DOS have been written by the designer of the C compiler for DOS keeping in mind how DOS deals with I/O operations. The functions are then packaged in a standard library. Similarly, the `scanf()`

and `printf()` for Unix have been written by the designer of the C compiler for Unix keeping in mind how Unix deals with I/O operations. The functions are then packaged in a standard library.

There are three types of I/O systems depending on the source devices for input and target devices for output. They are:

1. Console I/O
2. Disk I/O
3. Port I/O

The standard library of I/O functions for a platform will be provided by the designer of the compiler for that platform. We simply use them without bothering much about the intricacies of the functions. Since the prototypes of the functions are available in the header file `stdio.h`, we need to include it as part of our source program file with the help of the preprocessor directive `#include` as:

`#include <stdio.h>`

n this chapter, we deal with Console I/O only. Console I/O uses keyboard as the standard input device and screen as the standard output device.

4.2 THE `getchar()` AND `putchar()` FUNCTIONS

`getchar()` and `putchar()` are the simplest I/O functions and they are used to perform character input and output respectively.

`getchar()` is a function used to read a character through standard input, the keyboard. The syntax of its usage is as follows.

`c = getchar();`

where c is a variable of `char` type. As a result of this, a character typed at the keyboard is assigned to the variable c.

`putchar()` is the counterpart of `getchar()`. It is used to display a character on standard output, the screen. The syntax of using `putchar()` is as follows:

`putchar(c);`

where c represents a variable of type `char` or a character constant. It displays the character stored in c on the screen, or the character constant.

PROGRAM 4.1 To illustrate `getchar()` and `putchar()`

```
#include <stdio.h>

int main(void)
{
      char c;

      c = getchar();
      putchar(c);

      return 0;
}
```

Input–Output:

r

r

4.3 THE scanf() AND printf() FUNCTIONS

In many situations we need to input data of heterogeneous types. C language provides a more general input function namely scanf() which allows the user to input data of different types. The scanf() is used to accept mixed or same types of data through the keyboard. The syntax of its usage is as follows:

scanf("control string", arg1,arg2,........,argn);

Here, arg1, arg2, ..., argn are the addresses of the variables into which data are to be accepted. & symbol precedes each variable (except string variables) to obtain the address of the variable. control string consists of field specifications, which determine how the input data are to be interpreted, they include conversion specifier % , data-type specifier and an optional number, which indicates the width in which data are to be accepted. The general form of the field specifiers is : % [optional width specifier] [data-type specifier]. The data-type specifier indicates the type of the corresponding argument in the arguments-list.

Example 4.1

To accept a value into a variable **n** of **int** type, the following statement is used.

scanf("%d", &n);

Here **%d** is the format specifier for the int variable **n**. (format specifier is another name for data type specifier.)

Format specifiers for other data types available in C are given below.

Format specifiers	Meaning
%c	a character
%d	a decimal integer
%f	a floating point value
%e	a floating value
%h	a short integer
%ld	a long integer
%s	a string
%u	an unsigned integer
%o	an octal number
%x	a hexadecimal number
%[..]	a string of words

Some more example scanf() statements:

char c;

c is a variable of **char** type. The following scanf () statement is to accept a character into the variable **c**.

```
scanf("%c", &c);
```

Note that the format specifier used is %c.

```
float f;
```

f is a variable of float type. The following scanf () statement is to accept a floating point value into the variable **f**.

```
scanf("%f", &f);
```

Note that the format specifier used is %f.

To read values into three variables **i**, **f** and **c** of type **int**, **float** and **char** respectively using a single statement. The following statement is used.

```
scanf("%d%f%c", &i, &f, &c);
```

Note that the order of the format specifiers matches with that of the variables (arguments). This is a must when we are reading into more than one variable. The values entered must be delimited by spaces, tabs or newline characters.

A complementary operation similar to scanf () is printf (). This function is used to display data on the screen. The syntax of its usage is similar to that of scanf ():

```
printf("control string", arg1,arg2,......, argn);
```

Here, arg1, arg2, . . . , argn are the variables, the values of which are to be displayed on the screen. control string consists of the following three items.

1. Format specifiers similar to those discussed in the case of scanf ().
2. Some sequence of characters, which will be displayed on the screen as they are.
3. Characters like \n, \t and \b etc. These characters are called **Escape Sequence characters.**

Example 4.2

To display the value of the variable **n** of **int** type, the following statement is used.

```
printf("%d", n);
```

Here **%d** is the format specifier for the int variable **n**.

Format specifiers for other data types available in C is given below.

Table of format specifiers

Format specifiers	Meaning
%c	character
%d	decimal integer
%ld	long integer
%f	floating point value in decimal point notation
%e	floating point value in exponential form
%h	short integer

%lf	double
%s	string
%u	unsigned integer
%p	pointer
%o	octal number without the prefix 0
%x	hexadecimal number without the prefix 0x

Table of escape sequence characters

Escape sequence	Meaning
\n	New line
\t	Horizontal tab
\v	Vertical tab
\f	Form feed
\b	Backspace
\a	Alert character
\\	Backslash
\?	Question mark
\'	Single quote
\"	Double quote

Some more example `printf()` statements:

`char c;`

c is a variable of **char** type. The following `printf()` statement is to display the character stored in the variable **c**.

`printf("%c", c);`

Note that the format specifier used is `%c`.

`float f;`

f is a variable of **float** type. The following `printf()` statement is to display the floating point value stored in the variable **f**.

`printf("%f", f);`

Note that the format specifier used is `%f`.

To display the values stored in three variables **i**, **f** and **c** of type **int**, **float** and **char** respectively using a single statement. The following `printf()` statement is used.

`printf("%d%f%c", i, f, c);`

Note that the order of the format specifiers matches with that of the variables (arguments). This is a must when we are displaying values of more than one variable.

`printf("Welcome to Programming in C");`

Here, arguments are not provided. Displays the string "Welcome to Programming in C" on the screen. Many times, the printf() is used to display just some messages.

Note: Prompt messages cannot be included as part of the control string of scanf() statements. In an interactive program, normally, printf() statements are used for the purpose before scanf() statements.

Example 4.3

```
printf ("Enter a number \n");
scanf ("%d", &n);
```

Note:

printf() returns the number of characters displayed on the screen

```
    noi = printf ("Welcome");
```

Here the variable **noi** would collect 7, the number of characters in the message "Welcome".

PROGRAM 4.2   To illustrate scanf() and printff()

```
#include <stdio.h>

int main (void)
{
        int i;
        float f;
        char c;

printf ("Enter a character into c \n");
scanf ("%c", &c);
printf ("Enter a value for i \n");
scanf ("%d", &i);
printf ("Enter a value for f \n");
scanf ("%f", &f);
printf ("\n c = %c \n", c);
printf (" i = %d \n", i);
printf (" f = %f \n", f);

return 0;
}
```

Input–Output:

```
Enter a character into c
r
Enter a value for i
5
```

```
Enter a value for f
6

c = r
i = 5
f = 6.000000
```

PROGRAM 4.3   To display the minimum and maximum values of different data types

```
#include <stdio.h>
#include <limits.h>

int main(void)
{
        printf("CHAR_MIN =%d \n", CHAR_MIN);
        printf("CHAR_MAX =%d \n", CHAR_MAX);
        printf("SCHAR_MIN =%d \n", SCHAR_MIN);
        printf("SCHAR_MAX =%d \n", SCHAR_MAX);

        printf("INT_MIN =%d \n", INT_MIN);
        printf("INT_MAX =%d \n", INT_MAX);
        printf("UINT_MAX =%u \n", UINT_MAX);
        printf("SHRT_MIN =%d \n", SHRT_MIN);
        printf("SHRT_MAX =%d \n", SHRT_MAX);

        printf("LONG_MIN =%ld \n", LONG_MIN);
        printf("LONG_MAX =%ld \n", LONG_MAX);
        printf("ULONG_MAX = %lu \n", ULONG_MAX);

        return 0;
}
```

Input–Output:

```
CHAR_MIN =-128
CHAR_MAX =127
SCHAR_MIN =-128
SCHAR_MAX =127
INT_MIN =-32768
INT_MAX =32767
UINT_MAX =65535
SHRT_MIN =-32768
SHRT_MAX =32767
LONG_MIN =-2147483648
LONG_MAX =2147483647
ULONG_MAX = 4294967295
```

4.4   FORMATTING OF OUTPUTS

Formatting of outputs refers to displaying the outputs in a more readable and comprehensible manner. In other words, it is nothing but dressing up of the outputs. The main objective of formatting is to increase the degree of readability of outputs. It is accomplished with the specification of the width in which data items are to be displayed and making data items to be displayed justified in the required direction in the specified width. We will now understand how integers, float values and characters are formatted by dealing with them individually.

4.4.1   Formatting of Integers

Suppose i is a variable of type int. To display the value of i, we use the following printf() statement:

```
printf("%d", i);
```

As a result of the execution of the statement, the value of i will be displayed on the screen starting from the first column of the screen as follows.

```
3456
```

The value of i can be formatted by modifying the above control string. The modified control string would be %wd, where w is an integer specifying the width within which the value of i has to be displayed. The following examples illustrate formatting the value of i in different ways.

1. printf("%6d", i);

		3	4	5	6

   Since the width specified is six, six columns are allocated and the value of i is right-justified in the specified width.

2. printf("%3d",i);

3	4	5	6

   Since the width specified is less than the actual number of digits of the value in i, the width is ignored and the full value is displayed.

3. printf("%-6d", i);

3	4	5	6		

   Since – symbol is used before the width specifier 6, the value of i is left-justified.

4. printf("%06d", i);

0	0	3	4	5	6

   Since 0 is used before the width specifier 6, the leading blanks are filled with 0s. This is called **padding with 0s**.

PROGRAM 4.4   To illustrate the formatting of integers

```c
#include <stdio.h>

int main(void)
{
        int a = 6789;

        printf("%d\n", a);
        printf("%3d\n", a);
        printf("%6d\n", a);
        printf("%-6d\n", a);
        printf("%06d\n", a);

        return 0;
}
```

Input–Output:

```
6789
6789
    6789
6789
006789
```

4.4.2 Formatting of Floating Point Values

Suppose **f** is a variable of type **float**. To display the value of **f**, we use the following printf() statement:

```c
printf("%f", f);
```

As a result of the execution of the statement, the value of **f** will be displayed on the screen starting from the first column of the screen as follows:

3456.560000

The value of f can be formatted by modifying the above control string. The modified control string would be **%w.pf**, where **w** is an integer specifying the width within which the value of f has to be displayed and **p** denotes the number of digits to be displayed after the decimal point. The following examples illustrate formatting the value of **f** in different ways.

1. printf("%7.2f", f);

3	4	5	6	.	5	6

Since the width specified is seven, seven columns are allocated and the value of f is displayed as shown above. Note that the decimal point also occupies one location and only two digits are displayed after the decimal point.

2. `printf("%3.2f", f);`

3	4	5	6	.	5	6

Since the width specified is less than the actual number of digits of the value in f, the width is ignored and the full value is displayed.

3. `printf("%9.2f", f);`

		3	4	5	6	.	5	6

Since the width specified is nine which is greater than the number of digits in the given number, nine columns are allocated and the value of f is right justified in the specified width.

4. `printf("%-9.2f", f);`

3	4	5	6	.	5	6		

Since the width specified is nine which is greater than the number of digits in the given number, nine columns are allocated and the value of f is left justified in the specified width because of the presence of – symbol before the width specifier.

5. `printf("%09.2f", f);`

0	0	3	4	5	6	.	5	6

Since the symbol 0 is used before the width specifier, the leading blanks are filled with 0s. The number is said to have been padded with 0s.

6. `printf("%7.1f", f);`

	3	4	5	6	.	6

Since the number of digits after the decimal point to be displayed, which is one, is less than the actual number of digits (two) after the point in the given number, the value is rounded off to the first digit.

7. `printf("%e", f);`

3	.	4	5	6	5	6	0	e	+	0	3

Displays the floating point number in exponentiation form with six digits after the point in the mantissa.

8. `printf("%10.3e", f);`

		3	.	4	6	e	+	0	3

Displays the floating point number in exponentiation form with three before the point in the mantissa within the specified width. The display is right justified.

9. `printf("-10.3e", f);`

3	·	4	6	e	+	0	3		

Displays the floating point number in exponentiation form with three before the point in the mantissa within the specified width. The display is left justified because of the presence of minus symbol before the width.

PROGRAM 4.5   To illustrate the formatting of floating point values

---

```
#include <stdio.h>

int main(void)
{
    float f = 3456.56;

    printf("%f \n", f);
    printf("%7.2f \n", f);
    printf("%3.2f\n", f);
    printf("%9.2f\n", f);
    printf("%-9.2f\n", f);
    printf("%09.2f\n", f);
    printf("%7.1f\n", f);
    printf("%e\n", f);
    printf("%10.2e\n", f);
    printf("%-10.2e\n", f);

    return 0;
}
```

Input–Output:

```
3456.560059
3456.56
3456.56
   3456.56
3456.56
003456.56
   3456.6
3.456560e+03
   3.46e+03
3.46e+03
```

4.4.3 Formatting of Characters

Suppose c is a variable of type `char`. To display the character stored in the variable **c**, we use the following `printf()` statement:

```
printf("%c", c);
```

As a result of the execution of the statement, the character stored in **c** will be displayed on the screen in the current position of the cursor.

Similar to formatting of integers, characters also can be formatted. The modified control string to display a character is **%wc, w** is the width specifier.

1. `printf("%4c", c);`

   Since the width specified is four, four columns are allocated and the character stored in c is displayed right justified in the width as follows:

			a

2. `printf("%-4c", c);`

   Since the width specified is four, four columns are allocated and the character stored in c is displayed left justified in the specified width because of the presence of – symbol before the width specifier as follows:

a			

PROGRAM 4.6   To illustrate the formatting of characters

```c
#include <stdio.h>

int main(void)
{
    char c = 'a';

    printf("%c \n", c);
    printf("%4c \n", c);
    printf("%-4c \n", c);

return 0;
}
```

Input–Output:

```
a
    a
a
```

4.4.4 Displaying Data in Tabular Form

Often, we will be required to display data in multiple columns. For instance, consider the details of employees, which include Empno, Name and Salary. It would be more comprehensible if we display the details of the employees in columnar format given as follows:

Empno	Name	Salary
121	Shankar	23000
122	Vinay	33000

PROGRAM 4.7   To illustrate formatting of integer, real numbers and characters

```c
#include <stdio.h>

int main(void)
{
    int i1 = 10, i2 = 24, i3 = 56;
    float f1 = 12.34, f2 = 34.567, f3 = 456.67;
    char c1 = 'a', c2 = 'h', c3 = 'y';

    printf("Integers Float Values Characters \n");
    printf("%6d%13.2f%5c\n", i1, f1, c1);
    printf("%6d%13.2f%5c\n", i2, f2, c2);
    printf("%6d%13.2f%5c\n", i3, f3, c3);

    return 0;
}
```

Input–Output:

```
Integers    Float    Values Characters
   10        12.34           a
   24        34.57           h
   56       456.67           y
```

SUMMARY

- The operation of processing the given data to produce the required output is known as data processing
- Accepting the required inputs from input devices and displaying the produced results on output devices are referred to as Input/Output operations
- The standard library of I/O functions for a platform will be provided by the designer of the compiler for that platform
- The getchar() is a function used to read a character through standard input, the keyboard
- The putchar() is a function used to display a character on standard output, the screen.
- The scanf() is used to accept mixed or same types of data through the keyboard
- The printf() is used to display mixed or same types of data on the screen
- Formatting of outputs refers to displaying the outputs in more readable and comprehensible manner.

REVIEW QUESTIONS

4.1 Why does C language not have its own Input–Output statements?

4.2 Mention the character-oriented I/O functions.

4.3 Write the syntax of using `getchar()` and `putchar()`.

4.4 Explain `printf()`.

4.5 What does the control string of `printf()` consist of?

4.6 Explain `scanf()`.

4.7 Can we have prompt messages as part of `scanf()`?

4.8 What is the significance of fomatting of outputs?

PROGRAMMING EXERCISES

4.1 Write a program to accept length and breadth of a rectangle and find its area.

4.2 Write a program to accept two integers, two double values and display them. (Integers are to be left justified, double values are to be right justified and the number of decimal digits after the point is 2.)

4.3 Write a C program to display the number 567 in the following formats:

000567

0567

567

4.4 Write a program to accept an integer number and display the number in decimal, octal and hexadecimal system.

INTERVIEW QUESTIONS

4.1 What is the output of the following programs? Give reason to justify your answer.

(a)

```
#include <stdio.h>
int main(void)
{
    float f = 2.3456;
```

```
        int a = 1234;
        printf("%d\n", f);
        printf("%0.2f\n", f);
        printf("%5.1f \n", f);
        printf("%4.2f\n", a);
        return 0;
    }
```

(b)
```
    #include <stdio.h>
    int main(void)
    {
        int a = 6790;
        printf("%2d \n", a);
        printf("%f \n", a);
        printf("%.2d \n", a);
        return 0;
    }
```

(c)
```
    #include <stdio.h>
    int main(void)
    {
        float f = 67.9067;
        printf("%7.2f \n", f);
        printf("%f \n", f);
        printf("%5.1f \n", f);
        return 0;
    }
```

(d)
```
    #include <stdio.h>
    int main(void)
    {
        int a = 012;
        printf("%d\n", d);
        return 0;
    }
```

(e)
```
    #include <stdio.h>
    int main(void)
```

```
{
    int a=15;
    float b='a';
    float c = 45.24
    printf("%f", a);
    printf("%c", b);
    printf("%d", b);
    printf("%f", c);
    return 0;
}
```

4.2 Number of significant characters in an identifier depends on

(a) Machine   (b) Compiler   (c) Processor   (d) None

4.3 An example of legal identifier is

(a) int   (b) Main   (c) Float   (d) All of them

4.4 Can we print a string of characters using %c format specifier? Give an example.

4.5 What happens when a variable is redefined in a program given below?

```
#include<stdio.h>
int main(void)
{
    int a = 5;

    int a = 10;
    printf("%d", a);
    return 0;
}
```

4.6 Can we have the same variable name and the function name in a program?

5

Operators and Expressions

5.1 INTRODUCTION

A program operates on input data to produce the desired output. This requires processing of data and it is done by means of what is known as an **operator**. Data processing is done as per the instructions in the program. Same data when processed differently leads to different output. Operators are symbols which instruct computer to perform the specified manipulations over some data. They are useful for writing expressions in C. One of the real strengths of C is the availability of large number of operators. This rich set of operators available in C enable us to write efficient and concise programs and this fact serves to set C apart from any other programming languages. Even operators are also classified into three types depending on the number of operands used, i.e., 1. Unary operators, 2. Binary operators and 3. Ternary operators. A **unary operator** is one which is defined over a single operand. A **binary operator** is one which is defined over two operands. A **ternary operator** is one which is defined over three operands.

Operators can not be used in isolation. They have to be used in combination with either variables or constants or with combination of variables and constants. When used in combination, they are said to form what are called expressions. An **expression** in C is thus a combination of variables or constants and operators conforming to the syntax rules of the language. The variables or constants used with an operator are the ones which are subjected to the operation specified by the operator and hence they are called **operands** for the operator. Depending on the operators used, the expressions are further classified into **Arithmetic Expressions, Relational Expressions, Logical Expressions**, etc.

Depending on the type of operations they perform, they are classified into the following types.

- Assignment operator

  =
- Arithmetic operators

  +, -, *, /, %, unary +, unary -

- Relational operators
  `<, <=, >, >=, ==, !=`
- Logical operators
  `&&, ||, !`
- Increment/Decrement operators
  `++, --`
- Shorthand arithmetic assignment operators
  `+=, -=, *=, /=, %=`
- Conditional operator
  `?:`
- Bitwise operators
  `&, |, ^, <<, >>`
- `sizeof()` operator
- Comma operator
  `,`

and so on.

5.2 ASSIGNMENT OPERATOR [=]

The single equal symbol = is referred to as the assignment operator. It is used to assign the value of an expression to a variable. The statement used for this purpose is called the assignment statement. The general form of an assignment statement is as follows:

Variable = Expression;

The **Expression** can be a constant, variable or any valid C expression.

Example 5.1

```
int a;
a = 10;
```
The variable a is assigned the value 10.

Example 5.2

```
int a, b =10;
a = b;
```
The variable a is assigned the value of b.

Example 5.3

```
int a =5, b =10, c;
c = a + b;
```
Here, the value of the expression a + b, which is 15, is assigned to the variable c.

PROGRAM 5.1   To illustrate assignment operator [=]

```
#include <stdio.h>

int main(void)
{
    int a, b, c;

    a = 10;
    printf("a = %d \n", a);
    b = a;      /* Value of a is assigned to b */
    printf("b = %d \n", b);
    c = a + b;  /* Value of the expression a + b is assigned to c */
    printf("c = %d \n", c);

    return 0;
}
```

Input–Output:

```
A = 10
B = 10
C = 20
```

5.3 ARITHMETIC OPERATORS [unary +, unary -, +, -, *, /, %]

The arithmetic operators are used to perform arithmetic operations like addition, subtraction, multiplication, etc. over numeric values by constructing arithmetic expressions. An arithmetic expression is one which comprises arithmetic operators and variables or constants. Here variables and constants are called operands. The unary + and unary – are defined over a single operand and hence the name unary operators. Their usage is of the form + operand and –operand respectively. The unary + has no effect on the value of operand. But the unary – changes the sign of the operand.

Example 5.4

```
a = 10;
```
+a, -a are the valid arithmetic expressions.
+a evaluates to 10 only, the value of a.
-a evaluates to –10.

The remaining +, -, *, / and % are binary arithmetic operators since they are defined over two operands. Note that + and – play dual roles.

A simple arithmetic expression with binary arithmetic operators is of the form

```
operand1 operator operand2
```

where operator is any binary arithmetic operator, operand1 and operand2 can both be variables or constants or a combination of variable and constant.

Example 5.5

```
a + b
a - 7
4 * 9
a / 4
```
b % 3 are all valid arithmetic expressions.

If a and b are two operands

a + b is a simple arithmetic expression and it evaluates to the sum of a and b. The assignment statement s = a + b on its execution assigns the sum of a and b to the variable s.

a - b is a simple arithmetic expression and it evaluates to the difference between a and b. The assignment statement d = a - b on its execution assigns the difference between a and b to the variable d.

a * b is a simple arithmetic expression and it evaluates to the product of a and b. The assignment statement p = a + b on its execution assigns the product of a and b to the variable p.

a / b is a simple arithmetic expression and it evaluates to the quotient after division of a by b. The assignment statement q = a / b on its execution assigns the quotient after division of a by b to the variable q.

a % b is a simple arithmetic expression and it evaluates to the remainder after division of a by b. The assignment statement r = a % b on its execution assigns the remainder after division of a by b to the variable s. The operator % is defined over integers only.

Arithmetic operators			
+	Addition	4 + 5	9
-	Subtraction	4 - 5	-1
*	Multiplication	4 * 5	20
/	Division	4 / 5	0
%	Remainder	4 / 5	4

PROGRAM 5.2   To illustrate arithmetic operators [+, -, *, /, %]

```c
#include <stdio.h>

int main(void)
{

    int a, b, sum, diff, product, rem, quotient;

    printf("Enter two numbers \n");
    scanf("%d%d", &a, &b);

    sum = a + b;
    diff = a - b;
    product = a * b;
    quotient = a / b;
```

```
rem = a % b;

printf (" a = %d b = %d \n", a, b);
printf ("Addition: \t\t %d + %d = %d \n", a, b, sum);
printf ("Subtraction: \t\t %d - %d = %d \n", a, b, diff);
printf ("Multiplication: \t %d * %d = %d \n", a, b, product);
printf ("Division: \t\t %d / %d = %d \n", a, b, quotient);
printf ("Remainder: \t\t %d %% %d = %d \n", a, b, rem);

return 0;
}
```

Input–Output:

```
Enter two numbers
6   3

a = 6   b = 3

Addition:            6 + 3 = 9
Subtraction:         6 - 3 = 3
Multiplication:      6 * 3 = 18
Division:            6 / 3 = 2
Remainder            6 % 3 = 0
```

Explanation:

In the above program, all the assignment statements are of the form `Result = operand1 arithmetic-operator operand2;` In each of the assignments, the expression on the right-hand side of the assignment operator gets evaluated and the result of the expression is assigned to the variable on the left-hand side of the assignment operator. The values of the collecting variables are displayed.

5.3.1 Types of Arithmetic Expressions

Depending on the type of operands used, arithmetic expressions are further classified into

1. Integer mode expression
2. Real mode expression (Floating point mode expression)
3. Mixed mode expression

Integer mode expressions: If all the operands of an expression are integers (`char`, `unsigned char`, `int`, `short`, `long`, `unsigned int`), the expression is called an integer mode expression. The resultant value of an integer mode expression is always an integer.

Example 5.6

4 + 5	is an integer mode expression
= 9	is an integer

Example 5.7

```
int a, b;
long l, m;
```
a + b, l / m and a * l + m are all integer expressions.

Real mode expressions: If all the operands used in an expression are real values (float, double, long double) then it is called a real mode expression. The resultant value of a real mode expression is always value of real type.

Example 5.8

```
5.4 + 4.0      is a real mode expression
= 9.4          is a value of float type
```

Example 5.9

```
float f, g;
double d, e;
long double ld, le;
```
f + g, f + d and ld * le are all real mode expressions.

Mixed mode expressions: If some operands are of integer type and some are of real type in an expression, then it is called a mixed mode expression. The resultant value of a mixed mode expression will always be of real type.

Example 5.10

```
5.4 + 4              is a mixed mode expression
```

Example 5.11

```
int a;
float f;
long l;
double d;
```
a + f, a – d, l * f are all mixed mode expressions.

5.3.2   Precedence of Arithmetic Operators and Associativity

In reality, an arithmetic expression can even have more than one arithmetic operator wherein each operator is surrounded by two operands (except unary operators).

Example 5.12

```
int a = 4, b = 5, c = 6;
a + b * c
```

The above expression has two operators + and *. While evaluating the expression, if we consider part of the expression consisting of + first; and * next, the value obtained would be 9 * 6 = 54. On the other hand, if we take * first and + next, the value of the expression turns out to be 4 + 30 = 34. As observed, there are two possible outcomes, which make the outcome ambiguous. This problem is eliminated by associating relative precedence to the operators. **Operator precedence** determines the order of evaluation of an arithmetic expression and ensures that the expression produces only one value. The following is the precedence level and associativity of arithmetic operators.

Precedence level	Operators	Associativity
I	Unary+, Unary−	Right to Left
II	*, /, %	Left to Right
III	+, −	Left to Right

According to the operator precedence rules, the value of the above expression a + b * c would be 4 + 30 = 34. Since b and c are multiplied first and then the product and a are summed.

If an arithmetic expression has more than one operator, which are at the same level, then the order of evaluation is determined by a rule called **associativity**. In the case of arithmetic operators, they will be evaluated from left to right.

Example 5.13

```
int a = 4, b = 12, c = 6, d = 7;
a + b/c * d
```

In the above expression, since both / and * are present, which are at the same level, first / gets evaluated and then evaluation of * follows. After these, + gets evaluated. As a result of this, the value of the expression turns out to be:

```
4 + 12/6 * 7
= 4 + 2 * 7
= 4 + 14
= 18
```

However, we can override the default order of evaluation of an expression by using pairs of parenthesis. In this case, the sub-expressions enclosed within the parenthesis are given top priority while evaluating.

Example 5.14

```
int a = 4, b = 5, c = 6;
(a + b) * c
```

Here, even though * is at higher level than +, a and b are added first. c is then multiplied with the sum. The result of the expression would thus be:

```
(4 + 5) * 6
= 9 * 6
= 54
```

PROGRAM 5.3　To illustrate operator precedence in arithmetic operators
　　　　　　　　　[unary +, unary -, +, -, *, / and %]

```
#include <stdio.h>

int main(void)
```

```
{
    int a = 4, b = 6, c = 3, d, e, f, g;

    d = -a + b * c;
    e = (a + b) * c;
    f = a * b / c;
    g = a * (b / c);
    printf(" a = %d b = %d c = %d \n\n", a, b, c);
    printf(" -%d + %d * %d = %d \n", a, b, c, d);
    printf(" (%d + %d) * %d = %d \n", a, b, c, e);
    printf(" %d * %d / %d = %d \n", a, b, c, f);
    printf(" %d * (%d / %d) = %d \n", a, b, c, g);

    return 0;
}
```

Input–Output:

```
a = 4 b = 6 c = 3

-4 + 6 * 3 = 14

(4 + 6) * 3 = 30

4 * 6 / 3 = 8

4 * (6 / 3) = 8
```

Explanation:

In Program 5.3, the evaluation of the statement $d = -a + b * c$; proceeds as follows:

$d = -4 + 6 * 3$	The value of a, i.e., 4 gets negated since the operator unary enjoys the highest priority.
$= -4 + 18$	The values of b and c, 6 and 3 respectively are multiplied since the arithmetic operator * is at the next higher level.
$= 14$	The intermediate results are added and the sum is then assigned to the variable **d**.

The evaluation of the statement $e = (a + b) * c$; proceeds as follows:

$e = (a + b) * c$	
$= (4 + 6) * 3$	
$= 10 * 3$	The sub-expression $(4 + 6)$ gets evaluated first since it is enclosed within a pair of parentheses.
$e = 30$	10 and 3 are then multiplied to produce 30 which is then assigned to the variable **e**.

Note that in the above expression, even though the multiplication operator * is at a higher precedence level than that of the addition operator +, addition is performed first. This is because of the fact that the sub-expression $4 + 6$ is enclosed within a pair of parentheses. (The usage of the set of parentheses has thus overridden the precedence rule.)

The evaluation of the statement `f = a * b/c;` proceeds as follows:

```
f = a*b/c;
  = 4*6/3
  = 24/3        The sub-expression 4 * 6 gets evaluated first to produce 24 since both * and
                / are at the same precedence level and the associativity of the operators is
                from left to right.
f = 8           24 is divided by 3 to produce 8, which is then assigned to the variable f.
```

The evaluation of the statement `g = a * (b/c);` proceeds as follows:

```
g = a * (b/c);
  = 4 * (6/3)
  = 4 * 2       The sub-expression 6 / 3 gets evaluated first to produce 2 since the sub-
                expression is enclosed within a pair of parentheses.
g = 8           4 and 2 are multiplied to produce 8, which is then assigned to the variable g.
```

Note that in the above expression, even though the multiplication operator * and the division operator/are at the same level and their associativity is from left to right, the sub-expression $6 / 3$ is evaluated first. This is because of the fact that the sub-expression is enclosed within a pair of parentheses. The usage of the set of parentheses has thus overridden the associativity rule.

Examples of some mathematical expressions and their equivalent C expressions

Mathematical expressions	Equivalent C expressions
$(a + b)^2$	(a + b) * (a + b)
$a^2 + b^2 - 2ab$	a * a + b * b - 2 * a * b
$u^2 - 2as$	u * u - 2 * a * s
$ut + (1/2) at^2$	u * t + (1 / 2) * a * t * t
$(a - b) / a + b$	(a - b) / a + b

5.4 RELATIONAL OPERATORS [<, <=, >, >=, ==, !=]

The Relational Operators are used to construct Relational Expressions, which are used to compare two quantities. A relational expression is of the form **operand1 operator operand2**, where `operator` is any relational operator. `operand1` and `operand2` are variables or constants or a combination of both, which are being compared. The value of a relational expression in C is 1 or 0. 1 indicates that the condition is true and 0 indicates that the condition is false. A relational expression is also called a conditional expression or a Boolean expression.

Example 5.15

`a < b, a > 10, 5 == 10` are all valid relational expressions.

Relational expressions are excessively used as parts of decision-making and branching statements, and looping statements. We will see this later.

Relational operators			
<	Less than	4 < 5	1
<=	Less than or equal to	4 <= 5	1
>	Greater than	4 > 5	0
>=	Greater than or equal to	4 >= 5	0
==	Equal to	4 == 5	0
!=	Not equal to	4 != 5	1

PROGRAM 5.4   To illustrate relational operators [<, < =, >, >=, ==, ! =]

```
#include <stdio.h>

int main(void)
{
    int a, b, c, d, e, f, g, h;

    printf("Enter two numbers \n");
    scanf("%d%d", &a, &b);

    c = a < b;
    d = a < = b;
    e = a > b;
    f = a < = b;
    g = a = = b;
    h = a != b;
    printf("Less than: \t\t (%d < %d) = %d \n", a, b, c);
    printf("Less than or equal to: \t (%d <= %d) = %d \n",a,b,d);
    printf("Greater than: \t\t (%d > %d) = %d \n", a, b, e);
    printf("Greater than or equal to:(%d >= %d) = %d \n", a,b,f);
    printf("Equal to: \t\t (%d == %d) = %d \n", a, b, g);
    printf("Not equal to: \t\t (%d != %d) = %d \n", a, b, h);

    return 0;
}
```

Input–Output:

```
Less than:                  (5 < 6) = 1
Less than or equal to:      (5 <= 6) = 1
Greater than:               (5 > 6) = 0
Greater than or equal to:   (5 >= 6) = 1
Equal to:                   (5 == 6) = 0
Not equal to:               (5 != 6) = 1
```

Explanation:

In the above program, all the assignment statements are of the form **Result = operand1 relational-operator operand2;** In each of the statements, the expression on the right-hand side of the assignment operator gets evaluated and the result of the expression, which is either 1 (true) or 0 (false) is assigned to the variable on the left-hand side of the assignment operator.

Precedence levels and associativity within relational operators

Precedence level	Operators	Associativity
I	`<, <=, >, >=`	Left to Right
II	`==, !=`	Left to Right

5.5 LOGICAL OPERATORS [&&, ||, !]

These are used to construct compound conditional expressions. `&&` , `||` are used to combine two conditional expressions and `!` is used to negate a conditional expression.

Logical AND `&&`

The general form of a compound conditional expression constructed using `&&` is

    c1 && c2

where `c1` and `c2` are conditional expressions.

The working of `&&` is depicted in the following Truth Table.

c1	c2	c1&&c2
T	T	T
T	F	F
F	–	F

`c1` is first checked. If `c1` is true, then `c2` is checked. If `c2` is also true, then `c1&&c2` evaluates to true. If `c2` is false, then `c1&&c2` evaluates to false. (`c2` is checked only when `c1` is true). If `c1` itself is false, irrespective of whether `c2` is true or false (indicated by – for `c2`), `c1&&c2` evaluates to false.

Note: The resultant condition (`c1&&c2`) is true only when both the conditions `c1` and `c2` are true. Otherwise, it will be false.

Logical OR [||]

The general form of a compound conditional expression constructed using || is

    c1 || c2

where `c1` and `c2` are conditional expressions.

The working of || is depicted in the following Truth Table.

c1	c2	c1||c2
T	–	T
F	T	T
F	F	F

c1 is first checked. If c1 is true, irrespective of whether c2 is true or false (indicated by – for c2), c1 || c2 evaluates to true. If c1 is false, c2 is checked. If c2 is true, c1 || c2 evaluates to true. On the other hand, if c2 is false, c1 || c2 evaluates to false. c1 || c2 is checked only when c1 is false.

Note: The resultant condition (c1 || c2) is false, only when both the conditions c1 and c2 are false. Otherwise, it will be true.

Logical NOT [!]

The general form of a compound conditional expression using ! is as follows:

!c

where c is a test-expression.

c1	!c1
T	F
F	T

Here c1 is simply negated.

In all these cases, c1 and c2 can by themselves be compound conditional expressions. Knowledge of the working of these operators is essential while constructing compound conditional expressions to suit our requirement.

PROGRAM 5.5   To illustrate logical operators [&&, ||, !]

```
#include <stdio.h>

int main(void)
{
      int a = 5, b = 6, c = 7, d;

      printf("\n Working of Logical && \n\n");
      d = (a < b) && (b < c);
      printf("(%d < %d) && (%d < %d) = %d \n", a, b, b, c, d);
      d = (a < b) && (b > c);
      printf("(%d < %d) && (%d > %d) = %d \n", a, b, b, c, d);
      d = (a > b) && (b < c);
      printf("(%d > %d) && (%d < %d) = %d \n", a, b, b, c, d);
      d = (a > b) && (b > c);
      printf("(%d > %d) && (%d > %d) = %d \n", a, b, b, c, d);
      printf("\n Working of Logical || \n\n");

      d = (a < b) || (b < c);
      printf("(%d < %d) || (%d < %d) = %d \n", a, b, b, c, d);
      d = (a < b) || (b > c);
      printf("(%d < %d) || (%d > %d) = %d \n", a, b, b, c, d);
```

```
d = (a > b) || (b < c);
printf("(%d > %d) || (%d < %d) = %d \n", a, b, b, c, d);
d = (a > b) || (b > c);
printf("(%d > %d) && (%d > %d) = %d \n", a, b, b, c, d);

printf("\n Working of Logical NOT ! \n\n");
d = !(a < b);
printf("!(%d < %d) = %d \n", a, b, d);

d = !(a > b);
printf("!(%d > %d) = %d \n", a, b, d);

return 0;
}
```

Input–Output:

Working of Logical &&

```
(5 < 6) && (6 < 7) = 1
(5 < 6) && (6 > 7) = 0
(5 > 6) && (6 < 7) = 0
(5 > 6) && (6 > 7) = 0
```

Working of Logical ||

```
(5 < 6) || (6 < 7) = 1
(5 < 6) || (6 > 7) = 1
(5 > 6) || (6 < 7) = 1
(5 > 6) || (6 > 7) = 0
```

Working of Logical NOT !

```
!(5 < 6) = 0
!(5 > 6) = 1
```

Explanation:

The program serves the purpose of illustrating the working of all the logical operators. Note that for both logical OR (| |) and the logical (&&), all the four possible combinations of two conditions have been tested and the values of the resultant expressions are displayed. This reinforces the behaviour of the operators. Similarly, the working of the logical NOT (!) is also demonstrated.

Precedence levels within logical operators

Precedence level	Operators	Associativity
I	!	Right to Left
II	&&	Left to Right
III	||	Left to Right

5.6   SHORTHAND ARITHMETIC ASSIGNMENT OPERATORS

[+=, -=, *=, /=, %=]

Suppose a is a variable with the value 10. If its value is to be incremented by say, 5. With the available knowledge of arithmetic expressions and assignment statement, we would use a = a + 5. This assignment statement can now be written as a += 5; which produces the same effect as the assignment statement a = a + 5. Note that the variable a needs to be used only once.

Similarly,   a = a - 5 can be written as a -= 5
                a = a * 5 can be written as a *= 5
                a = a / 5 can be written as a /= 5
                a = a % 5 can be written as a %= 5

As the name itself indicates, these operators enable us to perform both arithmetic and assignment operations. The syntax of using these operators is as follows.

operand1 operator operand2,

where operator is any shorthand arithmetic assignment operator. operand1 should be a variable with an initial value and operand2 can be a variable, a constant or an arithmetic expression.

Example 5.16

```
a += 10;
a += b;
a += (b + c);
```

Shorthand arithmetic assignment operators a = 4		
+=	a += 5	a = 9
-=	a -= 5	a = -1
*=	a *= 5	a = 20
/=	a /= 5	a = 0
%=	a %= 5	a = 4

PROGRAM 5.6   To illustrate shorthand arithmetic assignment operators
                 [+=, -=, *=, /=, %=]

```
#include <stdio.h>

int main(void)
{
        int a, b, c, d, e;

        a = b = c = d = e = 10;
        printf("a = %d b = %d c = %d d = %d e = %d \n", a, b, c, d, e);
        a += 5;
        b -= 5;
```

```
        c *= 5;
        d /= 5;
        e %= 5;

        printf("a += 5\t a = %d\n", a);
        printf("b -= 5\t b = %d\n", b);
        printf("c *= 5\t c = %d\n", c);
        printf("d /= 5\t d = %d\n", d);
        printf("e %%= 5\t e = %d\n", e);

        return 0;
}
```

Input–Output:

```
a = 10  b = 10  c = 10  d = 10  e = 10

a += 5      a = 15
b -= 5      b = 5
c *= 5      c = 50
d /= 5      d = 2
e %= 5      e = 0
```

Explanation:

In Program 6.6 all the variables a, b, c, d and e are assigned the value 10 using the statement a = b = c = d = e = 10; This statement is perfectly valid in C. Here, the value 10 is assigned to the variable e; The value of the variable e is assigned to the variable d; The value of the variable d is then assigned to c. Likewise, the variable b will get the value of c and the variable a will get the value of b. As a result, all the five variables will get the same value 10.

When the statement a + = 5 gets executed, 5 gets added to the variable a and the value of a now becomes 15. Similarly, the other statements involving the shorthand arithmetic assignment operators change the value of the variable to the left of the operators appropriately.

5.7 INCREMENT/DECREMENT OPERATORS [++, −−]

Increment operator ++ is to increment the value of a variable by 1 and the decrement operator −− is to decrement the value of a variable by 1. The syntax of using ++ and −− is as follows.

operand++;   Here, ++ is said to have been suffixed to the operand

++operand;   Here, ++ is said to have been prefixed to the operand

operand−−;   Here, −− is said to have been suffixed to the operand

−−operand;   Here, −− is said to have been prefixed to the operand

Suppose a is a variable with an initial value, say, 10. If we have to increment it by 1, we will normally be inclined to use the assignment statement a = a + 1. Using increment operator ++, the assignment can now be written as a++;

There is no difference between suffixing and prefixing ++ if a++ and ++a are used as independent statements as:

```
a++;
++a;
```

Both have the effect of increasing the value of a by 1.

But, if they are used as part of an expression, the timing of incrementation will be different. For instance,

```
b = a++;
```

Here, ++ has been suffixed to the variable a. As a result, the value of a is assigned to b and then a gets incremented. That is, assignment precedes incrementation.

Now, consider the statement

```
b = ++a;
```

Here, ++ has been prefixed to the variable a. As a result, a gets incremented first and then it is assigned to the variable **b**. that is, incrementation precedes assignment.

Similar arguments hold good with respect to decrement operator -- also.

Increment/Decrement operators a = 6		
++	a++	a = 7
	++a	a = 7
--	a--	a = 5
	--a	a = 5

PROGRAM 5.7 To illustrate increment operator and decrement operators [++, --]

```c
#include <stdio.h>

int main(void)
{
        int a = 10, b;

        printf("a = %d\n", a);
        a++;
        printf("After a++; a = %d\n", a);
        ++a;
        printf("After ++a; a = %d\n", a);
        b = a++;
        printf("After b = a++; b = %d  a = %d\n", b, a);
        b = ++a;
        printf("After b = ++a; b = %d  a = %d \n", b, a);
        a--;
```

```
        printf("After a--; a = %d\n", a);
        --a;
        printf("After --a; a = %d\n", a);
        b = a--;
        printf("After b = a--; b = %d a = %d\n", b, a);
        b = --a;
        printf("After b = --a; b = %d a = %d \n", b, a);

        return 0;
}
```

Input–Output:

```
a = 10

After a++;    a = 11
After ++a;    a = 12
After b = a++;   b = 12    a = 13
After b = ++a;   b = 14    a = 14
After a--;    a = 13
After --a;    a = 12
After b = a--;      b = 12    a = 11
After b = --a;      b = 10    a = 10
```

5.8 CONDITIONAL OPERATOR [? :]

The conditional operator denoted by the symbol ? : is an unusual operator provided by C. It helps in two-way decision-making. The general form of its usage is as follows.

```
(Expression1)? (Expression2) : (Expression3);
```

Expression1 is evaluated. If it is true, Expression2 becomes the value otherwise expression3 becomes the value. Since three expressions are involved, the operator is called **Ternary operator**.

PROGRAM 5.8 To illustrate conditional operator [? :]

```
#include <stdio.h>

int main(void)
{
        int a, b, c, n;

        printf("Enter two numbers \n");
        scanf("%d%d", &a, &b);
        printf(" a = %d b = %d \n\n", a, b);
        c = (a > b) ? a : b;
```

```
        printf ("Largest = %d \n", c);

        printf ("Enter a number \n");
        scanf ("%d", &n);
        (n % 2) ? printf ("Odd"); : printf ("Even");

        return 0;
}
```

Input–Output:

```
Enter two numbers
5
6

a = 5 b = 6
Largest = 6

Enter a number
5
Odd
```

Explanation:

In the above program, the two-way decision-making ability of the conditional operator is used to find out the largest of the two numbers collected by the variables **a** and **b**. In the statement c = (a > b) ? a : b; If the expression a > b evaluates to true, **a** is assigned to the variable **c**. Otherwise, **b** is assigned to the variable **c**. So the variable c would collect the largest of the values in **a** and **b**.

Secondly, the conditional operator has also been used to find whether a number collected by the variable **n** is even or odd. The statement responsible for this is the following:

```
(n % 2) ? printf ("Odd"); : printf ("Even");
```

Here, if the expression n % 2 evaluates to true, then the statement printf ("Odd") gets executed displaying that the number in n is Odd. Otherwise, the statement printf ("Even") gets executed displaying that the number in n is Even. Note that the printf () statements are the other two operands for the conditional operator in addition to the expression n % 2.

5.8.1   Nesting of Conditional Operators

We know that the conditional operator denoted by the symbol ? : helps in making two-way decisions. The syntax of the operator usage is

```
(Expression1) ? (Expression2) : (Expression3);
```

Here Expression2 and Expression3 can themselves be two-way decision-making expressions. In which case, we come across nesting of one conditional operator within the other. Let us now write a program which calls for nesting of conditional operators.

PROGRAM 5.9   To illustrate nesting of conditional operators [?:]

```
#include <stdio.h>

int main(void)
{
        int a, b;

        printf("Enter the values of a and b \n");
        scanf("%d%d", &a, &b);
        (a > b) ? printf("a > b") : ((a < b) ? printf("a < b") : printf("a == b"));
        return 0;
}
```

Input–Output:

```
Enter two numbers
5
6
a < b
Enter two numbers
5
4
a > b
Enter two numbers
5
5
a == b
```

Explanation:

If the expression a >b evaluates to true, the true part of the expression, the statement printf
(`"a >b"`); gets executed displaying the string a > b. Otherwise, the false part of the expression
the statement ((a<b)? printf(`"a<b"`): printf(`"a==b"`)) gets executed. Note the
usage of one more conditional operator. Here if the expression a<b evaluates to true, printf
(`"a < b"`); gets executed displaying the string a < b. Otherwise, the statement printf
(`"a==b"`); gets executed displaying the string a== b.
The following program illustrates the usage of conditional operator to determine the biggest among
three numbers.

```
#include <stdio.h>
#include<conio.h>
int main(void)
{
        int a, b, c, large;
        clrscr();
```

```
printf("Enter three integer numbers\n");
scanf("%d %d %d", &a, &b, &c);
large = a > b? (a > c? a: c): (b > c? b: c);
printf("Biggest of %d  %d and %d is %d\n", a, b, c, large);
getch();
return 0;
}
```

5.9 THE sizeof() OPERATOR

The sizeof() operator is used to find the size of a variable or the size of a data type in terms of the number of bytes. The syntax of its usage is as follows:

sizeof(data-type)
         or
sizeof(variable)

Example 5.17

sizeof(float) evaluates to the value four, the number of bytes required by float type variables.

double d;

sizeof(d) evaluates to the value eight, the number of bytes required by the variable d, which is of double type.

Normally, sizeof() is used to find the size of user-defined data type.

PROGRAM 5.10   To illustrate the sizeof operator

```
#include <stdio.h>

int main(void)
{
    printf(" The number of Bytes occupied by: \n");
    printf(" char  = %d \n", sizeof(char));
    printf(" unsigned char = %d \n", sizeof(unsigned char));
    printf(" int = %d \n", sizeof(int));
    printf(" short int = %d \n", sizeof(short int));
    printf(" long int = %d \n", sizeof(long int));
    printf(" unsigned int = %d \n", sizeof(unsigned int));
    printf(" float  = %d \n", sizeof(float));
    printf(" double = %d \n", sizeof(double));
    printf(" long double = %d \n", sizeof(long double));

    return 0;
}
```

Input–Output:

The number of bytes occupied by:

```
char             = 1
unsigned char    = 1
int              = 2
short int        = 2
long int         = 4
unsigned int     = 2
float            = 4
double           = 8
long double      = 10
```

5.10 THE COMMA OPERATOR [,]

The comma operator is basically used to link two related expressions. The general form of its usage in its simplest form is as follows:

e1, e2

where e1 and e2 are two related expressions. The expressions are evaluated from left to right, so initially e1 is evaluated and then e2 is evaluated. The value of the comma separated expression is the value of the rightmost expression, e2 in this case.

i.e., the value of the sub-expression e2 becomes the value of the whole expression e2, e2 .

Example 5.18

a = 4, b = a + 2

Here initially 4 is assigned to the variable a. Then the variable b is assigned a + 2, i.e. 4 + 2 = 6 and 6 becomes the value of the whole expression.

If the comma separated expressions appear on the right-hand side of an assignment statement, the collecting variable collects the value of the rightmost expression in the list of expressions.

a = (b = 3, c = 4 + b)

Here firstly, b is assigned 3. The value of 3 is then used to get the value of c = 4 + 3 = 7. The value of the rightmost expression, which is 7, is then assigned to the variable **a**.

Similarly, the following three related expressions separated by comma operators, interchange the values of a and b,

a = a + b, b = a − b, a = a − b

PROGRAM 5.11   To illustrate comma operator

```
#include <stdio.h>

int main(void)
{
        int x = 2, y = 4, t;
```

```
        printf("x = %d y = %d\n", x, y),

        t = x, x = y, y = t;
        printf("x = %d y = %d", x, y);

        return 0;
}
```

Input–Output:

```
a = 5
x = 4   y = 2
```

Explanation:

The declaration assigns the values 2 and 4 to the variables x and y respectively. The values of these two variables are printed. The next statement consists of three expressions linked together by means of comma operator. The statement t = x assigns the values of x to t, the next statement x = y assigns the values of y to x and finally the statement y = t, assigns the value stored in the variable t (i.e. intital value of x) to the variable y so that the values of x and y are interchanged. Finally the output function prints the changed values of the variables x and y.

5.11 TYPE CONVERSION

We are now aware of the fact that C is rich in data types. It allows an expression to have data items of different types. It is quite interesting to understand how an expression gets evaluated and what the type of the expression would be.

Conversion takes place at two instances:

1. At the time of evaluation of an expression, whenever an expression has two data items which are of different types, lower type gets converted into higher type. The result of the expression will be in higher type mode.

2. At the time of assignment of the value of an expression or source variable to a target variable, the value of the expression on the right-hand side of an assignment statement gets converted into the type of the variable collecting it.

The hierarchy of data types in the increasing order is given below.

```
char  - the lowest data type
short
int
unsigned
long
float
double
long double - the highest data type
```

Example 5.19

```
int a = 10;
float f = 3.4;
```

Let us consider the expression a + f. The variable a is of int type and f is of float type. Since float is the dominating type. The value of a gets converted into float type first and then the summation proceeds. The sum also turns out to be of float type.

```
    a + f
  = 10 + 3.4
  = 10.0  +  3.4 10 gets converted into 10.0
  = 13.4
```

Now consider the assignment statement a1 = a + f; where a1 is a variable of int type. The right-hand side of the assignment statement gets evaluated to 13.4. But the variable a1 on the left-hand side collects only 13 since it is a variable of into type.

```
a1 = a + f
a1 = 13.4
a1 = 13
```

If the collecting variable a1 were of float type, it would have collected the exact result.

Under some circumstances, automatic type conversion does not work out for us. For instance, consider the arithmetic expression 5/2. In C, the value of this expression would be 2. Since both 5 and 2 are integers, the result of the expression would also be of int type. This is according to the rules of automatic type conversion. But the exact result of this expression is 2.5. How do we get it? **Type casting** or **forcible conversion** is the answer to this.

5.11.1 Forcible Conversion or Type Casting

The general form of casting a value is as follows:

```
(type-name) Expression
```

type-name is any data type supported by C or any user-defined type and expression may be a single variable, constant or an expression itself. By using the type-name, we are forcibly converting the type of the expression to type-name specified.

Example 5.20

(float) 5/2	will now evaluate to 2.5 as follows:
= 5.0 / 2	The operator float forcibly converts 5 to 5.0
= 5.0 / 2.0	Now, automatic conversion takes over. The denominator 2 also gets converted to 2.0
= 2.5	The result of the expression 5.0/2.0 would then be a float value 2.5.

PROGRAM 5.12   To illustrate automatic conversion and forcible conversion

```
#include <stdio.h>

int main(void)
```

```
{
        int i = 10, i1;
        float f = 8.5, f1;
        i1 = f;
        printf ("i1 = %d \n", i1);

        f1 = i;
        printf ("f1 = %f \n", f1);

        i1 = 5 / 2;
        printf (" i1 = 5 / 2 = %d \n", i1);

        i1 = 5.0 / 2;
        printf ("i1 = 5.0 / 2 = %d \n", i1);

        f1 = 5 / 2;
        printf ("f1 = 5 / 2 = %f \n", f1);

        f1 = 5.0 / 2;
        printf ("f1 = 5.0 / 2 = %f \n", f1);

        f1 = (float)5/2;
        printf ("f1 = %f \n", f1);

        return 0;
}
```

Input–Output:

```
i1 = 8
f1 = 10.000000
i1 = 5 / 2 = 2
i1 = 5.0 / 2 = 2
f1 = 5 / 2 = 2.000000
f1 = 5.0 / 2 = 2.500000
f1 = 2.500000
```

Explanation:

In the assignment statement i1 = f; the source variable f is of type float and the target variable i1 is of int type, so the variable i1 would collect only the integral part of f.

In the assignment statement f1 = i; the source variable i is of int type and the target variable f1 is of float type, so the variable f1 would collect the value of i with fractions.

Upon execution of the statement i1 = 5/2; the variable i1 would collect only 2 since both 5 and 2, the operands to / operator are integers. Upon execution of the statement i1 = 5.0/2, even though the RHS part of the statement produces exact result of division 2.5, the variable i1 being of integer type could collect only 2. As a result of the execution of the statement f = 5/2, the variable is assigned 2.0. but upon execution of the statements f = 5.0/2 and f = (float) 5/2, the variable f could collect the exact result of division of 5 by 2.

In general, the following rules apply in sequence during the automatic conversion.

Operands of type char or short int are by default converted into int type.
In an expression having two data items of different types

- If one of the operands is of type long double the other will also be converted to long double. the result of the expression is of type long double.

- Otherwise, if one of the operands is of type double the other will also be converted to double. the result of the expression is of type double.

- Otherwise, if one of the operands is of type float the other will also be converted to float. the result of the expression is of type float.

- Otherwise, if one of the operands is of type unsigned long int the other will also be converted to unsigned long int. the result of the expression is of type unsigned long int.

- Otherwise, if one of the operands is of type unsigned int and the other is of type long int then there are two cases.

  (a) If unsigned int can be converted into long int, the unsigned int is converted into long int and the result also will be of long int.
  (b) Otherwise, both are converted into unsigned long int and the result will also be of unsigned long int.

- Otherwise, if one of the operands is of type long int the other will also be converted to long int. The result of the expression is of type long int.

- Otherwise, if one of the operands is of type unsigned int the other will also be converted to unsigned int. The result of the expression is of type unsigned int.

5.12 PRECEDENCE LEVELS AND ASSOCIATIVITY AMONG ALL THE OPERATORS

Precedence	Operators	Description	Associativity
1	( )	Function call	Left to Right
	[]	Array indexing	
	->	Structure pointer	
	.	Structure member	
2	+	Unary +	Right to Left
	−	Unary −	
	++	Increment	
	−−	Decrement	
	~	1's complement	
	!	Logical negation	
	&	Address of	
	*	Value at address	
	(type)	Type casting	
	sizeof	Size in terms of bytes	

Precedence	Operators	Description	Associativity
3	*	Multiplication	Left to Right
	/	Division	
	%	Remainder	
4	+	Addition	Left to Right
	−	Subtraction	
5	<<	Left shift	Left to Right
	>>	Right shift	
6	<	Less than	Left to Right
	<=	Less than or equal to	
	>	Greater than	
	>=	Greater than or equal to	
7	==	Equal to	Left to Right
	!=	Not equal to	
8	&	Bitwise AND	Left to Right
9	^	Bitwise exclusive OR	Left to Right
10	|	Bitwise inclusive OR	Left to Right
11	&&	Logical AND	Left to Right
12	||	Logical OR	Left to Right
13	?:	Conditional operator	Right to Left
14	=	Assignment	Right to Left
	*= /=		
	%/		
	+= -= &=		
	^= |=		
15	,	Comma	Left to Right

SUMMARY

- C provides rich set of operators.
- Arithmetic operators include +, −, *, /, %, unary + and unary − and they perform arithmetic operations addition, subtraction, multiplication, division, etc. over the operands.
- The relational operators include <, <=, >, >=, == and != and they are used to construct conditional expressions, which in turn are used to change the flow of control of program execution.
- The logical operators include &&, || and ! and are used to construct compound conditional expressions. && and || operate on two conditional expressions whereas logical ! operates on a single conditional expression in their simplest forms.
- Increment (++) and decrement (−−) operators are used to increment and decrement the values of variables by 1 respectively.
- The shorthand arithmetic assignment operators +=, −=, *=, /=, %= perform both arithmetic and assignment operations.

- The conditional operator ?: is the unusual operator available in C which operates on three operand expressions. It is normally used to achieve two-way decision-making.
- The bit-wise operators operate on onl integers and they operate at bit level.
- If an expression has data items of different types, its evaluation takes place as per type conversion rules.

REVIEW QUESTIONS

5.1 What is an operator?

5.2 C is rich in operators. Justify.

5.3 What is an arithmetic expression? Mention different types of arithmetic expressions.

5.4 What do you mean by the terms precedence and associativity?

5.5 Give an account of precedence and associativity of arithmetic operators.

5.6 Why do we use relational operators? List out them in C.

5.7 What is a relational expression? Give an example.

5.8 Give an account of precedence and associativity of relational operators.

5.9 What is the significance of logical operators? List out logical operators in C.

5.10 Explain the working of logical && operator.

5.11 Explain the working of logical | | operator.

5.12 What is the use of logical ! operator?

5.13 Give an account of precedence and associativity of logical operators.

5.14 Differentiate between prefixing and suffixing ++ to a variable.

5.15 Give an account of shorthand arithmetic assignment operators.

5.16 Why do we use conditional operator ? : ? Why is it called a ternary operator?

State whether the following are true or false

5.1 The minus (–) operator can be used as both unary and binary operator.

5.2 An arithmetic expression can be used as a test-expression.

5.3 The operators +, – have higher precedence over *, / and %.

5.4 The operator / has higher priority than %.

5.5 Associativity of the arithmetic operators is from left to right.

5.6 Arithmetic operators and relational operators can be used in combination.

5.7 Relational operators have higher precedence than arithmetic operators.

5.8 Relational operators and logical operators have the same precedence.

5.9 All the relational operators have the same precedence.

5.10 b = ++a ; and b = a++ ; produce the same effect.

5.11 a += 6 and a = a + 6 are equivalent.

5.12 a += b += c; is a valid statement.

5.13 The shorthand arithmetic assignment operators are evaluated from left to right.

5.14 The conditional operator can be nested.

5.15 sizeof('a') and sizeof(char) produce the same result.

5.16 sizeof(a+b) and sizeof(int) produce the same result (a and b are variables of int type).

5.17 Conditional operator is called a ternary operator.

5.18 The comma operator has the highest priority.

5.19 The comma oerators are evaluated from left to right.

PROGRAMMING EXERCISES

5.1 Write a program to accept the number of seconds and display its equivalent number of hours, number of minutes and number of seconds. (Hint: Use / and % operators)

5.2 Write a program to find the area and circumference of a circle, given its radius r.
Area = 3.14 * r^2 Circumference = 2 * 3.14 * r

5.3 Write a program to accept the length and the breadth of a rectangle and display its area and perimeter. The area is given by the product of the length and the breadth, the perimeter is twice the sum of the length and the breadth.

5.4 If a and b are two numbers, find out the values of $(a + b)^2$ and $a^2 + b^2 + 2ab$.

5.5 If a and b are two numbers, find out the values of $(a - b)^2$ and $a^2 + b^2 - 2ab$.

5.6 Write a program to find the value of s, the distance travelled by an object
s = u * t + 0.5 * a* t^2
where u is the initial velocity, t is the time taken and a is the acceleration.

5.7 Write a program to find the value of v, the final velocity.
$v^2 = u^2 - 2 * a * s$

5.8 Write a program to calculate net salary of an employee given his basic pay.

Allowances

DA	45%
HRA	14%
CCA	10%

Deductions

PF	12%
LIC	15%

All the allowances are based on basic pay

Gross salary = Basic pay + Allowances
Net salary = Gross salary – Deductions

INTERVIEW QUESTIONS

5.1 Predict the output of the following C programs

(a)
```
int main(void)
{
    int a = 10;
    printf("%d %d %d\n", ++a, ++a, ++a);
    return 0;
}
```

(b)
```
int main(void)
{
    int a = 10, b = 5, c = 8, x;
    x = (a>b) || ( b != ++c)
    printf("%d %d %d  %d\n", a, b, c, x);
    return 0;
}
```

(c)
```
int main(void)
{
    int a = 10, b = 5, c = 8, x;
    x = (a<b) || ( b++ != ++c)
    printf("%d %d %d  %d\n", a, b, c, x);
    return 0;
}
```

(d)
```
int main(void)
{
    int a = 10, b = 5, t;
    t=a, a=b, b=t;
    printf("%d %d\n", a, b);
    return 0;
}
```

(e)
```
int main(void)
```

```
    {
        int a = 10, b = 5, c = 8, x;
        x = (++a = = 10) || (b+3 = c++)
        printf("%d %d %d  %d\n", a, b, c, x);
        return 0;
    }
```

(f)
```
int main(void)
    {
        int a = 1, b = 2, c = 3, x;
        x=a<b>c;
        printf("%d", x);
        return 0;
    }
```

(g)
```
int main(void)
    {
        int a = 1, b = 2, c = 3, x;
        x=(a++ == b) && (c!=++b);
        printf("%d%d%d%d", a,b,c,x);
        return  0;
    }
```

(h)
```
int main(void)
    {
        int a = 1, b = 2, c = 3, x;
        x=(!a = = b-1) && (++b = = c++);
        printf("%d", a,b,c, x);
        return 0;
    }
```

(i)
```
int main(void)
    {
        int a = 10;
        int x;

        x = a &5|7
         printf("%d", x);
         return 0;
    }
```

(j)
```
int main(void)

{
    int a=8, b=4, c=5, x
    x = b*c + a*b +(a>b?a:b);
    printf("%d", x);
    return 0;
}
```

(k)
```
int main(void)
{
    int h = 8;
    int b = 4 + 6 + 3 * 4 >  3 ? 8 : 3;
    printf("%d\n", b);
    return 0;
}
```

(l)
```
int main(void)
{
    char a = 't';
    char b = 's'
    int c = a && b || 70
    printf("%d\n", c);
    return 0;
}
```

(m)
```
int main(void)

{
    int a = 8, b = 0,c = 5;
    d = (a > b) ? (++a):(--b);
    printf("%d %d %d 5d", a, b, c, d);
    return 0;
}
```

(n)
```
int main(void)
{
    int a = 4, b = 6, c = 7, d;
    d = a + b * c;
```

```
        printf("%d", d);
        return 0;
    }
```

(o)
```
    int main(void)
    {
        int a = 4, b = 5, c = 7, d;

        d = (a - b) / c;
        printf("%d", d);
        return 0;
    }
```

(p)
```
    int main(void)
    {
        int a = 4, b = 5, c;

        c = a < b + 10;
        printf("%d", c);
        return 0;
    }
```

(q)
```
    int main(void)
    {
        int a;
        a = 4 > 5 && 5 > 3;
        printf("%d", a);
        return 0;
    }
```

(r)
```
    int main(void)
    {
        int a = 10, b = 6, c;
        c = a++ + b;
        printf("%d", c);
        c = ++a + b;
        printf("%d", c);
        return 0;
    }
```

(s)
```
int main(void)
{
    int a = 10, b = 6, c;
    c = a++ + b + a++;
    printf("%d", c);
    c = ++ a + b ++a;
    printf("%d", a);
    return 0;
}
```

(t)
```
int main(void)
{
    int a = 5;
    printf("%d%d%d", a++, a++, a++);
    printf("%d%d%d", a, a++, ++a);
    return 0;
}
```

(u)
```
int main(void)
{
    int a = 5;
    printf("%d%d%d", ++a, ++a, ++a);
    return 0;
}
```

(v)
```
int main(void)
{
    int a = 5, b = 10;
    printf("%d %d\n", a, b);
    a = a ^ b;
    b = a ^ b;
    a = a ^ b;
    printf("%d%d", a,b);
    return 0;
}
```

(w)
```
int main(void)
{
    int a = 5, b, c;
```

```
    b = a>>2;
    c = a<<1;
    printf("%d %d %d\n", a, b, c);
    return 0;
}
```

5.2 Which relational operator has the highest precedence?

5.3 Which is the least precedence operator in C?

5.4 Which bitwise operator is used for masking specific bit of a number?

5.5 Which bitwise operator is used to turn on specific bit of a number?

5.6 What is the significance of bitwise operator in C?

5.7 How do you multiply a number by two without using * operator?

5.8 How do you divide a number by 4 without using / operator?

6

Decision-making and Branching (Selection)

6.1   INTRODUCTION

The common thing shared by all the programs written so far is that in each of the programs, all the statements from the first statement till the last statement get executed without fail in a serial manner. That is, one after the other. This kind of execution of statements in a program is called **Sequential Execution**.

As we proceed towards the real programming world, we do realize that the circumstances which cannot be implemented using only **Sequential Execution** are in plenty. These programming circumstances require selecting some statements for execution if some condition is satisfied; skipping the block of statements if the condition is not satisfied, thereby, resulting in a change in the order of execution of statements. To be precise, selection of some statements for execution depends on whether a condition is true or false. This kind of execution of statements is called **Conditional Execution** or **Selection**.

For instance, suppose we have to write a program to find whether a number n is divisible by 5 or not. The program written for this purpose will have the statement r = n %5. We know that % is to get the remainder after division of one number by another. Here, the value of r determines whether n is evenly divisible by 5 or not. The program should thus check the value of r. If it finds that r takes 0, it should display that n is divisible by 5. If r takes a non-zero value, the program should display that the number is not divisible by 5. As seen, there is decision-making involved in the program.

C provides built-in decision-making structures to implement conditional execution in the form of **if** statement and its variations, **switch** statement and conditional operator. Let us now try to follow the syntax of each of these and illustrate each of these with example programs.

6.2 **THE** simple-if **STATEMENT**

The syntax of **if** statement in its simplest form

```
if (test-expression)
   {
           statements;
   }
```

The following flow chart reflects the logical flow of the **simple-if** statement.

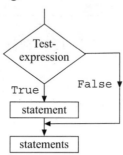

This is known as **simple-if** statement. The test-expression can be a relational expression, a logical expression or any other expression which evaluates to a non-zero (true) value or zero (false). The statements enclosed within the braces get executed when the test-expression evaluates to true. Otherwise, they will simply be skipped. The control gets transferred to the statement after the closing brace of the **if**-statement.

The set of statements enclosed within the opening brace and the closing brace of the if statement is called the **if-block**. If only one statement is to be executed when the test-expression of the if statement evaluates to true, enclosing it within the opening brace and the closing brace is optional.

A single statement is called a **Simple Statement**. A set of statements enclosed within a pair of opening and closing braces is called a **Compound Statement**.

Example 6.1

```
if (a == b)
      printf("a and b are equal");
```

If the values of the variables a and b are same, then only the printf() statement gets executed. Otherwise, it is skipped.

Example 6.2

```
if ((a > b) && (a > c))
      printf("a is the largest"):
```

If the value of the variable a is greater than the values of both b and c, then only the printf() gets executed. Otherwise, the statement is skipped.

Example 6.3

```
if (n % 2)
      printf("n is odd");
```

If the value of the variable n is not divisible by two, i.e. if the remainder after division of n by 2 is 1, then only the printf() statement gets executed. Otherwise, the printf() statement gets skipped.

Example 6.4

```
if ( a > b)
{
        t = a;
        a = b;
        b = t;
}
```

Only when the value of **a** is greater than the value of **b** the statements within the pair of braces get executed. Otherwise, the statements are skipped.

To find whether a number is even or odd

Input: A number, n
Output: Whether n is even or odd

If n is divisible by 2, it is even. If n in not divisible by 2, it is odd

Pseudocode to find whether a number is even or odd
```
Read n
r = n % 2;
if (r == 0)
        Display n is even
if (r != 0)
        Display n is odd
```
End pseudocode

PROGRAM 6.1   To find whether a number is even or odd

```c
#include <stdio.h>

int main(void)
{
        int number, rem;

        printf("Enter a number \n");
        scanf("%d", &number);

        rem = number % 2;
        if (rem == 0)
                printf("%d is even", number);

        if (rem != 0)
                printf("%d is odd", number);

        return 0;
}
```

Input–Output:

```
Enter a number
4
4 is even
Enter a number
5
5 is odd
```

Explanation:

number and rem are declared to be variables of int type. number is to collect a number (input). rem is to collect the remainder after division of number by 2.

If the relational expression (rem == 0) evaluates to true, which means number is evenly divisible by 2, then we display that number is even. If the relational expression (rem != 0) evaluates to true, which means number is not evenly divisible by 2, then we display that number is odd.

To find the largest of three numbers

Inputs: Three Numbers a, b, c
Output: The largest of a, b and c

Pseudocode to find the largest of three numbers

```
Read a, b, c
      largest = a
if (b > largest)
      largest = b;
if (c > largest)
      largest = c
Display largest
```

End pseudocode

PROGRAM 6.2   To find the largest of three numbers

```c
#include <stdio.h>

int main(void)
{
      int a, b, c, largest;

      printf("Enter three numbers \n");
      scanf("%d%d%d", &a, &b, &c);

/* Finding the largest begins */
```

```
        largest = a;

        if (b > largest)
        largest = b;

        if (c > largest)
        largest = c;

/* Finding the largest ends */

        printf("\n Given Numbers: a = %d b = %d c = %d \n", a, b, c);
        printf("\n Largest = %d \n", largest);

        return 0;
}
```

Input–Output:

```
Enter three numbers
2
3
4

Given Numbers: a = 2 b = 3 c = 4

largest = 4
```

Explanation:

a, b, c, and **largest** are declared to be variables of int type. a, b and c are to collect three numbers (inputs). **largest** is to collect the largest of the three numbers **(output)**.

We accept the values of three numbers into the variables a, b and c. In the process of finding out the largest of a, b and c, we start with the assumption that a is the largest and assign it to the variable **largest**. We then check if b is greater than largest. If it is, we assign b to largest. We then check if c is greater than largest. If it is, we assign c to largest, eventually largest collects the largest of a, b and c.

Variations of if Statement

It is obvious that the **simple-if** statement would not suffice to implement selection in all the cases. The following variations of **if** statement can be used depending on the complexity of the conditions to be checked.

The following are the variations of **if** structure.

1. The if-else Statement
2. The Nested if-else Statement
3. The else-if Ladder

We will now discuss the syntax and illustrate each of these variations by means of suitable programming examples.

6.3 THE `if-else` STATEMENT

The syntax of the **if-else** statement is as follows:

```
if (test-expression)
    {
            statements-1;
    }
    else
    {
            statements-2;
    }
```

The following flow chart reflects the logical flow of the **if-else** statement.

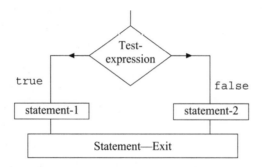

If `test-expression` evaluates to `true`, `statements-1` will be executed. `statements-2` will be skipped. On the other hand, if it evaluates to `false`, `statements-2` will get executed. `Statements-1` will be skipped. Thus, **if-else** structure acts as a selector of one block of statements out of two blocks. In both the situations, the final control goes to the Statement-Exit.

The set of statements enclosed within the braces following **if** is called `if-block` and the set of statements enclosed within the braces following **else** is called `else-block`.

Example 6.5

```
if(a > b )
        Printf("a is larger than b");
else
        Printf(" a is not larger than b");
```

Here if a is greater than b the message "a is larger than b" is displayed on the screen. Otherwise, i.e., if a is less than or equal to b the message " a is not larger than b" is displayed.

Example 6.6
```
if (n % 2)
    Printf ("n is odd");
else
    Printf ("n is even");
```
If n is not divisible by two, the expression n % 2 evaluates to true and the message "n is odd" is displayed. If n is divisible by two, then the message "n is even" is displayed.

Example 6.7
```
if (basic > 5000)
{
        da = basic * .65;
        hra = basic * 15;
        cca = 200;
}
else
{
        da = basic * 57;
        hra = basic * 12;
        cca = 150;
}
```
Here, if the basic is greater than ₹ 5000 then da and hra are calculated to be 65% and 15% of basic respectively and the cca is assigned ₹ 200. Otherwise, i.e. the basic is less than or equal to ₹ 5000 than da and hra are calculated to be 57% and 12% respectively and cca is assigned ₹ 150.

Note that in all the above three cases, one out of two alternatives gets selected.

Pseudocode to find whether an integer is even or odd
```
Read n
r = n % 2;
if (r == 0)
      Display n is even
else
      Display n is odd
```
End pseudocode

PROGRAM 6.3   To illustrate if-else statement

```c
#include <stdio.h>

int main(void)
{
        int number, rem;

        printf ("Enter a number \n");
        scanf ("%d", &number);
```

```
        rem = number % 2;
        if (rem == 0)
                printf("%d is even", number);
        else
                printf("%d is odd", number);

        return 0;
}
```

Input–Output:

First-Run:

```
Enter a number
4
4 is even
```

Second-Run:

```
Enter a number
5
5 is odd
```

Explanation:

In the above program, number and rem are declared to be variables of int type. The variable number is to collect a number (Input). rem is to collect the remainder after division of number by 2. The value of rem determines whether number is even or odd. If (rem == 0) evaluates to true, then number is displayed as even. Otherwise, (else part of if) number is displayed as odd.

To find whether a year is a leap year or not

A leap year is one which has 366 days in it. In the month of February of the year, the number of days would be 29. We say that a year is a leap year, if it is evenly divisible by 400 or if it is evenly divisible by 4 but not by 100.

Pseudocode to finding whether a year is a leap year or not.

```
Read year
r4   = year % 4;
r100 = year % 100;
r400 = year % 400;
if (( r4 == 0) && (r100 != 0) || (r400 == 0))
     Display "leap year"
else
     Display "not a leap year"
```

End pseudocode

PROGRAM 6.4   To find whether a year is a leap year or not

```
#include <stdio.h>

int main(void)
{
        int year, r4, r100, r400;

        printf("Enter a year \n");
        scanf("%d", &year);

        r4 = year % 4;
        r100 = year % 100;
        r400 = year % 400;

        if (( r4 == 0) && (r100 != 0) || (r400 == 0))
                printf("%d is a leap year", year);
        else
                printf("%d is not a leap year", year);

        return 0;
}
```

Input–Output:

First-Run:

```
Enter a year
2000
2000 is a leap year
```

Second-Run:

```
Enter a year
2001
2001 is not a leap year
```

Third-Run:

```
Enter a year
1900
1900 is not a leap year
```

Explanation:

year, r4, r100 and r400 are declared to be variables of int type. The variable year is to collect year number (Input); r4, r100 and r400 are to collect the remainders after division of year by 4, 100 and 400 respectively.

After accepting year number into the variable `year`, the variables `r4`, `r100` and `r400` are assigned the remainders after division of `year` by 4, 100 and 400 respectively. If `year` is divisible by 4 but not by 100 or divisible by 400 alone, the year is displayed as leap year. Otherwise, it is displayed as not leap year.

6.4 THE NESTED `if-else` STATEMENT

We now know that if execution of a block of statements is conditional, we can use one **if** statement. What if the conditional execution of the block of statements is itself conditional? Here, we need to enclose one **if** statement within another **if** statement. On the similar lines, we can even enclose an **if-else** within another **if-else**. If one **if-else** is enclosed within another **if-else**, the resulting structure is called **nested if-else**. The syntax of nested **if-else** is as follows:

```
if (test-expression 1)
    {
            if (test-expression 2)
            {
                    statements-1;
            }
            else
            {
                    statements-2;
            }
    }
    else
    {
            statements-3
    }
```

Here, one **if-else** is enclosed within another **if-else**. The **if** structure, which encloses another is called `outer-if`. The `if` structure, which is enclosed within another is called `inner-if`. `Statements-1`, `statements-2` and `statements-3` are three blocks of statements. Selection of one of these blocks of statements for execution proceeds as follows.

First, `test-expression1` is checked. If it evaluates to true, `test-expression2` is checked. If `test-expression2` also evaluates to true, then `statements-1` would get executed. If `test-expression2` evaluates to false, then `else`-block of the inner-if, `statements-2` would get executed. If `test-expression1` itself evaluates to false, then the `else`-block of the `outer-if`, `statements-3` would get executed. Thus, this variation acts as a selector of one out of three blocks of statements.

Example 6.8

The following program segment compares a and b.

```
if ( a >= b)
    if (a > b)
            printf ("a is larger than b");
```

```
        else
                printf ("a and b are equal");
else
        printf ("a is less than b");
```

Example 6.9

The following segment compares two values **a** and **b** and collects the largest of them in the variable **largest**.

```
if (a > b)
{
    if (a > c)
            largest = a;
    else
            largest = c;
}
else
{
    if (b > c)
            largest = b;
    else
            largest = c;
}
```

Note that in this case an **if-else** statement is enclosed within the **if** block and the else block of the outer if-else statement.

PROGRAM 6.5   To illustrate nested **if** statement

```
#include <stdio.h>

int main(void)
{
        int number;

        printf ("Enter a number \n");
        scanf ("%d", &number);

        if (number <= 0)
                if (number < 0)
                        printf ("%d is negative", number);
                else
                        printf ("Zero");
        else
                printf ("%d is positive", number);

        return 0;
}
```

Input–Output:

First-Run:

```
Enter a number
3
3 is positive
```

Second-Run:

```
Enter a number
-4
-4 is negative
```

Explanation:

number is declared to be variable of int type. It is to collect a number **(Input)**. We accept a number into the variable number. We then use **nested**-if-else to find whether number is positive, negative or 0. If the test expression in the **outer**-if, (number <= 0) evaluates to true, then the test expression in the inner-if, (number < 0) is checked; if (number < 0) also evaluates to true, then number is displayed as negative. If (number < 0) evaluates to false, then number is displayed as zero. If the test expression of the outer-if, (number <= 0) itself evaluates to false, the inner-if condition is not checked at all; number is displayed as positive.

PROGRAM 6.6   To illustrate the nested **if** statement

```c
#include <stdio.h>

int main(void)
{
        int a, b, c, largest;

        printf("Enter three numbers \n");
        scanf("%d%d%d", &a, &b, &c);
        if (a > b)
        {
                if (a > c)
                        largest = a;
                else
                        largest = c;
        }
        else
        {
                if (b > c)
                        largest = b;
                else
                        largest = c;
        }
```

```
        printf("\n Given Numbers: a = %d b = %d c = %d \n", a, b, c);
        printf("\n Largest = %d \n", largest);

            return 0;
}
```

Input–Output:

```
Enter three numbers

2 3 4

Given Numbers: a = 2 b = 3 c = 4

Largest = 4
```

6.5 THE else-if LADDER

The else-if ladder helps select one out of many alternative blocks of statements for execution depending on the mutually exclusive conditions. The syntax of the else-if ladder is as follows:

```
if (test-expression1)
    {
            statements-1;
    }
    else if (test-expression2)
    {
            statements-2;
    }
    else if (test-expression3)
    {
            statements-3;
    }
    :

    else if (test-expression-n)
    {
            statements-n;
    }
    else
    {
            statements;
    }
```

Here test-expression1, test-expression2, ..., test-expression-n are mutually exclusive. That is, only one test-expression of all will be true. There are n+1 blocks of statements.

Initially, test-expression1 is checked. If it is true, the block of statements statements-1 would get executed; all the other blocks of statements would be skipped. If test-expression1 is false, `test-expression2` is checked. If it is true, the block of statements `statements-2` would get executed; all the other statements would be skipped. If `test-expression2` is false, `test-expression3` is checked. If it is true, `statements-3` would get executed; all the other statements would be skipped. This continues. In general, ith test-expression is checked only when the first `i-1` test-expressions evaluate to false. If none of the expressions is found to be true, the last block of statements would get executed. Thus, **else-if** ladder acts as a selector of one out of n+1 blocks of statements.

Example 6.10

The following program segment checks the value of n for different intervals.

```
printf ("Enter a number \n");
scanf ("%d", &n);
if (n <= 10)
        printf ("n is less than or equal to 10");
else if (n <= 20)
        printf ("n lies between 11 and 20")
else if (n < = 30)
        printf ("n lies between 21 and 30")
else
        printf ("n is greater than 30");
```

Example 6.11

The program segment checks the content of the variable **ch** against the grades A, B and C and displays the appropriate grade.

```
ch = getchar ();
if (ch == 'A')
        printf ("Grade A");
else if (ch == 'B')
        printf ("Grade B");
else if (ch == 'C')
        printf ("Grade C");
else
        printf ("Grade D");
```

PROGRAM 6.7   To find whether a number is +ve, −ve or 0

```
#include <stdio.h>

int main (void)
{
        int number;
        printf ("Enter a number \n");
        scanf ("%d", &number);
/* Finding whether the given number is +ve, -ve or 0 begins */

        if (number > 0)
```

```
              printf("%d is positive", number);
        else if (number < 0)
              printf("%d is negative", number);
        else
              printf("zero");

/* Finding whether the given number is +ve, -ve or 0 ends */

        return 0;
}
```

Input–Output:

First-Run:

```
Enter a number
3
3 is positive
```

Second-Run:

```
Enter a number
-4
-4 is negative
```

Explanation:

number is declared to be a variable of int type. It is to collect a number, the input required by the program.

We accept a number into the variable number. To find whether the number entered is positive, negative or 0, we have used else-if ladder. We first check if the number is greater than 0. If it is, then we display that the number is positive. If the number is not greater than 0, then only we check whether it is less than 0. If it is, then we display that the number is negative. If the number is not found to be negative, the default option, it is displayed as 0.

PROGRAM 6.8   To find the largest of three numbers

```
#include <stdio.h>

int main(void)
{
        int a, b, c, largest;
        printf("Enter three numbers \n");
        scanf("%d%d%d", &a, &b, &c);

/* Finding the largest begins */

        if ((a > b) && (a > c))
```

```
                largest = a;
        else if ((b > a) && (b > c))
                    largest = b;
            else
                    largest = c;
```

```
/* Finding the largest ends */
```

```
        printf("\n Given Numbers: a = %d b = %d c = %d \n", a, b, c);
        printf("\n Largest = %d \n", largest);

        return 0;
}
```

Input–Output:

```
Enter three numbers
2
3
4

Given Numbers: a = 2 b = 3 c = 4

largest = 4
```

Explanation:

The integer variables a, b and c are to collect the three numbers (inputs), the largest of which is to be found out. The variable largest is to collect the largest of the numbers a,b and c.

The program uses the else-if ladder to accomplish the task. If the value in a is greater than the values in both b and c, a is assigned to the variable largest; if a is not greater than either b or c, b is checked against the values of both a and c . If the value in b is greater than the values in both a and c, b is assigned to the variable largest. Otherwise, the variable c is assigned to the variable largest. The value of the variable largest is then displayed.

PROGRAM 6.9   To accept a digit and display it in word

```
#include <stdio.h>

int main(void)
{
        int digit;
        printf("Enter a digit \n");
        scanf("%d", &digit);

        if (digit == 0)
                printf("Zero");
        else if (digit == 1)
                printf("One");
```

```
        else if (digit == 2)
              printf("Two");
        else if (digit == 3)
              printf("Three");
        else if (digit == 4)
              printf("Four");
        else if (digit == 5)
              printf("Five");
        else if (digit == 6)
              printf("Six");
        else if (digit == 7)
              printf("Seven");
        else if (digit == 8)
              printf("Eight");
        else if (digit == 9)
              printf("Nine");
        else
              printf("Not a digit");
              return 0;
}
```

Input–Output:

First-Run:

```
Enter a digit
4
Four
```

Second-Run:

```
Enter a digit
5
Five
```

Explanation:

digit is declared to be a variable of int type. It is to collect a digit, the input required by the program.

We accept a digit into the variable and use a series of conditions to match its content with the digits (0, 1, 2, etc.). If matching is found, then the digit is displayed in word. Note that anything. other than a digit accepted into the variable digit causes the program to report that input entered is not a digit (even in the case of multiple digit number).

PROGRAM 6.10   To accept the co-ordinates of a point and determine its position.

```
#include <stdio.h>
int main(void)
```

```
{
      int x, y;

      printf("Enter the x and y co-ordinates of the point \n");
      scanf("%d%d", &x, &y);
      if ((x==0) && (y==0))
            printf("The point is at the origin\n");

      else
      if ((x == 0))
            printf("The point lies on the y axis\n");

      else
      if ((y == 0))
            printf("The point lies on the x axis\n");

      else
      if ((x > 0) && (y > 0))
            printf("The point lies in the first quadrant\n");

      else
      if ((x < 0) && (y > 0))
            printf("The point lies on the second quadrant\n");

      else
      if ((x < 0) && (y <0))
            printf("The point lies on the second quadrant\n");

      else
            printf("The point lies on the fourth quadrant\n");
}
```

Explanation:

Here x, y are the variable declared as float. These two variables are used to specify the two coordinates (x and y) of the point. Each of the if statement checks the position of the point. If the point neither lies at the origin, nor on x and y axis and nor in any of the first three quadrant then it is considered to be lie on the fourth quadrant

Input-Output:

```
First Run
Enter the x and y co-ordinates of the point
2 5
The point lies in the first quadrant

Second Run
Enter the x and y co-ordinates of the point
```

```
-2.5 5.6
The point lies in the second quadrant

Third Run
Enter the x and y co-ordinates of the point
5.6 0
The point lies on the y axis
```

PROGRAM 6.11   To grade a student

```
#include <stdio.h>

int main(void)
{
        int m1, m2, m3, m4, m5, flag;
        float percent;

        printf("Enter marks in five subjects \n");
        scanf("%d%d%d%d%d", &m1, &m2, &m3, &m4, &m5);
        flag = 1;

        if (m1 < 35)
        {
                printf("Failed in subject1 \n");
                flag = 0;
        }

        if (m2 < 35)
        {
                printf("Failed in subject2 \n");
                flag = 0;
        }

        if (m3 < 35)
        {
                printf("Failed in subject3 \n");
                flag = 0;
        }

        if (m4 < 35)
        {
                printf("Failed in subject4 \n");
                flag = 0;
        }

        if (m5 < 35)
        {
```

```
            printf ("Failed in subject5 \n") ;
            flag = 0;
    }

    if (flag)
    {
            percent = (float) (m1 + m2 + m3 + m4 + m5) / 5;
            if (percent < 50)
                    printf ("\n Grade : Just Pass \n") ;
            else if (percent < 60)
                    printf ("\n Grade : Second class \n") ;
            else if (percent < 70)
                    printf ("\n Grade : First class \n") ;
            else
                    printf ("\n Grade : Outstanding \n") ;
    }

    return 0;
}
```

Input–Output:

```
Enter marks in five subjects
78 87 98 89 69

Subject1 : 78
Subject2 : 87
Subject3 : 98
Subject4 : 89
Subject5 : 69


Grade : Outstanding
```

Explanation:

m1, m2, m3, m4, m5 and flag are declared to be variables of int type. percent is declared to be a variable of type float. m1, m2, m3, m4 and m5 are to collect marks scored by a student in five subjects. The variable flag acts as a Boolean variable and is used to find whether the student has scored minimum passing marks in each subject or not. percent is to collect the percentage of marks.

We accept marks scored by a student in five subjects into the variables m1, m2, m3, m4 and m5. Before grading the student, we first verify whether he has scored passing marks (35) in all the five subjects or not. We use the flag variable flag for this purpose. We start with the assumption that he has passed in all the subjects and assign 1 to flag. Each subject marks are then checked. If the marks in a subject are below 35, then we display the message that he has failed in the subject and flag is set to 0.

If the variable flag retains 1, which means that the student has passed in all the five subjects, then only we grade him as just passed, Second class, First class or Outstanding depending on the percentage of marks.

6.6 THE switch STATEMENT

When we need to select one block of statements out of two alternatives, we use if-else structure. When we are to select one block of statements for execution out of n blocks of statements and associated with each block of statements is a condition and all conditions being mutually exclusive, we tend to use else-if **ladder**. Since the conditions are mutually exclusive, only one condition would evaluate to true at any point of time resulting in the selection of the corresponding block of statements. Even though the programming situation is implementable using else-if ladder, the code becomes more complex when the number of conditions increases since the degree of readability decreases. Fortunately C provides switch structure, an alternative to else-if ladder, which simplifies the code and enhances readability when we need to implement problems which involve selection of one out of many alternatives.

Syntax of switch structure:

```
switch (expression)
{
        case v1:
        statements-1;
            break;
        case v2:
            statements-2;
            break;
            .
            .
        case vn:
            statements-3;
            break;

        default:
            statements;
            break;
}
```

Here, expression is an integer or char expression. It evaluates to either an integer or a character. v1, v2, ... vn are the case labels. The expression of the switch statement can take any of the case labels. If it takes v1, statements-1 will get executed and the break statement following it causes the skipping of the switch structure. The control goes to the statement following the closing brace of the switch structure. If the expression takes v2, the corresponding block of statements-2 will get executed and the switch statement is exited, and so on. The block of statements to be executed depends on the value taken by the expression. If none of the values is taken by the expression, the statements following the default option will get executed. Thus, the switch statement acts as the selector of one block out of many blocks of statements.

Points to Remember:

- The case labels should not be float values or Boolean expressions.
- The case labels v1, v2 , ..., vn should be distinct.
- The order of their presence is immaterial.
- After each case, there should be a break statement.
- default case is optional.

Example 6.12

```
scanf ("%d" , &n) ;
switch(n)
{
      case 1: printf ("one")
            break;
      case 2: printf (two") ;
            break;
      default:
            printf ("Other than one or two \n") ;
}
```

If the value of n is 1, then the string "one" is displayed. If the value of n is 2, then the string "two" is displayd. In all the other cases, the string "other than one or two" is displayed.

PROGRAM 6.12   To accept a digit and display it in word

```
#include <stdio.h>

int main(void)
{
      int digit;

      printf ("Enter a number \n") ;
      scanf ("%d" , &digit) ;

      switch(digit)
      {
            case 0:
                  printf ("Zero") ;
                  break;
            case 1:
                  printf ("One") ;
                  break;
            case 2:
                  printf ("Two") ;
                  break;
            case 3:
                  printf ("Three") ;
                  break;
```

```
            case 4 :
                  printf ("Four") ;
                  break;
            case 5 :
                  printf ("Five") ;
                  break;
            case 6 :
                  printf ("Six") ;
                  break;
            case 7 :
                  printf ("Seven") ;
                  break;
            case 8 :
                  printf ("Eight") ;
                  break;
            case 9 :
                  printf ("Nine") ;
                  break;
            default:
               printf ("Not a digit") ;
      }

      return 0;
}
```

Input–Output:

First-Run:

```
Enter a digit
4
Four
```

Second-Run:

```
Enter a digit
5
Five
```

Explanation:

digit is declared to be a variable of int type and it is to collect a decimal digit (input). During the course of the execution of the program, a digit is accepted into the variable. The variable digit forms the expression of the switch structure used in the program. (The expression evaluates to an integer constant) the expression's value is first checked against 0, the label of the first case. If a match takes place, the string "zero" is displayed by the printf () corresponding to the label and the break statement following it will cause the control of the program to be transferred to the first statement after the closing brace of the switch structure. If the expression's value does not match with 0, then it is checked against 1. If a match takes place, the string "One" is displayed and the control is transferred to the first statement after the closing brace of the switch structure. This continues. If none of the values match with the value of the expression, then the statements under default option would get executed.

Example 6.13

The following program segment displays the grade depending on the content of the variable **ch**.

```
printf("Enter grade A, B or C \n");
ch = getchar();
switch(ch)
{
      case 'A': printf("A grade");
            break;
      case 'B': printf("B grade");
            break;
      case 'C': printf("C grade");
            break;
}
```

PROGRAM 6.13   To illustrate switch structure

```
#include <stdio.h>

int main(void)
{
      int a, b, sum, diff, product, rem;
      float quotient;
      char operator;

      printf("Enter two numbers \n");
      scanf("%d%d", &a, &b);
      fflush(stdin);
      printf("Enter an operator \n");
      operator = getchar();
      switch(operator)
      {
            case '+':
                  sum = a + b;
                  printf("Sum = %d \n", sum);
                  break;
            case '-':
                  diff = a - b;
                  printf("Difference = %d \n", diff);
                  break;
```

```
                    case '*':
                            product = a * b;
                            printf("Product = %d \n", product);
                            break;
                    case '/':
                            quotient = (float) a / b;
                            printf(" Quotient = %f \n", quotient);
                            break;
                    case '%':
                            rem = a % b;
                            printf(" Remainder =%d \n", rem);
                            break;
                    default:
                            printf("Not a valid operator");
            }

        return 0;
}
```

Input–Output:

```
Enter two numbers
6  8

Enter an operator
*

Product = 48
```

Explanation:

In the above program, a and b are declared to be variables of int type. operator is declared to be a variable of char type. a and b are to collect two numbers and operator is to collect an arithmetic operator [+, –, *, /, %]. The variable operator forms the expression of the switch structure and it evaluates to a character constant.

During the course of the execution of the program, two numbers are accepted into the variables a and b. an arithmetic operator is accepted into the variable operator. Within the switch structure, depending on the operator, the corresponding block of statements would be executed, which display the result of the arithmetic expression after which the control is transferred to the first statement after the closing brace of the switch structure. If none of the case labels match with the value of the expression, then the default option gets executed.

In the above example programs, we observed that for each case label, there is a separate block of statements. That is, there is one-to-one mapping between the case labels and blocks of statements. When the expression value matches with a case label, the corresponding block of statements would get executed. In addition to this, switch statement enables us to execute a common block of statements for more than one case label value.

Example 6.14

The following program segment accepts a character and displays whether it is a vowel or not.

```
ch = getchar();
Switch (ch)
{
      case 'a':
      case 'e':
      case 'o':
      case 'i':
      case 'u': printf("vowel");
                  break;
      default: printf(" not a vowel");
}
```

Example 6.15

The following program segment finds out whether n is even or odd.

```
printf("Enter an integer");
scanf("%d", &n);
r = n % 10;
switch ( r )
{
      case 0:
      case 2:
      case 4:
      case 6:
      case 8:   printf("n is even");
            break;
      default: printf("n is odd");
}
```

PROGRAM 6.14   To accept a month (number) and display the maximum number of days in the month

---

```
#include <stdio.h>

int main(void)
{
      int month, year, days;

      printf("Enter month number \n");
      scanf("%d", &month);
      printf("Enter year \n");
      scanf("%d", &year);

      switch(month)
```

```
        {
                case 1:
                case 3:
                case 5:
                case 7:
                case 8:
                case 10:
                case 12: days = 31;
                            break;
                case 4:
                case 6:
                case 9:
                case 11:
                            days = 30;
                            break;
                case 2:
                if (((year % 4 == 0) && (year % 100 != 0)) || (year % 400 == 0))
                            days = 29;
                else
                        days = 28;
                            break;
                default:
                            printf(" Not a valid month number ");
        }
        printf("Maximum number of days in month %d of the year %d= %d",
    month,year, days);

        return 0;
}
```

Input–Output:

First-Run:
```
Enter month number
4
Enter year
1998
Maximum number of days in month 4 of year 1998 = 30
```

Second-Run:
```
Enter month number
1
Enter year
2000
Maximum number of days in month 1 of year 2000 = 31
```

Third-Run:
```
Enter month number
2
Enter year
2000
Maximum number of days in month 2 of year 2000 = 29
```

Explanation:

In the above program, month, year and days are declared to be variables of **int** type. the variable **month** is to collect the month number (input) of a year [1-12], **year** is to collect year number. The year number is required to check the leap year condition, and **days** is to collect the number of days in the given month of the given year. The variable **month** forms the expression of the switch structure used in the program and it evaluates to an integer constant.

During the course of the execution of the program, month and year are accepted. Within the switch structure, the value of month is checked against 1, 3, 5, 7, 8, 10, 12 in a serial manner. If the value of the expression matches with any of these, then the variable days is assigned 31. This segment of the switch structure is equivalent to the following if statement.

```
if ( (month ==1) || (month == 3) || (month == 5) || (month == 7) || (month == 8)
|| (month == 10) || (month == 12))
    days = 31;
```

Similarly, if the value of the expression matches with any of the values 4, 6, 9 and 11, then days is assigned 30. This segment of the switch structure is equivalent to the following if statement.

```
if ( (month ==4) || (month == 6) || (month == 9) || (month ==11))
    days = 31;
```

If the value of the expression is 2, the following segment of the program gets executed which assigns the correct number of days in the month of February by verifying the leap year condition.

```
if (((year % 4 == 0) && (year % 100 != 0)) || (year % 400 == 0))
        days = 29;
    else
        days = 28;
        break;
```

If none of the labels match with the value of the expression, then the default option is executed. After each of the above cases, the control is transferred to the statement after the closing brace of the switch statement.

Note: The common thing that is shared by both else-if ladder and the switch statement is that both enable us to select one out of many blocks of statements for execution when the conditions are mutually exclusive. But the difference is in the case of else-if ladder the conditions may involve non-integers as well and the conditions may involve any relational operators <, <=, >, >= , == and != and the conditions can even have all the logical operators. In the case of switch statement, the conditions can only involve integral values and only == relational operator can be used.

All the programming situations which are implemented through switch statement can even be implemented through else-if ladder but the converse is not true.

switch statement is simpler than the else-if ladder in its appearance and hence offers better comprehensibility.

6.6.1 Nested switch Statement

On the lines of if statement and its variations, even switch statements also can be nested, if required. The following program makes use of this fact. Suppose there are two departments, namely sales and production. Sales department is denoted by the numeric Code 1 and production department is denoted by the numeric Code 2 and both of these departments have employees with two designations Manager and Asst. Manager. We will denote Manager by numeric Code 1 and Asst. Manager by numeric Code 2 for the ease of programming.

Dept	Code	Designation	Code
Sales	1	Manager	1
Production	2	Asst. Manager	2

The program should accept dept_code and dsg_code as inputs, and display the corresponding department name and designation name.

PROGRAM 6.15 To illustrate nesting of switch statements

```c
#include <stdio.h>
int main(void)
{
    int dept, dsg;

    printf("Enter dept code \n");
    scanf("%d", &dept);
    printf("Enter dsg code \n");
    scanf("%d", &dsg);

    switch(dept)
    {
        case 1: switch(dsg)
                {
                    case 1: printf("Manager in Sales Dept \n");
                            break;
                    case 2: printf("Asst.Manager in Sales Dept \n");
                            break;
                }
                break;

        case 2: switch(dsg)
                {
                    case 1: printf("Manager in Production Dept \n");
                            break;
                    case 2: printf("Asst.Mgr in Production Dept \n");
                            break;
```

```
                        }
                        break;
        }

        return 0;
}
```

Input–Output:

First-Run:
```
Enter dept_code
1
Enter dsg_code
2

Asst.Manager in Sales Dept
```

Second-Run:
```
Enter dept code
2
Enter dsg code
1

Manager in Production Dept
```

Explanation:

In the above program, the identifiers dept and dsg are declared to be variables of int type. The variable dept is to collect the dept_code and it forms the expression for the outer switch statement. The variable dsg is to collect dsg_code and it forms the expression for the inner switch statements. Depending on the value taken by the variables, the appropriate combination of designation and dept is displayed. It is important to note that the outer switch statement selects the department and the inner switch statement selects the designation of an employee.

6.7   THE goto STATEMENT

The goto statement is an unconditional branching statement. It causes the control to be transferred from one part to another part of the same function. The syntax of its usage is as follows:

goto label;

where label is a valid C identifier and it marks the place where the control has to be transferred to in a function. The statement to which the control is to be transferred is preceded by the label and a colon.

Forward Jumping
```
        goto abc;
        s1;
        s2;
abc:    s3;
        s4;
```

Backward Jumping

```
abc:    s1;
        s2;
        s3;
        goto abc;
```

However, liberal usage of goto statement is not advocated in C. This is because, its usage makes the programs hard to understand and most of the programming situations can be implemented without using the goto statement. It has to be used very rarely in situations like transferring control out of nested loops from the inner loops.

Jumping out of the innermost loop

```
        for(i = 1; i < 10; i++)
        {
                statements;
                for(j = 0; j < 10; j++)
                for(k = 0; k < 10; k++)
                {
                        if (some drastic condition)
                        goto abc;
                }
        }
abc: s1;
 s2;
```

SUMMARY

- Execution of a block of statements conditionally is called conditional execution.

- In C, conditional execution is achieved by the **if** statement and its variations and **switch** statement.

- The if statement includes its variations such as **if-else, nested if-else** and **else-if ladder**.

- **If-else** is to select one block of statements out of two blocks of statements and the **else-if** ladder is to select one out of many alternative blocks of statements.

- The **switch** statement can be used as an alternative to the **else-if** ladder because of its simple syntactic structure.

- The expression of the switch structure can take only integral values.

- All the problems which can be solved by **switch** statement can be solved by **else-if** ladder but the converse is not true.

- We can even have nested **switch** statements.

- The **goto** statement is an unconditional branching statement and is used to transfer the control from one part of the program to another and is used very rarely in inevitale situations only.

REVIEW QUESTIONS

6.1 What do you mean by conditional execution?

6.2 Differentiate between sequential execution and conditional execution.

6.3 What is a test-expression?

6.4 Find out whether the following text-expressions involving the variables a,b,c and d evaluate to true or false.

a = 3, b = 4, c = 5, d = 7

(a) a + b > c   (b) a > b + c   (c) a > b && a > c   (d) a + b < c + d

6.5 Write the syntax of `simple-if` structure.

6.6 Explain nested `if-else` structure.

6.7 What is the need for `else-if` ladder? Give an example of its requirement.

6.8 Write the syntax of `switch` structure.

6.9 Compare `else-if` ladder and `switch` structure.

6.10 Why is the usage of `goto` statement not recommended?

6.11 Give the syntax the usage of `goto` statement.

State whether the following are true or false

6.1 The expression of the `switch` statement can be any type.

6.2 The `switch` statements can be nested.

6.3 `switch` statement is a replacement for `else-if` ladder in all the cases.

6.4 Default option is a must in the `switch` statement.

6.5 a = 6
```
if (a)
        printf("a=6"); is a valid statement.
```

6.6 `goto` is a conditional branching statement.

Identify errors, if any, in the following

6.1
```
if (a > b);
        printf("a is greater than b");
```

6.2
```
if (n %2 == 0) then
        printf("Even");
```

6.3
```
if (a > b) and (b > c)
        printf("a is the greatest");
```

6.4
```
if (not(5>4))
        printf("false");
```

6.5
```
if (a > b) or (a < c)
        printf(" a is ideal");
```

6.6
```
switch (5)
{
        case 5.0: printf ("Five");
        case 5:printf ("Five");
}
```

6.7
```
if (1)
{
        printf ("Welcome to");
        printf ("Programming in C");
else
        printf ("Welcome to");
        printf ("Programming in C++");
}
```

6.8
```
if (n = 10)
        printf (" n = 10");
```

6.9
```
if (a + b)
{
        g = a;
}
```

6.10
```
if (a > b)
{
        g = a;
        printf ("g = %d \n", g);
}
        else
            g = a;
            printf ("g %d \n", g);
            }
```

PROGRAMMING EXERCISES

6.1 Write a program to validate a given date.

    Example: 12/3/1998 is valid

                 32/3/98 is not valid   Day exceeds 31

                 30/13/98 is not valid   Month exceeds 12

                 31/4/98 is not valid   Maximum number of days in the month of April is 30

6.2 Write a program to find whether one date is earlier than the other or not.

    Example: 12/3/98 is earlier than 20/4/99

                 12/3/98 is not earlier than 12/3/98

6.3 Write a program to accept a number and display whether it is divisible by 5 only or 6 only or by both 5 and 6.

6.4 Write a program to accept three sides a, b and c. Find whether the sides form a triangle or not. (A triangle can be formed out of a, b, and c if the sum of any two sides is greater than the remaining side.)

6.5 Write a program to find the value of y for the given value of x.

y = 2 * x + 100   if x < 50
  = 3 * x + 300   if x = 50
  = 5 * x – 200   if x > 50

6.6 An electricity supply company charges its consumers according to the following slab rates

Units   Charge
1–100   ₹ 1.50   per unit
101–300   ₹ 2.00   per unit for excess of 100 units
301–500   ₹ 2.50   per unit for excess of 300 units
501–above   ₹ 3.25   per unit for excess of 500 units

Write a program to accept the number of units, calculate the total charge and display it.

6.7 The following are the numeric codes assigned to different colours. Write a program to accept a colour code and display the appropriate colour in word.

Colour Code   **Colour**
1   Red
2   Blue
3   Green
4   Yellow
5   Purple

6.8 Write a program to accept three sides of a triangle and display the type of the triangle. Suppose a, b and c are three sides of the triangle.

(a) If all the three sides are equal then the triangle is called an equilateral triangle.

(b) If any two of the sides are equal then the triangle is called an isosceles triangle.

6.9 Write a program to accept three angles of a triangle and display the type of the triangle. Suppose a, b and c are three angles of the triangle

(a) If all the three angles are equal, then the triangle is called an equilateral triangle.

(b) If any two of the angles are equal, then the triangle is called an isosceles triangle.

(c) If any one of the angles is an obtuse angle (>90), the triangle is called obtuse angled triangle.

6.10 Write a program to find the roots of a quadratic equation.

A quadratic equation is of the form $ax^2 + bx + c = 0$,
The discriminant $d = sqrt(b^2 - 4ac)$
The roots of the equation are given by $x1 = (-b + d)/2$ $x2 = (-b - d)/2$
Roots are equal if $d = 0$
Roots are real and distinct if $d > 0$
Roots are complex numbers if $d < 0$

6.11 Write a program to accept the three sides of a triangle and find whether the triangle is a right angled triangle or not. (Use Pythagoras theorem)

6.12 Write a program to accept a point (x, y) and find whether it lies on the circle or inside the circle or outside the circle. The centre of the circle (0, 0) and radius of the circle is 5. Equation of a circle with (0,0) as the centre and r as the radius is given by $x^2 + y^2 = r^2$ where r is the radius.

If $x^2 + y^2 < r^2$ then the point (x, y) lies within the circle.

If $x^2 + y^2 > r^2$ then the point (x, y) lies outside the circle.

If $x^2 + y^2 = r^2$ then the point (x, y) lies on the circle.

6.13 A Commercial Bank accepts Fixed Deposits from the public. The rates of interest vary depending on the number of days for which the deposits are made. The following are the rates.

30 days to 60 days	6%
61 days to 90 days	6.5%
91 days to 180 days	7%
181 days to one year	8%
More than one year	8.5%

For senior citizens, additional 1% is offered for deposits more than 50,000.

Write a program to accept the amount deposited and the number of days for which the deposit is made and calculate the amount to be given to the customer after the given number of days.

6.14 Write a program using `switch` statement to accept a Roman letter and display its decimal equivalent.

Roman symbol	Decimal equivalent
I	1
V	5
X	10
L	50
C	100
D	500
M	1000

6.15 Given three numbers, write a C program that checks whether they form a pythagoras triplet or not.

6.16 Given the angle θ, convert the angle to radians and evaluate tan θ.

6.17 Calculate the income tax of an employee based on the following tax rates given as follows:

Taxable income	Tax rate
₹ 0–200000	Nil
₹ 200000–500000	10% the amount exceeding 200000
₹ 500000–800000	30000 + 20% of the amount exceeding 500000
₹ 800000–100000	90000 + 30% of the amount exceeding 800000
More than 10 lakhs	150000 + 40% of the amount exceeding 1000000 + 2% additional tax

INTERVIEW QUESTIONS

6.1 Predict the output of the following programs:

```
(a) #include<stdio.h>
    int main(void)
    {
        float x=0.5;
        if (x < 0.5)
            printf("TRUE");
        else
            printf("FALSE :-( ");
    return 0;
    }
```

```
(b) #include <stdio.h>
    int main(void)
    {
            int t = 0;
            if (t == 0)
        printf("Good");

            else
              printf("Morning");
              printf("Evening");
    return 0;
    }
```

```
(c) #include <stdio.h>
    int main(void)
    {
            int x = 0;

            if (x)
                printf("C is interesting Language");
            else
                printf("C is confusing");
        return 0;
    }
```

```
(d) #include<stdio.h>
    int x = 4; y = 2;

    int main(void)
    {
    switch(x%y)
    {

        case  0: printf("Zero\n");

        case 1: printf("One\n");

        case 2: printf("Two\n");

        default:printf("More than two\n");

        return 0;
    }
```

6.2 Write a C code to determine the largest among three numbers using conditional statement.

6.3 Write different ways of incrementing a variable in C.

6.4 Write a C code to display the series 1, –2, 3, –4, . . .

6.5 Write a C code to display the series 1, 4, 27, 64, . . .

(Hints: The series $1^1, 2^2, 3^3, 4^4, \ldots$)

6.6 Write a C program to swap two numbers using three different types of operators.
(Hint: Bitwise operator, Assignment Operator, Arithmetic Operator)

7

Looping Statements in C

7.1 INTRODUCTION

So far, we have come across two types of execution of statements in our earlier programs. One, **Sequence,** Where all the statements from the beginning till the end get executed without fail in the serial order. Two, **Selection**. Where some statements are executed and some are skipped depending on some condition. The common thing shared by both of these is that statements selected for execution get executed only once.

Under some circumstances, we may need to execute a block of statements repeatedly as long as some condition is true. For instance, suppose we need to find the sum of the first **n** natural numbers 1, 2, 3, ..., n. If the variable **s** expected to collect the sum, it is to be initialized with 0 to start with; Next 1 is to be added to the variable **s**; after 1 is added, next 2 is to be added to it; then 3 is to be added, and so on. Here, selection of the members of the series and adding them to the variable **s** constitute a repetitive process.

To be precise, the following statements are to be executed repeatedly

```
s += i
i++;
```

The repetition of execution of a block of statements as long as some condition is true is called **Looping**. Looping is also called **Iteration**.

PROGRAM 7.1 To find the sum of first n natural numbers using **if** and **goto** statements

---

```
#include <stdio.h>

int main(void)
{
        int n, i, sum;
```

136

```
          printf ("Enter a number \n");
          scanf ("%d", &n);

          sum = 0;
          i = 1;
          abc:
                  sum += i;                      \
                  i++;
                  if (i <= n) goto abc;

          printf ("Sum = %d \n", sum);

          return 0;
}
```

Input–Output:

First-Run:

```
Enter a number
5
sum = 15
```

Second-Run:

```
Enter a number
10
sum = 55
```

Explanation:

In the above program; n, i and **sum** are declared to be variables of **int** type. n is to collect a natural number; i is to collect each natural number starting from 1 to n; **sum** is to collect the sum of the natural numbers up to n.

First, we accept a number into the variable n; initialize **sum** and i with 0 and 1 respectively. The initial value of i, that is, 1 is added to **sum**. So the first member of the natural numbers series, 1, is added to **sum**. i is incremented by 1; The value of i now becomes 2, the second member of the natural numbers series. The condition i <= n is checked. If it is found to be true, the control is transferred to the statement following the label abc (Backward jumping). The value of i, that is, 2 is added to **sum** and i is once again incremented. i will now become 3. Once again i<= n is checked. If it is found to be true. The control is transferred to the statement following the label abc. 3 is added to **sum** and i is incremented again. This continues as long as i <= n. Once i exceeds n, the control is transferred to the statement printf ("sum=%d", sum); which displays the sum up to n natural numbers.

It is important to note that there are three steps employed to construct a loop.

1. Initialization
2. Checking Test-expression
3. Updation.

At least one variable should be involved in all these three steps. The variable involved is called **Control Variable**. In the first step, the control variable is given a value. In the second step, the test expression involving the control variable is checked to find whether it evaluates to true or false. If the test expression evaluates to true, then only the statements get repeatedly executed. In the last step, the variable's value gets changed. The updation of the control variable should be such that the test expression evaluates to false at some later point of time so that the loop is exited.

In the above program, the control variable is i. It is assigned the responsibility of selecting the natural numbers one by one. Initialization is i = 1. Test expression is i <= n and updation statement is i++, which increments i by 1.

In the above program, we have used if statement in combination with goto statement and effected backward jumping to construct a loop. We need not have to always rely on the combination of if and goto to construct loops. C provides its own looping constructs, which are simple and hence facilitate simplified coding. Let us now get to know the looping structures provided by C, their syntax and usage.

C provides three looping structures. They are

1. The **while** loop
2. The **do-while** loop
3. The **for** loop

we now know that to be able to execute a block of statements repeatedly as long as some condition is true (i.e., to construct a valid loop), there should be three things. 1. Initialization, 2. Test-expression, 3. Updation and at least one variable should be involved in all of these. Our previous program has thrown light on this account. All these three looping constructs are not exceptions to this fact. They do incorporate the above-mentioned three fundamental things in the process of construction of valid loops.

7.2 THE while LOOP

The while loop is the simplest and most frequently used looping structure in C. The syntax of the looping structure is given below:

```
while (test-expression)
    {
            statements
    }
```

As far as the syntax is concerned, it starts with the keyword while. The keyword is followed by a test-expression enclosed within a pair of parentheses. The test-expression can be an arithmetic expression, relational expression or a logical expression. The test-expression is then followed by a set of one or more statements, which are expected to be repeatedly executed, enclosed within a pair of braces.

As regards, the other two components, initialization and updation, required for a loop other than test-expression, one of the statements, written before the while loop, acts as initialisation statement and one of the statements in the body of the loop acts as updation statement.

Execution sequence effected by the looping construct is as follows: `test-expression` is evaluated. If `test-expression` evaluates to true, then the statements in the body of the loop get executed. The updation statement in the body of the loop updates the looping variable. Control goes back to the `test-expression`. The `test-expression` is again evaluated. If it evaluates to true, then once again the statements in the body of the loop would get executed. This is repeated as long as the `test-expression` remains evaluated to true. Once the `test-expression` evaluates to false, the loop is exited and the control goes to the first statement following the looping construct.

The execution sequence effected by `while` looping construct is best illustrated by the following flow chart segment.

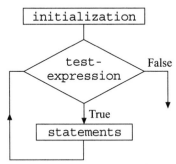

Since the `test-expression` is first evaluated before entering into the body of the loop, the looping construct is called **Entry-Controlled** or **Pre-Tested** looping construct. Since the test-expression is evaluated in the beginning itself, if it evaluates to false in the beginning itself, the body of the loop is not entered at all. The statements would simply be skipped and the control is transferred to the first statement following the looping construct.

Example 7.1

Consider the following segment of code

```
i = 1;
sum = 0;
While (i <= 10)
{
        sum += i;
        i++;
}
```

The purpose of the code is to find the sum of the first 10 natural numbers.

Example 7.2

Consider the following segment

```
ch = getchar();
while (ch != '\n')
{
        ch = getchar();
}
```

The segment of code enables us to accept characters one at a time till the new line character is entered and thus it can be used to accept a line of text.

After getting familiarized with the syntax and examples of the usage of the `while` loop, we will now write some programs which make use of it.

To find the sum of the digits of an integer

Given a multiple digit integer **n**, in order to find the sum of the digits in it, we need to set up a loop to extract each digit in the number and add it to a variable say, **s** repeatedly.

Pseudocode to find the sum of the digits of an integer

```
Read n
sum = 0
while (n > 0)
begin
        rem = n % 10
        sum = sum + rem
        n = n   / 10
  end
Display sum
```
End pseudocode

PROGRAM 7.2   To find the sum of the digits of an integer

```c
#include <stdio.h>

int main(void)
{
        int n, rem, sum;

        printf("Enter an integer \n");
        scanf("%d", &n);

        /* Finding the sum of the digits of n begins */
        sum = 0;
        while (n > 0)
        {
                rem = n %10;
                sum += rem;
                n /= 10;
        }

        /* Finding the sum of the digits of n ends */

        printf("sum = %d", sum);

        return 0;
}
```

Input–Output:

```
Enter an integer
234

sum = 9
```

Explanation:

In the above program n, rem and sum are declared to be variables of int type. The variable n is to collect an integer value (input). The variable sum is to collect the sum of the digits of the integer value in n and it is initialized to 0.

The following segment of the program is responsible for extracting each digit in n and adding the digit, collected by the variable rem, to the variable sum.

```
while (n > 0)
{
        rem = n %10;
        sum += rem;
        n /= 10;
}
```

The loop is exited once the value in n becomes 0 by which time the variable **sum** has collected the sum of all the digits in it. The value in **sum** is then displayed.

To find whether an integer is prime or not

A number is said to be a prime number if it is not divisible by any number other than 1 and itself.

Example 7.3

5 is a prime number

7 is a prime number

To find whether a number **n** is prime number or not, we need to check whether any number within the range 2 to **n/2** divides n exactly or not. If none of the numbers within the range divides **n**, we conclude that **n** is prime. Otherwise, we conclude that **n** is not prime.

Pseudocode to find whether an integer is prime or not

```
Read number
k = 2
flag = 1
while ((k <= number/2) && (flag == 1))
begin
        rem = number % k
        if (rem == 0)
                flag = 0
        k = k + 1
end
```

```
        if (flag == 1)
                Display "prime "
        else
                display "not prime"
```
End pseudocode

PROGRAM 7.3   To find whether a number is a prime number or not

---

```c
#include <stdio.h>

int main(void)
{
        int number, k, flag, rem;

        printf("Enter a number \n");
        scanf("%d", &number);
        k = 2;
        flag = 1;
        while ((k <= number / 2) && (flag == 1))
        {
                rem = number % k;
                if (rem == 0)
                        flag = 0;
                k++;
        }

        if (flag == 1)
                printf("%d is prime \n", number);
        else
                printf("%d is not prime \n", number);
        return 0;
}
```

Input–Output:

```
Enter a number

7
7 is prime

Enter a number

8
8 is not prime
```

Explanation:

In the above program, number, flag, k and rem are declared to be variables of int type. Variable number is to collect a number, which we have to find whether prime or not. k is to select the numbers in the range [2 to number/2]. **flag** is to take a value which is either 1 (true) or 0 (false). **rem** is to collect the remainder after division of **number** by **k**.

First, We accept a number into the variable **number**, and assign 2 to **k** since we need to start dividing **number** from **2**. We start with the assumption that **number** is prime by assigning 1 to **flag** (true). Within the **while** loop, we check whether any value of **k** divides **number** exactly. If any value of **k** is found to divide **number** exactly, **flag** is assigned 0 and the loop is exited. Otherwise, the loop completes without altering the value of **flag**. If none of the values of **k** divides **number** exactly, **flag** retains 1 only. If **flag** retains 1, then we conclude that **number** is prime. On the other hand, if **flag** gets 0 then we conclude that **number** is not prime. Thus, the value of **flag** would tell us whether **number** is prime or not.

To generate the members of the Fibonacci series

The first two members of the series are two 1s. The third member is the sum of the first two members, i.e., two. The fourth member is the sum of the second and the third member, and so on. In general, ith member of the series, where $i > 2$, is obtained by adding the $(i-1)$th and $(i-2)$th members.

Pseudocode to generate the members of Fibonacci series

```
Read n
f1 = 1
f2 = 1
Display f1
Display f2
i = 3
while (i <= n)
begin
      f3 = f1 + f2
      Display f3
      f1 = f2
      f2 = f3
      i = i + 1
end
```
End pseudocode

PROGRAM 7.4   To generate Fibonacci series

```c
#include <stdio.h>

int main(void)
{
      int n, i, f1, f2, f3;

      printf("Enter the number of members to be generated \n");
      scanf("%d", &n);
```

```
        printf ("First %d members of Fibonacci series \n", n);
        f1 = 1;
        f2 = 1;
        printf ("%d\n", f1);
        printf ("%d\n", f2);
        i = 3;
        while (i <= n)
        {
                f3 = f1 + f2;
                printf ("%d\n", f3);
                f1 = f2;
                f2 = f3;
                i++;
        }

        return 0;
}
```

Input–Output:

```
Enter the number of members to be generated
5

First 5 members of Fibonacci series

1
1
2
3
5
```

Explanation:

In the program, n, i, f1, f2 and f3 are declared to be variables of int type. n is to collect the number of members of the Fibonacci series to be generated. f1, f2 and f3 are used in the process of generation of the series. i is to keep track of the number of members generated during the course of generation.

First, we accept the number of members to be generated into the variable n. The first two members of the series 1 and 1 are assigned to f1 and f2 respectively. They are displayed. Note that i is assigned three. This is to indicate that the third member is to be generated.

On the entry into the loop, the third member is found out by summing f1 and f2. It is collected by f3 and also displayed. Fourth member is then generated by summing up second and third member. Likewise, the loop repeats till the required number of members of the Fibonacci series are generated by summing up the immediate previous two members to get the next member of the series.

7.3 THE for LOOP

The for loop is another looping structure provided by C excessively used in many situations because of its inherent simplicity. The simple nature of the loop is evident from its syntax itself.
The fllowing is the syntax of the for loop:

```
for (initialization; test-expression; updation)
    {
            statements;
    }
```

The general form of the looping construct starts with the keyword for. The keyword is followed by the three fundamental things to construct a loop, initialization, test-expression and updation all in one place, separated by semicolons and enclosed within a pair of parentheses. (However, initialization, test-expression and updation can be used in different places like the way they are used in while and do-while loop. Usage of them in one line in the for loop increases its simplicity and comprehensibility.) Then the body of the loop follows.
The execution sequence effected by for loop is as follows:

1. Initialization statement is executed.
2. Test-expression is evaluated.
3. If the test-expression evaluates to false, the loop is exited and the control goes to the first statement after the body of the loop, otherwise the body of the loop gets executed.
4. Control goes to the updation statement, the updation statement is executed, which changes the value of the loop variable. Now control is transferred to step 2.

The sequence is repeated as long as the text-expression evaluates to true. Once the text-expression evaluates to false, the loop is exited and the control is transferred to the first statement following the looping construct.
The execution sequence effected by the for looping construct can best be understood by the following flow chart segment.

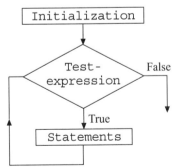

Similar to while loop, since the test-expression is evaluated first before entering into the body of the loop, the looping construct is called **Entry-Controlled or Pre-Tested** looping construct. If the test-expression evaluates to false in the beginning itself, the body of the loop is not entered at all. The control is transferred to the first statement following the loop.

Example 7.4

The following segment of code finds the sum of the natural numbers up to 10.

```
sum = 0;
for(i = 1; i <= 10; i++)
        sum += i;
```

Example 7.5

The following segment of code finds the factorial of the number 5.

```
fact = 1;
for(i = 5; i >=1; i--)
        fact *= i;
```

After getting familiarized with the syntax and examples of the usage of the `for` loop, we will now write some programs which make use of it.

Pseudocode to find the sum of first n natural numbers

```
Read n
sum = 0
for(i = 1; i <= n; i++)
        sum = sum + i
```

Display sum

End pseudocode

PROGRAM 7.5   To find the sum of the first n natural numbers using `for` loop

---

```c
#include <stdio.h>

int main(void)
{
        int n, i, sum;

        printf("Enter a number \n");
        scanf("%d", &n);

        sum = 0;
        for(i = 1; i <= n; i++)
                sum += i;

        printf("Sum = %d \n", sum);

        return 0;
}
```

Input–Output:

First-Run:

```
Enter a number
5
sum = 15
```

Second-Run:

```
Enter a number
10
sum = 55
```

Explanation:

In the above program; n, i and sum are declared to be variables of int type. n is to collect a natural number; i is to collect each natural number starting numbers from 1 to n; sum is to collect the sum of natural numbers up to n.

First, we accept a number into the variable n and initialize sum with 0. The following segment finds the sum of the first n natural numbers.

```
for (i = 1; i <= n; i++)
        sum += i;
```

the value of sum is then displayed.

To generate multiplication table of a number

Given a number n, in order to generate the multiplication table of the number, we definitely need to set up a loop to multiply n with the numbers in the range [1 – 10] and get the product of n and each number in the range. Here the multiplication is a repetitive process.

Pseudocode to generate multiplication table of a number

```
        Read number
        for (i = 1; i <= 10; i++)
        begin
                product = number * i
                Display number * i = product
end
```

End pseudocode

PROGRAM 7.6   To generate multiplication table of a number

```c
#include <stdio.h>

int main(void)
{
        int number, i, product;

        printf("Enter a number \n");
        scanf("%d", &number);
```

```
        for(i = 1; i <= 10; i++)
    {
            product = number * i;
            printf(" %d * %d = %d \n", number, i, product);
    }

        return 0;
}
```

Input–Output:

```
Enter a number
5
 5 * 1 = 5
 5 * 2 = 10
 5 * 3 = 15
 5 * 4 = 20
 5 * 5 = 25
 5 * 6 = 30
 5 * 7 = 35
 5 * 8 = 40
 5 * 9 = 45
 5 * 10 = 50
```

Explanation:

In the above program, **number, i** and **product** are declared to be variables of **int** type. The variable **number** is to collect a number (input), multiplication table of which is to be generated. The variables **i** and **product** are used in the process of generation of the table.

The segment of the program responsible for generating the table is:

```
for(i = 1; i <= 10; i++)
{
        product = number * i;
        printf(" %d * %d = %d \n", number, i, product);
}
```

In the **for** loop, the variable **i** ranges from 1 to 10. Initially **i** takes 1. Since i <= 10 becomes true, the body of the loop is entered and the product of **i** and **number** is found out and is displayed. **i** is then incremented and it becomes 2. Once again since i <= 10 evaluates to true, the product of **number** and **i** is found out and is displayed. This is repeated till **i** becomes greater than 10, by which event, the multiplication table of number has been generated.

7.3.1   Variations of for Loop

1. The for loop can have more than one initialization expression separated by comma operator.

    Example 7.6

    ```
            for(sum = 0, i = 1; i <= 10; i++)
                sum += i;
    ```

Note the presence of two initialization expressions **sum = 0** and **i = 1** separated by comma operator.

2. The `for` loop can have more than one updation expression also separated by comma operator.

Example 7.7

```
sum = 0;
for(i = 1; i <= 10; i++, sum += i)
```

Note the presence of two updation expressions **i++** and **sum + = 1** separated by comma operator.

3. The initialization expression and updation expression can both be displaced as follows. The resulting looping structure resembles `while` loop.

Example 7.8

```
sum = 0;
i = 1;
for(;i < =10; )
{
    sum += i;
    i++;
}
```

4. Consider the following segment of code:

Example 7.9

```
sum = 0;
for(scanf("%d", &n); n > 0; n /= 10)
{
        rem = n % 10;
        sum += rem;
}
```

The segment of code finds the sum of the digits of a number collected by the variable n. Note that the `scanf("%d", &n)` has been used as the initialization expression. This is perfectly valid and it is executed only once in the beginning similar to the normal initialization expression. Also note the updation expression n /= 10; which is different from normal incrementation/ decrementation. Since there are two statements to be executed repeatedly, they are enclosed within the braces.

5. Consider the following for statement. It does not have any of the three components required for loop. (But the two semicolons are mandatory.)

Example 7.10

```
for(; ;)
```

This sets up an infinite loop.

6. Some programming circumstances, which deal with events which are to be raised periodically with some time-gap between two successive events. The time-gap can be provided with the help of the following loop.

Example 7.11

```
for(i=0; i<=10000;i++);
{
    statements;
}
```

Here the variable i is initialized first with 0. Then it gets incremented by one repeatedly as long as the condition i <= 10000 is true. Once the condition becomes false, the loop is exited.

7.4 THE do-while LOOP

The do-while loop is another looping structure provided by C, which is less frequently used when compared to while loop and for loop. Unlike while loop and for loop, this is a post-tested or exit-controlled looping structure. The syntax of the looping structure is as follows:

```
do
{
    statements;
}
while (test-expression);
```

As far as the syntax is concerned, it starts with the keyword do. The keyword is followed by a block of one or more statements, which are expected to be executed repeatedly, enclosed within a pair of braces. The set of statements form the body of the loop. The set of statements are then followed by another keyword while, which is then followed by a test-expression enclosed within a pair of parentheses. Note the presence of semicolon after the closing parenthesis of the test-expression.

The execution sequence effected by do-while loop is as follows: The statements in the body of the loop get executed once and then the control goes to the test-expression. The test-expression is evaluated. If it evaluates to true then, the body of the loop is re-entered. After the statements in the body of the loop get executed for the second time, the control goes back to the test-expression. Once again the test-expression is evaluated. If it evaluates to true, again the body of the loop gets executed. This is repeated as long as the test-expression evaluates to true. Once the test-expression evaluates to false, the loop is exited and the control goes to the first statement following the looping construct.

The execution sequence effected by do-while looping construct can best be grasped by the following flow chart segment.

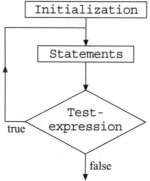

Since the `test-expression` is evaluated at the end, the looping construct is called **Exit-Controlled** or **Post-Tested** looping construct. The statements in the body of the loop are guaranteed to be executed at least once.

Example 7.12

Consider the following segment

```
i = 1;
sum = 0;
do
{
sum += i;
i++;
}while (i <= 10);
```

The statements in the body of the loop get repeatedly executed as long as i `<= 10` and it finds the sum of the first 10 natural numbers.

Example 7.13

Consider the following segment

```
ch = 'y';
do
{
        scanf ("%d", &n);
        printf ("Do you want to continue? y or n \n");
        ch = getchar ();
}while (ch == 'y');
```

The segment of code enables us to keep accepting integer value into the variable n as long as we enter 'y' to the variable ch. Once we input 'n' (or any other character) in response to the statement ch = getchar (); the loop is exited.

After getting familiarized with the syntax and examples of the usage of the do-while loop, we will now write some programs which make use of it.

Pseudocode to find the sum of first n natural numbers

```
Read n
i = 1
sum = 0
do
begin
    sum += i
    i = i + 1
end
while (i <= n)
display sum
```

End pseudocode

PROGRAM 7.7   To find the sum of first n natural numbers using do-while loop

---

```c
#include <stdio.h>

int main(void)
{
      int n, i, sum;

      printf("Enter a number \n");
      scanf("%d", &n);

      i = 1;
      sum = 0;
      do
      {
            sum += i;
            i++;
      }
      while (i <= n);
      printf("Sum = %d \n", sum);

      return 0;
}
```

Input–Output:

First-Run:

```
Enter a number
5
sum = 15
```

Second-Run:

```
Enter a number
10
sum = 55
```

Explanation:

In the above program, **n**, **i** and **sum** are declared to be variables of **int** type. **n** is to collect a natural number; **i** is to select each natural number starting numbers from 1 to **n**; **sum** is to collect the sum of natural numbers up to **n**.

First, we accept a number into the variable n and initialize **sum** with 0. The following segment finds the sum of the first **n** natural numbers.

```
do
{
      sum += i;
      i++;
}
while (i <= n);
```

The sum is collected by the variable **sum**. The value of the variable **sum** is then displayed.

PROGRAM 7.8   To accept two numbers and an arithmetic operator and display the result of the expression involving them

---

```
#include <stdio.h>

int main(void)
{
      int a, b;
      char ch, operator;
      ch = 'y';
      do
      {
            printf("Enter two numbers \n");
            scanf("%d%d", &a, &b);
            fflush(stdin);
            printf("Enter an operator \n");
            operator = getchar();

            switch (operator)
            {
                  case '+':    printf("sum = %d\n", a + b);
                               break;
                  case '-':    printf("Difference = %d\n", a - b);
                               break;
                  case '*':    printf("Product = %d\n", a * b);
                               break;
                  case '/':    printf("Quotient = %d\n", a / b);
                               break;
                  case '%':    printf("Remainder = %d\n", a % b);
                               break;
                  default:     printf("Not an operator");
            }
            printf("Do you want to continue y/n? \n");
            fflush(stdin);
            ch = getchar();
      }while (ch == 'y');

      return 0;
}
```

Input–Output:

```
Enter two numbers
3 4
Enter an operator
+

sum = 7

Do you want to continue y/n?
y
Enter two numbers
5 6
Enter an operator
*
Product = 30
Do you want to continue y/n?
n
```

Explanation:

In the above program, a and b are declared to be variables of int type. These variables are to accept two integer values. ch and operator are the variables of char type. The variable operator is to accept an arithmetic operator symbol [+, -, *, / and %] and the variable ch is to accept the characters 'y' or 'n'

The program is to accept two numbers and an arithmetic operator repeatedly and interactively as long as the variable ch has the value 'y'. Thus, the variable ch becomes the control variable for the loop used in the program. Initially, the variable ch is assigned the value 'y' and the loop is entered. Within the loop, we can accept two numbers into the variables a and b, and we can accept an arithmetic operator into operator. The switch statement incorporated into the loop takes care of evaluating the resultant expression and display the result on the screen. The above procedure is repeated as long as we accept 'y' into the variable ch. Once we accept 'n' into it, the loop is exited and eventually the program also terminates.

7.5 WHICH LOOP TO USE WHEN

As a matter of fact, all the three looping structures can be used in all the situations which require repetition of execution of statements as we have seen before through the programming examples. However, by keeping in mind the nature of the looping structures, we can choose them according to the following guidelines.

If the problem to be programmed requires the test-expression to be checked first before executing the statements and if the statements are to be executed fixed number of times, the for loop is ideal (as we have seen in the case of generation of multiplication table of a number).

If the problem to be programmed requires the test-expression to be checked first before executing the statements and if the statements are to be executed unknown number of times and the loop is to be exited when the specified condition becomes false, the while loop is ideal (as we have seen in the case of finding the sum of the digits of an integer value).

If the problem to be programmed requires the test-expression to be checked after executing the statements once and if the statements are to be executed an unknown number of times and the loop is to be exited when the specified condition becomes false, the do-while loop is ideal. This looping structure is rarely used.

7.6   JUMPS IN LOOPS

The break statement

We know that a loop enables us to execute a block of statements as long as some test-expression is true. The break and continue statements provided by C enable us to exercise some kind of control over the working of loops. Let us now understand the need for these statements and their working.

The test-expression is one of the important components of a loop. As long as it is true, the statements in the body of the loop get executed repeatedly. Under some circumstances, we require the loop be exited even when the loop's test-expression still evaluates to true. The break statement becomes handy in these situations. When used within a loop, it causes the premature exit from the loop.

The syntax of its usage is

```
break;
```

More importantly, a break statement used within a loop is expected to be associated with an **if** statement. It is when the test-expression of the **if** statement evaluates to true, the loop is exited prematurely.

```
while (test-expression1)
{
        statements-1;
        if (test-expression2)
                break;
        Statements-2;
}
```

Here during the course of iterations, for any iteration, if the **test-expression2** evaluates to true, the control reaches the **break** statement and the **break** statement, on its execution, causes the loop to be exited prematurely. The following program demonstrates the working of the **break** statement when enclosed in a loop. The **break** statement can be used in any of the looping structures.

PROGRAM 7.9   To illustrate **break** statement

```
#include <stdio.h>

int main(void)
{
```

```
        int n, i, sum = 0, number;

        printf("Enter the number of elements \n");
        scanf("%d", &n);
        printf("Enter %d numbers type -ve number to terminate \n", n);
        for(i = 1; i <= n; i++)
        {
                scanf("%d", &number);
                if (number < 0)
                        break;
                sum += number;
        }
        printf(" sum of %d positive numbers = %d \n", i - 1, sum);

        return 0;
}
```

Input–Output:

```
Enter the number of elements
5
Enter 5 numbers Type -ve number to terminate
1
2
3
-4
sum of 3 +ve numbers = 6
```

Explanation:

In the above program **n**, **i**, **sum** and **number** are declared to be variables of **int** type. The variable **n** is to accept the number of values to be summed up; the variable number is to collect n numbers on one by one basis; **i** is to range from 1 to n in the loop used and sum is to collect the sum of the numbers entered before a negative number is entered.

The segment of the program responsible for the summation is:

```
for(i = 1; i <= n; i++)
{
        scanf("%d", &number);
        if (number < 0)
                break;
        sum += number;

{
```

Using the above for loop, we try to accept n numbers and find their sum. During the course of accepting the numbers, if positive numbers are entered, they are added to the variable sum. But if a negative number is entered, then the control reaches the break statement, which, when executed causes the loop to be exited prematurely. The value of the variable sum is then displayed.

The `continue` statement

The `continue` statement exercises control over a loop in a slightly different way. When enclosed in a loop, the statement causes skipping of the statements following it in the body of the loop and also causes the control to be transeferred back to the beginning of the loop. Similar to `break` statement, the `continue` statement statement is also expected to be associated with an `if` statement.

```
  ┌─► while (test-expression1)
  │    {
  │        statements-1;
  │        if (test-expression2)
  └──────────────── continue;
           statements 2;
     }
```

Here for some iteration, when `test-expression2` evaluates to true, the statements-2 are skipped for those iterations and the control goes to the beginning of the loop. Note that the loop is not prematurely exited as in the case of `break` statement. The following program demonstrates this very fact.

PROGRAM 7.10   To illustrate `continue` statement

```c
#include <stdio.h>

int main(void)
{
        int n, i, sum = 0, number;

        printf("Enter numbers of numbers \n");
        scanf("%d", &n);
        printf("Enter %d numbers \n", n);
        for(i = 1; i <= n; i++)
        {
                scanf("%d", &number);
                if (number < 0)
                        continue;
                sum += number;
        }
        printf(" sum of +ve numbers = %d \n", sum);

        return 0;
}
```

Input–Output:

```
Enter the numbers of numbers
5
Enter 5 numbers both +ve and -ve
```

```
1
2
-3
4
-5
sum of +ve numbers = 7
```

Explanation:

In the above program n, i, sum and number are declared to be variables of int type. The variable n is to accept the number of values to be summed up; the variable number is to collect **n** numbers on one-by-one basis; i is to range from 1 to n in the loop used and sum is to collect the sum of only the positive numbers out of n numbers entered.

The segment of the program responsible for the summation is:

```
for (i = 1; i <= n; i++)
{
        scanf ("%d", &number);
        if (number < 0)
                  continue;
        sum += number;
}
```

Using the above **for** loop, we accept **n** numbers and find their sum. During the course of accepting the numbers, if positive numbers are entered, they are added to the variable **sum**. But if a negative number is entered, then the control reaches the **continue** statement, which, when executed, causes the skipping of the statements following it within the loop and causes the control to be transferred back to the beginning of the loop, so that the loop continues with its next iteration. This continues as long as the test-expression of the loop evaluates to true. Once it evaluates to false, the loop exits. The value of **sum**, the sum of only positive numbers, is then displayed.

Differences between break **and** continue **statements**

The break statement

- Can be used in switch statement
- Causes premature exit of the loop enclosing it
- The control is transferred to the statement following the loop
- The loop may not complete the intended number of iterations

The continue statement

- Cannot be used in switch statement
- Causes skipping of the statements following it in the body of the loop
- Control is transferred back to the loop
- The loop completes the intended number of iterations

7.7 NESTING OF LOOPS

We now know that looping refers to repeated execution of a block of statements as long as some condition is true. In all our earlier programs on looping structures, we used a single loop to repeatedly execute a block of statements. There are many programming circumstances which require repeated execution of a block of statements itself to be repeated a known number of times or as long as some other condition is true. In these circumstances, we naturally need to enclose one loop within another loop. C allows this. Enclosing one loop within another loop is called nesting of loops. The enclosing loop is called **Outer-Loop** and the enclosed loop is called **Inner-Loop**.

Suppose we are asked to write a program to generate multiplication table of a number n, the program segment would be,

```c
for(i = 1; i <= 10; i++)
{
        p = n * i;
        printf("%d\n", p);
}
```

What if we want to generate multiplication tables of numbers of a range of numbers say 11 to 20? The direct option would be using the above program segment 10 times, one for each number in the range. The problem with this approach is duplication of the program segment, which in turn, results in consumption of more memory space. This problem can be solved by embedding the above program segment within another loop as follows.

```c
for(i = 11; i <= 20; i++)
{
        for(j = 1; j <= 10; j++)
        {
                p = n * i;
            printf("%d\n", p);
        }
}
```

Here, **for**-loop with the control variable **j (inner-loop)** is said to be nested within the **for**-loop with the control variable **i (outer-loop)**.

PROGRAM 7.11   To generate multiplication tables of a range of numbers

---

```c
#include <stdio.h>

int main(void)
{
        int m, n, i, j, p;

        printf(" Enter Lower limit \n");
        scanf("%d", &m);
        printf(" Enter Upper limit \n");
        scanf("%d", &n);

        for(i = m; i <= n; i++)
        {
            for(j = 1; j <= 10; j++)
            {
```

```
                    p = i * j;
                    printf("%4d", p);
            }
            printf("\n");
    }

    return 0;
}
```

Input–Output:

```
Enter Lower limit
5

Enter Upper limit
10

     5  10  15  20  25  30  35  40  45  50
     6  12  18  24  30  36  42  48  54  60
     7  14  21  28  35  42  49  56  63  70
     8  16  24  32  40  48  56  64  72  80
     9  18  27  36  45  54  63  72  81  90
    10  20  30  40  50  60  70  80  90 100
```

Explanation:

m, n, i, j and p are declared to be variables of **int** type. The variables m and n are to collect the lower limit and upper limit of the range of values, whose multiplication tables are to be generated. Since the task is to generate multiplication tables of the given range of numbers, we need to nest one loop within another. The outer loop is to select each number in the range and the inner loop is to generate the multiplication table of the number selected by the outer loop. The variables i and j are used as the control variables in the outer loop and the inner loop respectively. The variable p is used in the process of obtaining the products.

In the outer loop, when i takes m, the lower limit, the inner loop generates the multiplication table of m. Once the inner loop completes, control goes to the outer loop again. i gets incremented it becomes m+1. Then the inner loop generates the multiplication table of m+1. This continues as long as the test-expression of the outer loop evaluates to true. Once it evaluates to false, the outer loop is exited, by which time, multiplication tables of all the numbers in the range [m-n] have been generated.

PROGRAM 7.12   To generate prime numbers within a range of numbers

```
#include <stdio.h>

int main(void)
{
        int m, n, i, j, k, flag;
```

```
        printf ("Enter Lower limit \n");
        scanf ("%d", &m);
        printf ("Enter Upper limit \n");
        scanf ("%d", &n);
        printf ("Prime numbers between %d and %d \n", m, n);
        for (i = m; i <= n; i++)
        {       k = i;
                flag = 1;
                for (j = 2; (j <= k / 2) && flag; j++)
                        if ( k % j == 0)
                                flag = 0;

        if (flag)
                printf ("%d \n", i);
        }

        return 0;
}
```

Input–Output:

```
Enter Lower limit
10

Enter Upper limit
20

Prime numbers between 10 and 20
11
13
17
19
```

Explanation:

m, n, i, j and flag are declared to be variables of **int** type. The variables **m** and **n** are to collect the lower limit and upper limit of the range of values, within which prime numbers are to be generated. Since the task is to generate prime numbers within the given range of numbers, we need to nest one loop within another. The outer loop is to select each number in the range and the inner loop is to find whether the number selected by the outer loop is prime or not. The variables **i** and **j** are used as the control variables in the outer loop and the inner loop respectively. The variable **flag** is used in the process of finding out prime numbers.

In the outer loop, when **i** takes **m**, the lower limit, the inner loop finds out whether m is prime or not. the value of flag tells this. If flag retains 1 then m is prime if it gets 0 within the inner loop then it is taken to be not prime. Outside the inner loop, if the value of flag is found to be equal to 1, then m is displayed as prime otherwise m is not displayed at all. Control goes back to the outer loop again, **i** gets incremented and it becomes **m+1**. The inner loop finds out whether m+1 is prime or not. If it is found to be prime, it is displayed. This continues as long as the test-expression of the outer loop evaluates to true. Once it evaluates to false, the outer loop is exited, by which time, all the prime numbers in the range [m–n] have been generated.

7.7.1   Jumps in Nested Loops

The break **statement in nested loops**

We have understood the working of the break statement in relation to a single loop. Many programming circumstances call for its usage even when the loops are nested. It is important to note that the break statement affects only the loop in which it is enclosed.

```
for(initialization1; test-expression1; updation1)
{
        for(initialization2; test-expression2; updation2)
        {
                if (test-expression3)
                           break;
}
        statements;
}
```

```
for(initialization1; test-expression1; updation1)
{
        for(initialization2; test-expression2; updation2)
        {
                statements2;
        }

        if (test-expression3)
                   break;
}
statements;;
```

PROGRAM 7.13   To illustrate **break** statement in the case of nested loops

---

```c
#include <stdio.h>

int main(void)
{
        int number, i, j, sum;

        for(i = 1; i <= 2; i++) /* Outer loop */
        {
                sum = 0;
                printf("Enter five numbers for set %d \n", i);
```

```
                for (j = 1; j <= 5; j++) /* Inner loop */
                {
                        scanf ("%d", &number);
                        if (number < 0)
                                break;
                        sum = sum + number;
                }
                printf ("Sum of %d numbers in set %d = %d\n", j - 1, i, sum);
        }
        return 0;
}
```

Input–Output:

```
Enter five numbers for set 1
1
2
-3

Sum of 2 numbers in set 1 = 3

Enter five numbers for set 2
4
5
6
-8

Sum of 3 numbers in set 2 = 15
```

Explanation:

In the above program, **number**, **i**, **j** and **sum** are declared to be variables of **int** type. The program is to accept two sets of numbers, each set consisting of maximum five numbers and find the sum of +ve numbers in each set before a –ve number is entered. It is important to note that the problem calls for nesting of two loops. The outer loop for selecting each set and the inner loop for enabling us to accept the elements of the set selected by the outer loop. The variables **i** and **j** act as the control variables of the outer loop and the inner loop respectively. Number is to collect each number of a set and sum is to collect the sum of +ve numbers in the sets before a –ve number is entered.

Initially, the outer loop control variable **i** takes **1** representing the first set. The inner loop control variable **j** then ranges from **1** to **5** enabling us to accept up to five numbers of the first set and find the sum of the numbers. Importantly, within the inner loop, break statement is enclosed. It gets executed when the number entered is negative. So, once a –ve number is entered for the set, the inner loop is prematurely exited. In which case, the variable **sum** would collect the sum of fewer than intended five numbers of the set. This is repeated even for the second set also.

Since break statement is enclosed within the inner loop, we notice that it causes the premature exit of the inner loop only.

The `continue` statement in nested loops

We have also understood the working of the `continue` statement in relation to a single loop. Many programming circumstances call for its usage even when the loops are nested. It is important to note that the `continue` statement also affects only the loop in which it is enclosed.

`continue` Statement enclosed in Inner Loop:

```
for(initialization1; test-expression1; updation1)
{
        for(initialization2; test-expression2; updation2)
        {
                if (test-expression3)
                        continue;
                statements-2;
        }
        statements-1;
}
```

`continue` Statement enclosed in Outer Loop:

```
for(initialization1; test-expression1; updation1)
{
        for(initialization2; test-expression2; updation2)
        {
                statements2;
        }

        if (test-expression3)
        continue;
}
        statements;;
```

PROGRAM 7.14 To illustrate `continue` statement in the case of nested loops

---

```c
#include <stdio.h>

int main(void)
{
        int number, i, j, sum, count;

        for(i = 1; i <= 2; i++)
        {
                sum = 0;
                count = 0;
                printf("Enter five numbers for set %d \n", i);
                for(j = 1; j <= 5; j++)
                {
```

```
                        scanf ("%d", &number);
                        if (number < 0)
                                continue;
                        count++;
                        sum = sum + number;
                }
                printf ("Sum of %d +ve numbers in set %d = %d\n", count, i, sum);
        }

        return 0;
}
```

Input–Output:

```
Enter five numbers for set 1
1
2
-3
4
-5

Sum of 3 +ve numbers in set 1 = 7

Enter five numbers for set 2
4
5
6
-8
4
Sum of 4 +ve numbers in set 2 = 19
```

Explanation:

In the above program, **number**, **i**, **j** and **sum** are declared to be variables of **int** type. The program is to accept two sets of numbers, each set consisting of maximum five numbers and find the sum of only +ve numbers in each set ignoring –ve numbers, if any. As in the case of the previous program, the problem calls for nesting of two loops. The outer loop for selecting each set and the inner loop for enabling us to accept the elements of the set selected by the outer loop. The variables **i** and **j** act as the control variables of the outer loop and the inner loop respectively. **number** is to collect each number of a set and **sum** is to collect the sum of only +ve numbers in the sets ignoring –ve numbers, if any. Initially, the outer loop control variable **i** takes **1** representing the first set. The inner loop control variable **j** then ranges from **1** to **5** enabling us to accept up to five numbers of the first set and find the sum of the positive numbers. Importantly, within the inner loop, continue statement is enclosed. It gets executed when the number entered is negative. So once a –ve number is entered for the set, the statements following it in the inner loop are skipped and the control goes back to the beginning of the inner loop itself. The variable **sum** would collect the sum of fewer than intended five numbers of the set in case negative numbers are entered. This is repeated for the second set also. Since `continue` statement is enclosed within the inner loop, we notice that it affects the inner loop only.

SUMMARY

- Repeated execution of a block of statements is called looping or iteraton.
- Initialization, Condition and Updation are the three components required to construct a valid loop. More importantly, all of the three things should have at least one variable in common.
- C provides three looping structures, namely `for` loop, `while` loop and `do-while` loop.
- `For` loop and `while` loop are pre-tested loops, whereas `do-while` loop is the post-tested loop.
- In the case of `do-while` loop, the statements in the body of the loop are guaranteed to get executed once, which is not guaranteed in the former looping structures.
- When we know the number of iterations in advance, **for** loop is preferable because of its simple structure.
- Loops can be nested, i.e. one loop can be used within the other. In this case, the inner loop completes for each value of the outer loop variable. In essence, nested loops implement repetition of executon of statements.
- The `break` statement when used within a loop causes the premature exit of the loop. More importantly, it should be associated with an `if` statement.
- The `continue` statement when used in a loop causes the skipping of the statements, which follow it for some iteratons and the loop completes.

REVIEW QUESTIONS

7.1 What is the need for looping?

7.2 Differentiate between selection and looping.

7.3 How do you construct a loop with the help of **if** and **goto** statements?

7.4 Mention the three necessary things required to construct a loop.

7.5 What will be the output of the following program?

```c
int main(void)
{
    int i;
    for(i = 1; i < 10; i—)
            printf("%d", i);
    return 0;
}
```

7.6 Explain `for` loop with its syntax.

7.7 Explain `while` loop with its syntax.

7.8 Explain `do-while` loop.

7.9 Differentiate between `while` loop and `do-while` loop.

7.10 Why do we need to nest loops?

7.11 Differentiate between `break` and `continue` statements.

State whether the following are true or false

7.1 Initialization, condition and updation, all the three, are a must to construct a loop.

7.2 A test-expression is always associated with a loop.

7.3 Absence of the `updation` statement leads to infinite loop.

7.4 `while` loop executes at least once.

7.5 `for` loop is a post-tested looping structure.

7.6 `do-while` loop does not execute the block even once.

7.7 `for` loop can be nested within `while` loop.

7.8 `break` statement causes the premature exit of the loop in which it is enclosed.

7.9 `continue` statement can be used only within a loop.

7.10
```
for (i = 0; i < 9; i++)
{
    continue;
}
```
is a valid statement.

7.11 Both `break` and `continue` statements should be associated with an `if` statement.

7.12 `continue` statement also terminates a loop prematurely.

Find out errors, if any, in the following

7.1
```
int i;
while(i <= 10)
{
    printf("%d", i);
    i++;
}
```

7.2
```
int j = 10, sum;
while(j >= 1)
{
    sum += j;
    j++:
}
```

7.3
```
for(i = 0; i < 10; i—)
    printf("%d", i);
```

7.4
```
for(j = 10; j < 1; j++)
    printf("*");
```

7.5
```
for(i = 0; i < 3; i++)
    while(j = 0; j < 3; j++)
        printf("$");
```

7.6
```
do while ('a' > 24)
{
    printf("*");
}
```

7.7
```
do
{

    printf("Welcome");
    ans = getchar();
}while (ans == 'y')
```

7.8
```
while(1)
{
    break;
}
```

7.9
```
hile (10)
{
continue;
}
```

PROGRAMMING EXERCISES

7.1 Write a program to find the factorial of a number.

(**Example:** Input = 4   Output = 24)

7.2 Write a program to find whether a number is an Armstrong number or not.

(A number is said to be an Armstrong number if the sum of the cubes of the digits of the number is equal to the number itself. **Example:** $153 = 1^3 + 5^3 + 3^3 = 1 + 125 + 27$)

7.3 Write a program to find the sum of the digits of a multiple digit integer.

(**Example:** Input = 2345   Output = 14)

7.4 Write a program to generate all the integers in the range m and n divisible by the integer d.

7.5 Write a program to generate all the divisors of an integer n.

7.6 Write a program to find the number of occurrences of a digit in a number.

7.7 Write a program to reverse a given integer.

(**Example:** Input = 2345   Output = 5432)

7.8 Write a program to find sum of the sequence

$1 - 1/2 + 1/3 - 1/4 \ldots$

7.9 Write a program to find sum of the sequence
$1/3 + 3/7 - 5/11 + 7/15$

7.10 Write a program to evaluate sine series
$$\sin(x) = x - x^3/3! + x^5/5! - x^7/7! + x^9/9! \ldots$$
The inputs are:
(a) The value of **x**
(b) **n**, the number of terms to be summed up

7.11 Write a program to evaluate cosine series
$$\cos(x) = 1 - x2/2! + x4/4! - x6/6! + \ldots$$
The inputs are:
(a) The value of **x**
(b) **n**, the number of terms to be summed up

7.12 Write a program to evaluate the exponential series
$$e^x = 1 + x + x^2/2! + x^3/3! + x^4/4! + \ldots + x^n/n!$$
The inputs are:
(a) The value of **x**
(b) **n**, the number of terms to be summed up

7.13 Write a program to generate Armstrong numbers between two numbers.

7.14 Write a program to display the following pattern

1 2 3
4 5 6
7 8 9

7.15 Write a program to display the following pattern

1
1 2
1 2 3
1 2 3 4

7.16 Write a program to display the following pattern

       1
     2 1 2
   3 2 1 2 3
 4 3 2 1 2 3 4

INTERVIEW QUESTIONS

7.1 Predict the output and give your explanation.

(a)
```c
#include<stdio.h>
int main(void)
{
    int x = 0;
    while (x++<=5)
    {
        printf("c programming\n");
    }
    while (x--  >= 5)
    {
        printf("programming in c\n");
    }
    return 0;
}
```

(b)
```c
#include<stdio.h>
int main(void)
{
    int x = 0;
    while (x=0)
    {
        printf("C Programming\n");
        x++;
    }
    printf(" Is very interesting\n");
    }

    while (x-->=5)
    {
        printf("Programming in C\n");
    }

    return 0;
}
```

```
(c) #include<stdio.h>
    int main(void)
    {
        int i, x=012;
        for(i=0;i<x;i+=3)
        {
            printf("%d", i);
        }

        return 0;
    }
```

```
(d) #include<stdio.h>
    int main(void)
        int i,j;
        i=j=2;
        while(++i&&j--)
            printf("%d %d",i,j);
        return 0;
    }
```

```
(e) #include<stdio.h>
    int main(void)
        int i;
        for(i=0;i<=5;i++);
        printf("%d",i)
        return 0;
    }
```

```
(f) #include<stdio.h>
    int main(void)
        char c=125;
        do
            printf("%d ",c);
        while(c++);

        return 0;
    }
```

```c
(g) #include<stdio.h>
    int main(void)
    {
        int i=1;
        for(;i++;)
            printf("%d",i);
        return 0;
    }
```

```c
(h) #include<stdio.h>
    int main()
    {
        int i,j;
        i=j=2,3;          // line 5
        while(--i&&j++)
        printf("%d %d\n",i,j);
        printf("%d %d\n",i,j);
        return 0;
    }
```

```c
(i) #include <stdio.h>
    int main(void)
    {
        int t1=1, t2=1;
        while (t1 < 5, t2 < 10)
        {
            t1++;
            ++t2;
        }
        printf("%d, %d\n", t1, t2);

        return 0;
    }
```

7.2 Write a C code to show that for loop is a pre-tested loop.

8

Functions

8.1 INTRODUCTION

One of the real strengths of C language is its ability to deal with large and complicated programs due to its capability to support **Structured Design** (Top–down approach). The basic idea behind which is to divide a big program into a number of relatively smaller and easily manageable subprograms. So far, in all our earlier programs, we have used only `main()` to solve problems. The algorithms involved in solving the problems were realized in terms of statements embedded in the `main()`. If a problem involves lengthy and complex algorithm, naturally, the length of the `main()` may increase to an extent where keeping track of the steps involved may become an Herculean task. In this case, it would be a nice proposition, if the problem can be divided into a number of logical units and each logical unit is programmed separately and eventually all the logical units are combined together. This is where the concept of functions comes into picture. Each subprogram in C is called a **Function**.

Because of the flexibility provided by C in defining functions and the fact that each logical unit of work is accomplished by means of a function, C is referred to as a **Language of Functions**.

> A function is defined to be a self-contained program which is written for the purpose of accomplishing some task.

8.2 ADVANTAGES OF FUNCTIONS

The functions offer the following advantages.

1. **Minimization of memory space usage:** Suppose we have five sets of numbers, each set consisting of three numbers and suppose we need to find the largest in each of the sets. If we use only `main()` to accomplish this task, we identify that the statements which are used to find the largest of three numbers have to be repeated five times. What if the

numbers of sets is more than five? Inevitably, we have to repeat the statements as many times as the numbers of sets. The repetition of the same code leads to more consumption of memory space. This problem can be avoided by defining a separate function embedding the statements responsible for finding the largest of three numbers within it. The function can then be made to work with each of the sets at different points of time.

2. **Improvization of overall organization of a program:** The overall organization of a program is improved by way of compartmentalization or modularization. Wherein, a program is divided into a number of subprograms depending on the functionality required by each subprogram. Each subprogram is viewed as a separate compartment or a module.

3. **Facilitation of teamwork:** Development of many real life applications calls for involvement of more than one programmer. This is mainly because of the larger size of the projects. The projects will normally be divided into a number of modules and each module is assigned to a different programmer. Naturally, the programmers implement their modules using functions, which will be integrated together at the final stage.

4. **Simplification of software engineering tasks like testing and debugging:** The errors encountered in the code can easily be identified and fixed. Ease of identifying the location of the errors and correcting them is once again attributed to the flexibility provided by functions.

8.3 CLASSIFICATION OF FUNCTIONS

We can categorize functions into two types: 1. **Built-in functions** and 2. **User-defined functions**.

Built-in functions are those which are already made available as part of C Library. They can be used by any programmer. `scanf()`, `printf()`, `strlen()`, `strcpy()` are some of the built-in functions which have been used in earlier programs, whereas a **User-defined function** is one which is written by a user to solve a problem. The strength of C lies in its flexibility in supporting development of user-defined functions at ease. The only user-defined function dealt with so far is `main()`

Since the built-in functions are already available for use as part of the C Library, it is enough if we know the purpose of the functions and the syntax of their usage. The list of most commonly used built-in functions, information about the functions like their syntax and their usage and the header file to be included are given in the Appendices towards the end of the book for reference.

We will now delve into the art of defining our own functions to accomplish the tasks which we come across. The general form of defining a function is as follows:

```
return-type function-name (arguments)
    {
        local variables;
        statements;
        return (expression);
    }
```

`return-type` refers to the data type of the value being returned by the function. `function-name` is the name given to the function which is referred to while using the function. It should be a valid identifier and it is better if it reflects the underlying purpose. The function name is followed by arguments declaration enclosed within a pair of parentheses. The first line consisting of return-type, function-name and arguments declaration enclosed within a pair of parentheses is usually referred to as the **Function Header**. The Function Header is followed by the local variables declaration part and a set of executable statements of the function enclosed within a pair of opening brace and closing brace. The local variables declaration part and the set of statements enclosed within the braces are referred to as the **Function Body**.

Function Header + Function Body = Function Definition

A function, which is defined, cannot be executed by itself. It has to be invoked by another function. It can be `main()` or any other function. A function which invokes another function is called **Calling Function** and the function which is invoked is termed **Called Function**.

In all our earlier programs, `scanf()` and `printf()` have been invoked by `main()`. So, the `scanf()` and `printf()` are Called Functions and `main()` is the Calling Function.

Sometimes, it is desirable that calling function and called function establish data communication. Arguments facilitate the data communication. Depending on the type of data communication, if any, functions are further classified into four types.

1. Functions with no arguments and no return value.
2. Functions with arguments and no return value.
3. Functions with arguments and return value.
4. Functions with no arguments but with return value.

8.4 FUNCTIONS WITH NO ARGUMENTS AND NO RETURN VALUE

Suppose `f()` is a function which does not require arguments to be passed and does not return any value to its calling program. The prototype of the function would be as follows:

```
void f(void);
```

and the function definition will have the form

```
void f(void)
{
    variables
    statements
}
```

The call to the function `f()` would be like an independent statement as shown below.

```
void fn()
{
    f();
}
```

where `fn()` is the calling function for the function `f()`.

Pictorially, the calling and returning sequence is shown as follows:

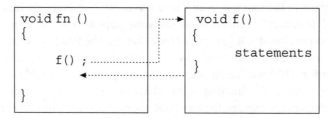

The sequence is as follows: The control is transferred to the function f () ; the statements of f () are executed; on completion of execution of f () , the control is transferred back to the calling function fn () ; The dotted lines with an arrow mark at their end indicate the transfer of control from fn () to f () and after the completion of execution of f () , transferring the control back to the calling function fn ()

Since the function f () does not require arguments to be passed from the calling function fn () and does not return any value back to it, there is no data communication between the function f () and its calling function. The following program uses a function which requires no arguments to be passed from the calling program and also does not return any value.

Pseudocode to find the largest of three numbers

```
Pseudocode largest ()
Read a, b, c
l = a;
if (b > l)
     l = b;
if (c > l)
     l = c;
display l
```

End pseudocode

PROGRAM 8.1   To find the largest of the three given numbers

```c
#include <stdio.h>

void largest (void);

int main (void)
{
     largest ();
     return 0;
}

void largest (void)
{
     int a, b, c, l;
```

```
        printf ("Enter three numbers \n");
        scanf ("%d%d%d", &a, &b, &c);

        l = a;
        if (b > l)
              l = b;
        if (c > l)
              l = c;

        printf ("Largest = %d \n", l);
}
```

Input–Output:

```
Enter three numbers
3 4 5
```

```
Largest = 5
```

Explanation:

The function largest () is to find the largest of the three numbers. Its header indicates that it requires no arguments and it does not return any value. In the body of the function, four variables are declared. **a, b** and **c** are to collect three numbers. The variable **l** is to collect the largest of them. The statements which follow, accept three numbers, find the largest of them and display it.

In the main (), largest () is invoked by just specifying its name and a pair of parentheses. The actual execution starts from and ends with main () only. When largest (); is encountered in main (), control is transferred to the function largest (). Upon completion of its execution, the control is regained by the main ()

Points to Remember

- If a function f1 () invokes another function f2 (), then f2 () is said to have been called by f1 ().
- A called function can be defined either before or after its calling function. In the above example programs, largest () (called function) has been defined after main () (calling function).
- If called function does not return any value, it has to be used as an independent statement.
- A function cannot be defined within the body of another function as it is treated as an external variable.

8.5 FUNCTIONS WITH ARGUMENTS AND NO RETURN VALUE

Suppose f () is a function which requires arguments to be passed and does not return any value to its calling program. The prototype of the function would be as follows:

```
void f (arguments);
```

and the function definition will have the form

```
void f (arguments)
{
    variables
    statements
}
```

The call to the function f () would be like an independent statement as shown below.

```
void fn ()
{
    f (actual-arguments) ;
}
```

where fn () is the calling function for the function f ()

Pictorially, the calling and the return sequence is shown as below:

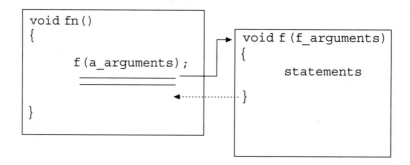

The sequence is as follows: The control is transferred to the function f () with the actual arguments having been copied to the formal arguments of f () ; the statements of f () are executed; on completion of execution of f (), the control is transferred back to the calling function fn () ; The dark line with the arrow mark indicates that the control is transferred from fn () to f () along with data transfer. The dotted line with the arrow mark indicates the transfer of control from f () back to fn (). Since the function f () requires arguments to be passed from the calling function fn () and does not return any value back to it, there is one-way data communication between the function f () and its calling function, i.e. from fn () to f () only.

The following program uses a function which requires arguments but does not return any value.

Pseudocode largest (a, b, c)

```
l = a;
if (b > l)
      l = b;
if (c > l)
      l = c;
display l
```

End pseudocode

PROGRAM 8.2   To illustrate a function with arguments and no return value

```c
#include <stdio.h>
void largest (int a, int b, int c)

int main (void)
{
      int a, b, c;
      int x, y, z;

      printf ("Enter values of a , b and c \n");
      scanf ("%d%d%d", &a, &b, &c);
      largest (a, b, c);

      printf ("Enter values of x , y and z \n");
      scanf ("%d%d%d", &x, &y, &z);
      largest (x, y, z);

      return 0;
}

void largest (int a, int b, int c)
{
      int l;

      l = a;
      if (b > l)
            l = b;
      if (c > l)
            l = c;

      printf ("Largest = %d \n", l);
}
```

Input–Output:

```
Enter values of a , b and c
3 4 5

Largest = 5

Enter values of x , y and z
6 3 2

Largest = 6
```

Explanation:

The function largest () is defined with three arguments **a**, **b** and **c** of **int** type. The arguments **a, b** and **c** are called formal arguments of the function. The purpose of the function is to find the largest of the three integer values passed to it. Within the function, one more variable **1**, is declared and it collects the largest of **a, b** and **c**.

In the main () **a, b, c, x, y** and **z** are declared to be variables of **int** type. Initially, the values of **a, b** and **c** are accepted and the function largest () is called by passing the values of **a, b** and **c** as largest (a, b, c); As far as the function call largest (a, b, c); is concerned, the values of **a, b** and **c** belonging to main () are called the actual arguments for the function call. Note that **a, b** and **c** specified as formal arguments of largest () and **a, b** and **c** (actual arguments) declared in main (), even though they have same names, are different in terms of storage. As a consequence of the function call largest (a, b, c); in main (), the values of **a, b** and **c** are copied to the formal arguments of largest () **a, b** and **c** rspectively as:

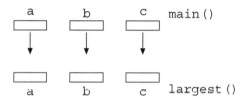

after the formal arguments of largest (), **a, b** and **c** get filled up, the function finds the largest of them assigns it to the variable **1**, which is then displayed. Control is regained by main ().

Next, three values are accepted into the variables **x, y** and **z** and again the function **largest ()** is called by passing **x, y** and **z** as largest (x, y, z); Now **x, y** and **z** become actual arguments. Similar to the previous case, as a consequence of the call largest (x, y, z); the values of **x, y** and **z** are copied to the formal arguments **a, b** and **c** respectively as shown below.

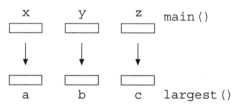

After the formal arguments of largest (), **a, b** and **c** get filled up, the function finds the largest of them assigns it to the variable **1**, which is then displayed. The control is regained by **main ()**

Points to Remember

- The names of the formal arguments and the names of the actual arguments can be same or different.
- The number of formal arguments and the number of actual arguments should be same.
- Types of the actual arguments should be compatible with those of the formal arguments.
- We can even pass constants as actual arguments. That is, largest (3, 6, 7); is a valid function call.

8.6 FUNCTIONS WITH ARGUMENTS AND RETURN VALUE

Suppose f() is a function which requires arguments to be passed and also returns a value to its calling program. The prototype of the function would be as follows:

```
data-type f(arguments);
```

and the function definition will have the form

```
data-type f(arguments)
{
      variables
      statements
      return (Expression);
}
```

The call to the function f() would be like a variable (part of an expression) as shown below.

```
void fn()
{
      variable = f(actual-arguments);
}
```

where fn() is the calling function for the function f()

Pictorially, the calling and the return sequence is shown as below:

The sequence is as follows: The control is transferred to f() with the actual arguments of fn() having been copied to the formal arguments of f(); the statements of f() are executed; on completion of execution of f(), the control is transferred back to the calling function fn(); The value returned by f() is assigned to variable in fn().

The dark lines connecting the functions indicate the transfer of control with data transfer in both the directions.

Since the function f() requires arguments and also returns a value back to its calling program, there is two-way data communication between the calling function fn() and the function f() The following program uses a function which requires arguments and returns a value to its calling program.

```
Pseudocode largest(a, b, c)
l = a;
if (b > l)
      l = b;
if (c > l)
      l = c;
return l
End Pseudocode
```

PROGRAM 8.3   To illustrate a function with arguments and return value

```c
#include <stdio.h>
int largest (int a, int b, int c)

int main (void)
{

        int a, b, c, lar;
        int x, y, z;

        printf ("Enter values of a, b and c \n");
        scanf ("%d%d%d", &a, &b, &c);
        lar = largest (a, b, c);
        printf (" Largest = %d \n", lar);

        printf ("Enter values of x, y and z \n");
        scanf ("%d%d%d", &x, &y, &z);
        lar = largest (x, y, z);
        printf ("Largest = %d \n", lar);
        return 0;
}

        int largest (int a, int b, int c)
{

        int largest;

        largest = a;
        if (b > largest)
                largest = b;
        if (c > largest)
                largest = c;

        return (largest);
}
```

Input–Output:

```
Enter values of a, b and c
3 4 5
Largest = 5

Enter values of x, y and z
4 5 6
Largest = 6
```

Explanation:

Here, as in the case of previous program, the `largest()` takes three arguments **a, b** and **c** of **int** type and finds the largest of the values collected by the arguments but unlike in the previous case, it does not display the largest value, but returns it back to the calling function (`main()`).

In the `main()`, the values of variables **a, b** and **c** are passed in the first call to the function `largest()`. Since `largest()` now returns a value, the function call is used on RHS of an assignment statement as `lar = largest(a, b, c);` the value returned by the function is collected by the variable **lar** and it is displayed.

In the second call to the function `largest()`, the values of **x, y** and **z** are passed. `lar = largest(x, y, z);` As a result, the function returns the largest of **x, y** and **z** and it is assigned to the variable **lar**, which is then displayed.

Points to Remember

- A function cannot return more than one value. By default, it returns a value of **int** type.
- If a function returns a value then, normally the function call would be like a variable. However, if the value being returned is not required, it can even be called as an independent statement. For example, both **scanf()** and **printf()** are called as independent statements even though they return values.

```
int i;
float f;
char c;

scanf("%d%f%c", &i, &f, &c);
```

If the values entered are

    12
    23.56
    w

The **scanf()** returns 3, the number of values that are read.

The `printf("%d%f%c\n", i, f, c);` displays 12, 23.56 and w and returns 8, the total number of characters that are displayed. The values returned by both of these functions can be used to verify whether the functions have worked correctly or not. We do not use these values assuming that the functions have done their job perfectly.

Similarly, there are a number of functions in the standard C Library, which return values but are called like independent statements. It is left to the readers to figure out them.

Pseudocode to find whether a number is prime or not

```
Pseudocode prime(number)
flag = 1
k = 2
while(k <= number - 1)
begin
        rem = number % k
        if (rem == 0)
                flag = 0
```

```
                break

        k++
end
return (flag);
```
End pseudocode

PROGRAM 8.4   To find whether a number is prime or not using a function

---

```c
#include <stdio.h>

int prime(int number)
{
        int k, rem, flag;

        flag = 1;
        k = 2;
        while(k <= number - 1)
        {
                rem = number % k;
                if (rem == 0)
                {
                        flag = 0;
                        break;
                }
                k++;
        }

        return (flag);
}

int main(void)
{
        int number;

        printf("Enter a number \n");
        scanf("%d", &number);

        if (prime(number))
                printf("%d is prime", number);
        else
                printf("%d is not prime", number);
        return 0;
}
```

Input–Output:

```
Enter a number
6
6 is not a prime number

Enter a number
7
7 is a prime number
```

Explanation:

The Function prime() is defined with one formal argument of int type and is made to return either 1 or 0 . The purpose of the function is to take an integer number and find out whether the number is prime or not. If the number is prime, it returns 1. Otherwise, it returns 0.

In the main(), an integer number is accepted into the variable number. A call is made to the function prime() by passing the value of number. Since the function returns either 1 or 0, the function call has been used as a conditional expression as (prime(number)) in main(). If prime(number) returns 1 then, the number is displayed as prime. Otherwise, the number is displayed as not prime.

Point to Remember
- If a function returns a value which is either 0 or 1 (or any non-zero value) can be used as a test-expression.

8.7 FUNCTIONS WITH NO ARGUMENTS BUT WITH RETURN VALUE

We can design functions which do not require arguments but return a value. There are a number of built-in functions which belong to this category. The function getch() is one such example. The getch() function does not require any arguments but it returns the character value it reads from the keyboard.

The sequence is as follows: The control is transferred from fn() to f(); after the completion of execution of f(), the control is transferred back to fn(); The value returned by f() is assigned to variable in fn();. Pictorially the calling and returning sequence is depicted as shown below:

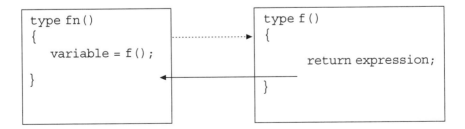

PROGRAM 8.5   To illustrate a function with no arguments but with return value

```c
#include <stdio.h>

int read_number(void);

int main(void)
{
        int number;

        number = read_number();
        printf("number = %d", number);
        return 0;
}

int read_number(void)
{
        int n;
        printf("Enter a number \n");
        scanf("%d", &n);
        return n;
}
```

Input–Output:

```
Enter a number
5
number = 5
```

Explanation:

In the above program, the function `read_number()` is defined with no arguments but it is made to return a value. Within the function n is declared to be a variable of `int` type and a value is read into it with the statement `scanf("%d", &n);` and the value is returned back to the calling program.

In the `main()`, the `read number()` is invoked in the statement `number = read_number();` Note that the function call appears on the right hand side of the assignment statement. The value returned by the function is collected by the variable number and it is displayed.

8.8 FUNCTIONS RETURNING A NON-INTEGER VALUE

We just learnt that a function, if returns a value, the value will be of type `int` by default. In the real programming situations, we may require to write functions which have to return a non-integer value to their calling programs. For instance, most of the built-in mathematical functions return double type values, for example: `sin()`, `cos()`, `tan()`, `pow()`, etc. In order to force a function to return a non-integer value, the function header should explicitly have the appropriate return-type name specified. If the function call precedes its definition, its prototype should also specify the appropriate return-type. Let us now write a program to illustrate this fact.

PROGRAM 8.6 To illustrate function returning a non-integer value

```
#include <stdio.h>

float largest (float, float);

int main(void)
{
    float a, b, c;

    printf ("Enter two float values \n");
    scanf ("%f%f", &a, &b);
    c = largest (a, b);
    printf (" largest = %f \n", c);

    return 0;
}

float largest (float f, float g)
{
    float l;
    l = f;
    if (g > l)
        l = g;
    return (l);
}
```

Input–Output:

```
Enter two float values
5.5
6.78
largest = 6.78
```

Explanation:

The function largest () is defined with two arguments of float type and is made to return value of type float. The purpose of the function is to find the largest of the two float values passed to it and return the result back to the calling program (main () in this case). Since the function is returning a value of float type (non-integer type), the function prototype starts with the keyword float. (function call precedes function definition). Similarly, the keyword float is used in the header of the function also while it is defined. These are to force the function to return a value of float type.

In the main (), two values of float type are read into the variables a and b. The function largest () is then called by passing a and b as the actual arguments as c = largest (a, b); Note that since the function is returning a value, the function call is like a variable or a part of an expression. The value returned by the function largest () is assigned to the variable c in main () and it is displayed.

Points to Remember

- Function prototype is defined to be the declaration of a function, which indicates the number of arguments, their types and return-type.
- Prototype for a function is mandatory if the function is defined after its call. However, it is optional if the call is made to the function after defining the function.
- When a function is made to return a value of non-integer type, it is expected to be assigned to a variable of the corresponding type to get the correct value returned by the function.

8.9 NESTING OF FUNCTIONS

Suppose f1(), f2() and f3() are three functions, f1() can invoke f2(), f2() in turn can invoke f3(). Practically, the nesting of function calls can be further extended if necessary. The following program illustrates this concept.

PROGRAM 8.7   To illustrate nesting of functions

```c
#include <stdio.h>

int fact(int);
int npr(int, int);

int main(void)
{
        int n, r, p;

        printf("Enter the values of n and r\n");
        scanf("%d%d", &n, &r);
        p = npr(n, r);
        printf("The number of permutations of %d items out of %d items = %d
", r, n, p);

        return 0;
}

int fact(int n)
{
        int i, f = 1;

        for(i = 1; i <= n; i++)
                f *= i;

        return f;
}

int npr(int n, int r)
{
```

```
        int p;

        p = fact(n) / fact(n - r);

        return p;
}
```

Input–Output:

```
Enter the values of n and r
4
3
The number of permutations of 3 items out of 4 items = 24
```

Explanation:

The function fact() is defined with an argument n of int type and it is made to return an int type value. The purpose of the function is to find the factorial of the number passed to it as the argument and return it to its calling function (npr() in this case).

The function npr() is defined with two arguments **n** and **r** of int type and is made to return a value of int type. The purpose of the function is to find the number of permutations of r items taken together out of n items and return it to the calling function (main() in this case).

In the main() the values of n and r are accepted. The statement p = npr(n, r); finds the number of permutations of r items out of n items and assign it to the variable p, which is then displayed. It is important to note that there are two levels of nesting in function calls. The main() calls npr(), which in turn calls fact().

8.10 RETURN STATEMENT VS. EXIT()

The exit() is a built-in function available as part of C library. The common thing shared by both the return statement and the exit() is that both are used to exit the function in which they are used. But, the difference lies in where the control is then transferred to after the exit of their corresponding functions. The return statement causes the exit of the function in which it is enclosed and transfers the control to the **Calling Function**. But the exit() enclosed within a function, on its execution, terminates the entire program and the control is transferred to the **underlying operating system** itself. To be able to use exit(), the program should include either **stdlib.h** or **process.h** header files. This is because, the prototype for the function is available in these files.

PROGRAM 8.8   To illustrate return statement vs. exit()

```
#include <stdio.h>
#include <process.h>
int fact(int);

int main(void)
```

```
{
        int n, f;

        printf ("Enter a number \n");
        scanf ("%d", &n);
        f = fact (n);
        printf ("Factorial = %d \n", f);

        return 0;
}


int fact (int n)
{
        int f = 1, i;
        if (n < 0)
        {
                printf ("The number entered is -ve \n");
                exit (0);
        }
        else
        {
                for (i = 1; i <= n; i++)
                f *= i;
        }
        return (f);
}
```

Input–Output:

First-Run:
Enter a number
-4
The number entered is –ve **(The control goes to the operating system)**

Second-Run:
Enter a number
5
Factorial = 120 **(The control is transferred to the main ())**

Explanation:

In the above program, if the number passed to the function fact () is negative, the entire program is terminated because the statement **exit(0);** gets executed and the control is transferred to the operating system. But if a positive integer is passed to the function fact (), its factorial is found out and the **return** statement in the function fact () on its execution returns the factorial value to the calling function (main ()).

8.11 RECURSION

Suppose f1(), f2() and f3() are three functions. The function f1() can call f2(), in turn, f2() can call f3(). Likewise, nesting of the function calls can be to any level depending on the requirement. There is one more possibility with regard to functions, which needs to be mentioned. That is, a function f() can call itself().The phenomenon of a function calling itself is called **Recursion**. The function involved in the process is referred to as a **Recursive Function**.

There are a number of problems, the solutions of which can be expressed in terms of recursive steps. A solution to a problem is said to be expressible in terms of recursive steps if it can be expressed in terms of its subsolutions. These can be implemented by the use of recursive functions. When a recursive function is employed to solve these problems, care needs to be taken to see to it that the function does not call itself again at some point of time by which the solution for the problem has been arrived at. This is accomplished with the help of a **Terminating Condition**.

Problem 1:

Finding the factorial of a number 4

Mathematically, factorial of 4 is denoted by 4 !

```
= 4 * 3 * 2!
= 4 * 3 * 2 * 1!
= 4 * 3 * 2 * 1
= 24
```

In general, factorial of a number n denoted by n! can be written as:

```
n! = n * (n-1)!
   = n * (n-1) * (n-2)!
              :
              :
   = n * (n-1) * (n-2) ......* 1!
   = n * (n-1) * (n-2) ......  * 1 * 0!
```

We know that factorial of 0 is 1. Thus, when n takes 0, we do not call the function fact() but we, simply return 1. This happens to be the terminating condition.

Pseudocode to find factorial of a number

```
Pseudocode fact(n)
if (n == 0)
      return (1);
else
      f = n * fact(n - 1);
return f;
End pseudocode
```

PROGRAM 8.9   To find factorial of a number

```c
#include <stdio.h>

int fact (int);

int main (void)
{
        int n, f;

        printf ("Enter a number \n");
        scanf ("%d", &n);
        f = fact (n);
        printf (" fact = %d \n", f);

        return 0;
}

int fact (int n)
{
        int f;

        if (n == 0)
                return (1);
        else
                f = n * fact (n - 1);

        return f;
}
```

Input–Output:

```
Enter a number
4
factorial of 4 = 24
```

Explanation:

The function fact () is defined with an argument of **int** type and is made to return a value of **int** type. The purpose of the function is to find the factorial of an integer number passed to it and to return the result back to the calling program (main () in this case).

Within the function fact (), the task of finding the factorial of n is expressed in terms of recursive steps. The function works as follows: In the simplest case, if the value of n is 0, the function returns 1. That is, factorial of 0 is returned back to the main ()

If n > 0 then, as long as n > 0, fact () is called recursively by passing one less than the previous number. once argument to fact () becomes 0 the function returns 1 to its calling function.

In this case the same function `fact()`, which had the argument as 1 [i.e. `fact(1)`]. Then the function `fact(1)` returns 1 to its calling function which once again is the `fact()` itself which had the argument as 2, [i.e. fact(2)] likewise each recently called function `fact()` returns the value it evaluates, to its calling `fact()` and ultimately, the `fact()` which was called by `main()` returns the factorial of the given number to the `main()`. Suppose n = 4, the function call `fact(4)` in `main()` gives rise to the following sequence.

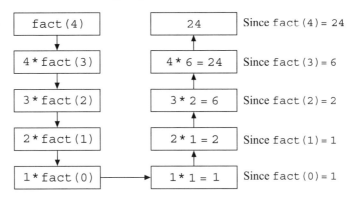

The factorial of 4 = 24 is then collected by the variable **f** in the `main()`

Problem 2:

Suppose we want to find the sum of digits of an integer number, we can see that the task can be expressed in recursive steps as given in the following example.

To find the sum of the digits of 456
If `sum()` is the function defined for this

```
sum(456)  = 6 + sum(45)
          = 6 + 5 + sum(4)
          = 6 + 5 + 4 + sum(0)
          = 6 + 5 + 4 + 0
          = 15
```

In general, if `sum()` is to find the sum of digits of a number n:
`sum(n)` is expanded to `n%10 + sum(n/10)` as long as the argument to `sum()` becomes 0. Once the argument becomes 0, `sum(0)` is replaced by 0. This becomes the terminating condition for the problem. The value of the resultant expression turns out to be the sum of the digits of the given number. Within the function, we keep checking the value of the argument passed, if the terminating condition is satisfied, the value 0 is returned.

Pseudocode to find the sum of digits of a number
```
Pseudocode sum(number)
if (number == 0)
      return 0
else
      s = number % 10 + sum(number/10)
      return s
End pseudocode
```

PROGRAM 8.10   To find the sum of digits of a number

```c
#include <stdio.h>

int sum(int);

int main(void)
{
        int number, s;

        printf("Enter a number \n");
        scanf("%d", &number);

        s = sum(number);

        printf(" sum =%d \n", s);

        return 0;
}

int sum(int number)
{
        int s;

        if (number == 0)
                return 0;
        else
                s = number % 10 + sum(number / 10);
        return s;
}
```

Input–Output:

```
Enter a number
456
sum = 15
```

Explanation:

The function sum() is defined with an argument of **int** type and is made to return a value of **int** type. The purpose of the function is to find the sum of digits of the number passed to it and return the sum back to the calling program. Within the function, the sum of digits of the number passed, is found out using recursive approach as follows. As long as number > 0, remainder after division of number by 10 is extracted and the remaining part of the number is once again passed to the function as in the statement s= number % 10 + sum(number/10). Once the argument to sum() becomes 0, the recursive calls to sum() are exited in the last in first out order. The first call made by main() to sum() on its exit returns the sum of the digits to the main(). The function sum() works as follows:

Suppose n = 465, the function call sum (465) in main () gives rise to the following sequence:

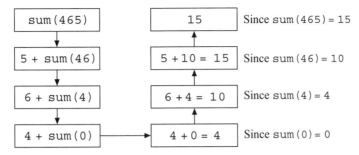

Sum of the digits of the number 465 = 15 is collected by the variable **s** in the main().

Problem 3:

Fibonacci series starts with two numbers 1 and 1. The next subsequent member of the series is obtained by summing the immediate previous two numbers. Generation of the series can be recursively expressed as follows.

```
fib(n) = fib(n-1) + fib(n-2)
```

i.e. **nth** member is the sum of **(n – 1)** th and **(n – 2)** th member of the series

and fib(1) = 1, fib(2) = 1

Thus, we have two terminating conditions. In either of these cases, the function exits without making another call to itself.

Pseudocode to generate Fibonacci series

```
Pseudocode fib(n)
if (n == 1)
      return 1;
else if (n == 2)
      return 1;
else
      f = fib(n - 1) + fib(n - 2);
      return f;
End pseudocode
```

PROGRAM 8.11   To generate Fibonacci series

```c
#include <stdio.h>

int fib(int);

int main(void)
{
      int n, i;
```

```
        printf("Enter a number \n");
        scanf("%d", &n);

        for( i = 1; i <= n; i++)
                printf("%d \n", fib(i));

        return 0;
}

int fib(int n)
{
        int f;

        if (n == 1)
                return 1;
        else if (n == 2)
                return 1;
        else
                f = fib(n - 1) + fib(n - 2);
        return f;
}
```

Input–Output:

```
Enter the number of members to be generated
5

1
1
2
3
5
```

Explanation:

The function fib() is defined with one argument of **int** type and is made to return a value of **int** type. The purpose of the function is to take an integer number n and generate nth member of Fibonacci series and return it to the calling program.

The following program segment is responsible for generating **n** members of the Fibonacci series.

```
for( i = 1; i <= n; i++)
        printf("%d \n", fib(i));
```

Here when i takes the value 1, the function call fib(1) returns 1, the first member of the series and it is displayed. In the next iteration, the control variable **i** takes the value 2, then the function call fib(2) returns 1, the second member of the series and it is displayed by the printf().

In the third iteration **i** takes 3, the function call becomes fib(3), the function call to fib() with 3 as the argument in turn makes two calls to itself by passing 2 and 1 as the arguments (fib(2)+fib(1)). Both these function calls return 1 to the function fib() itself(which was called with 3 as the argument), which in turn returns the sum of them, which is 2, the third member of the series to the main (). Similarly, when the variable **i** takes 4 the fourth member of the series is obtained, and so on.

To find the value of x to the power of y

The task of finding the value of x to the power of y can also be expressed in terms of recursive steps. Suppose we need to evaluate 2^3, let us express 2^3 in recursive terms as follows:

$$2^3 = 2 * 2^2$$
$$= 2 * 2 * 2^1$$
$$= 2 * 2 * 2 * 2^0$$
$$2 * 2 * 2 * 1$$

Note that 2^0 is replaced by 1. So the terminating condition for the recursive problem is: If the power value is 0, return 1.

Pseudocode to find x to the power of y (where x and y are integers)

```
Pseudocode power(x,y)
if (y == 0)
      return (1);
else if (y > 0)
      p =x * power(x, y - 1);
else

      p = 1/power(x, -y);

return (p);
```
End pseudocode

PROGRAM 8.12   To find x to the power of y

```
#include < stdio.h>

float power(int x, int y)
{
      float p;
      if (y == 0)
            return (1);
      else if (y > 0)
            p = x * power(x, y - 1);
      else
      {
            p = 1 / power(x, -y);
      }
      return (p);
}
```

```
int main(void)
{
        int x, y;
        float p;
        printf("Enter the values of x and y \n");
        scanf("%d%d", &x, &y);
        p = power(x, y);
        printf("%f", p);

        return 0;
}
```

Input–Output:

```
Enter the values of x and y
2
3

8.000000

Enter the values of x and y
2
-2

0.25

Enter the values of x and y
3
0

1
```

Explanation:

The function **power()** is defined with two arguments **x** and **y** of **int** type and it is also made to return a value of **float** type. The purpose of the function is to find the value of **x** to the power of **y** and return it to its calling program.

When $y = 0$ the function returns 1 since any number raised to the power of 0 is 1 and this happens to be the terminating condition for the recursive function. If the value of $y > 0$ (i.e. positive) the function is called recursively as in the statement p = x * power(x, y-1); Note that one less than the previous value of y is passed as the second argument in each successive recursive call till it becomes 0. Once it becomes 0 the function exits in the last in first out manner and ultimately it returns the value of x to the power of y to the calling program (main() in this case). If the value of $y < 0$ (i.e. negative) the function is called recursively as in the statement p = 1/x * power(x, -y); . This is because mathematically x^{-y} can be written as $1/x^y$. Here the value of x^y is found as in the previous case and the value of $1/x^y$ is returned to the calling program (main() in this case).

In the main(), **x** and **y** are declared to be variables of **int** type and **p** is declared to be a variable of type **float**. The values of **x** and **y** are accepted and the value of x^y is found out with the statement p = power(x, y); Here **p** collects the value of x^y and it is displayed.

when x = 2, y = 3

The following is the sequence of recursive calls to the function power() and at the end, the value of 2 to the power of 3 is assigned to the variable p in main() and it is displayed.

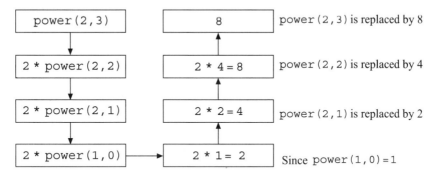

Recursion versus iteration

Recursion

- Near to the problem definition, easy to understand
- Consumes more memory space (stack memory)
- More CPU overhead
- Less efficient

Iteration

- Relatively more difficult to understand
- CPU overhead minimal
- Memory consumption is also minimal
- More efficient

8.12 STORAGE CLASSES

When we declare a variable of some type, associated with the variable are the variable name and its data type. It is identified by the given variable name and it is capable of storing a value of the specified type. In addition to these, two more important factors are associated with the variable—**scope** of the variable and **lifetime** of the variable.

Scope of a variable is defined to be the area of its existence in a program. That is, parts of the underlying program, whereas lifetime of a variable is defined to be the duration of time for which the variable exists. Depending on the scope and the lifetime of the variables, variables are made to fall into the following classification broadly. They are:

1. Internal variables
2. External variables

Internal variables are those which are declared within the body of a function. Internal variables are also called local variables. Internal variables are known only within the body of their enclosing functions.

External variables are those which are declared outside the functions. External variables are also called global variables. Global variables are accessible from the point of declaration till the end of the program.

Example 8.1

```
int k;
int main(void)
{
        int j;
}

void function1(void)
{
        int l;
}
```

j is an internal variable to main(). l is an internal variable in function1() whereas k is an external variable available in both main() and function1().

Scope of a variable is the area of its existence. Lifetime of a variable is the duration of its availability in a program. Depending on where a variable is allocated required storage, the area of its existence in a program (scope), and its longevity (lifetime), variables are further classified into what are called storage classes.

The following are the four storage classes:

1. Automatic
2. Static
3. Register
4. Extern

8.12.1   Automatic Storage Class

The variables declared within a function are by default of automatic storage class. The keyword **auto** can also be used to explicitly specify it. For instance,

```
void function(void)
{
   int i;
   auto int j;
}
```

Here, even though the keyword **auto** is not used while declaring **i**. Storage class of **i** would be **auto** by default. **j** has been explicitly declared with **auto** keyword.

Automatic variables are characterized by the following properties:

1. They get created on entry into their function.

2. They get automatically destroyed on the exit of their function.
3. They are visible within the function only.
4. Their lifetime is the duration of the function only.
5. If not initialized, they will have unpredictable values (garbage values).
6. If initialized, they would be reinitialized on each entry into the function.
7. They cannot be declared outside of functions.

8.12.2 Static Storage Class

Variables can be made to belong to static storage class by explicitly using the keyword `static` while declaring them. Unlike auto variables, the variables of static storage class may be declared either within or outside the functions. Here, let us confine our discussion to the static variables declared within the body of the functions.

```
void function2()
{
    static int a;
}
```

The variable **a** has been declared to be a `static` variable. `static` variables declared within the body of the functions are characterized by the following properties.

1. They get created on the entry into their enclosing function.
2. They are not destroyed on the function's exit.
3. They are initialized to 0 by default. However, the default can be defeated by initializing them with our own values.
4. They are not reinitialized on the re-entry into the function. The previous values persist.
5. They are visible within the function only.
6. Their lifetime is the duration of the entire program's duration.
7. They can be declared either within or outside of functions.

8.12.3 Register Storage Class

In order to understand the significance of `register` storage class, it is better to be aware of the roles of Memory and CPU in relation to programs and data.

Memory acts as workspace for programs and data. This is where programs and data are stored. CPU plays the role of Instruction Executor. CPU needs to fetch instructions and the required data from memory before acting upon them. `register` storage class enables us to tell the compiler that some variables are to be stored in CPU general purpose registers themselves. CPU can thus act upon these data readily without requiring to fetch from memory resulting in increase in the speed of execution of the program.

Note: Only local variables of type `int`, `char` can be declared with the keyword `register`. The number of register storage class variables is limited by the available number of general purpose registers. However, if the number of variables exceeds the limit, C Compiler itself converts the remaining into auto variables.

```
void f1()
{
        register int i j;
}
```

variables **i** and **j** are allocated two registers.

8.12.4   Extern Storage Class

In some situations, some variables need to be accessed by more than one function. Variables belonging to extern storage class serve this purpose. Since the variables are accessible by more than one function, the variables are called global variables.

Variables belonging to extern storage class are characterized by the following properties.

1. They are declared outside of functions.
2. The area of their existence is from the point of declaration till the end of the program. That is, all the functions defined after the variables declaration can access the variables. However, there is an exception to this fact. If a function has a local variable with the same name as that of the global variable, as far as the function is concerned, the local variable is given more priority. That is, global variable value cannot be accessed.
3. Their lifetime is the duration of the entire program. That is, they are created when the program is launched for execution and destroyed when the program is exited.

```
int i = 10;
void f1()
{
        printf("%d", i);
}

void f2()
{
        printf("%d", i);
}
int main(void)
{
        int i =5;
        printf("%d", i);

        return 0;
}
```

Here, variable **i** is declared before all the three functions f1(), f2() and main(). f1() and f2() can access the value of the variable **i**. But main() cannot, since it has a local variable with the same name.

```
#include <stdio.h>

extern int i = 10;

void show(void)
{
        printf("extern i within show() = %d \n", i);
}

void display(void)
{
        int j = 5;
        static int k = 5;

        j++;
        printf("auto variable j = %d \n", j);
        k++;
        printf("static variable k = %d \n", k);
}

int main(void)
{
        register int l = 10;

        printf(" register variable l = %d \n\n", l);
        printf(" extern i in main() = %d \n", i);
        show();
        printf("\n After first call to display()\n \n");
        display();
        printf("\n After second call to display() \n\n");
        display();

        return 0;
}
```

Input–Output:

```
register variable l = 10

extern i in main() = 10
extern i within show() = 10

After first call to display()
```

```
auto variable j = 6
static variable k = 6

After second call to display()

auto variable j = 6
static variable k = 7
```

Explanation:

In the above program, the variable **i** is declared to be a global variable. The value of the variable can thus be seen by all the functions defined after its declaration. That is, by show(), display() and main(). Within the function display(), **j** and **k** are declared to be **auto** and **static** variables respectively. Both the variables are initialized with the value 5 . They are displayed after incrementing them. Within the main(), **l** is declared to be a register class variable with an initial value and it is displayed. It is important to note that a CPU register is allocated for the variable. The value of the extern variable **i** is then displayed, which implies that the extern variable **i** is accessible even in main() also.

Two calls are made to the function display() to understand the difference between **auto** and **static** variables. As can be seen from the output, after the first call to it, the values of **j** and **k** are displayed to be 6. But after the second call to the function, the values of **j** and **k** are displayed to be 6 and 7 respectively. This is because, in the second call, the **auto** variable **j** was recreated and initialized with 5 again and redisplayed after incrementation. But the **static** variable **k** persisted even after the exit of the first call and in the second call, **k** was not reinitialized (recreated). The value of **k** was 6 and after incrementation, when it is displayed, it turned out to be 7.

8.13   MULTIFILE PROGRAMS

So far, each program that we have written was contained in one source file. This was true even in the case of multifunction programs. Many a time, the real programming environment calls for using multiple files. For instance, if a software project is being developed by a team of programmers, it is quite natural that each programmer writes code for the task assigned to him in his own source file. At a later stage, all the source files are combined before they are submitted to the compiler. The programs, which are spilt across multiple source files are termed **Multifile Programs**.

The multiple source files not only facilitate division of program modules among programmers, but also help in the compilation process, in the sense that if any changes are made in one source file, only that file needs to be recompiled again. The resultant object code can be integrated with the object codes of the remaining files.

Study of static and extern storage classes

When multiple source files are used, we definitely need to deal with the scope of the variables, which are used by the program. Some variables may be required to be shared by all the functions in the entire program or some variables may be required to be shared by all the functions in a specific source file only. The static and extern storage class variables are of use here.

If in a source file, **static** variables are declared before the definition of all the functions in it, then those variables are accessible by all the functions in that source file only. No other function in other files can access them.

Example 8.2

```static int i = 10;```
```void main()```
```{```
        ```i is accessible```
```}```
 	
```void function1()```
```{```
        ```i is accessible```
```}```
	```void function2()```
	```{```
	        ```static i of file1.c is not```
	        ```accessible here```
	```}```
	
	```void function3()```
	```{```
	        ```static i of file1.c is not```
	        ```accessible here```
	```}```

file1.c	**file2.c**

If in a source file, a global variable is declared before the definition of all the functions in it and if the variable is declared as **extern** in the beginning of all other source files, then the global variable can be accessed by all the functions in all the source files.

```int i = 10;```
```int main(void)```
```{```
        ```i is accessible```
```}```
 	
```void function1(void)```
```{```
        ```i is accessible```
```}```
	```extern int i;```
	```void function2(void)```
	```{```
	        ```i of file1.c is accessible```
	        ```here also```
	```}```
	
	```void function3(void)```
	```{```
	        ```i of file1.c is accessible```
	        ```here also```
	```}```

file1.c	**file2.c**

SUMMARY

- A function is a self-contained program written for the purpose of accomplishing a task.
- Writing a multifunction program helps compartmentalize a big program and makes it manageable. Once we define a function, it can be called any number of times and anywhere in a program. As a result, functions help optimize memory space usage.

- Broadly, there are two classifications: 1. Built-in Functions, and 2. User-defined Functions.
- Built-in functions are those which are already made available as part of the C Library.
- User-defined functions, as the name itself indicates, are those which are defined by users (programmers) to solve problems.
- Further, depending on the kind of data communication between a calling function and a called function, there are four categories: 1. Functions without arguments and no return value, 2. Functions with arguments but no return value, 3. Functions with arguments and return value, and 4. Functions without arguments but with return value.
- In the category number 1, there is no data communication between a calling and a called function. In the category number 3, there is two-way data communication between a calling and a called function. In the other two categories, data communication is one way.
- Formal arguments are those which are specified while a function is defined. Actual arguments are those which are specified while calling a function.
- Lifetime of a variable is the duration of the variable for which it exists, whereas Scope of a variable is the area of a program in which the variable is accessible.
- Automatic variables are local to functions in which they are declared. They get created on entry into the functions and get destroyed on the exit, whereas static variables declared within a function do not get destroyed even after the exit of the function.
- By default, static variables will have 0 value.
- The scope of the global variables is from the point of declaration till the end of the program.
- A static variable declared outside of a function is accessible by all the functions following the declaration in the entire source file.
- The `extern` variables can be accessed in different files.
- Recursion is the phenomenon of a function calling itself.
- The function involved in ecursion is called recursive function.

REVIEW QUESTIONS

8.1 What is the need for functions?

8.2 What is a function?

8.3 Explain the general form of defining a function.

8.4 What are formal arguments?

8.5 What are actual arguments?

8.6 What is function header?

8.7 What do you mean by function call?

8.8 Differentiate between built-in functions and user-defined functions. Give examples.

8.9 Define function prototype.

8.10 What is a calling function?

8.11 What is a called function?

8.12 Mention the categories of functions depending on the existence of data communication between calling and called functions.

8.13 How many values can a function return?

8.14 The number of actual arguments and the number of formal arguments should be same when a function is called. True/False.

8.15 One function can be defined within another function. True/False.

8.16 What is meant by the scope of a variable?

8.17 What is meant by lifetime of a variable?

8.18 Mention different storage classes.

8.19 Give an account of characteristics of variables belonging to automatic storage class.

8.20 Give an account of characteristics of variables belonging to static storage class.

8.21 Give an account of characteristics of variables belonging to register storage class.

8.22 Give an account of characteristics of variables belonging to extern storage class.

8.23 Define recursion and recursive function.

8.24 What is the significance of terminating condition in recursion?

State whether the following are true or false

8.1 Functions reduce memory space usage.

8.2 Once a function is defined, it can be called anywhere.

8.3 A function can return any number of values.

8.4 A function returns float value by default.

8.5 A function, which does not take any arguments, cannot return any value.

8.6 The names of the formal arguments and the names of the actual arguments should be same.

8.7 A function whose formal argument is of type int can take a float value as its actual argument.

8.8 A function whose formal argument is of type char can take an int value as its actual argument.

8.9 C supports recursion.

8.10 Scope of a variable is the duration of time for which its value is available.

8.11 Variables declared within functions are by default of static storage class.

8.12 Automatic variables have default values.

8.13 An external static variable has the entire file scope.

8.14 The name of a global variable and that of a local variable can be same.

8.15 Variables of float type can be made to belong to register storage class.

8.16 Only local variables can be of register storage class.

8.17 There is no limit on the number of register variables.

8.18 Static variables retain their values between function calls.

Identify errors, if any, in the following

8.1
```
int sum(int a, int b);
{
    int s;

    s = a + b;
    return s;
}
```

8.2
```
void disp msg (char s[])
{
    printf ("%s", s);
}
```

8.3
```
int mean(int a, b, c, d)
{
    return (a+b+c+d)/4;
}
```

8.4
```
main()
{
    void display(int a)
    {
        printf("%d", a);
    }
}
```

8.5
```
void sum(int a, int b)
{
    int s;
    s = a + b;
    return s;
}
```

8.6
```
int sum(int, int);
int sum(int, int, int);
main()
{
    printf("%d", sum(3,5));
    printf("%d", sum(4, 5, 6));
}
    int sum(int a, int b)
    {
        return a + b;
    }
    int sum(int a, int b, int c)
    {
        return a + b+ c;
    }
}
```

PROGRAMMING EXERCISES

8.1 Write a program to find the reverse of a number using a function.

8.2 Write a program to grade a student using a function.

8.3 Write a program to find out the value of an expression v1 op v2 where v1 and v2 are two values of int type and op is an arithmetic operator using a function.

8.4 Write a program to find out whether a number is a perfect number or not using a function. [A number is said to be a perfect number if the sum of all its divisors (except the number itself) is equal to the number].
   (**Example:** 6 is a perfect number since $6 = 1 + 2 + 3$)

8.5 Write a program to find out whether a number is an Armstrong number or not using a function. (A number is said to be an Armstrong number if the sum of the cubes of the digits is equal to the number itself.)

8.6 Write a program to generate multiplication table of a number using a funcion.

8.7 Write a program to calculate $n_{p_r} = $ n! / (n − r)!
   (Use a function to find out factorial of a numer)

8.8 Write a program to calculate $n_{c_r} = $ n! / n! * (n − r)!
   (Use a function to find out factorial of a number)

8.9 Write a program to convert from decimal number to its binary equivalent using a function.

8.10 Write a program to reverse an integer using a recursive function.
   Example: Input: 3456   Output: 6543

8.11 Given month and year, write a program to find the number of days in the month in the given year using a function.

Example:	Month = 4	Year = 2000
	Days = 30	
	Month = 2	Year = 2000
	Days = 28	
	Month = 12	Year = 1999
	Days = 31	

8.12 Write a program with a funcion to calculate the definite integral $\int_b^a f(x)\, dx$ using Simpson's rule with *n* strips. The approximation to the integral is given by

```
h / 3 {f(a) + 4f(a + h) + 2f(a + 2h) + ...+2f(a + (n-2)h) + 4f(a + (n-1)h)
+ f(b)}
```

where $h = (b − a) / n$.

INTERVIEW QUESTIONS

8.1 Is main() a user defined or a library function? Justify.

8.2 What is the output of the following programs?

(a)
```c
#include<stdio.h>
int main(void)
{
    int x = 10;
    printf("%d", x);
    f(x);
    printf("%d", x);
    return 0;
}
f(int x)
{
    ++x;
}
```

(b)
```c
#include<stdio.h>
int main(void)
{
    int x = 10, y = 20;
    printf("%d %d\n", x, y);
    f(x, y);
    printf("%d %d\n", x, y);
    return 0;
}
void f(int x, int y)
{
    int t;
    t = x;
    x = y;
    y = t;
}
```

(c)
```c
#include<stdio.h>
int main(void)
{
```

```
    int x = 10, i;

    for (i = 1; i <= 5; i++)
{
    funct(i);
}
    return 0;
}

    funct(int i)
{
        static int j = 1;
        j = j + 1;
        printf("%d %d\n", i, j);
}
```

(d)
```
#include<stdio.h>
int main(void)
{
    int test(int);
    int result = fun(5);
    printf("%d\n", ++result);
     return 0;
}
int test(int x)
{
     return (x++);
}
```

(e)
```
#include<stdio.h>
int main(void)
{
    int f(int, int);
    int result = f(6,7);
    printf("%d\n",  result);
    return 0;
}
int f(int x, int y)
{
    return((x > y)? ++x: --y)
}
```

(f)
```
#include<stdio.h>
int main(void)
```

```
{
    int fun(int);
    int i = 3;
    i = fun(fun(fun(i)));
    printf("%d\n", i);
    return 0;

}

int test(int i)
{
    i++;
    return i;
}
```

8.3 How many times a recursive function is executed if the terminating condition is not specified?

8.4 What is the maximum number arguments a C function can take?

9

Arrays

9.1 INTRODUCTION

Suppose a C program is required to accept five integer values, find their sum and the program needs access to each value even after finding their sum. We can declare five variables of **int** type in the program as follows.

```
int a, b, c, d, e;
```

As a result of this declaration, five memory locations get allocated to store these values. The program segment to accept five values into these variables and find their sum is as follows.

```
scanf("%d%d%d%d%d", &a, &b, &c, &d, &e);
s = a + b + c + d + e ;
```

As can be seen, all the five variables have to be explicitly specified both in the **scanf()** statement and in the arithmetic expression of the assignment statement following it.

What, if the number of values to be summed up is more than five, say 10 or even 100? If we use ordinary variables to store these, we need to declare so many variables and need to explicitly specify all the variables in the corresponding **scanf()** statement and the arithmetic expression. Declaration of all of these variables and explicit specification of each of the variables in the **scanf()** statement and in the required arithmetic expression become laborious.

Here, accepting values into five locations and finding the sum of them are two examples of collective manipulations. A **Collective Manipulation** over a group of values is one, which requires access to each value in the group or in its selected subgroup. Other collective manipulations include, searching for a value in a list of values, finding the maximum value in a list of values, etc. Collective manipulations, in general, cannot be performed over a group of data items stored in ordinary variables in an easier manner.

The problems stated above can be overcome, if we can form a group of data items by making them share a common name and use subscripts to indicate a data item, for example, **a[1]** to denote first value, **a[2]** to denote second value and so on. Here **a** is said to be subscripted or indexed. This is where the concept of arrays comes into picture. We will soon realize that the problems encountered above are overcome with the help of one-dimensional array of **int** type.

9.2   DEFINITION OF AN ARRAY

> An array is defined to be a group of fixed number of data items of similar type, stored in contiguous memory locations, sharing a common name but distinguished by subscript(s) values.

Depending on the number of subscripts used, arrays are classified into one-dimensional arrays, two-dimensional arrays, and so on.

9.3   ONE-DIMENSIONAL ARRAYS

An array with only one subscript is termed **One-Dimensional array or 1-D array**. It is used to store a list of values, all of which share a common name (1-D array name) and are distinguishable by subscript values.

Declaration of one-dimensional arrays

The syntax of declaring a `one-dimensional array` is as follows:

```
data-type variable-name [size];
```

data-type refers to any data type supported by C, **variable-name** refers to array name and it should be a valid C identifier, **size** indicates number of data items of type **data-type** grouped together.

Each element in the array is identifiable by the array name (`variable-name`), followed by a pair of square brackets enclosing a subscript value. The subscript value ranges from 0 to `size - 1`. When the subscript value is 0, first element in the array is selected, when the subscript value is 1, second element is selected, and so on.

Example 9.1

```
int a[5];
```

Here, **a** is declared to be an array of **int** type and of size five. Five contiguous memory locations get allocated as shown below to store five integer values.

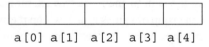

Each data item in the array **a** is identified by the array name followed by a pair of square brackets enclosing a subscript value. The subscript value ranges from 0 to 4, i.e., **a[0]** denotes first data item, **a[1]** denotes second data item, and so on. **a[4]** denotes the last data item.

Since all the five locations share a common name and are distinguishable by index values 0 to 4, to perform a collective manipulation, we can set up a loop (preferably a `for` loop because of its inherent simplicity) with the control variable of the loop ranging from 0 to 4 to identify the five data items.

Example 9.2

To accept five values into the array, the following segment can be used.

```
for(i = 0; i < 5; i++)
    scanf("%d", &a[i]);
```

Here, initially the control variable **i** takes 0. As a result, the value for a[0] is accepted. When i takes 1, the value for the location a[1] is accepted and this is continued till the last location a[4] of the array gets a value. So when the loop completes, the array **a** gets filled up.

Similarly, to display the elements of the array a, the following segment can be used.

```
for(i = 0; i < 5; i++)
    printf("%d", a[i]);
```

Here also, initially, the control variable **i** takes 0. As a result, the value in a[0] is displayed, when i takes 1, value in the location a[1] is displayed and this is continued till the value of the last location a[4] of the array is displayed. So when the loop completes, all the elements of the array a are displayed.

By looking at the declaration of the array variable a and, the program segments for accepting values into it and displaying the array elements, we definitely feel the advantage offered by arrays.

PROGRAM 9.1   To accept values into an array and display them

```
#include <stdio.h>

int main(void)
{
    int a[5], i;

    printf("Enter five values \n");
    for(i = 0; i < 5; i++)
        scanf("%d", &a[i]);
    printf("The values in the array are \n");
    for(i = 0; i < 5; i++)
        printf("a[%d] = %d\n", i, a[i]);
    return 0;
}
```

Input–Output:

```
Enter five values
10 13 43 65 87
```

The values in the array are

```
a[0] = 10
a[1] = 13
a[2] = 43
a[3] = 65
a[4] = 87
```

Initialization of one-dimensional arrays

Just as we initialize ordinary variables, we can also initialize one-dimensional arrays if we know the values of the locations of the arrays in advance, i.e. locations of the arrays can be given values while they are declared.

The syntax of initializing an array of one dimension is as follows:

```
data-type variable-name[size] = {value0, value1, value2, ...};
```

`data-type` refers to the data type of the array elements, and `variable-name` refers to the name of the array. {`value0, value1, ..., valuesize-1`} are constant values of type `data-type` or convertible into values of data type `data-type`. The values {`value0, value1, ..., valuesize-1`} are collectively called `initializer-list` for the array.

In short, the syntax of initializing a 1-D array can now be written as

```
data-type variable-name[size] = {initializer-list};
```

Example 9.3

```
int a[5] = { 2, 5, 6, 8, 9 };
```

As a result of this, memory locations of **a** get filled up as follows:

2	5	6	8	9
a[0]	a[1]	a[2]	a[3]	a[4]

If the number of values in `initializer-list` is less than the size of an array, only those many first locations of the array are assigned the values. The remaining locations are assigned 0.

Example 9.4

```
int a[5] = { 2, 4, 5 };
```

The size of the array **a** is 5. `initializer-list` consists of only three values. As a result of this, only the first three locations would get these values. The last two locations get 0 assigned to them automatically, as follows.

2	4	5	0	0
a[0]	a[1]	a[2]	a[3]	a[4]

If a **static** array is declared without `initializer-list`, then all the locations are set to 0.

Example 9.5

```
static int a[5];
```

0	0	0	0	0

a[0] a[1] a[2] a[3] a[4]

PROGRAM 9.2   To illustrate initialization of arrays of one dimension

---

```c
#include <stdio.h>

int main(void)
{
    int a[5] = {4, 5, 7, 9, 2};
    int b[5] = {6, 8, 5};
    static int d[5];
    int i;

    printf("Elements in the array a \n");
    for(i = 0; i < 5; i++)
            printf("a[%d] = %d\n", i, a[i]);
    printf("\n");

    printf("Elements in the array b \n");
    for(i = 0;i < 5; i++)
            printf("b[%d] = %d\n", i, b[i]);
    printf("\n");

    printf("Elements in the static array d \n");
    for(i = 0; i < 5; i++)
            printf("d[%d] = %d\n", i, d[i]);
    printf("\n");

    return 0;
}
```

Input–Output:

```
Elements in the array a
a[0] = 4
a[1] = 5
a[2] = 7
a[3] = 9
a[4] = 2

Elements in the array b
b[0] = 6
b[1] = 8
```

```
b[2] = 5
b[3] = 0
b[4] = 0
```

```
Elements in the static array d
d[0] = 0
d[1] = 0
d[2] = 0
d[3] = 0
d[4] = 0
```

Points to Remember

1. If the number of values listed within `initializer-list` for an array is greater than the size of the array, the compiler raises an error (too many initializers).

   Example 9.6

   ```
   int a[5] = { 2, 3, 4, 5, 6, 7, 8};
   ```

   The size of the array **a** is 5. But the number of values listed within the `initializer-list` is seven. This is illegal.

2. There is no array bound checking mechanism built into C-compiler. It is the responsibility of the programmer to see to it that the subscript value does not go beyond `size-1`. If it does, the system may crash.

   Example 9.7

   ```
   int a[5];
   a[6] = 10;
   ```

   Here, **a[6]** does not belong to the array **a**, it may belong to some other program (e.g. operating system) writing into the location may lead to unpredictable results or even to system crash.

3. Array elements cannot be initialized selectively

   Example 9.8

   An attempt to initialize only 2nd location is illegal.

   i.e. `int a[5] = { , 2 }` is illegal.

4. If `size` is omitted in a 1-D array declaration, which is initialized, the compiler will supply this value by examining the number of values in the initializer-list.

   Example 9.9

   ```
   int a[] = { 2, 4, 6, 7, 8 };
   ```

   Since the number of values in the `initializer-list` for the array **a** is 5, the size of **a** is automatically supplied as 5.

2	4	6	7	8
a[0]	a[1]	a[2]	a[3]	a[4]

   Similar to arrays of **int** type, we can even declare arrays of other data types supported by C, also.

Example 9.10

char s[10];

s is declared to be an array of **char** type and size 10 and it can accommodate 10 characters.

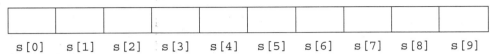

| s[0] | s[1] | s[2] | s[3] | s[4] | s[5] | s[6] | s[7] | s[8] | s[9] |

An array of **char** is used to store a string. The concept of string manipulations is so important that it deserves to be dealt with in detail. A separate chapter is meant for discussing this, which is to follow:

float f[10];

f is declared to be an array of **float** type and size 10 and it can accommodate 10 values of **float** type. The following is the scheme of memory allocation for the array f.

| f[0] | f[1] | f[2] | f[3] | f[4] | f[5] | f[6] | f[7] | f[8] | f[9] |

Note:

> A one-dimensional array is used to store a list of values. A loop (preferably, for-loop) is used to access each value in the list.

Processing one-dimensional arrays

We have understood that a one-dimensional array is used to store a list of values. The list of values may represent the salary of the number of employees, marks obtained by a student in different subjects, etc. The commonly performed operations over lists of values include finding the sum of them, finding the largest or the least among them, arranging the values in the increasing order or decreasing order, and so on. Let us now proceed to understand the flexibility provided by one-dimensional arrays in processing lists of values.

To find the sum and average of a list of values

Suppose we have a list of five values consisting of 5, 6, 7, 10 and 12, to find the sum of these values we use a variable say, sum set to zero to begin with. We add the first value 5 to the variable sum and we then add the second value 6 to the variable sum and this is repeated for all the remaining values 7, 10 and 12 in the list. The variable sum would then have sum of the list of values. We then divide the value in sum by five, the number of values in the list, to get the average value of the list.

Input: A list of values
(We need to have a one-dimensional array to store the list of values)
Output: Sum and average values of the list of values

Pseudocode to find the sum and average of a list of values

```
        // Read n values
        for( i = 0; i < n; i++)
            read a[i]
```

```
// Finding the sum and average begins

        sum = 0;
        for( i = 0; i < n; i++)
            sum += a[i];

        avg = (float) sum / n;

//   Finding the sum and average ends
        display sum
        display avg
End pseudocode
```

PROGRAM 9.3   To find the sum and average of the values in a 1-D array

---

```
#include <stdio.h>

int main(void)
{
        int a[10], i, n, sum;
        float avg;

        printf("Enter the number of elements [1-10] \n");
        scanf("%d", &n);

        printf("Enter %d numbers \n", n);
        for( i = 0; i < n; i++)
            scanf("%d", &a[i]);

        printf("The numbers are \n");
        for( i = 0; i < n; i++)
            printf("%4d", a[i]);

/* Finding the sum and average begins */

        sum = 0;
        for( i = 0; i < n; i++)
            sum += a[i];

        avg = (float) sum / n;

/* Finding the sum and average ends */
        printf("\n Sum = %d\n", sum);
        printf("\n Average = %f\n", avg);

        return 0;
}
```

Input–Output:

```
Enter the number of elements [1-10]
5

Enter 5 numbers
1 2 3 4 5

The numbers are
1 2 3 4 5

Sum = 15

Average = 3.000000
```

Explanation:

a is declared to be an array of int type and of size 10. Maximum 10 numbers can be written into the array. **n, i** and **sum** are declared to be variables of **int** type. **n** is to collect the number of values to be read into the array **a,** which lies within 1 and 10. **i** is to traverse all the values in a. **sum** is to collect the sum of the values in a. avg is declared to be a variable of float type and it is to collect the average of values in **a**.

In the process of finding the sum of all the n values, initially sum is set to 0. A for loop is used to select each number in the array and it is added to sum with the statement sum += a[i].

The statement **avg = (float) sum/n;** on its execution, assigns average value to **avg** . Note that we have used type-casting to convert **sum** forcibly to **float** to get the exact result. Otherwise, the expression (**sum/n**) produces only integral part of the quotient since both **sum** and **n** are integers. Both **sum** and **avg** are then displayed.

To find the minimum and the maximum in a list of values

Suppose we have a list of five values consisting of 7, 3, 2, 9 and 10, to find the minimum of the values we assume that the first value 7 in the list itself is the minimum by assigning it to a variable say, min.

We then compare min value (7) with the second value 3. Since 3 is less than 7, the value 3 is assigned to min. Next the third value 2 is compared with min value (3). Since 2 is less than 3, the value 2 is assigned to min. This is repeated for the remaining values 9 and 10. At the end the variable min collects the minimum of the values in the list which is 2.

Using the similar logic, maximum value in the list of values is also found out.

Input: A list of values
(We need to have a one-dimensional array to store the list of values)
Output: The minimum and maximum values in the list of values

Pseudocode to find the minimum and the maximum in a list of values
```
// Read n values
for(i = 0; i < n; i++)
      read a[i]
```

```
// Finding the minimum begins
min = a[0];
for(i = 1; i < n; i++)
     if (a[i] < min)
          min = a[i];
// Finding the minimum ends

// Finding the maximum begins
max = a[0];
for(i = 1; i < n; i++)
    if (a[i] > min)
         max = a[i];
// Finding the maximum ends

Display min
Display max
End pseudocode
```

PROGRAM 9.4   To find the minimum and the maximum in a list of values

```
#include <stdio.h>

int main(void)
{
       int a[10], i, n, min, max;

       printf("Enter the number of values 1-10 \n");
       scanf("%d", &n);

       printf("Enter %d values \n", n);
       for(i = 0; i < n; i++)
            scanf("%d", &a[i]);

       min = a[0];
       for(i = 1; i < n; i++)
            if (a[i] < min)
                 min = a[i];

       max = a[0];
       for(i = 1; i < n; i++)
            if (a[i] > max)
                 max = a[i];

       printf("Minimum in the array = %d \n", min);
       printf("Maximum in the array = %d \n", max);

       return 0;
}
```

Input–Output:

```
Enter the number of values 1-10
5
Enter 5 values
4
2
5
6
7
Minimum in the array = 2
Maximum in the array = 7
```

Explanation:

In the above program, a is declared to be an array of int type and of size 10. Maximum 10 values can be accepted into the array. The variable n is to collect the number of values [1-10]. The variables min and max are to collect the minimum and the maximum of the values in the array.

The following program segment is for finding the minimum in the array:

```
min = a[0];
for(i = 1; i < n; i++)
        if (a[i] < min)
                min = a[i];
```

Here, we start with the assumption that the first element in the array a[0] is the least and then we start comparing the remaining the elements with the value of min. If any value in the array is found to be less than the value in the variable min, min is overwritten by the value in the array. This is repeated till the array elements exhaust. Ultimately, the variable min collects the minimum of the array elements. The same logic is used to find the maximum in the array and both min and max are displayed.

9.4 MULTIDIMENSIONAL ARRAYS

An array with more than one subscript is generally called a multidimensional array. We can think of arrays of two dimensions (2-D arrays), arrays of three dimensions (3-D arrays), arrays of four dimensions (4-D arrays), and so on. We do require these in real life situations.

9.4.1 Two-dimensional Arrays (2-D arrays)

An array with two subscripts is termed a two-dimensional or 2-D array. A 2-D array can be thought of as a group of one or more 1-D array(s), all of which share a common name (2-D array name) and are distinguishable by subscript values. So, a 2-D array is essentially, an array of 1-D arrays. We know that a 1-D array can store a row of elements. So, a 2-D array enables us to store multiple rows of elements. That is, **a Table of values** or **a Matrix**. For this reason 2-D arrays are very much associated with matrices and have turned out to be the perfect data structures for storing matrices.

Declaration of two-dimensional arrays

The syntax of declaring a 2-D array is as follows:

```
data-type variable-name [rowsize] [colsize];
```

`data-type` refers to any valid C data type, `variable-name` (a valid C identifier) refers to the name of the array, `rowsize` indicates the number of rows and `colsize` indicates the number of elements in each row.

`rowsize` and `colsize` should be integer constants or convertible into integer values. Total number of locations allocated will be equal to `rowsize * colsize`. Each element in a 2-D array is identified by the array name followed by a pair of square brackets enclosing its row-number, followed by a pair of square brackets enclosing its column-number, where row-number ranges from 0 to `rowsize-1` and column-number ranges from 0 to `colsize-1`.

Example 9.11

```
int b[3][3];
```

b is declared to be an array of two dimensions and of data type `int`. `rowsize` and `colsize` of b are 3 and 3 respectively. Memory gets allocated to accommodate the array b as follows. It is important to note that b is the common name shared by all the elements of the array.

		Column numbers		
		0	1	2
	0	b[0][0]	b[0][1]	b[0][2]
Row numbers	1	b[1][0]	b[1][1]	b[1][2]
	2	b[2][0]	b[2][1]	b[2][2]

Each data item in the array b is identifiable by specifying the array name b followed by a pair of square brackets enclosing row number, followed by a pair of square brackets enclosing column number, row-number ranges from 0 to 2, that is, the first row is identified by row-number 0. The second row is identified by row-number 1, and so on. Similarly, column-number ranges from 0 to 2. The first column is identified by column-number 0, the second column is identified by column-number 1, and so on.

b[0][0] refers to data item in the first row and the first column
b[0][1] refers to data item in the first row and the second column

---

PROGRAM 9.5   To accept and display a matrix

```c
#include <stdio.h>

int main(void)
{
        int a[3][3], i, j;

        printf("Enter the elements of a \n");
```

```
        for (i = 0; i < 3; i++)
        for (j = 0; j < 3; j++)
        scanf ("%d", &a[i][j]);

        printf ("The matrix a \n");
        for (i = 0; i < 3; i++)
        {
                for (j = 0; j < 3; j++)
                        printf ("%4d", a[i][j]);
                printf ("\n");
        }

        return 0;
}
```

Input–Output:

```
Enter the elements of a
3 4 5 6 7 8 9 10 2
The matrix a
 3  4  5
 6  7  8
 9 10  2
```

Explanation:

In the above program, **a** has been declared to be an array of two dimensions, with `rowsize` 3, `colsize` 3, and thus it can accommodate a table of values (matrix) consisting of 3 rows and 3 columns. As can be seen, both while reading into the array and reading from the array to display them, two loops have been used. The outer loop (`i` loop) is used to select each row of the table, the inner loop (`j` loop) is used to select each element in the row selected by `i` loop.

When   `i = 0` (first row)
         `j` ranges from 0 to 2 to select all the elements of the first row.
         `i = 1` (second row)
         `j` ranges from 0 to 2 to select all the elements of the second row.
         `i = 2` (third row)
         `j` ranges from 0 to 2 to select all the elements of the third row.

All the elements of the table are thus accessed.

Initialization of two-dimensional arrays

We can initialize a 2-D array also while declaring it, just as we initialize 1-D arrays. There are two forms of initializing a 2-D array.

First form of initializing a 2-D array is as follows:

```
data-type variable-name [rowsize] [colsize] = {initializer-list};
```

data-type refers to any data type supported by C, variable-name refers to array name, rowsize indicates the number of rows, and colsize indicates the number of columns of the array. initializer-list is a comma separated list of values of type data-type or compatible with data-type.

If the number of values in initializer-list is equal to the product of rowsize and colsize, the first colsize values in the initializer-list will be assigned to the first row, the second colsize values will be assigned to the second row of the array, and so on.

Example 9.12

```
int a[2][3] = { 2, 3, 4, 5, 6, 7};
```

Since colsize is 3, the first 3 values of the initializer-list are assigned to the first row of a and the next three values are assigned to the second row of a as shown below.

2	3	4
5	6	7

Note: If the number of values in the initializer-list is less than the product of rowsize and colsize, only the first few matching locations of the array would get values from the initializer-list row-wise. The trailing unmatched locations would get 0s.

Example 9.13

```
int a[2][3] = { 2, 4, 5};
```

The first row of **a** gets filled with the values in the initializer-list. The second row gets filled with 0s.

2	4	5
0	0	0

A static 2-D array is initialized with 0s by default. However, they can be overridden by initializing explicitly.

```
static int a[2][3];
```

0	0	0
0	0	0

While initializing a 2-D array, rowsize is optional but columnsize is mandatory.

Example 9.14

```
int a[][3] = { 1,4,5,3,6,8};
```

Since two rows can be constructed with the elements, rowsize 2 will be provided by the compiler automatically. Memory allocation for the array a will be as follows:

1	4	5
3	6	8

PROGRAM 9.6   To illustrate initialization of a 2-D array

```c
#include <stdio.h>

int main(void)
{
        int a[2][2] = { 1, 2, 3, 4};
        int b[2][2] = { 1,2 3};
        static int c[2][2];
        int d[][3] = { 1,4,5,3,6,8};
        int i, j;

        printf("matrix a \n");
        for(i = 0; i < 2; i++)
        {
                for(j = 0; j < 2; j++)
                        printf("%4d", a[i][j]);
                printf("\n");
        }
        printf("\n");
        printf("matrix b \n");
        for(i = 0; j < 2; i++)
        {
                for(j = 0; j < 2; j++)
                        printf("%4d", b[i][j]);
                printf("\n");
        }
        printf("\n");

        printf("matrix c \n");
        for(i = 0; i < 2; i++)
        {
                for(j = 0; j < 2; j++)
                        printf("%4d", c[i][j]);
                printf("\n");
        }
        printf("\n");

        printf("matrix d \n");
        for(i = 0; i < 2; i++)
        {
                for(j = 0; j < 3; j++)
                        printf("%4d", d[i][j]);
                printf("\n");
        }

        return 0;
}
```

Input–Output:

```
matrix a
  1 2
  3 4

matrix b
  1 2
  3 0

matrix c
  0 0
  0 0
matrix d
  1 4 5
  3 6 8
```

The second form of initializing a 2-D array has the following general syntax

```
data-type variable-name [rowsize] [colsize] = { {initializer-list1},
                                                {initializer-list2},

                                                ....... };
```

The values in `initializer-list1` are assigned to the locations in the first row. The values in `initializer-list2` are assigned to the locations in the second row, and so on.

Example 9.15

```
int a [2] [3] = { { 4, 5, 9 },
                  {6, 7, 8 }};
```

As a result of this, the array a gets filled up as follows.

4	5	9
6	7	8

Note:

1. If the number of values specified in any `initializer-list` is less than `colsize` of a, only those many first locations in the corresponding row would get these values. The remaining locations in that row would get `0`.

Example 9.16

```
int a [2] [3] = { { 3, 4 }, { 4, 5, 6 } };
```

Since the first `initializer-list` has only two values, a [0] [0] is set to 3, a [0] [1] is set to 4, and the third location in the first row is automatically set to 0.

3	4	0
4	5	6

PROGRAM 9.7   To illustrate initialization of a 2-D array

```c
#include <stdio.h>

int main(void)
{
        int a[2][2] = { {1, 2}, {3, 4}};
        int b[2][2] = { {1,2}, {3}};
        int i, j;
        printf("matrix a \n");
        for(i = 0; i < 2; i++)
        {
                for(j = 0; j < 2; j++)
                        printf("%4d", a[i][j]);
                printf("\n");
        }
        printf("\n");
        printf("matrix b \n");
        for(i = 0; i < 2; i++)
        {
                for(j = 0; j < 2; j++)
                        printf("%4d", b[i][j]);
                printf("\n");
        }

        return 0;
}
```

Input–Output:

```
matrix a
  1  2
  3  4

matrix b
  1  2
  3  0
```

Points to Remember

1. If the number of values specified in any `initializer-list` is more than `colsize` of a, compiler reports an error too many initializers.

    Example 9.17

    ```c
    int a[2][3] = {{ 2, 3, 4, 5},
                   { 4 , 6 , 7}};
    ```

    `colsize` is 3, but the number of values listed in the first row is 4. This results in compilation error (too many initializers).

2. Array elements cannot be initialized (in each row) selectively.

3. It is the responsibility of the programmer to ensure that the array subscripts do not exceed the `rowsize` and `colsize` of the array. If they exceed, unpredictable results may be produced and even the program can result in system crash sometimes.

4. A 2-D array is used to store a table of values (matrix).

   Similar to 2-D arrays of `int` type, we can declare 2-D arrays of any other data type supported by C, also.

   Example 9.18

   ```
   float s[5][6];
   ```

   s is declared to be 2-D array of **float** type with 5 rows and 6 columns

   ```
   double d[10][20];
   ```

   d is declared to be 2-D array of **double** type with 10 rows and 20 columns

Note: A two-dimensional array is used to store a table of values. Two loops (preferably `for` loops) are used to access each value in the table, the first loop acts as a row selector and the second loop acts a column selector in the table.

Processing two-dimensional arrays

We have understood that a 2-D array is used to store a table of values (matrix). The table of values may represent marks obtained by a number of students in different subjects (each row representing a student and each column representing marks in a subject) or sales figures of different salesmen in different months (each row representing a salesman and each column representing a month). The commonly performed operations over lists of values include finding the sum of each row or column, finding the largest or the least in each row or each column, and so on. Let us now proceed to understand the flexibility provided by 2-D arrays in processing tables of values.

Pseudocode to find the sum of each row and each column of a matrix

```
Read the elements of a matrix of order m * n
      for( i = 0; i < m; i++)
      for( j = 0; j < n; j++)
            read a[i][j]

// Finding sum of each row begins
for( i = 0; i < m; i++)
begin
      s[i] = 0;
      for( j = 0; j < n; j++)
            s[i] += a[i][j];
      display "sum of values in row number i = s[i]"
end
/* finding sum of each row ends */
```

```
/* Finding sum of each column begins */
for( i = 0; i < n; i++)
begin
      s[i]=0;
      for( j = 0; j < m; j++)
           s[i] += a[j][i];
display "sum of values in column number i = s[i]"
end
```
End pseudocode

PROGRAM 9.8   To find the sum of each row and each column of a matrix

---

```
#include <stdio.h>

int main(void)
{
      int a[10][10], i, j, s[10], m, n;

      printf("Enter the number of rows 1-10 \n");
      scanf("%d", &m);
      printf("Enter the number of columns 1-10 \n");
      scanf("%d", &n);

      printf("Enter the elements of matrix a \n");
      for( i = 0; i < m; i++)
      for( j = 0; j < n; j++)
      scanf("%d", &a[i][j]);

      printf(" matrix a \n");

      for( i = 0; i < m; i++)
      {
            for(j = 0; j < n; j++)
            printf("%4d", a[i][j]);
      printf("\n");
      }

/* Finding sum of each row begins */

for( i = 0; i < m; i++)
{
      s[i] = 0;
      for( j = 0; j < n; j++)
           s[i] += a[i][j];
      printf("sum of values in row number %d = %d\n", i, s[i]);
}
```

```
/* Finding sum of each row ends */

/* Finding sum of each column begins */

for( i = 0; i < n; i++)
{
      s[i]=0;
      for( j = 0; j < m; j++)
            s[i] += a[j][i];
      printf("sum of values in column number %d = %d\n", i, s[i]);
}

/* Finding sum of each column ends */

      return 0;
}
```

Input–Output:

```
Enter the number of rows 1-10
3
Enter the number of columns 1-10
4
Enter the elements of matrix a 3
1 2 3 4 5 6 7 8 9 10 11 12

Matrix a

1  2  3  4
5  6  7  8
9  10 11 12

sum of elements in row number 0 = 10
sum of elements in row number 1 = 26
sum of elements in row number 2 = 42
sum of elements in column number 0 = 15
sum of elements in column number 1 = 18
sum of elements in column number 2 = 21
sum of elements in column number 3 = 24
```

Explanation:

In the above program, a is an array of size 10 and 10. m and n are to collect the number of rows and the number of columns respectively, which lie within 1 and 10. First, the m * n elements of the matrix are accepted into the array a. The array elements are displayed in matrix form. To find the sum of each row and column, we use a 1-D array, namely **s** of size 10, s[0] is made to collect the sum of the first row or column, s[1] is made to collect the sum of the second row or column, and so on.

The following segment is responsible for finding the sum of each row:

```
for( i = 0; i < m; i++)
{
        s[i] = 0;
        for( j = 0; j < n; j++)
                s[i] += a[i][j];
        printf("sum of values in row number %d = %d\n", i, s[i]);
}
```

Note that the outer loop is to select each row of the matrix a. When i = 0 the first row is selected. After the execution of the statements in the body of the loop, s[0] collects the sum of the first row and it is displayed. When i becomes 1, s[1] collects the sum of the elements in the second row and it is displayed so on.

Similarly, the sum of the elements in each column are also found out and displayed with the program segment.

```
for( i = 0; i < n; i++)
{
        s[i] = 0;
        for( j = 0; j < m; j++)
                s[i] += a[j][i];
        printf(" sum of values in column number %d = %d\n", i, s[i]);
}
```

Note that this time the outer loop selects each column in the matrix.

To find the sum of two matrices

If a and b represent two matrices with the order m1*n1 and m2*n2 respectively, they are said to be compatible for addition, if both of them are of the same order. That is, the number of rows of a is same as that of b (m1=m2) and the number of columns of a is same as that of b (n1=n2). Addition operation over a and b produces another matrix c, which is also of the same order as a and b. The element in ith row and jth column of c is obtained by summing the elements in ith row and jth column of a and b.

Example 9.19

$$a = \begin{pmatrix} 2 & 3 & 4 \\ 1 & 2 & 6 \\ 5 & 7 & 8 \end{pmatrix}$$

$$b = \begin{pmatrix} 1 & 4 & 7 \\ 2 & 5 & 9 \\ 2 & 4 & 7 \end{pmatrix}$$

$$a+b = \begin{pmatrix} 2+1 & 3+4 & 4+7 \\ 1+2 & 2+5 & 6+9 \\ 5+2 & 7+4 & 8+7 \end{pmatrix}.$$

$$a + b = \begin{pmatrix} 3 & 7 & 1 \\ 3 & 7 & 15 \\ 7 & 11 & 15 \end{pmatrix}$$

Pseudocode to add two matrices

```
Read no. of rows and columns of matrix a
Read m1 n1
Read no. of rows and columns of matrix b
Read m2 n2

// check for compatibility for addition
if (( m1 != m2 ) || ( n1 != n2 ))
begin
     Display "Matrices not compatible for addition"
     exit
end

Read the elements of matrix a
Read the elements of matrix b

// Summation begins

for( i = 0; i < m1; i++)
for( j = 0; j < n1; j++)
s[i][j] = a[i][j] + b[i][j];

// Summation ends

Display the matrix a
Display the matrix b
Display the matrix s
```
End pseudocode

PROGRAM 9.9   To add two matrices

```c
#include <stdio.h>
#include <process.h>

int main(void)
{
     int a[10][10], b[10][10], s[10][10], m1, n1, m2, n2, i, j;

     printf("Enter the number of rows and the number of columns of matrix
a \n");
     scanf("%d%d", &m1, &n1);
```

```
    printf ("Enter the number of rows and the number of columns of matrix
b \n") ;
    scanf ("%d%d", &m2, &n2) ;

    if (( m1 != m2 ) || ( n1 != n2 ))
    {
        printf ("Matrices not compatible for addition \n") ;
        exit (1) ;
    }

    printf ("Enter the elements of matrix a \n") ;
    for ( i = 0; i < m1; i++)
    for ( j = 0; j < n1; j++)
        scanf ("%d", &a [i] [j]) ;

    printf ("Enter the elements of matrix b \n") ;
    for ( i = 0; i < m2; i++)
    for ( j = 0; j < n2; j++)
        scanf ("%d", &b [i] [j]) ;

    /* Summation begins */

    for ( i = 0; i < m1; i++)
    for ( j = 0; j < n1; j++)
        s [i] [j] = a [i] [j] + b [i] [j] ;

    /* Summation ends  */

    printf ("Matrix a \n") ;
    for ( i = 0; i < m1; i++)
    {
        for ( j = 0; j < n1; j++)
            printf ("%4d", a [i] [j]) ;
        printf ("\n") ;
    }

    printf ("\n\n") ;

    printf ("Matrix b \n") ;
    for ( i = 0; i < m2; i++)
    {
        for ( j = 0; j < n2; j++)
            printf ("%4d", b [i] [j]) ;
        printf ("\n") ;
    }
```

```
        printf("\n\n");

        printf("Sum Matrix \n");
        for ( i = 0; i < m1; i++)
        {
                for ( j = 0; j < n1; j++)
                        printf("%4d", s[i][j]);
                printf("\n");
        }

        return 0;
}
```

Input–Output:

```
Enter the number of rows and the number columns of the matrix a
3 4
Enter the number of rows and the number of columns of the matrix b
3 4

Enter the elements of a
1 2 3 4 5 6 7 8 9 10 11 12
Enter the elements of b
1 2 3 4 5 6 7 8 9 10 11 12

Matrix a
1  2  3  4
5  6  7  8
9 10 11 12

Matrix b
1  2  3  4
5  6  7  8
9 10 11 12

Sum Matrix
2  4  6  8
10 12 14 16
18 20 22 24
```

Explanation:

In the above program, a, b and s are declared to be arrays of two dimensions of int type and size $10 * 10$. a and b represent the two input matrices, which are to be added. s represents the resultant sum matrix. Variables m1 and n1 are to collect the number of rows and columns of a. Variables m2 and n2 are to collect the number of rows and the number of columns of b. We know that, for a and b to be added, both a and b should be of the same order. That is, m1 = m2 and n1 = n2. This compatibility for addition is first checked. If a and b are not compatible, the program exits reporting the appropriate error. This is accomplished by the following segment of the program.

```
if (( m1 != m2 ) || ( n1 != n2 ))
    {
            printf("Matrices not compatible for addition \n");
            exit(1);
    }
```

After the matrices are found to be compatible for addition, summation begins. The segment responsible for summation is,

```
/* Summation begins */

    for( i = 0; i < m1; i++)
    for( j = 0; j < n1; j++)
            s[i][j] = a[i][j] + b[i][j];


/* Summation ends */
```

After finding the sum matrix, all the three matrices are displayed.

To find the product of two matrices

Suppose **a** and **b** represent two matrices of order m1*n1 and m2*n2 respectively. They are said to be compatible for multiplication, if the number of columns of **a** is same as the number of rows of **b**. That is, n1 = m2. Multiplication operation over a and b produces another matrix c, which is of the order m1*n2. The element in ith row and jth column of c is obtained by summing the products of the pairs of elements in the corresponding positions of ith row of a and jth column of b.

Example 9.20

$$a = \begin{pmatrix} 1 & 4 \\ 2 & 5 \end{pmatrix}$$

$$b = \begin{pmatrix} 4 & 7 \\ 5 & 9 \end{pmatrix}$$

$$a*b = \begin{pmatrix} 1*4+4*5 & 1*7+4*9 \\ 2*4*+5*5 & 2*7+5*9 \end{pmatrix}$$

$$a*b = \begin{pmatrix} 24 & 43 \\ 33 & 59 \end{pmatrix}$$

```
Pseudocode to multiply two matrices

Read no. of rows and columns of matrix a
Read m1 n1
Read no. of rows and columns of matrix b
Read m2 n2
```

```
// check for compatibility for multiplication
if ( n1 != m2 )
begin
      Display "Matrices not compatible for multiplication
      exit
end

Read the elements of matrix a
Read the elements of matrix b

      // Multiplication of matrices a & b begins

      for( i = 0; i < m1; i++)
      for( j = 0; j < n2; j++)
      {
            p[i][j] = 0;
            for( k = 0; k < n1; k++)
                  p[i][j] += a[i][k] * b[k][j];

      }

      // Multiplication of matrices of a & b ends

Display the matrix a
Display the matrix b
Display the matrix p
```

End pseudocode

PROGRAM 9.10   To multiply two matrices

```c
#include <stdio.h>
#include <process.h>

int main(void)
{
      int a[10][10], b[10][10], p[10][10], m1, n1, m2, n2, i, j, k;

      printf("Enter no. of rows and columns of matrix a \n");
      scanf("%d%d", &m1, &n1);
      printf("Enter no. of rows and columns of b \n");
      scanf("%d%d", &m2, &n2);

      if ( n1 != m2 )
      {
            printf("Matrices are not compatible \n");
```

```
            exit(1);
    }

    printf("Enter the elements of a \n");
    for( i = 0; i < m1; i++)
    for( j = 0; j < n1; j++)
            scanf("%d", &a[i][j]);

    printf("Enter the elements of b \n");
    for( i = 0; i < m2; i++)
    for( j = 0; j < n2; j++)
            scanf("%d", &b[i][j]);

    /* Multiplication of matrices a & b begins */

    for( i = 0; i < m1; i++)
    for( j = 0; j < n2; j++)
    {
            p[i][j] = 0;
            for( k = 0; k < n1; k++)
                    p[i][j] += a[i][k] * b[k][j];

    }

    /* Multiplication of matrices of a & b ends */

    printf("Matrix a \n");
    for( i = 0; i < m1; i++)
    {
            for( j = 0; j < n1; j++)
                    printf("%4d", a[i][j]);
        printf("\n");
    }

    printf("Matrix b \n");
    for( i = 0; i < m2; i++)
    {
            for( j = 0; j < n2; j++)
                    printf("%4d", b[i][j]);
            printf("\n");
    }
    printf("Product Matrix p \n");
    for( i = 0; i < m1; i++)
    {
            for( j = 0; j < n2; j++)
                    printf("%4d", p[i][j]);
            printf("\n");
```

```
      }

      return 0;
}
```

Input–Output:

```
Enter the number of rows and number of columns of matrix a
2 3
Enter the number of rows and columns of b
3 4

Enter the elements of a
1 2 3 4 5 6

Enter the elements of b
1 2 3 4 5 6 7 8 9 10 11 12

Matrix a

1  2  3
4  5  6

Matrix b

1  2  3  4
5  6  7  8
9 10 11 12

Product Matrix p

38 44 50 56
83 98 113 128
```

Explanation:

In the above program, **a**, **b** and **p** are declared to be arrays of two dimensions of type **int** and size 10 * 10. **a** and **b** represent two input matrices, which are to be multiplied. **P** represents the resultant product matrix. Variables **m1** and **n1** are to collect the number of rows and columns of **a**. Variables **m2** and **n2** are to collect the number of rows and columns of **b**. The number of rows and columns values for both **a** and **b** are expected to lie within 1 and 10. Before proceeding to multiply **a** and **b**, we first find whether the matrices are compatible for multiplication. If they are not, the program exits reporting the appropriate error. The following segment does this.

```
if ( n1 != m2 )
{
      printf("Matrices are not compatible \n");
      exit(1);
}
```

After the matrices **a** and **b** are found to be compatible for multiplication, multiplication of them proceeds, which is accomplished by the following segment.

```
/* Multiplication of matrices a & b begins */

    for( i = 0; i < m1; i++)
    for( j = 0; j < n2; j++)
    {
            p[i][j] = 0;
            for( k = 0; k < n1; k++)
                    p[i][j] += a[i][k] * b[k][j];


    }

    /* Multiplication of matrices of a & b ends */
```

After multiplication, all the three matrices **a**, **b** and **p** are displayed.

9.4.2 Three-dimensional Arrays

An array with three subscripts is termed a three-dimensional or 3-D array. A 3-D array is a collection of one or more 2-D arrays, all of which share a common name and are distinguishable by values of the first subscript of the 3-D array. A 3-D array is thus an array of 2-D arrays. We know that a 2-D array is used to store a table of values. So, a 3-D array enables us to form a group of tables and perform collective manipulations over them in a fairly easier manner.

Declaration of three-dimensional arrays

Syntax of declaration of a 3-D array is as follows.

```
data-type variable-name [size1] [size 2] [size 3];
```

`data-type` refers to any data type supported by C, `variable-name` refers to the array name, and `size1` indicates the number of tables being grouped together. `size2` indicates the number of rows of each table. `size3` indicates the number of columns of each table.

Each element in a 3-D array is identified by the array name followed by a pair of square brackets enclosing a table-number, followed by a pair of square brackets enclosing a row-number, followed by a pair of square brackets enclosing a column number. Table-number ranges from 0 to `size1−1`. When the table-number is 0, the first table is selected. When the table-number is 1, the second table is selected, and so on. Row-number ranges from 0 to `size2 - 1`. When row-number is 0, the first row is selected. When row-number is 1, the second row is selected, and so on. Column-number ranges from 0 to `size3-1`. When column-number is 0, the first column is selected. When column-number is 1, the second column is selected, and so on.

Example 9.21

`int a[2][4][5];`

a is declared to be a 3-D array. It can accommodate two tables of values, each table having four rows and five columns. Each element in the array is identified by the array name a, followed by a pair of square brackets enclosing a table-number, followed by a pair of square brackets enclosing a row-number, followed by another pair of square brackets enclosing a column-number. Table-number for a ranges from 0 to 1. Row-number ranges from 0 to 3 and column-number ranges from 0 to 4.

a[0][0][0] indicates data item in the first table, first row, and first column.

a[1][0][0] indicates data item in the second table, first row, first column.

a[1][1][2] indicates data item in the second table, second row, third column.

Note: A three-dimensional array is used to store logically related group of tables of values. Three loops (preferably, for loops) are used to access each element in the tables. The first loop is to select each table. The second loop is to select each row of the selected table. The third loop is used to access each value in the row and table selected.

PROGRAM 9.11   To accept the elements of a 3-D array and display them

---

```c
#include <stdio.h>

int main(void)
{
        int a[2][2][2], i, j, k;

        printf("Enter the elements of a of order 2*2*2 \n");

        for( i = 0; i < 2; i++)
        {
                for( j = 0; j < 2; j++)
                for( k = 0; k < 2; k++)
                        scanf("%d", &a[i][j][k]);
}

        printf("\n The 3-D array a \n\n");
        for( i = 0; i < 2; i++)
        {
                printf("a-Table %d \n\n", i + 1);
                for(j = 0; j < 2; j++)
                {
                        for(k = 0; k < 2; k++)
                                printf("%4d", a[i][j][k]);
                printf("\n");
                }

                printf("\n\n");
        }

        return 0;
}
```

Input–Output:

```
Enter the elements of a of order 2*2*2 (Two tables of size 2*2)
1 2 3 4 5 6 7 8

The 3-D array a

a-Table 1
  1 2
  3 4

a-Table 2

  5 6
  7 8
```

Explanation:

In the above program, **a** has been declared to be a 3-D array of size 2*2*2. The array **a** can thus accommodate two tables, each with two rows and two columns. The outermost loop (**i** loop) is to select each table. **j** loop is used to select each row of the table selected by **i**. The innermost loop (**k** loop) is used to select the elements of the row selected by **j**.

When   i = 0 (The first table),

  j = 0 (The first row in first table),

   k ranges from 0 to 1 to select all the elements in the first row of the first table.

  j = 1 (The second row in first table)

   k ranges from 0 to 1 to select all the elements in the second row of the first table.

All the elements of the first table have now been accessed.

When   i = 1 (The second table)

  j = 0 (The first row in second table),

   k ranges from 0 to 1 to select all the elements in the first row of the second table.

  j = 1 (The second row in second table)

   k ranges from 0 to 1 to select all the elements in the second row of the second table.

All the elements of the second table have now been accessed.

On the similar lines, we can think of arrays of four dimensions, arrays of five dimensions and so on. (An array of n-dimension can be thought of as a group of one or more logically related arrays of dimension n − 1). The limit on the dimensionality is dependent on the C compiler being used and availability of memory.

Initialization of three-dimensional arrays

Even the 3-D arrays can also be initialized. The following program illustrates this. The initializers' list can have a list of values separated by commas in its simplest form. It can specify the values for each table of the array separately by enclosing them within inner pairs of braces. In the following program, we demonstrate these. It is left as an exercise to the readers to test the other variations on the lines of the variations of 2-D arrays initialization.

PROGRAM 9.12   To illustrate initialization of 3-D arrays

```c
#include <stdio.h>
int main(void)
{
    int a[2][2][2] = {1, 2, 3, 4, 5, 6, 7, 8};
    int b[2][2][2] = { {{1, 2}, {3, 4}},
                                        {{5, 6}, {7, 8}}};
    int i, j, k;
    printf("Array a \n");
    for(i = 0; i < 2; i++)
    {
        for(j = 0; j < 2; j++)
        {
            for(k = 0; k < 2; k++)
                printf("%4d", a[i][j][k]);
            printf("\n");
        }
        printf("\n");
    }
    printf("Array b \n");
    for(i = 0; i < 2; i++)
    {
        for(j = 0; j < 2 ; j++)
        {
            for(k = 0; k < 2; k++)
                printf("%4d", b[i][j][k]);
            printf("\n");
        }
        printf("\n");
    }
    return 0;
}
```

Input–Output:

```
Array a
 1  2
 3  4

 5  6
 7  8

Array b
 1  2
 3  4

 5  6
 7  8
```

Suppose there are two salesmen, who are assigned the job of selling two products for a week's time and we need to store the sales figures of both the salesmen in each day of the week, we are forced to use a 3-D array. The number of items of the products sold in each day of the week by a salesman can be captured in a 2-D array, each row representing a product and each column representing a day of the week. But here we need to record the sales figures of two salesmen, which means two 2-D arrays are required to do so. Instead of using two different 2-D arrays, we choose a 3-D array for want of easier collective manipulation, which is declared as follows:

```
int sales[2][2][7];
```

The size value within the first pair of square brackets representing the number of salesmen. The size value within the second pair of square brackets representing the number of products and the size value within the third pair of square brackets representing the number of days in a week.

PROGRAM 9.13   To illustrate three-dimensional array

```
#include <stdio.h>

int main(void)
{
        int sales[2][5][7], i, j, k;

        printf("Enter the Sales Figures of two Salesmen\n");
        for(i = 0; i < 2; i++)
        {

                for(j = 0; j < 2; j++)
                {
                printf("Enter Sales Figures of item %d by Salesman %d for a
week \n", i + 1, j + 1);
                        for(k = 0; k < 7 ; k++)
                                scanf("%d", &sales[i][j][k]);
                }
        }

                for(i = 0; i < 2; i++)
                {
                        printf("Weekly Sales Figures of Salesman %d each row
                                representing an item\n", i + 1);
                        for(j = 0; j < 2; j++)
                        {
                                for(k = 0; k < 7; k++)
                                        printf("%4d", sales[i][j][k]);
                                        printf("\n");
                        }
                        printf("\n\n");
                }
        return 0;
}
```

Input–Output:

```
Enter the Sales Figures of two Salesman

Enter Sales Figures of item 1 by Salesman 1 for a week
12 54 34 54 65 76 87

Enter Sales Figures of item 1 by Salesman 2 for a week
89 12 43 45 65 67 76

Enter Sales Figures of item 2 by Salesman 1 for a week
87 78 32 98 89 65 89

Enter Sales Figures of item 2 by Salesman 2 for a week
32 65 56 87 90 27 28

Weekly Sales Figures of Salesman 1 each row representing an item
12 54 34 54 65 76 87
89 12 43 45 65 67 76

Weekly Sales Figures of Salesman 2 each row representing an item
87 78 32 98 89 65 89
32 65 56 87 90 27 28
```

9.5 ARRAYS AND FUNCTIONS

We now know that arrays facilitate collective manipulations over a group of similar data items in a fairly easier way. The collective manipulations may be displaying the elements in an array, summing up the elements in an array, finding the largest element in an array or sorting the elements in an array in some order, etc. So far, the collective manipulations have been accomplished through the statements in `main()` only. If a collective manipulation, say, displaying a list of numbers, has to be repeated for more than one array, then we would be definitely inclined to think of defining a function for the purpose with an array itself as its argument. C does permit passing arrays as arguments to functions. Once an array is passed as an argument to a function, all the elements of the array can be operated upon by the statements of the function.

One-dimensional arrays as arguments to functions

To make a function take an array of one dimension as its input to be provided by a calling program, we need to define the function with two formal parameters: 1. Array name with data type specified and 2. The number of elements of the array being passed, while defining the function as

```
data-type function-name(data-type array_name[], int size)
{


}
```

Example 9.22

```
void display(int a[], int n)
{

}
```

Note the presence of a pair of square brackets after `array_name`. These are required to indicate that we are passing an array.

After the function is defined, while calling it, we need to pass just the array name of actual array belonging to the calling program and the number of elements in the array.

Example 9.23

```
int b[10];
```

If b is an array declared in the calling program, then invoking `display()` by passing the array b is as follows:

```
display(b, 10);
```

PROGRAM 9.14   To display the elements of a 1-D array

```
#include <stdio.h>

void display(int[], int);

int main(void)
{
        int a[20], i, n;

        printf("Enter the number of values \n");
        scanf("%d", &n);
        printf("Enter %d Values \n", n);
        for(i = 0; i < n; i++)
        scanf("%d", &a[i]);
        printf("The elements are \n");
        display(a, n);

        return 0;
}

void display(int a[], int n)
{
        int i;

        for(i = 0; i < n; i++)
        printf("%4d", a[i]);
}
```

Input–Output:

```
Enter the number of values
4
Enter 4 Values
1 2 3 4

The elements are
1 2 3 4
```

Explanation:

The function **display()** is defined with two arguments. A pair of square brackets after the name of the first argument **a** indicates an array of **int** type is being passed and the second argument **n** of **int** type indicates the number of elements in the array. The purpose of the function is to display the elements of the array passed to it.

In the **main()**, **a** is declared to be an array of **int** type and of size 20. Maximum 20 elements can be accepted into the array. **i** and **n** are declared to be variables of **int** type. The variable **i** is to traverse the elements of the array and **n** is to collect the number of elements of the array which should lie within 1–20.

After accepting the number of elements into the variable **n**, **n** elements are accepted into the array **a**. The function display() is then invoked by passing the array name a and the number of elements of the array **n** (actual arguments) to it. As a result, control gets transferred to **display()**. The **display()** displays the elements of the array **a**. The function exits after displaying and the control is regained by the main().

To find the sum of the elements in a 1-d array

```
Pseudocode sum(a[0..n-1])
s = 0
for(i = 0; i < n; i++)
    s += a[i];
return s
End pseudocode
```

PROGRAM 9.15   To find the sum of the elements in a 1-D array

```c
#include <stdio.h>

int sum(int[], int);

int main(void)
{
    int a[20], i, n, s;

    printf("Enter the number of values \n");
    scanf("%d", &n);
    printf("Enter %d Values \n", n);
```

```
        for (i = 0; i < n; i++)
        scanf ("%d", &a[i]);

        s = sum(a, n);
        printf ("Sum = %d \n", s);

        return 0;
}
int sum(int a[], int n)
{
        int s = 0, i;

        for (i = 0; i < n; i++)
                s += a[i];

        return (s);
}
```

Input–Output:

```
Enter the number of elements
5

Enter 5 elements
3 4 5 6 7

sum = 25
```

Explanation:

The function **sum()** is defined with two arguments. The first argument indicates that we pass an array of **int** type and the second argument, which is of **int** type, indicates the number of elements in the array being passed. The function is also made to return a value of **int** type. The purpose of the function as indicated by its name is to find the sum of the elements of the array being passed and return the sum to the calling program (main() in this case). Within the sum() two local variables i, s of **int** type are declared. If i is to traverse the elements of the array a, the variable s is to collect the sum of the elements in the array. After the sum is found out, the value of **s** is returned back to the calling program main().

Within main(), **a** is declared to be an array of **int** type with size 20. Maximum 20 elements can be accepted into the array. i, n and s are declared to be variables of **int** type. i is to traverse the elements of **a**, n is to accept the number of elements of the array **a** and s is to collect the sum of the elements in the array returned by the function sum(). After accepting n elements into the array a, **sum()** is called by passing the array name **a** and the size of the array n as s = sum (a, n). Upon execution of the sum(), the variable s in main() would collect the sum of the array elements which is then displayed.

Note that the variables n, i and s of **sum()** are different from those in **main()**.

To find the mean, variance and standard deviation of a list of values

Arrays of one dimension are used to store lists of sample values which are then subjected to statistical calculations. We normally come across the statistical terms like **Mean**, **Variance** and **Standard Deviation** of sample values representing some real life data like population in different cities, amount of rainfall in different seasons in a year, etc. Mean of a list of values is defined to be the average of the values in it. Variance is defined to be the average of the squares of the differences between each element and the mean of the list and Standard Deviation of a list of values is given by the square root of the variance of the list. We will now write a program to find Mean, Variance and Standard Deviation of a list of values.

```
Pseudocode find_mean(a[0..n-1], n)
sum = 0
for(i = 0; i < n; i++)
      sum += a[i]
avg = (float) sum / n;
return avg;
End pseudocode
```

```
Pseudocode find_variance(a[0..n-1],n)
sum_sqrs = 0
mean = find_mean(a, n)

for(i = 0; i < n; i++)
begin
      deviation = a[i] - mean;
      sum_sqrs += deviation * deviation;
end
variance = sum_sqrs / n;
return variance;
End pseudocode
```

```
Pseudocode find_stddev(a[0..n-1], n)
variance = find_variance(a, n);
stddev = sqrt(variance);
return stddev;
End pseudocode
```

PROGRAM 9.16   To find out the standard deviation of a list of values

---

```
#include <stdio.h>

void read(int a[], int n);
void display(int a[], int n);
float find_mean(int a[], int n);
float find_variance(int a[], int n);
float find_stddev(int a[], int n);
```

```
int main(void)
{
        int a[10], n;
        float mean, variance, stddev;

        printf("Enter the number of values \n");
        scanf("%d", &n);

        printf("Enter the values of the array \n");
        read(a, n);

        printf("The list of values \n");
        display(a, n);

        mean = find_mean(a, n);
        printf("mean = %f \n", mean);

        variance = find_variance(a, n);
        printf("Variance = %f \n", variance);

        stddev = find_stddev(a, n);
        printf("stddev = %f \n", stddev);
        return 0;
}

void read(int a[], int n)
{
        int i;
        for(i = 0; i < n; i++)
                scanf("%d", &a[i]);
}

void display(int a[], int n)
{
        int i;

        for(i = 0; i < n; i++)
                printf("%4d", a[i]);
}
float find_mean(int a[], int n)
{
        float sum = 0, avg;
        int i;

        for(i = 0; i < n; i++)
                sum += a[i];
```

```
        avg = (float) sum / n;

        return avg;
}

float find_variance(int a[], int n)
{
        float mean, sum_sqrs = 0, variance;
        int i;

        mean = find_mean(a, n);

        for(i = 0; i < n; i++)
        {
                deviation = a[i] - mean;
                sum_sqrs += deviation * deviation;
        }

        variance = sum_sqrs / n;

        return variance;
}

float find_stddev(int a[], int n)
{
        float variance, stddev;

        variance = find_variance(a, n);
        stddev = sqrt(variance);

        return stddev;
}
```

Input–Output:

```
Enter the number of values
5

Enter the values of the array
3 5 7 6 9

The list of values
3  5  7  6  9

mean = 6.000000
variance = 4.000000
stddev = 2.000000
```

Explanation:

In the above program, the function read() is defined with two formal arguments a and n. The formal arguments represent the array name and the number of elements of the array respectively. The purpose of the function is to accept the given number of values into the array specified while calling it.

The function `display()` is also defined with the same two formal arguments a and n. The formal arguments represent the array name and the number of elements of the array respectively. The purpose of the function is to display the elements of the array specified while calling it.

The functions find_mean(), find_variance() and find_stddev() are to find the mean, variance and standard deviation of the elements in an array respectively. Note that all these functions are also defined with the two arguments, array name and number of elements.

Also note that the function find_variance() calls find_mean() and find_stddev() in turn calls find_variance().

Passing two-dimensional arrays to functions

To be able to make a function take a 2-D array as its argument, we need to specify three formal arguments: 1. 2-D array name followed by two pairs of square brackets with constant enclosed within the second pair of square brackets preceded by the data type of the array, 2. The no. of rows in the array (int), and 3. The number of columns in the array (int). The last two arguments are not required when the function has to deal with the array of the same size as that of the actual argument.

The syntax of the function definition is as follows:

```
data-type function-name(data-type array_name[] [size2], int rowsize, int
colsize)
{
        local variables
        statements
}
```

Note that the specification of size within the second pair of square brackets for the array is mandatory since the compiler needs to be aware of the size of each row. It is to help the compiler generate appropriate code so that the function selects appropriate elements when it moves to different rows. However, specification of size within the first pair of square brackets is optional.

Example 9.24

```
void display(int a[] [10], int m, int n)
{
        local variables
        statements
}
```

The size specified within the second pair of square brackets should be same as that of the actual array to be passed. While calling the function, the calling program needs to pass just the array name (with no square brackets), number of rows and number of columns as:

```
display(b, m, n)
```

where **b** is a two-dimensional array declared in the calling program, **m** and **n** provide the number of rows and number of columns of the array respectively

PROGRAM 9.17 To display the elements of a matrix

```
#include <stdio.h>

void display(int [] [10], int, int);

int main(void)
{
        int a[10] [10], m , n, i, j;

        printf("Enter the size of the matrix \n");
        scanf("%d%d", &m, &n);
        printf("Enter the elements of matrix a \n");
        for(i = 0; i < m; i++)
        for(j = 0; j < n; j++)
        scanf("%d", &a[i] [j]);
        display(a, m, n);

        return 0;
}

void display(int a[] [10], int m, int n)
{
        int i, j;
        for(i = 0; i < m; i++)
        {
                for(j = 0; j < n; j++)
                        printf("%4d", a[i] [j]);
                printf("\n");
        }
}
```

Input–Output:

```
Enter the size of the matrix
2 3
Enter the elements of the matrix a
1 2 3 4 5 6
The matrix
1 2 3
4 5 6
```

Note: A function can receive arrays as arguments, but cannot return an array of automatic storage class to the calling function. However, it can return an array of static storage class declared within it and a dynamically created array within it to the calling function by returning the address of the first element of the array. You can explore the possibility of returning a static array or a dynamically created array to the calling function later after getting an insight into the relationship between arrays and pointers.

Pseudocode accept(a[0..m-1, 0..n-1])

```
for(i = 0; i < m; i++)
for(j = 0; j < n; j++)
       read a[i][j]
```

End pseudocode

Pseudocode display(a[0..m-1, 0..n-1])

```
for(i = 0; i < m; i++)
for(j = 0; j < n; j++)
       display a[i][j]
```

End pseudocode

Pseudocode subtract(a[0..m-1, 0..n-1],

b[0..m-1, 0..n-1],

c[0..m-1, 0..n-1])


```
for(i = 0; i < m; i++)
for(j = 0; j < n; j++)
       c[i][j] = a[i][j] - b[i][j];
```

End pseudocode

PROGRAM 9.18   Program to subtract one matrix from another matrix

---

```c
#include <stdio.h>
void accept(int a[][10],int m, int n);
void display(int a[][10], int m, int n);
void subtract(int a[][10], int b[][10], int c[][10], int m, int n);

int main(void)
{
       int a[10][10], b[10][10], c[10][10], m , n;
       printf("Enter the number of rows and columns of the matrices \n");
       scanf("%d%d", &m, &n);
```

```
        printf ("Enter the elements of matrix a \n") ;
        accept (a, m, n) ;
        printf ("Matrix a \n") ;
        display (a, m, n) ;
        printf ("Enter the elements of matrix b \n") ;
        accept (b, m, n) ;
        printf ("Matrix b \n") ;
        display (b, m, n) ;
        subtract (a, b, c, m, n) ;
        printf ("Resultant matrix c\n") ;
        display (c, m, n) ;

        return 0;
}

void accept (int a [] [10] , int m , int n)
{
        int i, j;

        for (i - 0; i < m; i++)
        for (j = 0; j < n; j++)
                scanf ("%d", &a [i] [j] ) ;
}

void display (int a [] [10] , int m , int n)
{
        int i, j;

        for (i = 0; i < m; i++)
        {
                for (j = 0; j < n; j++)
                        printf ("%4d", a [i] [j] ) ;
                        printf ("\n") ;
        }
}

void subtract (int a [] [10] , int b [] [10] , int c [] [10] , int m, int n)
{
        int i, j;

        for (i = 0; i < m; i++)
        for (j = 0; j < n; j++)
                c [i] [j] = a [i] [j] - b [i] [j] ;
}
```

Input–Output:

```
Enter the number of rows and columns of the matrices
2 2
Enter the elements of matrix a
6 7 8 9
Matrix a
  6  7
  8  9
Enter the elements of matrix b
2 3 4 5
Matrix b
  2  3
  4  5
Resultant matrix c
  4  4
  4  4
```

Explanation:

The function accept() is defined with three formal arguments a (2-D array name), m (int) and n (int). The arguments m and n represent the number of rows and the number of columns of the 2-D array respectively. The purpose of the function is to accept the elements of a 2-D array. The function display() is also defined with the same types of arguments and it is to display the elements of a 2-D array.

The function subtract() is the important part of the program since it serves the purpose of the program. Within the function the matrix represented by the formal argument b is subtracted from the matrix a and the resultant matrix is collected by c with the help of the following segment.

```
for(i = 0; i < m; i++)
for(j = 0; j < n; j++)
   c[i][j] = a[i][j] - b[i][j];
```

It is important to note that all the formal arguments representing 2-D arrays are provided with the value of the second subscript.

9.5.1 Passing Three-dimensional Arrays to Functions as Arguments

To be able to make a function take a 3-D array as its argument, we need to specify four formal arguments: **1.** Three-dimensional array name followed by three pairs of square brackets with constants enclosed within the second and third pairs of square brackets preceded by the data type of the array, **2.** The number of tables (int), **3.** The number of rows in the array (int), and **4.** The number of columns in the array (int). The last three arguments are not required when the function has to deal with the array of the same size as that of the actual argument.

The syntax of the function definition is as follows:

```
data-type function-name(data-type array_name[ ][size2][size3], int tab-
size, int rowsize, int colsize)
```

```
{
        local variables
        statements
}
```

Note that the specification of size within the second and the third pairs of square brackets for the array are mandatory since the compiler needs to be aware of the size of each table and the size of each row in each table. It is to help the compiler generate appropriate code so that the function selects appropriate elements when it moves to different tables and different rows in each table. However, specification of size within the first pair of square brackets is optional.

Example 9.25

To display the elements of a 3-D array a. The function looks as follows:

```
void display (int a [ ] [10] [10] , int t, int r, int c)
{
        local variables
        statements
}
```

The sizes specified within the second and the third pair of square brackets should be same as those of the actual array to be passed. While calling the function, the calling program needs to pass just the array name (with no square brackets), the number of tables, the number of rows and the number of columns as:

```
display (b, t, r, c)
```

where b is a 3-D array declared in the calling program, t, r and c provide the number of tables, the number of rows and number of columns of the array respectively.

PROGRAM 9.19   To illustrate passing the 3-D arrays to functions as arguments

---

```
#include <stdio.h>
void display (int a [] [2] [2] , int t, int r, int c);

int main (void)
{
        int a [2] [2] [2] = { 1, 2, 3, 4, 5, 6, 7, 8};

        display (a, 2, 2, 2);
        return 0;
}

void display (int a [] [2] [2] , int t, int r, int c)
{
    int i, j, k;

    for (i = 0; i < t; i++)
    {
```

```
        printf("Table - %d \n", i + 1);
        for(j = 0; j < r; j++)
        {
                for(k = 0; k < c; k++)
                        printf("%4d", a[i][j][k]);
                printf("\n");
        }
        printf("\n");
    }
}
```

Input–Output:

```
Table 1

1 2
3 4

Table 2

5 6
7 8
```

Explanation:

The function display() is defined with four formal arguments. The first argument a is a 3-D array of int type. The fact that it is a 3-D array is indicated by using three pairs of square brackets after the array name. Note that the last two pairs of square brackets enclose the constant values representing the number of rows and columns in each table (as specified in the declaration of the array in the calling program. The next three arguments represent the number of tables, the number of rows and the number of columns respectively. The purpose of the function is to display a 3-D array with the number of rows and the number of columns in each table being equal to two.

In the main(), the function display() is invoked by passing the array a and the number of tables, the number of rows and the number of columns into it as display(a, 2, 2, 2).

SUMMARY

- An array is a group of data items of similar type stored in contiguous locations sharing a common name, but distinguished by subscript values.
- Arrays facilitate collective manipulation in an easier and flexible way.
- An array of 1-D represents a list of values, which are logically related, whereas an array of two dimensions represents a table of values, which are otherwise called matrices.
- Like ordinary variables, arrays can also be initialized while they are declared.
- A single loop is used to access all the elements of a one-dimensional array.
- Two loops, one nested within the other, are used to access all the elements of a 2-D array.

- We can even pass arrays to functions as arguments.
- While we define a function to take a 2-D array, we must specify the column size within the second pair of square brackets.
- While we define a function to take a 3-D array, we must specify both the row size and the column size within the second and the third pairs of square brackets.

REVIEW QUESTIONS

9.1 Explain the need for arrays.

9.2 Define an array.

9.3 What do you mean by dimensionality of an array?

9.4 Explain the syntax of declaring a 1-D array with an example.

9.5 Explain the syntax of initializing a 1-D array while declaring.

9.6 Write a program segment to accept values through keyboard into an integer array a of size 10.

9.7 Find out errors, if any, in the following
   (a) `int a(9);`   (b) `float b[];`   (c) `int c[x];`
   (d) `double 1d[10];`   (e) `int bc[4];`   (f) `int b[10]`

9.8 Explain the syntax of declaring a 2-D array with an example.

9.9 Explain the syntax of initializing a 2-D array while declaring with an example.

9.10 Write a program segment to accept values through keyboard into an integer array a of two dimensions of size 5*4.

9.11 Explain the syntax of declaring a 3-D array with an example.

9.12 Explain the syntax of initializing a 3-D array while declaring with an example.

9.13 Write a program segment to accept values through keyboard into an integer array a of three dimensions of size 5*4*3.

State whether the following are true or false

9.1 Arrays facilitate collective manipulations.

9.2 In an array, there can be data of different types.

9.3 The size of an array can be a real number.

9.4 The array index starts with one.

9.5 Arrays can be initialized.

9.6 `int a[] = {3, 4, 5};` is a valid initialization.

9.7 `float f[2] = {3, 5};` is a valid initialization.

9.8 Any looping structure can be used to access the elements of an array.

9.9 Two loops are used to access the elements of a 2-D array.

9.10 Int a [] [] = {1, 2, 3, 4} is a valid initialization of the 2-D array a.

9.11 Three loops are used to access the elements of a 3-D array.

9.12 There is a limit on the dimensionality of arrays in C.

9.13 Arrays can be passed to functions as arguments.

9.14 An array can be returned from a function.

9.15 While passing a 2-D array as an argument to a function, the number of columns should be specified within the second pair of square brackets.

Find out errors, if any, in the following

9.1 `int a(9)(9);`

9.2 `float b[][];`

9.3 `int c[x][y];`

9.4 `double 1d[10][3];`

9.5 `int b c[4][3];`

9.6 `int b[10][4]`

9.7 `int [3,4];`

9.8 `int a(3,4);`

9.9 `int a[] = { 1, , 2};`

9.10
```
int main(void)
{
        int a[][2] = {1, 2, 3, 4}, i, j;

        for(i = 1; i <= 2; i++)
        for(j = 1; j <= 2; j++)
                printf("%d\n", a[i][j]);
        return 0;
}
```

9.11
```
int identity(int a[][], m, n)
{
        int flag = 1, i, j;

        for(i = 0;i <= m; i++)
        for(j = 0; j <= n; j++)
        {
                if ((i == j) && (a[i][j] != 1))
                        flag = 0;
                if ((i != j) && (a[i][j] != 0))
                        flag = 0;
        }
        return flag;
}
```

9.12 `int a[10];`
`scanf("%d", a);`

PROGRAMMING EXERCISES

9.1 Write a program to generate Fibonacci series using an array.

(Hint: First two members of the series are 1 and 1.

```
a[0] = 1,
a[1] = 1,
a[i] = a[i-1] + a[i-2], i ranging from 2 to n )
```

9.2 Write a program to find the sum of odd numbers and sum of even numbers in an integer array.

9.3 Write a program to display only prime numbers in an integer array.

9.4 Write a program to insert an element into an array of one dimension.

9.5 Write a program to delete an integer into an array of one dimension.

9.6 Write a program to delete duplicates in an array.

9.7 a and b are two arrays of one dimension of size 10. Write a program to find the array c such that

```
C[0] = a[0] + b[9]
C[1] = a[1] + b[8]
     :
     :
     :
C[8] = a[8] + b[1]
C[9] = a[9] + b[0]
```

9.8 Write a program to find the intersection of two arrays a and b with size m and n respectively.

Example:

```
int a[3] = {1, 2, 3, 4, 5};
int b[2] = {1, 4, 6};
```

Result of intersection of a and b is another array c with the elements which are common in both a and b.

```
c[] = { 1, 4}.
```

9.9 Write a program to find the union of two arrays **a** and **b** with size **m** and **n** respectively.

Example:

```
int a[3] = {1, 2, 3, 4, 5};
int b[2] = {1, 4, 6};
```

Result of union of a and b is another array c with the elements which are either in a or in b or in both.

```
c[] = { 1,2, 3, 4, 5, 6}.
```

9.10 Write a program to find the largest element in an array using a function.

9.11 Write a program to find the number of prime numbers in an array using a function.

9.12 Write a program to search for a number in a list of numbers using linear search method. (Use a recursive function to implement linear search method)

9.13 Write a program to search for a number in a list of numbers using binary search method. (Use a recursive function to implement binary search method. For the binary search method to work, the list is expected to be in increasing or decreasing order. Suppose the list is in the increasing order, the number being searched for is compared with the middle element in the list. If the number is less than the middle element, the first half of the list only is considered. If the number is greater than the middle element, only the second half of the list is considered. This continues till the number is found or the list gets exhausted.)

9.14 Write a program to find whether a matrix is symmetric or not.

9.15 Write a program to find out whether a matrix is an identity matrix or not.
(A square matrix is said to be an identity matrix if all the principal diagonal elements are 1s and all the remaining elements are 0's.)
Example:

$$
\begin{array}{ccc}
1 & 0 & 0 \\
0 & 1 & 0 \\
0 & 0 & 1
\end{array}
$$

9.16 Write a program to find whether a matrix is a lower triangular matrix or not.
(A square matrix is said to be a lower triangular matrix if all the elements below the principal diagonal elements are non-zero values and the remaining elements are all 0s.)
Example:

$$
\begin{array}{ccc}
0 & 0 & 0 \\
2 & 0 & 0 \\
7 & 8 & 0
\end{array}
$$

9.17 Write a program to find whether a matrix is an upper triangular matrix or not.
(A square matrix is said to be an upper triangular matrix if all the elements above the principal diagonal elements are non-zero values and the remaining elements are all 0s.)
Example:

$$
\begin{array}{ccc}
0 & 3 & 5 \\
0 & 0 & 7 \\
0 & 0 & 0
\end{array}
$$

9.18 Write a program to transpose a matrix.
Example:

Given matrix:

$$
\begin{array}{ccc}
1 & 2 & 3 \\
4 & 5 & 6 \\
8 & 7 & 9
\end{array}
$$

Transposed matrix: 1   4   8
                      2   5   7
                      3   6   9

9.19 Write a program to sort a matrix row-wise.
(Elements in each row should be in the increasing order.)

9.20 Write a program to sort a matrix column-wise.
(Elements in each column should be in the increasing order.)

9.21 Write a program to find the trace of a matrix.
(Trace of a matrix is defined to be the sum of the diagonal elements in the matrix.)

9.22 Write a program to find the norm of a matrix.
(Norm of a matrix is defined to be the square root of the sum of the squares of the elements of the matrix.)

9.23 Write a program to check whether a matrix is orthogonal or not.
(A matrix is said to be orthogonal if the product of the matrix and its transpose turns out to be an identity matrix.)

9.24 Write a program to find the sum of the elements above and below the diagonal elements in a matrix.

9.25 Write a program to find the saddle points in a matrix.

(A saddle point is one which is the least element in the row and is the largest element in the column.)

9.26 Write programs to perform the tasks of the Questions 9.1–9.25 using functions.

9.27 Modify the Program 9.15 to calculate the total number of items of each product sold in a week by both salesmen.

INTERVIEW QUESTIONS

9.1 What is the output of the following C programs?

```
(a) #include<stdio.h>
    int main(void)
    {
        int a[5] = {1,2,3,4,5};
        int s = 0;

        for(i=4; i>=0; i--)
        {
            s=s+a[i];
            printf("%d %d\n", i, s);
        }
    }
```

(b)
```c
#include<stdio.h>
int main(void)
{
    int a[5] = {1,2};
    int s = 0;

    for(i=0; i<=4; i++)
    {
        s=s+a[i];
        printf("%d %d\n", i, s);
    }
}
```

(c)
```c
#include<stdio.h>
int main(void)
{
    int a[5] = {1,2,3,4,5};
    int s = 0;

    for(i=0; i>=4; i++)

        s=s+a[i];
        printf("%d %d\n", i, s);

}
```

(d)
```c
#include<stdio.h>
int main(void)
{
    int a[4][4] = {{1},{2},{3}];
    int s = 0;

    for(i=0; i>=4; i++)
    {
    for(j=0; j<=4; j++)

            s=s+a[i][j];
    }
```

```
        printf("%d", s);


    }


(e) #include<stdio.h>
    int main(void)
    {
        int s[5] = {2,4,5,6};

        printf("%d", ++s);
    }


(f) #include<stdio.h>
    int main(void)
    {
        int s[5] = {2,4,5,6};

        printf("%d", s[2]++ + --s[4]);
    }
```

9.2 What happens when we try to access an array element out of position?

9.3 Predict the output:

```
#include<stdio.h>

int main(void)
{
    int a[5] = {3, 6, 9,12,15};
    int i, j, k;
    i = ++a[0];
    j = a[4]++;
    k = a[i++];
    printf("%d, %d, %d", i, j,k);
    return 0;

}
```

9.4 What is a base address?

9.5 How do you print the base address of an array and the corresponding element stored in the base address?

9.6 Can you change the size of the array dynamically?

9.7 What is the output of the following program?

```
#include<stdio.h>
int main(void)
        {
        int a[2][3][3] = {1,3,5,7,9,10, 12, 34, 45, 56, 0, 8,
        6, 4, 13, 15, 50, 100};
        printf("%d",a[1][0][2]);
        return 0;


        }
```

9.8 What will be output of the following C code? Give explanation.

```
#include<stdio.h>
int main(void)
{
        int Test[10]={10};
        printf("%d %d",Test[1],Test[8]);
        return 0;
}
```

9.9 What are the advantages of an array?

9.10 Write two different ways of initializing a two-dimensional array C.

10

Strings

10.1 INTRODUCTION

Consider the statement printf("Welcome"); The printf() statement displays the message "Welcome" on the screen. Let us now understand how the message "welcome" is stored in memory and how the printf() works. The message "Welcome" is stored in memory as follows.

w	e	l	c	o	m	e	\0

Note that the last location in the memory block has the special character '\0'. The special character is automatically appended to the end of the message by the compiler.

In the statement printf("Welcome"); the printf() is provided with the starting address of the memory block. That is, the address of the first character 'w'. printf() will then continue to pick each character from the block and display it till the '\0' is reached. This is how the message is displayed. Here, the message "Welcome" is a **String**. To be precise, it is a **String Constant**.

A string in C is defined to be a sequence of characters terminated by the special character '\0' The special character '\0' is called the null character and it is to indicate the end of a string.

Strings constitute the major part of data used by many C programs. In real programming environment, we need to perform many more operations over strings. Like accepting strings through keyboard, extracting a part of a string, etc. String I/O operations and other manipulations over strings need variables to store them. The type of the variables inarguably happens to be an array of **char** type.

An array of **char** type to store the above string is to be declared as follows.

```
char s[8];
```

s[0]	s[1]	s[2]	s[3]	s[4]	s[5]	s[6]	s[7]
w	e	l	c	o	m	e	\0

An array of **char** is also regarded as a **String Variable**, since it can accommodate a string and it permits us to change its contents. In contrast, a sequence of characters enclosed within a pair of double quotes is called a **String Constant**.

Example 10.1

"Welcome" is a string constant

10.2 STRING I/O

10.2.1 The scanf() and printf() Functions

Syntax of using scanf() to accept a string into a string variable s is as follows.

```
scanf("%s", s);
```

accepts a string into s up to a white space character (Blank Space, New Line character, Tab space). The null character '\0' will be automatically appended to the string. The size of s is thus expected to be large enough to collect even the null character. %s is the format specifier for strings. Note that s is not preceded by symbol & (address of operator). This is because, the string variable name s itself gives the address of the string.

Example 10.2

```
char str[10];

scanf("%s", str);
```

if the input given is

```
abcd xyz
```

only abcd would be taken by str. Any subsequent scanf() to accept a string would read the string xyz.

Example 10.3

```
char str1[10], str2[10];

scanf("%s%s", str1, str2);
```

if the user input is

```
abcd xyz
```

"abcd" would be taken by str1 and "xyz" would be taken by str2.
Syntax of using printf() to display a string

```
printf("%s", s);
```

displays the string contained in s. %s is the format specifier for strings, s is a string variable the contents of which are to be displayed.

Example 10.4

`char s[10];`

If s has the string "abcd xyz",

`printf("%s",s);` would display "abcd xyz".

PROGRAM 10.1   To illustrate string I/O using `scanf()` & `printf()`

```
#include <stdio.h>

int main(void)
{
        char s[10];

        printf("Enter a string into s\n");
        scanf("%s", s);
        printf("s = %s \n", s);

        return 0;
}
```

Input–Output:

First-Run:
Enter a string into s
Programming

s = Programming

Second-Run:
Enter a string into s
abc xyz
s = abc

Note: In addition to the conversion specifier %s, the `scanf()` supports two other general conversion specifiers. They are %[characters] and %[^characters]. The conversion specifier %[characters] indicates to the `scanf()` that the characters specified within the opening square bracket and the closing square bracket only be accepted into the specified string variable and on encountering any other character, the reading process be terminated. The conversion specifier %[^characters] indicates to the `scanf()` that the characters other than those specified within the opening square bracket and the closing square bracket only be accepted into the specified string variable and on encountering any character specified within the brackets, the reading process be terminated.

Example 10.5

```
scanf("%[abcde]", s);
abcf
```

Here, only abc will be accepted by s

Example 10.6

```
scanf("%[^abcde]", s);
hkkhjkb
```

Here, only hkkhjk will be accepted by s

Example 10.7

```
scanf("%[a-z]", s);
 abcf7
```

Here, only abcf will be accepted by s

Example 10.8

```
scanf("%[^a-z]", s);
ASDDr
```

Here, only ASDD will be accepted by s

The statement scanf("%[^\n]", s); where s is an array of char type enables us to accept a string of characters terminated by the newline character. The string can consist of blank spaces. Note that the format specifier % s is replaced by [^\n]. The format specifier means that any character other than the newline character \n can be made a part of the string. The caret symbol ^ preceding \n is to indicate that the newline character is to be rejected by the scanf() in the process of accepting the string.

10.2.2 The getchar() and putchar() Functions

getchar() is a macro used to read a character through standard input, keyboard. The syntax of its usage is as follows.

```
c = getchar();
```

where c is a variable of **char** type. As a result of this, a character typed at the keyboard is assigned to the variable c.

This can be used iteratively to accept a line of text.
putchar() is the counterpart of getchar() It is used to display a character on the standard output screen. The syntax of using putchar() is as follows.

```
putchar(c);
```

where c represents variable of type char or a character constant. It displays the character stored in c on the screen. putchar() can be used iteratively to display a line of text.

PROGRAM 10.2   To accept a line of text and display it using getchar() and putchar()

```c
#include <stdio.h>
int main(void)
{
        char text[80], c;
        int i;

        printf("Enter a line of text \n");
        i = 0;
        c = getchar();
        while( c != '\n')
        {
                text[i] = c;
                c = getchar();
                i++;
        }
        text[i] = '\0'; /* The line of text is now available in text */

/* Displaying the line of text using putchar() */

        printf(" The line of text entered is \n");
        for( i = 0; text[i] != '\0'; i++)
        putchar(text[i]);

        return 0;
}
```

Input–Output:

```
Enter a line of text

I am going to Delhi.


The line of text entered is

I am going to Delhi.
```

10.2.3 The gets() and puts() Functions

The purpose of gets() is to accept a string up to a newline character into a string variable. It automatically appends the null character '\0' to the end of the string.

Prototype of gets() is as follows.

```c
char* gets(char*);
```

The function accepts a pointer to char type as the argument and returns a pointer to char type. We will learn later that a pointer to char type represents a string.

Example 10.9

```
char str[40];

gets(str);
```

enables us to accept a string up to a new line character into s. If the string given is "i am going", the entire string gets accepted by s.

The purpose of puts() is to display a string contained in a string variable. It also adds the newline character '\n' to the string automatically, as a result of which the cursor is moved down by one line after the string is displayed.

The prototype of puts() is as follows:

```
int puts(char*);
```

Example 10.10

```
char str[20];
```

If **str** has the string "I am going", puts(str) would display the entire string "I am going" and moves the cursor to the beginning of the next line.

PROGRAM 10.3   To accept a line of text using gets() and display it using puts()

```
#include <stdio.h>

int main(void)
{
      char str[40];

      printf("Enter a line of text \n");
      gets(str);
      printf("The line of text entered is \n");
      puts(str);

      return 0;
}
```

Input–Output:

```
Enter a line of text
I am going to Delhi.

The line of text entered is
I am going to Delhi.
```

10.2.4 The sprintf() and sscanf() Functions

The syntax of the sprintf() is similar to that of the printf() except the presence of buffer address as its first parameter and it is as follows.

```
void sprintf(char *s, char *fmt, arguments);
```

The argument s is the buffer address, fmt represents the control string. The function writes the values of the arguments into the memory area identified by s.

The syntax of the sscanf() is similar to that of the scanf() except the presence of buffer address as its first parameter and it is as follows:

```
void sscanf(char *s, char *fmt, arguments);
```

The argument s is the buffer address, fmt represents the control string. The function reads the values in s into the arguments.

PROGRAM 10.4   To illustrate sscanf() and sprintf() functions

---

```
#include <stdio.h>

int main(void)
{
    char str100];
    int a;
    float f;
    char s[10];

    sprintf(str, "%d %f %s", 12, 23.4, "sdg");
    puts(s);
    sscanf(str, "%d %f %s", &a, &f, s);
    printf("a = %d f = %f s = %s", a, f, s);

    return 0;
}
```

Input–Output:

```
12 23.400000 Mysore
a = 12 f = 23.400000 s = Mysore
```

10.3   INITIALIZATION OF ARRAYS OF char TYPE

The syntax of initializing a string variable has two variations.

Variation 10.1

```
char str1[5] = { 'a', 's', 'd', 'f', '\0' };
```

Here, str1 is declared to be a string variable with size 5. It can accommodate a maximum of five characters. The initializer-list consists of comma separated character constants. Note that the null character '\0' is explicitly listed. This is required in this variation.

Variation 10.2

```
char str2[5] = { "asdf" };
```

Here, str2 is also declared to be a string variable of size 5. It can accommodate a maximum of five characters including null character. The initializer-list consists of a string constant. In this variation, null character '\0' will be automatically appended to the end of string by the compiler.

In either of these variations, the size of the character array can be skipped, in which case, the size, the number of characters in the initializer-list would be automatically supplied by the compiler.

Example 10.11

```
char s1[] = { "abcd" };
```

The size of s1 would be 5, four characters plus one for the null character '\0'.

```
char s2[] = { 'a', 'b', 'c', '\0'};
```

The size of s2 would be four—three characters plus one for null character '\0'.

The strings being initialized can have white spaces (blank spaces, new line character and tab space character, etc.)

```
char s[20] = {"Programming with strings \n"};
```

Note the presence of the blank spaces and a new line character as part of the string.

PROGRAM 10.5   To illustrate strings initialization

```
#include <stdio.h>

int main(void)
{
        char s1[10] = { "Welcome" };
        char s2[10] = { 'a', 'd', 'f', 'g', '\0'};
        char s3[] = { "Welcome"};
        char s4[] = { "Programming with strings \n");

        printf("s1 = %s \n", s1);
        printf("s2 = %s \n", s2);
        printf("s3 = %s \n", s3);
        printf("s4 = %s n", s4);

        return 0;
}
```

Input–Output:

```
s1 = Welcome
s2 = adfg
s3 = Welcome
s4 = Programming with strings
```

10.4 ARITHMETIC AND RELATIONAL OPERATIONS ON CHARACTERS

Character variables and character constants can be included as part of arithmetic and relational expressions. When included, the ASCII values of the characters participate during their evaluation. (This is applicable to the computers, which use ASCII codes to represent characters. With computers supporting other computer codes, the corresponding numeric values equivalent are subjected to the operations. Here we assume that the underlying computers use ASCII codes). For example, consider the arithmetic expression 5 + 'a'. This is certainly valid in C. The value of the expression would be 5 + 97 = 102 where 97 is the ASCII value of 'a'.

Now consider the arithmetic expression 'b' − 'a'. The value of this expression turns out to be 1. Since ASCII value of 'b' is 98 and that of 'a' is 97.

Similarly, consider the relational expression 'a' > 50. The expression evaluates to true since the ASCII value of 'a' is 97 and 97 > 50 is certainly true. Consider another relational expression 'a' > 'z'. This expression evaluates to false since the ASCII value of 'z' is 122.

We know that a string is nothing but an array of char type. Similar to arrays of numeric type (int, float), individual characters of a string can be accessed by using the array name and the appropriate subscript values. The characters can be subjected to arithmetic and relational operations.

PROGRAM 10.6   To encrypt and decrypt a string

```
#include <stdio.h>

int main(void)
{
        char name[20];
        int i;

        printf("Enter a name \n");
        scanf("%s", name);
        printf("%s \n", name);
        for(i = 0; name[i] != '\0'; i++)
                name[i] = name[i] + 1;
        printf("Encrypted name = %s \n", name);

        for(i = 0; name[i] != '\0'; i++)
                name[i] = name[i] - 1;
        printf("Decrypted name = %s \n", name);

        return 0;
}
```

Input–Output:

```
Enter a name

Harsha
Encrypted name = Ibstib
Decrypted name = Harsha
```

Explanation:

name is declared to be a string variable and it can accommodate maximum 20 characters. It is to collect a name (input). **i** is declared to be a variable of int type and it is to access each character of the input string. In the body of the first for loop, 1 is added to the ASCII value of each character of the string with the statement name[i] = name[i] + 1. As a result, each character in the string is replaced by its next character in the ASCII sequence and encrypted name is displayed.

In the body of the second **for** loop, one is subtracted from the ASCII value of each character of the string with the statement name[i] = name[i] − 1. As a result, each character in the string is replaced by its preceding character in the ASCII sequence. As a result, the original name is obtained and it is displayed.

To find the number of occurrences of a character in a string

There are two inputs to the program. 1. String of characters, and 2. A single character. We use an array of char type to collect a string and a variable of type char to collect a character, and we keep a counter which is incremented when a character in the string is found to match with the given character during the course of traversing of the string from the first character till the last character is encountered.

Pseudocode   to find the number of occurrences of a character in a string

```
// Read a character to search for
Read ch
// Read a string
Read str

// Finding the number of occurrences of c in str begins
    count = 0;
    for( i = 0; str[i] != '\0'; i++)
        if (str[i] == ch)
            count++;
// Finding the number of occurrences of c in str ends
Display count
```

End pseudocode

PROGRAM 10.7   To find the number of occurrences of a character in a string

```
#include <stdio.h>

int main(void)
```

```
{
      char str[20], ch;
      int i, count;

      printf("Enter a character \n");
      scanf("%c", &ch);
      fflush(stdin);
      printf("Enter a string \n");
      gets(str);

      /* Finding the number of occurrences of c in str begins */

      count = 0;
      for( i = 0; str[i] != '\0'; i++)
           if (str[i] == ch)
                  count++;
      /* Finding the number of occurrences of c in str ends */
      printf("The number of occurrences of %c in %s is %d", ch, str, count);
      return 0;
}
```

Input–Output:

```
Enter a character
s

Enter a string
asdfgs

The number of occurrences of s in asdfgs is 2
```

Explanation:

str is declared to be a string variable of size 20. It can thus accommodate 20 characters and is to collect a string (input). **ch** is declared to be a variable of **char** type and it is to collect a character (input), the number of occurrences of which in **str** is to be found out. **i** and **count** are declared to be variables of **int** type. The variable **i** is to traverse the characters in **str** and **count** is to collect the number of occurrences of **ch** in **str** (output).

After a string is accepted into **str**, a **for** loop is set up to traverse each character of the string. Within the body of the loop, each character of the string is checked against **ch** for equality. In case of a match, the variable **count** is incremented. When the loop exits, the variable **count** will have the number of occurrences of the given character in the given string.

To count the number of upper case, lower case letters, digits and special characters in a string

There is only one input to the program, i.e. a string of characters. We use an array of char type to collect a string and we keep separate counters which are incremented when a character in the string is found to lie within the range of respective category of characters during the course of traversing the string from the first character till the last character is encountered.

Pseudocode to count the number of upper case, lower case letters, digits and special characters in a string

```
// Read a string
Read str

lc = 0
uc = 0
dc = 0
sc = 0
length = strlen(str);
for(i = 0; i < length; i++)
begin
      if ((str[i] >= 'a') && (str[i] <= 'z')) // lower case
            lc++;
      else if ((str[i] >= 'A') && (str[i] <= 'Z')) // upper case
            uc++;
      else if((str[i] >= '0') && (str[i] <= '9')) // digits
            dc++;
      else
            sc++;   //other characters
end
      display "Number of upper case letters = uc"
      display "Number of lower case letters = lc"
display "Number of Digits = dc"
      display "Number of special characters = sc
```

End pseudocode

PROGRAM 10.8 To count the number of upper case, lower case letters, digits and special characters in a string

---

```
#include <stdio.h>
#include <ctype.h>
#include <string.h>

int main(void)
{
      char str[40];
      int uc, lc, dc, sc, length, i;

      clrscr();
      printf("Enter a string \n");
      gets(s);

      lc = uc = dc = sc=0;
```

```
length = strlen(str);
for(i = 0; i < length; i++)
{
        if ((str[i] >= 'a') && (str[i] <= 'z'))
              lc++;
        else if ((str[i] >= 'A') && (str[i] <= 'Z'))
              uc++;
        else if((str[i] >= '0') && (str[i] <= '9'))
              dc++;
        else
              sc++;
}
printf(" The number of upper case letters = %d \n", uc);
printf(" The number of lower case letters = %d \n", lc);
printf(" The number of digits = %d \n", dc);
printf(" The number of special characters = %d \n", sc);

return 0;
}
```

Input–Output:

```
Enter a string
ASDhgjh134*&^

Given line of text
ASDhgjh134*&^

The number of upper case letters = 3
The number of lower case letters = 4
The number of digits = 3
The number of special characters = 3
```

Explanation:

In the above program, str is declared to be a string variable of size 40. The variables lc, uc, dc, sc, l and i are declared to be of int type. str is to collect a line of text. Maximum 39 characters can be accepted into it. lc is to collect number of lower case letters; uc is to collect number of upper case letters; dc is to collect number of digits; sc is to collect number of special characters in the given line of text.

First, a line of text is accepted into the string variable str. The length of str is then found out and is assigned to the variable l. lc, uc, dc and sc are set to 0. The for loop is to traverse each character in the line of text. As each character is taken, it is checked whether it is a lower case letter with the condition str[i] >= 'a' && str[i] <='z' If the condition is found to be true, lc is incremented. Similarly, for upper case letters, digits and special characters and the corresponding variables are incremented.

To find whether a string is palindrome or not

A string is said to be a palindrome if the string and its reverse are same.

Example 10.12

"madam" is a palindrome
The string "liril" is another example of a palindrome.

Pseudocode to find out whether a string is palindrome or not
```
// Read a string
Read str
l = strlen(str);
flag = 1;
for(i = 0; i <= l/2; i++)
      if ( str[i] != str[l - i - 1])
      begin
            flag = 0;
            break;
      end
      if (flag == 1)
            display "palindrome"
      else
            display "not a palindrome"
```
End pseudocode

PROGRAM 10.9   To find out whether a string is palindrome or not

```c
#include <stdio.h>

int main(void)
{
      char str[20];
      int l, i, flag;

      printf("Enter a string \n");
      gets(str);
      l = strlen(str);
      flag = 1;
      for(i = 0; i <= l/2; i++)
            if ( str[i] != str[l - i - 1])
            {
                  flag = 0;
                  break;
            }
      if (flag)
            printf("%s is a palindrome \n", str);
      else
      printf("%s is not a palindrome", str);

      return 0;
}
```

Input–Output:

```
Enter a string
madam
madam is a palindrome

Enter a string
ganesh
ganesh is not a palindrome
```

Explanation:

In the above program, str is declared to be a string variable and it is to collect a string (input). i and l are declared to be variables of int type. The variable i is to scan through the string and the variable l is to collect the length of the string.

After accepting a string into the variable str, it is subjected to the test of palindrome property. The segment of the program, responsible for finding out whether the string in str is palindrome or not, is the following.

```
l = strlen(str);
flag = 1;
for(i = 0; i <= l/2; i++)
    if ( str[i] != str[l - i - 1])
    {
        flag = 0;
        break;
    }
```

The length of the string is found out and it is assigned to the variable l. The variable flag is assigned 1 before the loop is entered and we assume that the string is palindrome. Within the body of the loop, the first character s[0] is checked against the last character s[l-1] if they match, the second character s[1] is matched against the last but one character s[l-2]. If they also match, the third character s[2] is checked against the last but two character s[l-3] and this is repeated till a mismatch is found or till half of the string is traversed, whichever occurs first. If there is any mismatch, the variable flag is assigned 0 and the loop is exited prematurely. Ultimately, the value of flag determines whether the string in str is palindrome or not. If flag retains 1, the string is displayed to be palindrome. Otherwise, it is displayed to be not a palindrome.

10.5   STRING MANIPULATIONS

The most commonly performed operations over strings are:

1. Finding the length of a string
2. Copying one string to another string
3. Concatenation of two strings
4. Comparing two strings
5. Searching substring in a string

All these operations are to be performed on a character by character basis. Let us now try to understand the logic involved and the built-in functions provided by C to perform these operations. Each of these operations is implemented using the underlying logic and using the built-in functions in the programs to follow. Since the string manipulation built-in functions are declared in the header file string.h, this file has to be included in all the programs which use these functions with the help of preprocessor directive #include.

To find the length of a string

Length of a string is defined to be the number of characters in it excluding the null character '\0'. To find the length of a string, we need to scan through the string; count the number of characters till the null character is reached. C provides a built-in function namely strlen() to find the length of a string. The prototype of strlen() is as follows.

```
int strlen(s );
```

Argument **s** represents a string. It can be a string constant or a string variable. The function returns an integer value, which is the length of the string.

Example 10.13

```
char s[20] = { "anbfdd" };
int l;
l = strlen(s);
```

l collects the length of **s** .

Pseudocode to find the length of a string
```
// Read a string
Read str

// finding the length begins
length = 0;
for( i = 0; str[i] != '\0'; i++)
     length++;
// finding the length ends

display length
End pseudocode
```

PROGRAM 10.10   To find the length of a string

```
#include <stdio.h>
#include <string.h>

int main (void)
{
      char str[20];
      int i, length;
```

```
      printf("Enter a string \n");
      scanf("%s", str);
```

```
/* Finding the length of s without using strlen() begins */
```

```
      length = 0;
      for( i = 0; str[i] != '\0'; i++)
            length++;
   printf("Length of %s = %d \n", str, length);
```

```
/* Finding the length of str without using strlen() ends */
```

```
length = strlen(str);
printf("Length of %s using strlen() = %d \n", str, length);
```

```
return 0;
}
```

Input–Output:

```
Enter a string
Ganguly
Length of "Ganguly" = 7
Length of "Ganguly" using strlen() = 7
```

Explanation:

str is declared to be an array of char type and of size 20. length and i are declared to be variables of int type. str is to collect the input string. variable length is to collect the length of the string in str. The variable i is to scan through the string accessing each character.

A string is read into str through the keyboard. The following segment finds the length of str without using strlen()

```
length = 0;
for( i = 0; str[i] != '\0'; i++)
      length++;
```

length is initialized to 0 before scanning through the string begins. When the loop is entered, scanning through the string begins. During the course of scanning, if the character is found to be not null character '\0', length is incremented by 1. The loop is exited when the null character is reached. So when the loop completes, length collects the length of str.

The length of str is found out using strlen() built-in function also.

To copy one string to another string

Suppose s1 and s2 are two string variables and s1 has the string "abcd". If we want to make a copy of s1 in s2, we cannot use the assignment statement s2 = s1. The assignment operator = is not defined over strings. Copying s1 to s2 should be done on a character by character basis. The first character in s1 should be assigned to the first location of s2, second character in s1 should be assigned to second location of s2 and so on till the null character in s1 is encountered. C provides `strcpy()` built-in function to copy one string to another. The syntax of the usage of `strcpy()` is as follows.

```
strcpy(s2, s1);
```

Here the string contained in s1 is copied to s2.

S1 can be a string constant or a string variable. But s2 should be a string variable and it should be large enough to collect the string in s1.

Example 10.14

```
char s1[20]={"abcd"}, s2[20];

strcpy(s2, s1);
```

As a result of this, s1 gets copied to s2. s2 now contains "abcd"

```
strcpy(s1, "xyz");
```

Here, the string constant "xyz" gets copied to s1. s1 now contains "xyz"

Pseudocode to copy one string to another string

```
// Read a string
Read str1
// copying str1 to str2 begins
     for( i = 0; str1[i] != '\0'; i++)
          str2[i] = str1[i];
     str2[i] = '\0';
// copying str1 to str2 ends
```

End pseudocode

PROGRAM 10.11   To copy one string to another string

```c
#include <stdio.h>
#include <string.h>
int main(void)
{
     char str1[20]="abcd", str2[20], str3[20], str4[20];
     int i;

     printf("String in str1 = %s \n", str1);

     /* Copying str1 to str2 without using strcpy() begins */

     for( i = 0; str1[i] != '\0'; i++)
          str2[i] = str1[i];
     str2[i] = '\0';
     printf("string in str2 = %s \n", str2);
```

```
        /* Copying str1 to str2 without using strcpy() ends */

        strcpy(str3, str1);    /* Copying string in a string variable */
        printf("string in str3 = %s \n", str3);
        strcpy(str4, "mno");    /* Copying a string constant */
        printf("string in str3 = %s \n", str4);

        return 0;
}
```

Input–Output:

```
string in str1 = abcd
string in str2 = abcd
string in str3 = abcd
string in str4 = mno
```

Explanation:

str1, str2, str3 and str4 are declared to be string variables of size 20. Each of the variables can thus accommodate up to 20 characters including the null character '\0'. The variable i is to scan through the strings. String variable str1 is initialized to "abcd" and it is displayed. The following segment of the program copies str1 to str2 without using strcpy().

```
for( i = 0; str1[i] != '\0'; i++)
    str2[i] = str1[i];
str2[i] = '\0';
```

The for loop is to scan through the string in str1 and assign its each character to the corresponding position in str2. When i takes 0, the first character in str1 is assigned to the first position in str2. When i takes 1, the second character in str1 is assigned to the second position in str2 and so on. The loop is terminated when the null character in str1 is encountered. Note that the null character '\0' is assigned to the last position in str2. This is required to mark the end of the string in it.

strcpy() is then used to copy string in str1 to str3 and a string constant "mno" to str4. The contents of both str3 and str4 are then displayed.

To compare two strings

Comparison of two strings is another most commonly performed operation over strings. We require this while searching for a string in a list of strings, while sorting a list of strings, etc. Suppose s1 and s2 are two strings. To find whether s1 is alphabetically greater than s2, we cannot use relational expression s1 > s2. To find whether s1 is alphabetically lower than s2, we cannot use relational expression s1 < s2. Similarly, s1 == s2 cannot be used to find whether s1 and s2 are equal or not. The relational operators are not defined over strings. So, comparison of two strings also should be done on a character by character basis. That is, comparison of the first pair of characters of s1 and s2, comparison of second pair of characters, and so on. C provides strcmp() built-in function to compare two strings.

The prototype of `strcmp()` is as follows.

```
int strcmp(s1, s2);
```

`s1` and `s2` represent two strings being compared. `s1` can be a string constant or a string variable. Similarly `s2` also. The function returns the numerical difference between the first non-matching pair of characters of `s1` and `s2`. It returns a positive value when `s1` is alphabetically greater than `s2`. It returns a negative value when `s1` is alphabetically lower than `s2`. It returns 0 when `s1` and `s2` are equal.

Example 10.15

```
char s1[20]={ "abc"}, s2[20]={"aac"};
int i;
i = strcmp(s1,s2);
```

`i` gets 1 since the numerical difference between the first non-matching pair 'b' of `s1` and 'a' of `s2` is 1.

```
char s1[20]={ "aac"}, s2[20]={"abc"};
    int i;
    i = strcmp(s1,s2);
```

`i` gets -1 since the numerical difference between the first non-matching pair 'a' of `s1` and 'b' of `s2` is -1.

```
char s1[20]={ "abc"}, s2[20]={"abc"};
    int i;
    i = strcmp(s1,s2);
```

`i` gets 0 since both the strings are equal.

Pseudocode to compare two strings

```
// Read a string
Read str1
// Read another string
Read str2
// comparing str1 and str2 begins
    i = 0
    while ((str1[i] == str2[i]) && (str1[i] != '\0'))
        i++
    diff = str1[i] - str2[i]
    display "Difference between str1 and str2 = diff"

// comparing str1 and str2 ends
```

End pseudocode

PROGRAM 10.12 To compare two strings

```
#include <stdio.h>
#include <string.h>
int main(void)
```

```
{
        char str1 [20] = {"abc"} , str2 [20] = {"aac"}, str3 [20] = {"abc"};
        int i, diff;

        printf ("str1 = %s str2 = %s \n", str1, str2);

/* comparing str1 and str2 without using strcmp() begins */

        i = 0;
        while ((str1[i] == str2[i]) && (str1[i] != '\0') &&
(str2[i]!='\0'))                         i++;
        diff = str1[i] - str2[i];
        printf ("Difference between %s and %s = %d \n", str1, str2, diff);

/* comparing str1 and str2 without using strcmp() ends */

        diff = strcmp(str1, str2); /* comparison using strcmp() */
        printf ("Difference between %s and %s = %d \n", str1, str2, diff);

        diff - strcmp(str2, str1);
        printf ("Difference between %s and %s = %d \n", str2, str1, diff);

        diff = strcmp(str1, str3);
        printf ("Difference between %s and %s = %d \n", str1, str3, diff);

        return 0;
}
```

Input–Output:

str1 = abc str2 = aac

Difference between abc and aac = 1
Difference between abc and aac = 1
Difference between aac and abc = -1
Difference between abc and abc = 0

Explanation:

str1, str2 and str3 are declared to be arrays of char type and all have been initialized. the integer variable i is to scan through the strings. diff is to collect the numeric difference of the ASCII values of the first non-matching pair of characters of two strings. The following segment of the program is to compare the strings str1 and str2 without using strcmp().

```
    i = 0;
    while((str1[i] == str2[i]) && ((str1[i] != '\0') && (str2[i] != '\0')))
i++;
    diff = str1[i] - str2[i];
```

The while loop repeats as long as the pairs of characters in str1 and str2 are same or the end of any of the strings is not reached. Once mismatch is found or the end of any of str1 and str2 is reached, the loop is terminated and the numerical difference between the non-matching pair of characters is assigned to diff.

Then, three calls are made to strcmp() In the first call, strings str1 and str2 are passed to strcmp(). The function returns 1, the numerical difference between the first non-matching pair (b, a) of str1 and str2 respectively indicating that str1 is alphabetically greater than str2.

In the second call, the strings str2 and str1 are passed to strcmp() The function returns -1, the numerical difference between the first non-matching pair (a, b) of str2 and str1 respectively indicating that str2 is alphabetically lower than str1.

In the third call, the strings str1 and str3 are passed to strcmp(). The function returns 0, indicating that both the strings are same.

To concatenate two strings

The process of appending one string to the end of another string is called concatenation. If s1 and s2 are two strings and when s2 is appended to the end of s1, s1 and s2 are said to be concatenated. The string s1 then contains its original string plus the string contained in s2. Similar to copying and comparing, appending s2 to s1 should be done on a character by character basis. C provides strcat() built-in function to concatenate two strings.

The prototype of strcat() is as follows.

```
strcat(s1,s2);
```

appends s2 to s1. s2 can be a string variable or a string constant. But s1 should be a string variable and the size of s1 should be large enough to collect even s2 also in addition to its own string.

Example 10.16

```
char s1[10] = { "abc" }, s2[10] = { "xyz" };

strcat(s1,s2);
```

s1 will now collect "abcxyz"

```
Pseudocode to concatenate two strings
// Read a string
Read str1
// read another string
Read str2
    // Concatenation of str1 and str2 begins

        for( i = 0; str1[i] != '\0'; i++)
        begin
        end

        for( j = 0; str2[j] != '\0'; j++)
            str1[i + j] = str2[j]
        str1[i + j] = '\0'
```

```
          display "After concatenation = str1"
```

```
   /* Concatenation of str1 and str2 ends
```
End pseudocode

PROGRAM 10.13   To concatenate two strings

```c
#include <stdio.h>
#include <string.h>

int main(void)
{
      char str1[20] = { "abc" }, str2[20] = { "def" }, str3[20] ={ "ghi"};
      int i, j;

      printf("str1 = %s str2 = %s \n", str1, str2);

/* Concatenation of str1 and str2 without using strcat() begins */
      for(i = 0; str1[i] != '\0'; i++);

      for(j = 0; str2[j] != '\0'; j++)
         str1[i + j] = str2[j];

      str1[i + j] = '\0';
      printf("After concatenation str1 = %s \n", str1);

/* Concatenation of str1 and str2 without using strcat() ends */

      strcat(str1, str3);
      printf(" str1 = %s \n", str1);
      strcat(str1, "jkl");
      printf(" str1 = %s \n", str1);

      return 0;
}
```

Input–Output:

```
str1 = abc str2 = def

After concatenation

str1 = abcdef

str1 = abcdefghi

str1 = abcdefghijkl
```

Explanation:

str1, str2 and str3 are declared to be arrays of char type and all are initialized strings. the integer variables i and j are to traverse the strings. String in str2 is appended to the end of the string in str1 by the following segment of the program.

```
for( i = 0; str1[i] != '\0'; i++);

for( j = 0; str2[j] != '\0'; j++)
        str1[i + j] = str2[j];

str1[i + j] = '\0';
```

The first for loop is to simply scan through the string str1. When the loop completes, the variable i points to the position of null character '\0' in str1. The second loop is to scan through the second string str2 till the end of it is reached. When j takes 0, the first character in str2 is assigned to the position of null character in str1. So, the null character in str1 is overwritten by the first character in str2. Subsequently, the remaining characters in str2 are appended to str1 and lastly, the null character '\0' is assigned to the last position of str1. The string in str1, "abcdef" is then displayed.

Then two calls are made to strcat(). In the first call, strcat(str1, str3), str3 is appended to str1. Since str3 had "ghi", str1 now becomes "abcdefghi" and is displayed. In the second call, strcat(str1, "jkl"), the string constant "jkl" is appended to str1. The new string "abcdefghijkl" in str1 is again displayed.

To find the position of one string in another string (indexing)

We will now write a program to find the position of occurrence of one string in another string. The C library provides a built-in function by name strstr() to perform this task. The program would thus simulate the working of the function.

Pseudocode to find the position of one string in another string (Indexing)

```
// Read the first string
Read str1
// Read the second string
Read str2
// Find the length of str1
len_str1 = strlen(str1);

// Find the length of str2
len_str2 = strlen(str2);

if (len_str2 > len_str1)
begin
            display  str2 can not be found in str1
            exit
end
```

```
for(i = 0; i < (len_str1 - len_str2 + 1); i++)
{
    flag = 1;
    for(j = 0; j < len_str2; j++)
        if (str1[i + j] != str2[j])
        {
            flag = 0;
            break;
        }
        if (flag)
            break;
}
if (flag == 1)
    display str2 is found in str1 at position i
else
    display str2 is not found in str1
```
End pseudocode

PROGRAM 10.14   To find the position of one string in another string (indexing)

```
#include <stdio.h>
#include <string.h>
#include <process.h>

int main(void)
{
    char str1[20], str2[20];
    int len_str1, len_str2, i, j, flag;


    printf("\n Enter the first string \n");
    scanf("%s", str1);
    printf("\n Enter the second string \n");
    scanf("%s", str2);

    len_str1 = strlen(str1);
    len_str2 = strlen(str2);

    if (len_str2 > len_str1)
    {
        printf("%s cannot be found in %s", str2, str1);
        exit(0);
    }
    for(i = 0; i < (len_str1 - len_str2 + 1); i++)
```

```
        {
                flag = 1;
                for(j = 0; j < len_str2; j++)
                        if (str1[i + j] != str2[j])
                        {
                                flag = 0;
                                break;
                        }
                        if (flag)
                        break;
        }
        if (flag)
                printf("%s is found in %s at position %d", str2, str1, i);
        else
                printf("%s is not found in %s", str2, str1);

        return 0;
}
```

Input–Output:

```
Enter the first string
abcdef

Enter the second string
bc

bc is found in abcdef at position 1
```

Explanation:

`str1` and `str2` are declared to be string variables of size 20. Both can collect strings consisting of maximum 19 characters. `str1` is to collect main string; `str2` is to collect a string, the position of occurrence of which in `str1` is to be found. `len_str1` and `len_str2`, i, j and flag are declared to be variables of `int` type. `len_str1` and `len_str2` are to collect the lengths of `str1` and `str2` respectively. i and j are to traverse the strings in `str1` and `str2` character by character.

len_str1 and len_str2 are assigned the lengths of the strings `str1` and `str2` respectively with the following statements

```
len_str1 = strlen(str1);
len_str2 = strlen(str2);
```

For the string `str2` to be a part of `str1`, essentially the length of `str2` should be less than or equal to that of `str1`. Otherwise, the question of occurrence of `str2` in `str1` does not arise. So the following segment of the program causes the program to exit gracefully with a proper message.

```
if (len_str2 > len_str1)
{
    printf("%s can not be found in %s", str2, str1);
    exit(0);
}
```

If the above condition is not true, then the procedure of finding the occurrence of str2 in str1 starts with the following segment.

```
for(i = 0; i < (len_str1 - len_str2 + 1); i++)
{
      flag = 1;
      for(j = 0; j < len_str2; j++)
            if (str1[i + j] != str2[j])
            {
                  flag = 0;
                  break;
            }
            if (flag)
            break;
}
```

Note that there are two loops, one nested within the other. The outer loop is to select the characters of the string str1 and the inner loop is to select the characters of the string str2. Also note the usage of the variable flag. During each iteration of the outer loop, it is assigned the value 1. When the inner loop is entered and if a mismatch occurs between the characters of str1 and str2 , the flag variable is assigned 0 and the inner loop is prematurely exited. If the string str2 is found in str1 the flag variable, the inner loop completely executes and the variable flag retains 1. Once the value of flag is not changed to 0 within the inner loop, the outer loop is exited prematurely indicating that the string str2 is found in str1.

10.6   TWO-DIMENSIONAL ARRAY OF char TYPE

We now know that we can use a character array to store a string. Suppose we need to deal with a list of five strings. Even though we can use 5-character arrays to store them by declaring them as follows:

```
char s1[20], s2[20], s3[20], s4[20], s5[20];
```

it would not be a wise idea. This is because the list of strings cannot be treated as a group in the programming environment. Therefore, we cannot perform collective manipulations over the list of names. The ideal data structure would be an array of character arrays, in other words, an array of two dimensions of char type which would be declared as follows.

```
char s[5][10];
```

Here, s is declared to be a 2-D array of **char** type and it can accommodate 5 strings with each string having maximum 10 characters including the null character ' \0 ' . Each string is identifiable by the array name followed by a pair of square brackets enclosing a subscript value. s [0] represents the first string, s [1] represents the second string and so on. As observed, all the five strings share a common name and are distinguishable by a subscript value.

s[0]	**S**	h	y	a	m	\0			
s[1]	**R**	a	g	h	u	\0			
s[2]	**R**	a	j	\0					
s[3]	**S**	h	a	n	k	a	r	\0	
s[4]	**M**	a	n	j	u	n	a	t	h	\0

PROGRAM 10.15 To accept a list of names and display them

```c
#include <stdio.h>

int main(void)
{
        char names[5][20];
        int i;

        printf("Enter five names \n");
        for( i = 0; i < 5; i++)
        scanf("%s", names[i]);

        printf("List of Names \n");
        for( i = 0; i < 5; i++)
        printf("%s \n", names[i]);

        return 0;
}
```

Input–Output:

```
Enter five names

Devaraj
Shobha
Girija
Jayanthi
Shantha

List of Names

Devaraj
Shobha
Girija
Jayanthi
Shantha
```

Explanation:

Here, **names** is declared to be two-dimensional array of **char** type of size 5*20. At maximum it can accommodate five names and the number of characters in each name can be up to 20 characters. The following segment of the program

```
for ( i = 0; i < 5; i++)
      scanf ("%s", names [i] );
```

is to accept five names into the 2-D array. Within the loop, when i takes 0, the first string is read into names [0], when i takes 1, the second string is read into names [1] and so on.

Similarly, the segment

```
for ( i = 0; i < 5; i++)
      printf ("%s \n", names [i] );
```

displays all the five names on the standard output.

10.6.1 Initialization of a 2-D Array of char Type

Just as we initialize arrays of two dimensions of numeric type, we can even think of initializing two-dimensional arrays of char type. We know that a two-dimensional array of char type is used to store a collection of strings. The initializer-list contains string constants separated by commas and the number of string constants should not exceed the size specified within the first pair of square brackets. Note that the size within the second pair of square brackets is a must and the size within the first pair of square brackets is optional.

PROGRAM 10.16   To illustrate initialization of strings

```
#include <stdio.h>
int main (void)
{
      char names [5] [10] = { "Raghav", "Nishu", "Harshith", "Asha", "Veena" };
      int i;

      printf ("List of Names \n");
      for (i = 0; i < 5; i++)
            printf ("%s\n", names [i] );

      return 0;
}
```

Input–Output:

```
List of names
Raghav
Nishu
Harshith
Asha
Veena
```

Note that in the above program, the initialization statement could have been written as:

```
char names[][10] = {"Raghav", "Nishu", "Harshith", "Asha", "Veena"};
```

where the size within the first pair of square brackets is omitted. In which case, the compiler finds the size by looking at the number of strings enclosed within the braces. Note also that the size specified within the second pair of brackets should be large enough to collect the largest string in the list and a null character.

To search for a name in a list of names

We use a two-dimensional array of `char` type to accommodate a list of names and a one-dimensional array of type `char` to store a name to be searched. We employ the linear search method to search for the name in the given list of names.

Pseudocode to search for a name in a list of names using linear search

```
//Read the number of names
Read n

// Read n names
for( i = 0; i < n; i++)
     read names[i]

// Read the name to be searched
Read sname

// Searching for sname in names begins

     flag = 0;
     for( i = 0; i < n; i++)
          if(strcmp(names[i], sname) == 0)
          begin
               flag = 1;
               break;
     end

// Searching for sname in names ends

     if (flag == 1)
          display sname is found
     else
          display sname is not found
End pseudocode
```

PROGRAM 10.17   To search for a name in a list of names

```
#include <stdio.h>
#include <string.h>
```

```c
int main(void)
{
    char names[10][20], sname[20];
    int i, flag;

    printf("Enter 10 Names \n");
    for( i = 0; i < 10; i++)
        scanf("%s", names[i]);

    printf("List of Names \n");
    for( i = 0; i < 10; i++)
    printf("%s \n", names[i]);

    printf("Enter name to be searched \n");
    scanf("%s", sname);

/* Searching for s in names begins */

    flag = 0;
    for( i = 0; i < 10; i++)
    if(strcmp(names[i], sname) == 0)
    {
        flag = 1;
        break;
    }

/* Searching for s in names ends */

    if (flag)
        printf("%s is found \n", sname);
    else
    printf("%s is not found \n", sname);

    return 0;
}
```

Input–Output:

```
Enter 5 Names
Nishu
Harsha
Devaraj
Shyam
Nitin

List of Names
Nishu
```

```
Harsha
Devaraj
Shyam
Nitin

Enter name to be searched
Nishu

Nishu is found
```

Explanation:

names is declared to be a two-dimensional array of char type of size 10 * 20. Maximum 10 names can be stored in it and each name can have up to 20 characters including the null character '\0'. sname is declared to be one-dimensional array of char type. It can accommodate a single name with the maximum length of 19 characters. 10 names are read into names. The name to be searched is read into sname. The following segment of the program is to search for sname in names.

```
flag = 0;
for( i = 0; i < 10; i++)
if(strcmp(names[i], sname) == 0)
{
      flag = 1;
      break;
}
```

The variable flag acts as a Boolean variable. Before searching for sname in names begins (before the for loop is entered), flag is set to 0. The for loop is to select each name in names and try to match them with sname by calling strcmp(). If any name in names is found to be matching with sname, flag is set to 1 and the loop is prematurely exited. The value of flag would thus determine whether sname is found in names or not. If flag retains 0, then it means that sname is not found in names. On the other hand, if flag gets 1 then it means that sname is found in names.

To sort a list of names alphabetically in the increasing order

Here also, we should use a two-dimensional array of char type to accommodate a list of names. After accepting a list of names into the 2-D array, we can use any sorting technique to sort the list. Let us employ the exchange sort method to arrange the names alphabetically in the increasing order. We know that sorting requires comparison and swapping of names, if needed, to be done repeatedly till the list is sorted. We use the built-in functions strcmp() and strcpy() to perform comparison and swapping respectively.

Pseudocode to sort a list of names alphabetically in the increasing order

```
// Read the number of names
Read n
//Read n names
for( i = 0; i < n; i++)
      read names[i]
```

```
// Sorting begins

for( i = 0; i < n - 1; i++)
for( j = i + 1; j < n; j++)
if (strcmp(names[i], names[j])>0)
     begin
            strcpy(tname, names[i]);
            strcpy(names[i], names[j]);
            strcpy(names[j], tname);
     end

// Sorting ends

// Sorted List
for( i = 0; i < n; i++)
     display names[i]
```
End pseudocode

PROGRAM 10.18   To sort a list of names alphabetically in the increasing order

---

```
#include <stdio.h>
#include <string.h>

int main(void)
{
     char names[5][20], tname[20];
     int i, j;

     printf("Enter 5 Names \n");
     for( i = 0; i < 5; i++)
          scanf("%s", names[i]);

     printf("Unsorted List of Names \n");
     for( i = 0; i < 5; i++)
          printf("%s \n", names[i]);

     /* Sorting begins */

     for( i = 0; i < 4; i++)
     for( j = i + 1; j < 5; j++)
     if (strcmp(names[i], names[j])>0)
     {
          strcpy(tname, names[i]);
          strcpy(names[i], names[j]);
          strcpy(names[j], tname);
     }
```

```
        /* Sorting ends */

        printf("Sorted List \n");
        for( i = 0; i < 5; i++)
                printf("%s \n", names[i]);

        return 0;
}
```

Input–Output:

```
Enter 5 Names
Nishu
Devaraj
Girija
Asha
Harsha

Unsorted List of Names
Nishu
Devaraj
Girija
Asha
Harsha

Sorted List
Asha
Devaraj
Girija
Harsha
Nishu
```

Explanation:

names is declared to be a two-dimensional array of **char** type of size 5 * 20. Maximum five names can be read into it and each name can have up to 20 characters including the null character '\0'. **tname** is declared to be a one-dimensional array of **char** type. It is used to store a name temporarily while sorting the list of names. Five names are read into the array names and they are displayed. The following segment of the program sorts the list of names.

```
for( i = 0; i < 4; i++)
for( j = i + 1; j < 5; j++)
if (strcmp(names[i], names[j])>0)
{
        strcpy(tname, names[i]);
        strcpy(names[i], names[j]);
        strcpy(names[j], tname);
}
```

The outer `for` loop is to select each name from the list one by one starting from the first name till the last but one, as indicated by the range of values `[0-3]` taken by i. The inner `for` loop is to select the next remaining names in the list of names. When i takes 0, the first name is selected. It is compared with all the remaining names, which are selected by j with the help of `strcmp()`. If necessary, the pair of strings being compared are interchanged. This produces the first alphabetically name, and it is placed in the first position of the array names. Note that three calls are made to `strcpy()` to interchange a pair of names. This is because, the assignment operator = is not defined over strings. This is repeated for all values of i. As a result, the list of names gets sorted. The sorted list is then displayed.

10.7 STRINGS AND FUNCTIONS

Strings can be passed as arguments to functions and within the body of the functions the strings can be subjected to required kind of manipulation. Later we understand that when we pass a string as an argument to a function, what we are passing is the address of the first character of the string. A function can even return a string (except automatic storage class) to the calling program. This is done by returning the starting address of the string.

10.7.1 Passing 1-D Arrays of `char` Type as Arguments to Functions

Arrays of `char` type can also be passed to functions as arguments on the lines of passing arrays of numeric type. The following are some examples of the functions which require strings as arguments.

simulation of `strlen()`

```
int str_len(char s[])
{
    int i, l = 0;

    for(i = 0; s[i] != '\0'; i++)
        l++;
    return (l);

}
```

simulation of `strcpy()`

```
void str_copy(char t[], char s[])
{
    int i;

    for(i = 0; s[i] != '\0'; i++)
        t[i] = s[i];
    t[i] = '\0';
}
```

simulation of `strcat()`

```
void str_cat(char t[], char s[])
{
        int i, l;
        for(i = 0;t[i] != '\0'; i++);
        for(j = 0; s[j] != '\0'; j++)
                t[i + j] = s[j];
        t[i + j] = '\0';
}
```

simulation of `strcmp()`

```
int str_cmp(char s[], char t[])
{
        int i;
        i=0;
        while (( s[i] == t[i]) && (s[i] !='\0') && (t[i] != '\0'))
                i++;
        return (s[i] - t[i]);
}
```

10.7.2 Passing 2-D Arrays of `char` to Functions

Passing 2-D arrays of `char` type is similar to passing 2-D arrays of numeric type. Specification of the size within the second pair of square brackets is a must for the array argument in the function prototype and in the function definition.

PROGRAM 10.19   To display a list of strings using a function

```
#include <stdio.h>
void display(char names[] [20], int n);

int main(void)
{
        char names[10] [20];
        int n, i;

        printf("Enter the number of names [1-10]\n");
        scanf("%d", &n);
        printf("Enter %d names \n", n);
        for(i = 0; i < n; i++)
                scanf("%s", names[i]);

        printf("The names are \n");
        display(names, n);

        return 0;
}
```

```
void display(char names[][20], int n)
{
        int i;

        for(i = 0; i < n; i++)
                printf("%s\n", names[i]);
}
```

Input–Output:

```
Enter the number of names [1-10]
3
Enter 3 names
Nitin
Raghu
Girish

The names are
Nitin
Raghu
Girish
```

Explanation:

The function display() is defined with a two-dimensional array of char type names and an integer value n as its formal arguments. The purpose of the function is to display n names in the list of names represented by the 2-D array names. Note that the size within the second pair of square brackets for the array is specified. This is required since the function should know the starting address of each name in the list of names. Within the function, a loop is set up to access each name in the list of names and it is displayed. In the main(), the function display() is called with the name of the 2-D array of char type and the number of names to be displayed as the actual arguments as display(names, n).

SUMMARY

- A string in C is a sequence of characters terminated by the null character '\0'.
- The string I/O is performed with the help of the functions scanf()–printf(), getchar()–putchar() and gets()–puts().
- The arrays of char type (string variables) can also be initialized while they are declared. The C language provides the programmers the complete control over the string manipulations.
- The most commonly performed manipulations include: Finding the length of a string, copying one string to another, concatenating two strings, comparison of two strings.
- The standard C library provides built-in functions namely strlen(), strcpy(), strcat() and strcmp() to carry out these operations.
- A two-dimensional array of char type can be used to store a list of strings.
- We can even pass a string or a list of strings to a function.

REVIEW QUESTIONS

10.1 Define a string.

10.2 What data structure is used to store a string?

10.3 Give an account of different functions used to input strings.

10.4 Give an account of different functions used to output strings.

10.5 Define the length of a string.

10.6 Explain the syntax and working of `strcpy()`.

10.7 Explain the syntax and working of `strcat()`.

10.8 Explain the syntax and working of `strcmp()`.

10.9 Explain the syntax and working of `strchr()`.

State whether the following are true or false

10.1 A string is a sequence of characters terminated by the null character `'\0'`.

10.2 C supports string built-in data type.

10.3 `scanf()` accepts even white spaces while accepting strings.

10.4 `gets()` reads a line of text terminates on encountering `'\n'`

10.5 `printf()` will stop displaying a string on encountering a white space.

10.6 `Puts()` replaces `'\0'` by `'\n'` on displaying a string.

10.7 We can pass strings to functions as arguments.

10.8 We can return a string from a function.

10.9 The function prototype `void display(char names[][], int n);` is valid.

10.10 `strchr()` returns the position of the first occurrence of a character in a string.

Identify errors, if any, in the following

10.1 `char str[] = {'a', 'b', 'c'};`

10.2 `strcpy("abc", "xyz");`

10.3 `int l;`
     `l = strlen(strcpy(s, "xyzl"));`

10.4 `if (strcmp("abc", "ABC") == 0)`
     `printf("abc and ABC are equal");`

10.5 `char names[][] = {"abc", "xyz"};`

PROGRAMMING EXERCISES

10.1 Write a program to count the number of words in a line of text.

10.2 Write a program to accept a string and display the ASCII character equivalent of each character in the string.

10.3 Write a program to convert a decimal integer number into its hexadecimal number equivalent.

Example: Decimal Number   126
          Hexadecimal Number   7E

10.4 Write a program to convert an hexadecimal integer number into its decimal number equivalent.

Example: Hexadecimal Number   7E
          Decimal Number   126

10.5 Modify the program 3 to convert a decimal real number into its hexadecimal number equivalent.

10.6 Modify the program 4 to convert an hexadecimal real number into its decimal number equivalent.

10.7 Write a program to convert an hexadecimal number into its binary equivalent.

Example: Hexadecimal Number   A23
          Equivalent Binary Number   1010 0010 0011

Note that each hexadecimal digit is replaced by its four bit binary equivalent.

10.8 Write a program to convert a binary number into its hexadecimal equivalent.

Example: Equivalent Binary Number   1010 0010 0011
          Hexadecimal Number   A23

Note that each group of four bits in the binary number is replaced by a hexadecimal digit.

10.9 Write a program to delete a given character in a string.

Example: Given String "abcdebfd"
          Given Character 'b'
          New String   "acdefd"

10.10 Write a program to extract left part of a string and display it. Inputs to the program are a string and the number of characters.

Example: Given String   "Bangalore"
          The number of characters 4
          Extracted string   Bang

10.11 Write a program to extract right part of a string and display it. Inputs to the program are a string and the number of characters.

Example:	Given String	"Bangalore"
	The number of characters	4
	Extracted string	"lore"

10.12 Write a program to extract a part of a string and display it. Inputs to the program are a string, starting position of the string and the number of characters.

Example:	Given String	"Bangalore"
	Starting Position	3
	The number of characters	4
	Extracted string	"ngal"

10.13 Write a program to find the number of occurrences of a substring in a string.

Example:	Given String	"abcdefcd"
	Substring	"cd"

Number of occurrences of "cd" in the given string = 2

10.14 Write a program to insert a substring at the specified position into a string.

Example:	Given String	"abcde"
	Substring	"xyz"
	Position	2
	Output string	"abxyzcde"

10.15 Write a program to delete a given substring from a string.

Example:	Given String	"abcde"
	Substring	"bc"
	Output string	"ade"

10.16 Write a program to search for a name in a list of names using binary search method.

10.17 Write a program to simulate strcmpi()

The function strcmpi() ignores the case of the letters while comparing. For example, the strings "abc" and "ABC" are treated to be equal.

10.18 Write a program to simulate strncpy()

The function strncpy() copies the specified number of characters of the source string to the target string.

10.19 Write a program to simulate strncat()

The function strncat() concatenates the specified number of characters of the source string to the target string.

10.20 Accept dates in 'dd-mm-yyyy' format into string variables and perform the following.
   (a) Validate the given date.
   (b) Find the difference between two dates.
   (c) Find whether date d1 is earlier than or later than or equal to the date d2.

10.21 Write a program to accept two strings s1 and s2 and delete each character in s1 that matches with any character in s2.

   Example: s1: abcdefg
                s2: xyahyd

   Resultant string: bcefg

10.22 Write a program to accept two strings s1 and s2 and display the first position in s1 where any character of s2 occurs.

   Example: s1: abcdefg
                s2: xyahyd

   Output: 0 (since the character 'a' of s2 is found in 0th position in s1.)

10.23 Write a program to accept n words (which form a sentence) one word at a time and output them on the screen as a sentence with a full stop at the end.

10.24 Write a program to accept a string and find whether it comprises of a decimal integer.

10.25 Write a program to accept a string and find whether it comprises of an octal integer.

10.26 Write a program to accept a string and find whether it comprises of a hexadecimal integer.

10.27 Write a program to accept a string and find whether it is a valid C identifier.

10.28 Write a program to accept a string and find whether it comprises of a decimal integer and convert it into an integer.

10.29 Write a program to accept a string and find whether it comprises of an octal integer and convert it into an octal integer.

10.30 Write a program to accept a string and find whether it comprises of a hexadecimal integer and convert it into a hexadecimal integer.

10.31 Write a program to accept an integer and convert into a string of decimal digits.

10.32 Write a program to accept an octal integer and convert into a string of octal digits.

10.33 Write a program to accept a hexadecimal integer and convert into a string of hexadecimal digits.

INTERVIEW QUESTIONS

10.1 What is the output of the following programs

```
(a) int main(void)
    {
        char a[5];
        a[0]='G';
        a[1]='O';
        a[2]='D';
        printf("%s",a);
```

```
      getch();
      return 0;
   }
(b) #include<stdio.h>
   int void main(void)
   {
      char x = 'A';
      printf("%d %d", sizeof(x), sizeof('A'));
      return 0;

   }
(c) #include<stdio.h>
   int main(void)
   {
      char s[] = "computer";
      s[5] = '(';
      printf("%s", s);

      printf("%c", s);
      return 0;
   }
(d) #include<stdio.h>
   int main(void)
   {
      char s[] = "computer";
      char t[] = "Science";
      char p[] = "Department";
      printf("%s", strcat(strcpy(s,t), p));
      return 0;

   }
```

10.2 What is the difference between char s[5]={'A', 'B', 'C', 'D', '\0'} and char s[5] = "ABCD"?

10.3 What is the difference between character array and a string?

10.4 Write a C code to print the string in reverse order.

10.5 Identify the error in the following program (if any).

```
#include<stdio.h>
int main(void)
{
    char s[10] = "Computer Science";
    printf("%c %s", s, s);
    return 0;
}
```

10.6 What is the difference between strcmp() and strncmp()?

11

Structures and Unions

11.1 INTRODUCTION

Each entity in the world is described by a number of characteristics. These descriptive characteristics of an entity are called its attributes. For instance, the entity, employee, is characterized by the attributes empno, name, designation, salary, etc. The entity, book is characterized by its author, title, publisher, number of pages and price. It can be noticed that the attributes of an entity may be of different types. If we consider the entity book, author, title and publisher are strings, the number of pages is of `int` type and price may be of **float** type. To store the details of a book, no doubt, we can declare the following variables and use them.

```
char author[20], title[20], publisher[20];
int pages;
float price;
```

Even though these variables can be used to store a book's details, the problem is, these variables are not treated as a single unit and hence do not necessarily reflect the fact that all these describe a single book. What if we have to deal with more than one book? Say 10 books. This approach turns out to be prohibitive since it is difficult to establish mapping between a book and its details.

We now know that an array enables us to identify a group of similar data items by a common name and thus facilitates easier collective manipulation. In many programming situations such as discussed above, we do require to identify a group of data items, which may be of dissimilar types, also by a common name with a provision for accessing individual data items.

The concept of structures accomplishes this. The concept of structures is analogous to the concept of records, a database terminology, and helps in coining new user-defined data types or derived types.

11.2 DEFINITION OF STRUCTURE TEMPLATE

Structure Template Definition helps in creating a format or prototype of the user-defined data type. The format or prototype of the user-defined data type allows us to logically relate a group of data items which may be of different types.

The syntax of defining a `structure template` is as follows.

```
struct tag-name
    {
            data-type member1;
            data-type member2;
            .
            .
            data-type membern;
    };
```

where **struct** is a keyword. `tag-name` is a user-defined name, it is the name of the structure, a valid C identifier. `data-type` refers to any valid data type supported by C and `member1`, `member2`, ..., `membern` are the members of the structure. It is important to note that `member1`, `member2`, ..., `membern` are not variables by themselves. So, no memory locations get allocated at this juncture. Memory locations get allocated only when variables of the structure are declared.

11.3 DECLARATION OF STRUCTURE VARIABLES

Syntax of declaring a variable of structure type:

```
struct tag-name variable-name;
```

As a result of this, n memory locations get allocated. Each location is identified by the structure variable name followed by a dot followed by the member name. Dot is used to access each individual member and it is called `member operator`. The dot operator expects the structure variable name to the left of it and member name to the right of it. `variable-name.member1` is used to access the value of `member1`, `variable-name.member2` is used to access value of member2 of the structure, and so on.

Example 11.1

```
struct emp
{
      int empno;
      char name[20];
      float salary;
};
```

`empno`, `name` and `salary` are now logically grouped.

struct `emp e;`

e is declared to be a variable of **struct** emp type. This results in allocation of three locations which are contiguous in nature, as follows.

    e.empno   e.name   e.salary

All the three data items share the common name e. and are distinguishable by members empno, name and salary. The operator. (dot) called member operator enables us to access each data item separately. A data item is referred to by structure variable name followed by a. (dot), followed by the corresponding member name. e.empno refers to employee number, e.name refers to employee name and e.salary refers to the salary of employee.

It is important to note that e.empno is a variable of **int** type, e.name as an array of **char** type and e.salary is a variable of **float** type when taken in isolation.

We can even declare variables of structure type while defining the structure template itself. The syntax of this kind of declaration is as follows.

```
struct tag-name
      {
              data-type member1;
              data-type member2;
              data-type member3;
                 .
                 .
                 .
              data-type membern;
      } variable_1, variable_2,…., variable_n;
```

Example 11.2

```
struct emp
{
      int empno;
      char name[20];
      float salary;
} e1, e2;
```

where **e1** and **e2** are variables of **struct** emp type.

Definition of Structure

> A structure can be defined to be a group of logically related data items, which may be of different types, stored in contiguous memory locations, sharing a common name, but distinguished by its members.

The following statements can be used to provide values to members of the structure variable.

```
e.empno = 121;
strcpy(e.name, "Raghav");
e.salary = 12000;
```

The locations allocated for e get filled up as follows.

e.empno	e.name	e.salary
121	Raghav	12000

The following `scanf()` and `printf()` statements are used to accept and display an employee's details.

```
scanf("%d%s%f", &e.empno, e.name, &e.salary);
printf("%d%s%f", e.empno, e.name, e.salary)
```

PROGRAM 11.1   To accept and display the details of two employees

---

```
#include <stdio.h>

struct emp
{
        int empno;
        char name[20];
        float salary;
};

int main(void)
{
        struct emp e;

        printf("Enter empno, name and salary of the employee \n");
        scanf("%d%s%f", &e.empno, e.name, &e.salary);
        printf("Details of the employee \n");
        printf("%6d%15s%8.2f\n", e.empno, e.name, e.salary);
        return 0;
}
```

Input–Output:

```
Enter empno, name and salary of the employee
123 Bhaskar 23000

Details of the employee
123 Bhaskar   23000.00
```

11.4   INITIALIZATION OF STRUCTURE VARIABLES

If we know the values of structure variables in advance, we can even think of initializing structure variables also. The syntax of initializing a structure variable is as follows.

```
struct tag-name variable-name = {member1-value, member2-value, ...,
                                          membern-value };
```

If a member is of **char** type, its value should be enclosed within single quotes. If a member is an array of **char** type, its value should be enclosed within double quotes.

Example 11.3

To initialize a variable of type **struct** emp:

```
struct emp e = { 121, "Anju", 20000 };
```

e.empno	e.name	e.salary
121	Raghav	12000

If the number of values listed in the `initializer-list` is less than the number of members of the structure, trailing members that are unmatched to initializers are implicitly initialized to 0 (null character in the case of strings).

Example 11.4

```
struct emp e = {124};
```

Here only the first member empno gets the value. The other two remaining members name and salary are set to null character and 0 respectively as shown below.

e.empno	e.name	e.salary
124	\0	0

The members of a structure variable belonging to static storage class are automatically initialized with 0s in the case of numeric data types and null characters in the case of strings.

Example 11.5

```
static struct emp e;
```

e.empno	e.name	e.salary
0	/0	0

PROGRAM 11.2   To illustrate initialization of structure variables while declaring

---

```
#include <stdio.h>

struct emp
{
        int empno;
        char name[20];
        float salary;
};

int main(void)
{
        struct emp e1 = {123, "Harshith", 23456};
        struct emp e2 = {124};
```

```
    static struct emp e3;

    printf("Details of the employee e1 \n");
    printf("%6d%15s%8.2f\n", e1.empno, e1.name, e1.salary);
    printf("Details of the employee e2 \n");
    printf("%6d%15s%8.2f\n", e2.empno, e2.name, e2.salary);
    printf("Details of the employee e3 \n");
    printf("%6d%15s%8.2f\n", e3.empno, e3.name, e3.salary);

    return 0;
}
```

Input–Output:

```
Details of the employee e1
   123        Harshith 23456.00

Details of the employee e2
   124                     0.00

Details of the employee e3
     0                     0.00
```

Note: The members of a structure variable cannot be initialized selectively.

11.5 OPERATIONS ON STRUCTURES

The number of operations which can be performed over structures is limited. The following are the permissible operations.

1. Accessing the individual members of a structure variable with the help of member operator (dot operator).

   Example 11.6
   In the case of a variable of type struct emp,

   ```
   struct emp e;
   e.empno = 10;
   ```

   10 is assigned to empno member of e .

   ```
   strcpy(e.name, "Ram");
   ```

   the string "Ram" is copied to name member of e.

2. Assigning one structure variable to another of the same type.

   Example 11.7

   ```
   struct emp e1= { 12, "Ram", 2900}, e2;
   e2 = e1;
   e1  has been assigned to e2 .
   ```

3. Retrieving the size of a structure variable using `sizeof()` operator.

   ```
   struct emp e;
   int s;
   s = sizeof(e);
   ```

4. Retrieving the address of a structure variable using `&` (`address of`) operator.

   ```
   struct emp e;
   &e gives the address of e.
   ```

5. Passing and returning a structure variable value to and from a function.
6. Checking whether two structure variables of same type are equal using `==` if `s1` and `s2` are two variables of the same structure type, `s1==s2` returns `1` if all the members of `s1` are equal to the corresponding members of `s2`, otherwise it returns `0`.
7. Checking whether two structure variables of same type are not equal using `!=` if `s1` and `s2` are two variables of the same structure type, `s1!=s2` returns `1` if all the members of `s1` are not equal to the corresponding members of `s2`, otherwise it returns `0`.

Note that not all compilers support the last two operations. For example, in case of Microsoft C each pair of the corresponding members should be compared separately.

PROGRAM 11.3   To illustrate the concept of structures and permissible operations over them

---

```c
#include <stdio.h>

struct emp
{
        int empno;
        char name[20];
        float salary;
};

int main(void)
{
        struct emp e1, e2;
        int size;

        printf("Enter empno, name and salary \n");
        scanf("%d%s%f", &e1.empno, e1.name, &e1.salary);
        size = sizeof(e1);
        printf("\n the number of bytes required for e1 =%d \n\n", size);
        e2 = e1;
        printf("After assigning e1 to e2 \n\n");
        printf("e2.empno = %d\n", e2.empno);
        printf("e2.name = %s\n", e2.name);
        printf("e2.salary = %8.2f\n\n", e2.salary);
        printf("Address of e1 = %u \n", &e1);

        return 0;
}
```

Input–Output:

```
Enter empno, name and salary
123 Nishu 3456
The number of bytes required for e1 = 26

After assigning e1 to e2

e2.empno = 123
e2.name = Nishu
e2.salary = 3456.00

Address of e1 = 65498
```

Explanation:

e1 and e2 are declared to be variables of struct emp type, both can accommodate details of an employee. Details of an employee are accepted into the variable e1. The number of bytes occupied by a variable of struct emp type is found out with the help of the operator sizeof () by passing e1 to it. The value returned by sizeof () is then displayed. To illustrate the fact that structure variables assignment is permissible, e1 is assigned to e2. The contents of e2 are then displayed. The address of operator & is used with e1 to obtain its address and it is then displayed.

11.6 ARRAYS AND STRUCTURES

Arrays can be treated in conjunction with the concept of structures in two different ways: One, by arraying structures themselves and two, by making arrays as members of structures.

11.6.1 Array of Structures

So far, we have dealt with arrays of fundamental data types (e.g. **int**, **float**, **char**) supported by C. Let us now explore the need for and possibility of using arrays of user-defined data type, structures, as well.

We know that a variable e of type **struct** emp can accommodate details (empno, name and salary), of a single employee. If we are required to deal with more than one employee's details, say 5 or even 10, Declaration of so many variables of **struct** emp type and using those variables would not be a wise idea. This is because collective manipulations cannot be performed over them easily. We would naturally be inclined to use the concept of array of **struct** emp type because of the flexibility provided by arrays in performing collective manipulations. C does support arraying of structures.

Suppose 5 employees' details are to be dealt with, we would declare an array of **struct** emp of size 5 as follows.

struct emp e[5];

Memory for the array gets allocated as follows:

	empno	name	salary
e[0]			
e[1]			
e[2]			
e[3]			
e[4]			

Here, the array elements e[0],e[1], ...,e[4] are variables of **struct** emp type and thus each can accommodate an employee's details. Since all the variables share a common name e and are distinguishable by subscript values [0–4], collective manipulation over the structure elements becomes easy.

PROGRAM 11.4 To illustrate an array of structures

```c
#include <stdio.h>

struct emp
{
        int empno;
        char name[20];
        float salary;
};

int main(void)
{
        struct emp e[10];
        int i, n;

        printf("Enter the number of employees [1-10]\n");
        scanf("%d", &n);

        printf("\n Enter %d employees' details \n", n);
        for( i = 0; i < n; i++)
                scanf("%d%s%f", &e[i].empno, e[i].name, &e[i].salary);
        printf("\n Employees' details \n");
        for( i = 0; i < n; i++)
                printf("\n %4d%15s%7.2f \n", e[i].empno, e[i].name, e[i].salary);

        return 0;
}
```

Input–Output:

```
Enter the number of employees [1-10]
2
```

```
Enter 2 employees' details
123 Nishu 25000
124 Harsha 20000

Employees' details
123 Nishu 25000.00
124 Harsha 20000.00
```

Explanation:

In the above program, **e** is declared to be an array of **struct** emp type and size 10, maximum 10 employees' details can be stored in it. The variable **n** is to collect the number of employees which should lie between 1 and 10 inclusive. **i** ranges from 0 to n-1 in the **for** loop used, thereby selecting each employee one-by-one. After accepting the number of employees to be stored in **e** into the variable **n**, **n** employees' details are accepted and they are displayed by the program segments

```
for( i = 0; i < n; i++)
scanf("%d%s%f", &e[i].empno, e[i].name, &e[i].salary)
```

and

```
for( i = 0; i < n; i++)
printf("\n %4d%15s%7.2 \n", e[i].empno, e[i].name, e[i].salary);
```

respectively.

Initialization of arrays of structures

Just as we initialize arrays of built-in type, we can initialize arrays of structures also. The following program illustrates initializing the elements of arrays of structures.

PROGRAM 11.5   To illustrate initialization of arrays of structures

```
struct emp
{
        int empno;
        char name[20];
        float salary;
};


int main(void)
{
        struct emp e[2] = { {121, "Nishu", 2345},
                            {122, "Harshith", 23498}};

        printf("Employee details \n");
        for(i = 0; i < 2; i++)
        printf("%6d%20s%8.2f\n", e[i].empno, e[i].name, e[i].salary);
        return 0;
}
```

Input–Output:

Employee details

```
121        Nishu 2345.00
122        Harshith 23498.00
```

To search for an employee in a list of employees using linear search method

Suppose we have a list of employees' details and we are to search for an employee in the list with the help of the value of any field (like empno, name) of the employees' details. Here, in the program that we develop, we use the concept of array of structures to store the employees' details and a variable of appropriate type to collect the field value and employ the search procedure to search for the required employee in the list employees. The following program accomplishes the task of searching for an employee by means of empno.

Pseudocode to search for an employee in a list of employees using linear search method

```
// Read the no. of employees
Read n

// Read n employees' details
for( i = 0; i < n; i++)
      read e[i].empno, e[i].name, e[i].salary

//Read empno of the employee to be searched
Read eno

// Searching begins
flag = 0
for( i = 0; i < n; i++)
      if (eno == e[i].empno)
      begin
            flag = 1;
            break;
      end

// Searching ends
if (flag == 1)
      display found
else
      display Not found
End pseudocode
```

PROGRAM 11.6   To search for an employee in a list of employees

```c
#include <stdio.h>
#include <string.h>

struct emp
{
        int empno;
        char name[20];
        float salary;
};

int main(void)
{
        struct emp e[10];
        int i, n, flag;
        char sname[20];

        printf("Enter the number of employees \n");
        scanf("%d", &n);

        printf("Enter %d employees' details \n", n);
        for( i = 0; i < n; i++)
        scanf("%d%s%f", &e[i].empno, e[i].name, &e[i].salary);
        printf("Enter the name of the employee to be searched \n");
        scanf("%s", sname);

        printf("%d employees' details \n", n);
        for( i = 0; i < n; i++)
        printf("\n%5d%10s%10.2f \n", e[i].empno, e[i].name, e[i].salary);

        printf("\n the name of the employee to be searched \n");
        printf("\n %10s \n", sname);

        /* Searching begins */

        flag = 0;
        for( i = 0; i < n; i++)
        if (strcmp(e[i].name, sname)==0)
        {
                flag = 1;
                break;

        }

        /* Searching ends */
```

```
        if (flag == 1)
                printf ("found");
        else
                printf ("Not found");

        return 0;
}
```

Input–Output:

```
Enter the number of employees
2

Enter 2 employees' details
123 Nishu 24000 124 Harsha 34000

Enter the name of the employee to be searched
Nishu

Employees' details
123    Nishu 24000.00
124    Harsha 34000.00

The Name of the employee to be searched
Nishu

found
```

Explanation:

e is declared to be an array of **struct** emp type and of size 10. It is to store a list of employees. Maximum 10 employees' details can be accepted into it. **sname** is declared to be an array of **char** type and this is to collect the name of an employee to be searched in the list. **i**, **n** and **flag** are declared to be variables of **int** type. **n** is to collect the number of employees, **i** is to traverse the structure elements and **flag** is to collect 1 (true) or 0 (false) depending on whether the employee being searched is found in the list or not.

After accepting the number of employees into the variable n, n employees' details are accepted into the variable e, the list of employees' details is now available in e, and the name of the employee to be searched is accepted into the string variable sname. Searching for an employee with the name sname in the list is accomplished by the following segment of the program.

```
flag = 0;
for ( i = 0; i < n; i++)
if (strcmp (e[i].name, sname) ==0)
{
        flag = 1;
        break;
}
```

Initially, flag is set to 0 (false) assuming that employee with the name in sname is not found in the list. The `for` loop selects each employee one by one and the selected employee's name is compared with the name in sname (note the use of `strcmp()`). If there is found to be a match, flag is set to 1 (true) and the loop is exited. So flag is set to 1 (true) only when a match is found between the name of an employee in the list and sname, otherwise flag retains 0 (false) only. Thus, the value of flag determines whether the employee being searched is found in the list or not. After the searching process, depending on the value of the variable flag, the result is displayed.

To sort a list of employees

The concept of array of structures is useful even when we need to arrange a list of records in some order. Suppose we have a list of employees' details and we are to sort the records in the increasing order of salary, we tend to use an array of structure with the structure template having the members like empno, name, salary, designation etc. and work on it. The following program sorts the employees' details in the increasing order of salary.

To sort a list of employees using exchange sort method

Pseudocode to sort a list of employees using exchange sort method
```
//Read the no. of employees
Read n
//Read n employees' details
for( i = 0; i < n; i++)
        read e[i].empno, e[i].name, e[i].salary


// sorting begins
for( i = 0; i < n - 1; i++)
for( j = i + 1; j < n; j++)
        if ( e[i].salary > e[j].salary)
                swap e[i] and e[j]


// sorting ends

//Sorted List
for( i = 0; i < n; i++)
        display e[i].empno, e[i].name, e[i].salary
```
End pseudocode

PROGRAM 11.7   To sort a list of employees in the increasing order of salary

---

```c
#include <stdio.h>

struct emp
{
        int empno;
        char name[20];
        float salary;
};
```

```c
int main(void)
{
        struct emp e[10], temp;
        int i, j, n;

        printf("Enter the number of employees [1-10]\n");
        scanf("%d", &n);

        printf("Enter %d employees' details \n", n);
        for(i = 0; i < n; i++)
        scanf("%d%s%f", &e[i].empno, e[i].name, &e[i].salary);

        printf("Unsorted list of employees' details \n");
        for(i = 0; i < n; i++)
        printf("%4d%15s%7.2f\n", e[i].empno, e[i].name, e[i].salary);

        /* sorting begins */

        for(i = 0; i < n - 1; i++)
        for(j = i + 1; j < n; j++)
                if (e[i].salary > e[j].salary)
                {
                        temp = e[i];
                        e[i] = e[j];
                        e[j] = temp;
                }

        /* sorting ends */

        printf("sorted List \n");
        for( i = 0; i < n; i++)
                printf("%4d%15s%7.2f\n", e[i].empno, e[i].name, e[i].sal-
ary);

        return 0;
}
```

Input–Output:

```
Enter the number of employees [1-10]
2

Enter 2 employees' details
123 Nishu 35000
124 Harsha 23000
```

Unsorted list of employees' details

```
123        Nishu     35000.00
124        Harsha    23000.00
```

Sorted List

```
124        Harsha    23000.00
123        Nishu     35000.00
```

Explanation:

e is declared to be an array of struct emp type with size 10, maximum 10 employees' details can be accepted and stored in it. So **e** is to store the details of a list of employees, which are to be sorted in the increasing order of salary. **temp** is also declared to be a variable of struct emp type and it is used to temporarily collect details of an employee during the process of sorting. **i**, **j** and **n** are declared to be variables of **int** type. **i** and **j** are to traverse the structure elements and **n** is to collect the number of employees.

After accepting the number of employees into the variable n, details of n employees are accepted into the array variable e and are displayed. The employee records are sorted in the increasing order of salary by the following segment of the program.

```
for(i = 0; i < n - 1; i++)
for(j = i + 1; j < n; j++)
      if ( e[i].salary > e[j].salary)
      {
            temp = e[i];
            e[i] = e[j];
            e[j] = temp;
      }
```

Sorting proceeds as follows: when **i** takes 0, first employee in the list is selected. Salary of the first employee is compared with those of the remaining employees. The remaining employees are selected by the inner-loop. **j** ranges from 1 to n-1. If need be, employees records being compared are interchanged. When the inner-loop completes, employee record with the lowest salary is made available in the first position, i.e. e[0]. When i takes 1, the second employee is selected, his salary is compared with that of the remaining employees. During the process, if need be, two employees records being compared are interchanged. When the inner-loop completes, employee record with the second lowest salary is made available in the second position of the array, i.e. e[1]. This is repeated till the outer-loop completes.

11.6.2 Arrays within Structures

We have already explored the need for and the possibility of using arrays within structures. In the previous programs, we used an array of **char** type as a member of **struct** emp to store name of an employee. However, the array was treated in its entirety. The array name was used to refer to the entire sequence of characters forming a name.

Now let us try to make an array of **int** type as a member of a structure, where we need to deal with each integer value of the array. Suppose we need to maintain a list of students' details (Reg_no, Name, Marks in five subjects). The structure template definition will be as follows.

```
struct student
{
    int regno;
    char name[20];
    int marks[5];
};
```

PROGRAM 11.8   To create a list of students' details and display them

```
#include <stdio.h>

struct student
{
    int reg_no;
    char name[20];
    int marks[5];
    int total;
    float percent;
};

int main(void)
{
    struct student s[10];
    int i, n, j;

    printf("Enter the number of students \n");
    scanf("%d", &n);
    for( i = 0; i < n; i++)
    {
        printf("Enter reg_no, name of student-%d \n", i+1);
        scanf("%d%s", &s[i].reg_no, s[i].name);
        printf("Enter marks in five subjects of %s \n", s[i].name);
        for( j = 0; j < 5; j++)
            scanf("%d", &s[i].marks[j]);
    }

    /* Finding the total and percentage begins */

    for( i= 0; i < n; i++)
    {
        s[i].total = 0;
        for( j = 0; j < 5; j++)
            s[i].total += s[i].marks[j];
        s[i].percent = (float)s[i].total/5;
    }
```

```
            /* Finding the total and percentage ends */
            printf("\n Reg-No Name Percentage \n");
            for( i = 0; i < n; i++)
                    printf("%6d%15s%7.2f \n", s[i].reg_no, s[i].name, s[i].per-
cent);

            return 0;
}
```

Input–Output:

```
Enter the number of students
2
Enter reg_no, name of student-1
1234      Nishchith
Enter marks in five subjects of Nishchith
67 78 76 59 90

Enter reg_no, name of student-2
1235 Harshith

Enter marks in five subjects of Harshith
87 67 65 59 89
```

Reg_No	Name	Percentage
1234	Nishchith	74.00
93	Harshith	73.40

Explanation:

struct student is defined with members **regno** (int), **name** (array of char), **marks** (an array of int with size 5), **total** (float), **percent** (float). A variable of **struct** student can thus capture Register number, Name, Marks scored in five subjects, Total marks and Percentage of marks of a student.

In main(), **s** is declared to be an array of **struct** student type with size 10. It can thus accommodate maximum 10 students' details. **n** and **i** are declared to be variables of **int** type. **n** is to accept the number of students [1-10]. **i** is to traverse the structure elements.

After accepting the number of students into the variable **n**, **n** students' details are accepted into the array variable **s** by the segment of the program.

```
for( i = 0; i < n; i++)
{
        printf("Enter reg_no, name of student-%d \n", i+1);
        scanf("%d%s", &s[i].reg_no, s[i].name);
        printf("Enter marks in five subjects of %s \n", s[i].name);
        for( j = 0; j < 5; j++)
                scanf("%d", &s[i].marks[j]);
}
```

Note the nesting of two loops. The outer-loop (i-loop) is to select each student. The inner-loop (j-loop) is to select marks in five subjects for each student.

After the details are fed into the array **s**, total marks and percentage of each student are found out by the following segment of the program.

```
for( i= 0; i < n; i++)
{
      s[i].total = 0;
      for( j = 0; j < 5; j++)
            s[i].total += s[i].marks[j];
      s[i].percent = (float)s[i].total/5;
}
```

when **i** takes 0, the first student is selected. **s[0].total** is set to 0 initially. Then the inner-loop selects marks of the first student in five subjects and adds them to **s[0].total**. Percentage of marks of the student is then assigned to **s[0].percent**. This is repeated for all values of **i** .

Register number, Name and Percentage of marks of all the students are then displayed in tabular form.

11.7   STRUCTURE WITHIN STRUCTURE

We know that structure enables us to make a group of heterogeneous types of data items. So far, our discussion was confined to heterogeneity with respect to fundamental data types **int, float, char**, etc. Let us now explore the possibility of making a group of data items of user-defined types also in addition to data items of built-in type. This is where the concept of nesting one structure within another comes into picture. Structures of one type are made the members of another structure.

Example 11.8
```
struct date
{
      int day, month, year;
};

struct emp
{
      int empno;
      char name[20];
      struct date doj;
      float salary;
};
```
Here, the structure template for date includes three members d, m and y. A variable of **struct** date type can be used to store a date. Within the structure template for employee, a variable of type **struct** date doj has been used as a member. A variable of **struct** emp type thus can accommodate empno, name, date of joining and salary of an employee.

struct emp e;

Here, e can represent the details of an employee with e.empno, e.name, e.salary and e.doj representing empno, name, salary and date of joining of the employee respectively. Since e.doj becomes a variable of **struct** date type. e.doj.day, e.doj.month and e.doj.year represent day, month and year part of doj. Note the use of two dots.

e.empno
e.name
e.doj is a variable of struct date type

PROGRAM 11.9   To illustrate the concept of structure within the structure

---

```c
#include <stdio.h>

struct date
{
        int day, month, year;
};

struct emp
{
        int empno;
        char name[20];
        struct date doj;
        float salary;
};

int main(void)
{
        struct emp e;

        printf("Enter empno, name, doj and salary \n");
        scanf("%d%s%d%d%d%f", &e.empno, e.name, &e.doj.day, &e.doj.month,
&e.doj.year, &e.salary);

        printf("Empno = %d \n", e.empno);
        printf("Name = %s \n", e.name);
        printf("DOJ = %d/%d/%d \n", e.doj.day, e.doj.month, e.doj.year);
        printf("Salary = %7.2f \n", e.salary);

        return 0;
}
```

Input–Output:

```
Enter empno, name, doj and salary
1234 Raghav 12 3 2001 3456
```

```
Empno:    1234
Name:     Raghav
DOJ:      12/3/2001
Salary:   3456.00
```

Explanation:

struct date is defined with three members **day**, **month** and **year** all of **int** type. A variable of **struct** date type can thus represent a date. struct emp, another structure, is defined with members **empno** (int), **name** (array of char), **doj** (struct date) and **salary** (float). A variable of **struct** emp type can thus accommodate employee Number, Name, Date of joining and Salary of an employee.

In main(), **e** is declared to be an array of **struct** emp type. The above discussed details of an employee are accepted into it and then they are displayed.

In the above program, we saw that we can nest one structure within another structure and understood how the members of the nested structure are accessed (two dots). In fact, nesting of structures can be to any level. If need be, we can nest structure A within structure B, in turn structure B can be nested within another structure C, and so on.

Initialization of a structure containing another structure

Just as we initialize the variables of some structure type when the members of the structure are of basic type, we can even initialize the variables of structures which themselves contain some other structures as members (nesting of structures). The following program demonstrates this.

PROGRAM 11.10   To illustrate initialization of a structure containing another structure

```
struct date
{
      int day, month, year;
};

struct emp
{
      int empno;
      char name[20];
      struct date doj;
      float salary;
};

int main(void)
{
      struct emp e1 = {123, "Raghav", 12,04,1998, 13450};
      struct emp e2 = {124, "Madhav", {12,05,1999}, 23450};

      printf("%6d%-15s%d/%d/%d%10.2f \n", e1.empno, e1.name, e1.doj.
day, e1.doj.month, e1.doj.year, e1.salary);
```

```
        printf("%6d%-15s%d/%d/%d%10.2f \n", e2.empno, e2.name, e2.doj.
day, e2.doj.month, e2.doj.year, e2.salary);

        return 0;
}
```

Input–Output:

123Raghav	12/4/1998	13450.00
124Madhav	12/5/1999	23450.00

Explanation:

In the above program, a structure with the tag name date is defined with three members **day**, **month** and **year,** all of int type. Any variable of type struct date would thus represent a date. Another structure with tag name emp is defined with the members empno (int), name (array of char), doj (struct date) and salary (float). Any variable of struct emp type would thus denote the details of an employee, which include empno, name, date of joining and salary. While initializing a variable of struct emp type the members of struct date may be listed one after the other separated by commas as in the following statement.

```
    struct emp e1 = {123, "Raghav", 12,04,1998, 13450};
```

or the members of struct date type can be enclosed within a pair of braces as in the statement.

```
    struct emp e2 = {124, "Madhav", {12,05,1999}, 23450};
```

Consider the following example:

```
struct measure
{
      int feet;
      float inches;
};

struct room
{
      struct measure length, breadth;
};

struct building
{
      struct room r1, r2;
};
```

Let us declare a variable of type **struct** building

```
struct building b;
```

b represents a building.

b.r1 and b.r2 represent two rooms of the building b.

`b.r1.length` represents the length of room `r1` of building `b`
`b.r1.breadth` represents the breadth of room `r1` of building `b`

`b.r1.length.feet` represents feet part of length of room `r1` of building `b`
`b.r1.length.inches` represents inches part of length of room `r1` of building `b`
`b.r1.breadth.feet` represents feet part of breadth of room `r1` of building `b`
`b.r1.breadth.inches` represents inches part of breadth of room `r1` of building `b`

Similarly,

`b.r2.length.feet` represents feet part of length of room `r2` of building `b`
`b.r2.length.inches` represents inches part of length of room `r2` of building `b`
`b.r2.breadth.feet` represents feet part of breadth of room `r2` of building `b`
`b.r2.breadth.inches` represents inches part of breadth of room `r2` of building `b`

Note that the nesting of structure within another structure increases the readability of the variable names.

11.8 STRUCTURES AND FUNCTIONS

The concept of structures can be treated in combination with the concept of functions in two different ways: One, by passing structures as arguments to functions; and two, by returning a structure from a function. Both are supported by ANSI C.

11.8.1 Passing Structures to Functions as Arguments

There are three approaches to passing a structure to a function.

1. Passing members of a structure individually
2. Passing entire structure at once
3. Passing address of structure

Passing members of a structure individually

Passing the members of a structure individually boils down to passing basic types of data to a function which we have dealt with so far. If `f()` is a function which requires the members of a variable of some structure type, the fact that we are passing the members of it individually to the function `f()` should be indicated by both while declaring and defining the function.

Example 11.9

If the `f()` requires a variable of type `struct emp` as its argument, the declaration of the function would be as:

`void f(int empno, char name[], float salary);`

and the function definition would be as:

```
void f(int empno, char name[], float salary)
{
        statements;
}
```

and the function call would be as:

f (e.empno, e.name, e.salary); where e is a variable of type struct emp.

Note that the individual members are explicitly specified in the function declaration, function definition and the function call.

PROGRAM 11.11 To illustrate passing the individual members of a structure to a function

```c
#include <stdio.h>

struct student
{
        int reg_no;
        char name[20];
        float percent;
};

void display(int, char[], float);

int main(void)
{
        struct student s;

        printf("Enter reg_no, name and percent \n");
        scanf("%d%s%f", &s.reg_no, s.name, &s.percent);
        display(s.reg_no, s.name, s.percent);

        return 0;
}

void display(int reg_no, char name[], float percent)
{
        printf("%6d%15s%6.2f", reg_no, name, percent);
}
```

Input–Output:

```
Enter reg_no, name and percent
123
Nishu
89

123    Nishu 89.00
```

The limitations encountered in this approach are: 1. If the number of members of the structure to be passed is more, this method turns out to be prohibitive, and 2. If some changes are made to the members of the structure by the called function, the called function cannot be made known about the changes. (Only one value can be returned by a function).

Passing entire structure at once

Passing an entire structure as an argument is another way of passing the structure values to a function. If f () is a function which requires a variable of some structure type as its argument, the fact that we are passing the entire structure to the function f () should be indicated both while declaring and defining the function.

Example 11.10

If f () requires a variable of type struct emp as its argument, the declaration of the function would be as:

```
void f (struct emp e) ;
```

and the function definition would be as:

```
void f (struct emp e)
{
        statements;
}
```

and the function call would be as:

f (e) ; where e is the actual argument, a variable of type struct emp.

PROGRAM 11.12   To illustrate passing an entire structure to a function

---

```
#include <stdio.h>

struct student
{
        int reg_no;
        char name[20];
        float percent;
};

void display(struct student);

int main(void)
{
        struct student s;

        printf("Enter reg_no, name and percent \n");
        scanf("%d%s%f", &s.reg_no, s.name, &s.percent);
        display(s);

        return 0;
}

void display(struct student s)
{
        printf("%6d%15s%6.2f\n", s.reg_no, s.name, s.percent);
}
```

Input–Output:

```
Enter reg_no, name and percent
123
Nishu
89

123    Nishu 89.00
```

Explanation:

The structure `struct student` is defined with the three members `reg_no, name, percent;` Any variable of the structure type would thus denote a student. The function `display()` is defined with an argument of type `struct student`. The purpose of the function is to display the details of a student. In the `main()` a student's details are accepted into the variable `s` and the variable is passed as the actual argument to the function `display()` with the statement `display(s);` The function on its execution displays the contents of `s` and returns to the `main()`.

Passing address of a structure variable

Passing the address of a structure variable is another and efficient way of passing the members of a structure variable to a function. If `f()` is a function which requires the address of a variable of some structure type, the fact that we are passing the address of the variable to the function `f()` should be indicated both while declaring and defining the function.

Example 11.11

If the `f()` requires the address of a variable of type `struct emp` as its argument, the declaration of the function would be as:

```
void f(struct emp*);
```

and the function definition would be as:

```
void f(struct emp *ep)
{
       statements;
}
```

and the function call would be as:

```
f(&e);
```

where `e` is a variable of type `struct emp`.

PROGRAM 11.13   To illustrate passing the address of a structure to a function

---

```
#include <stdio.h>

struct student
{
       int reg_no;
       char name[20];
       float percent;
};
```

```
void display(struct student*);
int main(void)
{
      struct student s;
      printf("Enter reg_no, name and percent \n");
      scanf("%d%s%f", &s.reg_no, s.name, &s.percent);
      display(&s);

      return 0;
}

void display(struct student *sp)
{
      printf("%6d%15s%6.2f\n", sp->reg_no, sp->name, sp->percent);
}
```

Input–Output:

```
Enter reg_no, name and percent
123
Nishu
89


123    Nishu 89.00
```

In fact, we can read values into a structure variable with the help of a function by passing the address of the structure variable.

```
void read(struct student *sp)
{
      scanf("%d%s%f", &sp->reg_no, sp->name, &sp->percent);
}
    read(&s);
```

enables us to accept reg_no, name and percent of a student into the variable **s**.

Passing a structure variable vs. passing address of a structure variable

If a structure variable itself is passed to a function, the function operates on a copy of the structure variable thereby protecting its original contents. Passing a structure variable amounts to passing all the members of the structure, which is tedious. If any changes are made to the members of the structure variable in the called function, the entire structure needs to be returned to the calling function if it wants to manipulate on the changed values.

Passing address of a structure variable to a function is quite simple since only one value (address) needs to be passed. However, by means of the address all the members of the structure variable can be accessed in the called function. We do not need to return the structure to the calling function even if any changes made to the members of the structure by the called function since the changes made are visible to the calling function also. The disadvantage of this approach is that there is always a chance of altering the contents of the structure inadvertently.

Passing arrays of structures to functions

Similar to the way, we pass arrays of basic type (char, int, float, etc.) to functions, we can even think of passing arrays of structures to functions as arguments. We know that to be able to pass an array of basic type to a function, we need to pass the array name (address of the first element in the array) and the number of elements in the array. Same is true even in the case of arrays of structures type. The prototype of the function which takes an array of structures type as an argument and the header of the function should reveal the argument type.

PROGRAM 11.14   To illustrate passing an array of structures to a function

```c
#include <stdio.h>

struct emp
{
        int empno;
        char name[20];
        float salary;
};

void display(struct emp[], int);

int main(void)
{
        struct emp e[10];
        int i, n;


        printf("Enter the number of employees \n");
        scanf("%d", &n);
        printf("Enter %d employees' details \n", n);
        for(i = 0; i < n; i++)
                scanf("%d%s%f``", &e[i].empno, e[i].name, &e[i].salary);
        printf("The list of employees \n");
        display(e, n);

        return 0;
}

void display(struct emp e[], int n)
{
        int i;
        for(i = 0; i < n; i++)
                printf("%6d%15s%8.2f \n", e[i].empno, e[i].name, e[i].salary);
}
```

Input–Output:

```
Enter the number of employees
2

Enter 2 employees' details
123 Nishu 23000
124 Harshith 45000

The list of employees
123        Nishu        23000.00
124        Harshith     45000.00
```

Explanation:

We have defined a structure by name **struct emp.** It involves three members empno, name and salary. A variable of **struct emp** type can accommodate empno, name and salary of an employee. An array of **struct emp** type can thus accommodate details of a list of employees. The function display() is to display the details of a list of employees passed to it. The prototype of display() indicates that it requires two arguments: 1. Array name, and 2. The number of structure elements.

In the main(), e is declared to be an array of struct emp type and of size 10. Maximum 10 employees' details can be accepted. **i** and **n** are declared to be variables of int type. **i** is to traverse the structure elements and n is to collect the number of employees. After accepting the number of employees into the variable **n**, we accept **n** employees details into the array **e**. The array name **e** and **n** are passed to display(), which in turn displays the list of employees' details.

11.8.2   Returning a Structure from a Function

When a function is made to accept and return a structure from and to the calling program, the function declaration and its definition should reflect the same. We will now write a program which illustrates not only passing a structure to a function but also illustrates returning a structure from the function.

PROGRAM 11.15   To illustrate passing and returning structure to and from a function

```c
#include <stdio.h>

struct book
{
        char author[20];
        char title[20];
        int pages;
        float price;
};

struct book update(struct book b, int p, float pr);
int main(void)
```

```
{
        struct book b = { "Manjunath", "Basic Electronics", 288, 125}, ub;
        int p;
        float pr;

        printf("Enter the number of pages increased by \n");
        scanf("%d", &p);
        printf("Enter the price increased by \n");
        scanf("%f", &pr);
        ub = update(b, p, pr);
        printf("Updated book details \n");
        printf("Author = %s \n", ub.author);
        printf("Title = %s \n", ub.title);
        printf("Pages = %d \n", ub.pages);
        printf("Price = %6.2f \n", ub.price);

        return 0;
}
struct book update(struct book b, int p, float pr)
{
        b.pages += p;
        b.price += pr;

        return b;
}
```

Input–Output:

```
Enter the number of pages increased by
20
Enter the price increased by
15

Updated book details
Author = Manjunath
Title = Basic Electronics
Pages = 308
Price = 140.00
```

Explanation:

The structure **struct book** is defined with four members author (array of char), title (array of char), pages (int) and price (float). A variable of **struct book** type would thus represent the details of a book. The function update() is defined with three formal arguments **b** of **struct book** type, **p** of **int** type and **pr** of **float** type representing the details of a book, the number of pages increased by and the price increased by, respectively. The purpose of the function is to update the values of the members pages and price of the book passed to it and return the updated structure value back to the calling program.

In the `main()`, the structure variable **b** is initialized with values and the number of pages and the price increased by, are accepted into the local variables **p** and **pr** respectively. A call is made to the function `update()` through the statement `ub = update(b, p, pr);` after the execution of the statement, the variable **ub** gets the updated values and they are displayed.

11.9 UNION

The concept of union is derived from the concept of structure. The common thing shared by both the structure and the union is that both enable us to identify a group of data items which may be of different types by a common name. But the difference lies in their storage allocation scheme. In the case of structure, the number of locations allocated would be equal to the number of members in the structure; whereas in the case of union, only one location which is large enough to collect the largest data type member in the union gets allocated. This single location can accommodate values of different types one at a time. This feature provided by union has helped in a big way while developing system software.

Before instantiating variables of some union type, the data items which are to share a common name should be grouped together. This is done with the help of union template. The syntax of defining a union template is as follows.

```
union tag_name
    {
            data-type member1;
            data-type member2;
               :
               :
               :
            data-type membern;
    };
```

union is a keyword. `tag-name` is any user-defined name, which should be a valid C identifier. `data-type` is any valid data type supported by C or user-defined type. `member1`, `member2`, ..., `membern` are the members of the union. Note the similarity between a union template and a structure template except the keyword **union** in the former and the keyword **struct** in the latter.

The syntax of declaring a variable of union type is as follows.

```
union tag_name variable_name;
```

As a result of this, a memory location gets allocated, the size of which is equal to that of the largest of the members `member1`, `member2`, `member3`, ..., `membern`. Accessing the members of a union is similar to accessing the members of a structure. Dot operator is used to access each individual member. Dot operator expects union variable to its left and member name to its right.

Example 11.12

```
union temp
{
```

```
        int i;
        float f;
        char c;
};
```

union temp makes a group of three data items of type **int**, **float** and **char**

> **union** temp t;

A variable t is declared to be of type **union** temp. As a result of this, only one memory location gets allocated. It can be referred to by any one individual member at any point of time. Note that the size of the memory location is four bytes, which happens to be the size of the largest sized data type **float** n the member-list.

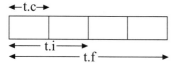

PROGRAM 11.16   To differentiate between structure and union

```
#include <stdio.h>

struct temp
{
        int i;
        float f;
        char c;
};

union temp1
{
        int i;
        float f;
        char c;
};

int main(void)
{
        struct temp st;
        union temp1 ut;

        printf(" size of struct temp = %d \n", size of(st));
        printf(" size of union temp = %d \n", size of(ut));

        st.i = 10;
        st.f = 3.45;
        st.c = 's';

        printf(" st.i = %d \n", st.i);
```

```
    printf(" st.f = %f \n", st.f);
    printf(" st.c = %c \n", st.c);

    ut.i = 10;
    printf(" ut.i = %d \n", ut.i);
    ut.f = 3.45;
    printf(" ut.f = %d \n", ut.f);
    ut.c = 's';
    printf(" ut.c = %c \n", ut.c);

    return 0;
}
```

Input–Output:

```
size of struct temp = 7
size of union temp = 4

st.i = 10
st..f = 3.450000
st.c = s
ut.i = 10
ut.f = 0
ut.c = s
```

Explanation:

In the above program, structure template **struct** temp logically relates three data items **i**, **f** and **c** of type **int**, **float** and **char** type respectively. **st** is declared to be a variable of type **struct** temp. Intentionally, the same three types of data items are grouped together even in the union template **union** temp. and **ut** is declared to be a variable of type **union** temp.

First, the size of **st** is displayed. It turns out to be seven bytes, the sum of the size of its members, then the size of ut is displayed. Note that it turns out to be only four bytes, the size of the largest data type, **float** member in the union.

Values of corresponding type are assigned to the members of **st** and they are displayed. An integer value is assigned to **ut.i** and it is displayed. Then a float value is assigned to **ut.f** and it is also displayed. It is important to note that when **ut.f** is assigned a value, **ut.i** ceases to exist since it is overwritten by **ut.f**. Lastly, **ut.c** is assigned a character. Now **ut.f** ceases to exist, since **ut.c** overwrites it. So at any point of time, only one of **ut.i**, **ut.f** and **ut.c** is accessible.

11.9.1 Unions within Structures

We can even nest unions within structures definitions. The following example demonstrates this. Here the program creates a table (a typical symbol table maintained by the compilers) with three columns of information data type specifier, variable name, and the value of the variable.

PROGRAM 11.17   To illustrate union within structure

```c
#include <stdio.h>

union utemp
{
      int i;
      float f;
      double d;
};

struct stemp
{
      int type;
      char name[20];
      union utemp u;
};

int main(void)
{
      struct stemp s[3];
      int i, t;
      float f, *fp;

      fp = &f;

      for(i = 0; i < 3; i++)
      {
            printf("Enter type [1 for int, 2 for float, 3 for double \n"]);
            scanf("%d", &t);
            printf("Enter name \n");
            scanf("%s", s[i].name);
            if (t == 1)
            {
                  printf("Enter an integer value \n");
                  scanf("%d", &s[i].u.i);
            }
            else if (t == 2)
            {
                  printf("Enter a float value \n");
                  scanf("%f", &s[i].u.f);
            }
            else
            {
                  printf("Enter a double value \n");
                  scanf("%lf", &s[i].u.d);
```

```
                }
                s[i].type = t;
        }

        for(i = 0; i < 3; i++)
        {
                if (s[i].type == 1)
                        printf("integer%-10s %4d", s[i].name, s[i].u.i);
                else if (s[i].type == 2)
                        printf("float %-10s %6.2f", s[i].name, s[i].u.f);
                else
                        printf("double %-10s %6.2lf", s[i].name, s[i].u.d);
                printf("\n");
        }

        return 0;
}
```

Input–Output:

```
Enter type [1 for int, 2 for float, 3 for double]
1
Enter name
counter
Enter an integer value
10
Enter type [1 for int, 2 for float, 3 for double]
2
Enter name
salary
Enter a float value
23000
Enter type [1 for int, 2 for float, 3 for double]
3
Enter name
Total
Enter a double value
2340000.00

integer    counter      10
float      salary       23000.00
double     total        2340000.00
```

Explanation:

The union template **utemp** is defined with three members i, f and d of type int, float and double respectively. We know that a variable of union utemp type can store any one of the types of values at a given point of time. The structure `struct stemp` is defined with three members type, name and u of type `int`, `char array` and union utemp type respectively. So a variable of type `struct stemp` would thus store a record of the symbol table with three fields integer value (type), name of the variable (name) and its value (u). Note that in the array s of type `struct stemp` the member u of different records stores either an integer or a float value or a double value and the type of the value stored in u is remembered by storing the numeric codes assigned to the types (1 for integer, 2 for float and 3 for double).

11.9.2 Structures within Unions

On the lines of embedding unions within structure, we can even think of making structures as members of unions. The following example illustrates this.

```
struct date
{
      int day, month, year;
};

union emp
{
      int age;
      struct date dob;
};
```

A variable of `union emp` type can be used to store either the age of a person of his date of birth.

11.9.3 Arrays within Unions

The following example illustrates the fact that we can have arrays as members of unions.

```
union student
{
      int reg_no;
      char name[20];
};
```

In a variable of **union student** type, either `reg_no` or `name` of a student can be stored.

11.10 ENUMERATED DATA TYPE

Enumerated data type offers us a way of inventing our own data type. The invented new data type enables us to assign symbolic names to integer constants, thereby increasing the degree of readability and maintainability of programs. Variables of enumerated data type are very often used in conjunction with structures and unions.

Like unions, enumerated data type also resembles structures as far as its template definition and declaration of its variables are concerned. The syntax of defining an enumerated type is as follows.

```
enum tag_name
    {

            enumerator-1,
            enumerator-2,
            enumerator-3,
            .
            .
            .

            enumerator-n
        };
```

enum is a keyword. **tag_name** is any user-defined name. It is better if the **tag-name** happens to be a collective name reflecting the set of enumerators. **enumerator-1**, **enumerator-2**, etc. are the symbolic names representing the integer constants 0, 1 etc. by default. However, the default integer constants of the enumerators can be overridden by assigning our own values.

The syntax of declaring a variable of enum type is similar to that used while declaring variables of structure or union type.

```
enum tag name variable;
```

Example 11.13

```
enum boolean
{
      false,
      true
};

enum boolean flag;
```

   flag = false;   The enumerator false is assigned to the variable flag.

Example 11.14

```
enum colors
{
      red,
      green,
      blue,
      yellow,
      white,
      black
}color;
```

Note that color is declared to be a variable of type enum colors.

color = red;   The enumerator red is assigned to the variable color.

Let us now write programs which use the enumerated data type.

PROGRAM 11.18   To illustrate enumerated data type

```c
#include <stdio.h>

enum subjects
{
        kannada,
        english,
        physics,
        maths,
        computers
};


int main(void)
{
        int marks[5];
        enum subjects subject;

        printf("Enter marks in five subjects \n");
        for(subject = kannada; subject <= computers; subject++)
            scanf("%d", &marks[subject]);

        printf("Marks in Different Subjects \n");

        printf("Kannada : %d \n", marks[kannada]);
        printf("English : %d \n", marks[english]);
        printf("Physics : %d \n", marks[physics]);
        printf("Maths    : %d \n", marks[maths]);
        printf("Computers : %d \n", marks[computers]);

        return 0;
}
```

Input–Output:

```
Enter marks in five subjects
78 79 80 98 99

Marks in Different Subjects
Kannada : 78
English : 79
Physics : 80
Maths    : 98
Computers : 99
```

Explanation:

In the above program, an enumerated data type with the name **enum subjects** is defined with the enumerators Kannada, English, Physics, Maths and Computers. **marks** is declared to be an array of **int** type of size five. The array is to collect the marks obtained by a student in five subjects mentioned above. **subject** is declared to be a variable of type **enum subjects** and it can take any one of the enumerators listed within the definition of **enum subjects**. Since the enumerators will have the values starting from 0, they are used as the indices with the array in the following program segment.

```
for(subject = kannada; subject <= computers; subject++)
        scanf("%d", &marks[subject]);
```

which accepts marks in five subjects.

Here, `marks[kannada]` (marks obtained in Kannada) is same as `marks[0]`. `marks[english]` (marks obtained in English) is same as `marks[1]`, and so on. Note the increase in the degree of readability.

PROGRAM 11.19 To illustrate the concept of enumerated data type

---

```c
#include <stdio.h>

enum week_day
{
        sunday = 1,
        monday = 2,
        tuesday = 3,
        wednesday = 4,
        thursday = 5,
        friday = 6,
        saturday = 7
};

int main(void)
{
        int n;

        printf("Enter the day number [1-7] \n");
        scanf("%d", &n);

        switch(n)
        {
                case sunday:
                        printf("Sunday");
                        break;
                case monday:
                        printf("Monday");
                        break;
```

```
                case tuesday:
                        printf("Tuesday");
                        break;
                case wednesday:
                        printf("Wednesday");
                        break;
                case thursday:
                        printf("Thursday");
                        break;
                case friday:
                        printf("Friday");
                        break;
                case saturday:
                        printf("Saturday");
                        break;
                default: printf("Invalid day number");
        }
    return 0;
}
```

Input–Output:

```
Enter the day number [1-7]
2
Monday

Enter the day number [1-7]
8
Invalid day number
```

Explanation:

In Program 11.19, note that the enumerators [Sunday–Monday] are assigned the integer values starting from 1 to 7 overriding the default values which range from 0 to 6. So, the program not only illustrates that the enumerators can be assigned our own values but also it illustrates that the enumerators can be used as case labels in the switch structure.

11.11 typedef

typedef, a facility provided by C, enables us to rename existing built-in data types and user-defined data types and thereby helps in increasing the degree of readability of source code. The syntax of its usage is as follows:

```
typedef old-name new-name;
```

where old-name is the name of the existing data type and new-name is the new name given to the data type identified by old name.

Example 11.15

```
typedef unsigned int TWOWORDS;
```

We can now declare variables of unsigned int type using the new name as

```
TWOWORDS i;
```

i has been declared to be a variable of unsigned int type

Example 11.16

```
struct emp
{
      int empno;
      char name[20];
      float salary;
};
```

```
typedef struct emp EMP;
```

variables of struct emp can now be declared using EMP as the type specifier as
EMP e; where e has been declared to be a variable of struct emp type.

PROGRAM 11.20   To illustrate the usage of typedef

```c
#include <stdio.h>

struct book
{
      char author[20];
      char title[20];
      int pages;
      float price;
};

typedef struct book BOOK;
int main(void)
{
      BOOK b;

      printf("Enter the details of a book \n");
      scanf("%s%s%d%f", b.author, b.title, &b.pages, &b.price);
      printf("Author : %s \n", b.author);
      printf("Title : %s \n", b.title);
      printf("Pages : %d \n", b.pages);
      printf("Price : %7.2f \n", b.price);

      return 0;
}
```

Input–Output:

```
Enter the details of a book
John Programming 270 260
Author : John
Title : Programming
Pages : 270
Price : 260.00
```

Explanation:

In the above program, a structure with the name **struct book** is defined with four fields **author**, **title**, **pages** and **price**. A variable of type **struct book** thus denotes a book. The facility typedef is used to rename the type struct book as BOOK. A variable b is declared to be of type struct book with the new name BOOK. The details of a book are then accepted into b and they are displayed.

SUMMARY

- The concept of structures in C enables us to make a group of data items which may be of different types sharing a common name and each data item in the group being uniquely distinguishable.
- Once a structure template is defined, variables of the structure type can be declared.
- Similar to basic type variables, structure variables can also be initialized while they are declared.
- The permissible operations over structures include: Retrieving the address of a structure variable (the **address of** operator &), accessing each member in a structure (dot operator .); assigning one structure variable to another of similar type. Obtaining the size of a structure; and, passing and returning a structure to and from a function.
- C supports arraying of structures and making arrays as members within structures.
- We can even nest one structure within another.
- The concept of unions enables us to refer to a common location by different names each referring to a different type of data item.
- Using structures as members of unions; using unions as members of structures and using arrays as members of unions are all possible.
- The enumerated data type enables us to assign meaningful name to constant values in an enumeration and the keyword typedef is used to assign an alternative name for an existing basic and user-defined data type.

REVIEW QUESTIONS

11.1 Explain the need for the concept of structure.

11.2 What is structure template?

11.3 Explain syntax of defining structure template with an example.

11.4 Define structure.

11.5 Explain the syntax of declaring a structure variable.

11.6 Can we initialize structure variables while they are declared? If yes, explain the syntax with an example.

11.7 Give an account of the operations which can be performed over structure variables.

11.8 What is the need for array of structures? Give an example.

11.9 Can we make an array as a member of a structure? If yes, give an example its requirement.

11.10 Can we nest one structure within another structure? If yes, give an example of its requirement.

11.11 How do we pass a structure variable as an argument to a function? Give an example.

11.12 What is union?

11.13 Differentiate between structure and union.

11.14 What is enumerated data type? Give an example of its usage.

11.15 Give the syntax of defining enumerated data type.

11.16 What is the significance of `typedef`? Give an example.

State whether the following are true or false

11.1 In a structure, the member data should be of different types.

11.2 Structure variables can be initialized.

11.3 Arrays can be made as members of structures.

11.4 `union temp`
```
    {
        int i;
        float f;
    };
```
The size of the union is six bytes.

11.5 Unions can be used as members of structures and vice versa.

11.6 Structures can be nested.

11.7 The keyword `typedef` is to create new data type.

11.8 The enumerators in the enumerated data type are of float type.

11.9 Structures can be passed and returned to and from functions.

11.10 The default values of the enumerators in the enumerated data type cannot be changed.

11.11 Unions cannot be arrayed.

11.12 Strings cannot be used as members of unions.

Identify errors, if any, in the following

11.1.
```
struct temp
{
    int i;
    int j;
    int k;
} a;
```

11.2.
```
struct temp
{
    int i;
    int j;
    int k;
};

main()
{
    struct temp t = (1, 4.6, 's');
}
```

11.3
```
struct item
{
    int code;
    float quantity;
}
main()
{
        struct item t;
}
```

11.4
```
struct A
{
    int i;
};

struct B
{
    int j;
};

main()
{
    struct A a = {10};
    struct B b;

    b = a;
}
```

11.5
```
struct temp
{
    int i = 10;
    float f = 19.8;
    char c = 'a';
}t;
```

11.6
```
enum colors
{
    white;
    red;
    blue;
};
```

11.7
```
typedef integer int;
```

11.8
```
union temp
{
    int i;
    float f;
    char c;
};

main()
{
    union tep t = {1, 3.4, 'a'};
}
```

PROGRAMMING EXERCISES

11.1 Write a program to create a list of books' details. The details of a book include title, author, publisher, publishing year, number of pages, price.

11.2 Perform the following with respect to the list of books created in the above exercise.

    (a) Display the details of books written by a given author

    (b) Sort the details of books in the increasing order of price.

    (c) Display the details of books published by a given publisher in a given year.

    (d) Sort the list of books in the increasing order of two fields, author and title of the books.

11.3 Define a structure by name date with members day, month and year of `int` type. Perform the following.

    (a) Validate a date.

    (b) If `d1` and `d2` are two dates, find whether `d1` is earlier than `d2` or `d1` is later than `d2` or both are equal.

    (c) Find the difference between two dates. If `d1` and `d2` are two dates, the difference between `d1` and `d2` is the number of days between them.

(d) Increment a date by one day, that is, to get next date for a given date.

(e) If d is a date and n is the number of days, to get the next date after adding n days to the date d.

11.4 Define a structure by name time with members seconds, minutes and hours of int type. A variable of the structure type would thus represent time. If t1 and t2 are two variables of the structure type, write a program to find the sum of the two times using a function.

11.5 Write a program to search for an employee in a list of employees by means of empno using binary search method. (Use structure concept with empno, name and salary as the fields)

11.6 A complex number is of the form $a + ib$, where a is the real part and b is the imaginary part. Define a structure with real part and imaginary part of a complex number as its member data. Write a program to perform the following operations over two complex numbers.

(a) Addition, (b) Subtraction, (c) Multiplication, (d) Division

11.7 Given the co-ordinates (x, y) of 10 points, write a program which will output the co-ordinates of all the points which lie inside or on the circle with unit radius with its centre (0, 0). (**Hint:** Define a structure by name **point** with the **x** and **y** of **int** type as its members. Each variable of the structure type represents a point. The equation of a circle with centre (0,0) is given by

$x^2 + y^2 = r^2$.

The point (x, y) lies on the circle if $x^2 + y^2 = r^2$.

The point (x, y) lies inside the circle if $x^2 + y^2 < r^2$.)

11.8 Develop a program to sort a list of employees on two keys (primary key and secondary key). Suppose the employees details include empno, name, dept, salary, sort the list using dept as the primary key and the salary as the secondary key (After sorting, the list in its entirety should be in the order of dept and within each dept the employees should be in the order of salary).

11.9 Write a program to search for an employee in a list of employees using binary search method.

11.10 Write a program to sort a list of employees on salary using selection sort method.

11.11 Write a program to sort a list of employees on salary using bubble sort method.

11.12 Write a program to sort a list of employees on salary using insertion sort method.

11.13 Write a program to sort a list of employees on salary using quick sort method.

11.14 Write a program to sort a list of employees on salary using merge sort method.

INTERVIEW QUESTIONS

11.1 Can we define a union inside a structure?

11.2 Can we compare two structure variable using = = operator? If not, how do you compare two structure variables?

11.3 When a structure is passed as an argument to a function, what is actually passed?

11.4 How do you initialize a union?

11.5 What is the output of the following programs?

(a)
```c
union example
{
    int a;
    float b;
    long c;
} e;
int main(void)
{
    e.a=10;

    printf("%d",e.a);
    printf("%f", e.b);
    printf("%ld", e.c);
    return 0;
}
```

(b)
```c
union example
{
    int a;
    float b;
    long c;
} e;
int main(void)
{
    e.a=10;
    printf("%d %d %d %d\n", sizeof(e.a), sizeof(e.b),
sizeof(e.c), sizeof(e));
    return 0;
}
```

(c)
```c
union example
{
    int a;
    float b;
    long c;
} e[4];

int main(void)
{
    printf("%d", sizeof(e));
    return 0;
}
```

```
(d) struct example
    {
        int a;
        float b;
        long c;
    } e[4];

    int main(void){
        printf("%d", sizeof(e));
            return 0;
    }
```

11.6 What is the purpose of typedef in structure declaration?

12

Pointers

12.1 INTRODUCTION

Pointers are a powerful concept in C and add to its strength. Mastery over pointers empowers a C programmer to deal with system level jargon. Let us begin by enumerating the advantages offered by pointers. The following are the advantages: pointers

1. Enable us to write efficient and concise programs
2. Enable us to establish inter-program data communication
3. Enable us to dynamically allocate and de-allocate memory
4. Enable us to optimize memory space usage
5. Enable us to deal with hardware components
6. Enable us to pass variable number of arguments to functions

It would be a wise idea to have an overview of the organization of memory before stepping into the concept of pointers. This is because understanding of pointers and their significance depends on understanding of this.

Memory is organized as an array of bytes. A byte is a basic storage and accessible unit in memory. Each byte is identifiable by a unique number called address. Suppose we have 1 KB of memory. Since 1 KB = 1024 Bytes, the memory can be viewed as an array of locations of size 1024 with the subscript range [0–1023]. 0 represents the address of the first location; 1 represents the address of the second location, and so on. The last location is identified by the address 1023.

Address   Location

We know that variables are to be declared before they are used in a program. Declaration of a variable tells the compiler to perform the following.

1. Allocate a location in memory. The number of bytes in the location depends on the data type of the variable.
2. Establish a mapping between the address of the location and the name of the variable.

Example 12.1

The declaration int i; tells the compiler to reserve a location in memory. We know that the size of a variable of **int** type is two bytes. So the location would be two bytes wide.

If the location is

Variable Name   Address of the location

   i   100

A mapping between the variable name and the address of the location is established. Note that the address of the first byte of the location is the address of the variable. The address of a variable is also a number, numeric data item. It can also be retrieved and stored in another variable. A variable which can store the address of another variable is called a **pointer**.

12.2 POINTER OPERATORS &, *

C provides two special operators known as pointer operators. They are **&** and *****. **&** stands for 'Address of' and it is used to retrieve the address of a variable. ***** stands for 'value at address' and it is used to access the value at a location by means of its address.

Since a pointer is also a variable, it also should be declared before it is used.

The syntax of declaring a pointer variable is as follows.

```
data-type *variable_name;
```

`data-type` is any valid data type supported by C or any user-defined type and `variable-name` is the name of the pointer variable. The presence of * before `variable_name` indicates that it is a pointer variable.

Example 12.2

```
int *ip;
```

`ip` is declared to be a pointer variable of **int** type.

```
float *fp;
```

`fp` is declared to be a pointer variable of **float** type.

We can see that both `ip` and `fp` are only declared but not defined, i.e. they are not assigned the addresses, such pointers are called wild pointers.

PROGRAM 12.1 To illustrate the concept of pointers and pointer operators [&, *]

```
#include <stdio.h>

int main(void)
{
        int i = 10, *ip;
        float f = 3.4, *fp;
        char c = 'a', *cp;

        printf("i = %d \n", i);
        printf("f = %f \n", f);
        printf("c = %c \n", c);

        ip = &i;
        printf("\nAddress of i = %u \n", ip);
        printf("Value of i = %d \n", *ip);
```

```
        fp = &f,
        printf("\nAddress of f = %u \n", fp);
        printf("Value of f = %f \n", *fp);

        cp = &c;
        printf("\nAddress of c = %u \n", cp);
        printf("value of c = %c \n", *cp);

        return 0;
}
```

Input–Output:

```
i = 10
f = 3.400000
c = a

Address of i = 65524
Value of i = 10

Address of f = 65520
Value of f = 3.400000

Address of c = 65519
value of c = a
```

Explanation:

In the above program, i, f and c are declared to be variables of int, float and char type respectively. ip, fp and cp are declared to be pointer variables of type int, float and char respectively.

The initial values of i, f and c are displayed. The pointer variable ip is assigned the address of i using the statement ip = &i; The address of i and its value are displayed through the pointer variable. The same thing is repeated for char and float variables. [Note however that the addresses of the variables may be different from those given here.]

12.3 POINTER ARITHMETIC

The following are the operations that can be performed over pointers.

1. We can add an integer value to a pointer.
2. We can subtract an integer value from a pointer.
3. We can compare two pointers if they point to the elements of the same array.
4. We can subtract one pointer from another pointer if both point to the same array.
5. We can assign one pointer to another pointer provided both are of same type.

But the following operations are not possible:

1. Addition of two pointers
2. Subtraction of one pointer from another pointer when they do not point to the same array

3. Multiplication of two pointers
4. Division of one pointer by another pointer

Suppose p is a pointer variable to integer type, the pointer variable p can be subjected to the following operations.

1. We can increment it using increment operator ++.
   Suppose the address stored in p initially is 100, after the statement p++; is executed, the content in p gets incremented by 2, the size of int type. So it becomes 102.
2. We can decrement it using decrement operator −−.
   Suppose the address stored in p initially is 100, after the statement p−−; is executed, the content in p gets decremented by 2, the size of int type. So it becomes 98.
       In general, if a pointer variable is incremented using ++, it gets incremented by the size of its data type, i.e., a char pointer gets incremented by 1, the size of char type. A float pointer gets incremented by 4, the size of float data type. In the case of decrement operator, a pointer variable gets decremented by the size of its data type.
3. An integer value can be added to it.
   Example 12.3
   p = p + integer value
   The content of p will now get incremented by the product of integer value and the size of int type.
4. An integer value can be subtracted from it.
   Example 12.4
   p = p − integer value.
   The content of p will now get decremented by the product of integer value and the size of int type.

PROGRAM 12.2   To illustrate the concept of pointer arithmetic

---

```
#include <stdio.h>

int main(void)
{
        int i, *ip;

        ip = &i;
        printf("ip = %u \n", ip);
        ip++;
        printf("After ip++        ip = %u \n", ip);
        ip--;
        printf("After ip--        ip = %u \n", ip);
        ip = ip + 2;
        printf("After ip= ip+2    ip = %u \n", ip);
        ip = ip - 2;
        printf("After ip=ip-2     ip = %u \n", ip);

        return 0;
}
```

Input–Output:

```
ip = 65524

After ip++        ip = 65526
After ip--        ip = 65524
After ip=ip+2     ip = 65528
After ip=ip-2     ip = 65524
```

Explanation:

In the above program; **i** is declared to be a variable of **int** type and **ip**, a pointer to **int** type. initially, the address of **i** is assigned to **ip** and it is displayed. The pointer variable **ip** is incremented using ++ operator. As can be seen, the value in **ip** gets incremented by two, the size of **int** type. The pointer variable **ip** is then decremented using −− operator. Now, the value in **ip** is decremented by 2, the size of **int** data type. Then, an integer constant 2 is added to **ip**. As a result, the value of ip gets incremented by 4, i.e. 2*sizeof **int** type. On the execution of the statement ip = ip - 2; the value of **ip** gets decremented by 4, i.e. 2 * sizeof (**int**).

12.3.1 Pointer Expressions

Once we assign the address of a variable to a pointer variable, the value of the variable pointed to can be made to participate in all the manipulations by means of the pointer itself. This is required when we pass the addresses of variables to functions as arguments. Let us now write a program to illustrate 'performing manipulations over variables' values by means of their pointers.

PROGRAM 12.3   To illustrate pointer expressions

```c
#include <stdio.h>

int main(void)
{
        int a = 4, b = 2, *ap, *bp, *sp;
        int s, d, p, q, r, t;

        ap = &a;
        bp = &b;

        s = *ap + *bp;
        d = *ap - *bp;
        p = *ap * *bp;
        q = *ap / *bp;
        r = *ap % *bp;

        sp = &t;
        *sp = *ap + *bp;
        printf("Sum = %d \n", s);
        printf("Difference = %d \n", d);
```

```
        printf("Product = %d \n", p);
        printf("Quotient = %d \n", q);
        printf("Remainder = %d \n", r);
        printf("Sum = %d \n", t);

        return 0;
}
```

Input–Output:

```
Sum = 6
Difference = 2
Product = 8
Quotient = 2
Remainder = 0
Sum = 6
```

Explanation:

In the above program, **a** and **b** are declared to be variables of **int** type and they are initialized also. **ap** and **bp** are declared to be pointers to **int** type. The pointer variables **ap** and **bp** point to the integer variables **a** and **b** respectively because of the statements ap = &a; and bp = &b; All the five basic arithmetic operations are performed over the values of a and b by means of **ap** and **bp** respectively and the results of the operations are assigned to the variables of **int** type. Here ***ap** and ***bp** represent the values of **a** and **b** respectively.

The fact that the de-referencing expression (i.e. *ptr) can be used on the left-hand side of an assignment statement is also illustrated with the statement *sp = *ap + *bp; here the sum of the values of a and b is assigned to the variable pointed to by sp i.e. t. Here we say that the de-referencing expression is used as an **Lvalue**. (Lvalue is one which has a location and which can be assigned a value).

12.4   POINTERS AND ARRAYS

We are now acquainted with both Arrays and Pointers. In our earlier discussions, we treated them as separate entities. But in C, there is a close relationship between them. Elements of an array are accessed through pointers internally. Let us now try to unravel the bonding between them.

12.4.1   Pointers and One-dimensional Arrays

Let us first consider relationship between one-dimensional arrays and pointers. Suppose a is a one-dimensional array of int type and of size 10, which is declared as follows:

int a[10];

We know that a block of memory consisting of 10 contiguous locations gets allocated and all the locations share common name **a** and are distinguishable by subscript values [0-9].

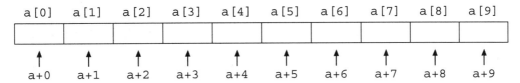

Here, the array name **a** gives the base address of the array. That is, the address of the first element a[0] of the array. So **a** being equivalent to &a[0] can be regarded as a pointer to integer but in the capacity of a constant pointer. That is, **a** cannot be incremented or decremented.

Since **a** is the address of **a[0]**, ***a** is the element stored in the first location. Since a is a constant pointer, it cannot be incremented to point to the next location. But the expression (a+1) gives the address of the second element a[1] of the array. *(a+1) gives the element itself stored at a[1]. Similarly, (a+2) is the address of a[2] and *(a+2) is the value at a[2].

```
*a =    * (a + 0) = a[0]
        * (a + 1) = a[1]
        * (a + 2) = a[2]
        * (a + 3) = a[3]
        * (a + 4) = a[4]
                .
                .
                .
        * (a + i) = a[i]
```

In general, (a + i) gives the address of ith element in the array **a** and *(a + i) is the element stored in the ith location of the array.

PROGRAM 12.4 To illustrate processing one-dimensional arrays using pointers

```c
#include <stdio.h>

int main(void)
{
        int a[10], n, i;

        printf("Enter the number of elements \n");
        scanf("%d", &n);

        printf("Enter %d elements \n", n);
        for(i = 0; i < n; i++)
                scanf("%d", a + i);

        printf("The list of elements \n");
        for(i = 0; i < n; i++)
                printf("%d \n", *(a + i));

        return 0;
}
```

Input–Output:

```
Enter the number of elements
5
Enter 5 elements
1 2 3 4 5
The list of elements
1 2 3 4 5
```

Explanation:

a is declared to be an array of **int** type of size 10. **n** and **i** are declared to be variables of **int** type. The variable **n** is to accept the number of elements to be accepted into the array **a**, the value of which should lie within 1 and 10 and the variable **i** is to select each location of the array. We know that the array name **a** gives the address of the first location of the array and the expression **a + i** gives the address of **i**th location of the array. The following segment of the above program enables us to accept **n** values into the array.

```
for (i = 0; i < n; i++)
    scanf ("%d", a + i);
```

Note that the second argument $a + i$ is equivalent to $\&a[i]$.

$*(a + 0)$ gives the value at the first location of the array and in general, $*(a + i)$ gives the value at i^{th} location of the array a. The following segment of the above program displays the n values stored in the array.

```
for (i = 0; i < n; i++)
    printf ("%d \n", * (a + i));
```

Note that the second argument $*(a + i)$ is equivalent to $a[i]$.

PROGRAM 12.5   To find out the minimum and maximum values in a list of values

```
#include <stdio.h>
int main (void)
{
        int a[10], i, n, min, max;

        printf ("Enter the number of values [1-10] \n");
        scanf ("%d", &n);
        printf ("Enter %d values \n", n);
        for (i = 0; i < n; i++)
                scanf ("%d", a + i);

        /* Finding the minimum starts */
        min = * (a + 0);
        for (i = 1; i < n; i++)
                if (* (a + i) < min)
                        min = * (a + i);
        /* Finding the minimum ends */
```

```
/* Finding the maximum starts */
max = * (a + 0) ;
for (i = 1; i < n; i++)
        if (* (a + i) > max)
                max = * (a + i) ;
/* Finding the maximum ends */

printf ("Minimum = %d \n", min) ;
printf ("Maximum = %d \n", max) ;

return 0;
}
```

Input–Output:

```
Enter the number of values [1-10]
5
Enter 5 values
2 3 4 5 6

Minimum = 2
Maximum = 6
```

Explanation:

a is declared to be an array of **int** type of size 10. **n** and **i** are declared to be variables of **int** type. The variable **n** is to accept the number of elements to be accepted into the array **a**, the value of which should lie within 1 and 10 and the variable **i** is to select each location of the array. The integer variables **min** and **max** are to collect the minimum and the maximum of the values in the list.

After accepting **n** values into the array, the minimum of the values is found out with the following segment of the program.

```
min = * (a + 0) ;
for (i = 1; i < n; i++)
        if (* (a + i) < min)
                min = * (a + i) ;
```

We start with the assumption that the first value in the array itself is the minimum and assign it to the variable **min**. Note that the statement min = * (a + 0) is same as min = a [0]. The **for** loop selects the remaining values in the array and if any other value is found to be less than the value in **min**, the variable **min** is replaced with the lesser value.

Note that the segment

```
if (* (a + i) < min)
        min = * (a + i) ;
```

is same as

```
if (a [i] < min)
        min = a [i] ;
```

Similarly, the maximum in the array is also found out.

PROGRAM 12.6   To access the elements of an array through a pointer variable

```
#include <stdio.h>

int main(void)
{

        int a[5] = { 4, 6, 7, 5, 2};
        int *p1, *p2;

        p1 = a;
        p2 = &a[4];
        printf("The elements of the array a \n");
        while (p1 < = p2)
        {
                printf("%3d", *p1);
                p1++;
        }

        return 0;
}
```

Input–Output:

```
The elements of the array a
4   6   7   5   2
```

Explanation:

a has been declared to be an array of **int** type and it is also initialized. **p1** and **p2** are declared to be pointers to **int** type. **p1** is assigned the address of the first element of the array with the statement p1 = a; the pointer variable **p2** is assigned the address of the last element of the array with the statement p2 = &a[4] ; . Since the pointers **p1** and **p2** point to the elements of the same array, they can be compared. The while loop, that is set up is to traverse the elements of the array and display them. As long as p1 <= p2 the loop repeats and displays the value pointed to by **p1**. Since **p1** is getting incremented each time, once it exceeds the address in **p2**, the test-expression p1<= p2 evaluates to false and the loop is exited.

Because of the same reason, p2 - p1 is also a valid expression.

12.4.2   Pointers and Two-dimensional Arrays

Suppose **a** is an array of two dimensions of **int** type, which is declared as follows.

```
int a[5][5];
```

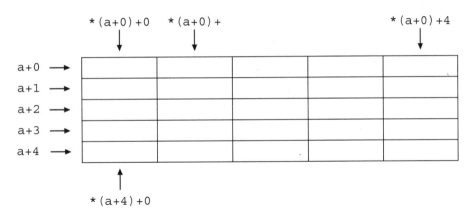

We know that a 2-D array is essentially an array of 1-D arrays. So each element in a 2-D array happens to be a 1-D array.

Here also, the array name **a** gives its base address. That is, the address of its first element. First element in this case is the first 1-D array. So **a** is the address of its first 1-D array . So **a** is a pointer to its first 1-D array. As we have seen earlier, since 1-D array itself is a pointer, **a** can now be regarded as a pointer to pointer to `int` type. Note the two levels of indirections.
a + 1 is the address of the second 1-D array of a, and so on.

(a + 0) is the address of the first 1-D array	* (a + 0) is the first 1-D array
(a + 1) is the address of the second 1-D array	* (a + 1) is the second 1-D array
(a + 2) is the address of the third 1-D array	* (a + 2) is the third 1-D array
⋮	⋮
(a + n - 1) is the address of the nth 1-D array	* (a + n - 1) is the nth 1-D array

Now * (a + i), (i + 1)th 1-D array of a is similar to any 1-D array, say b, which is declared as follows:

`int b[10];`   Here, we know that the array name b gives the address of its first element.
On the similar lines,

* (a + 0) = * (a + 0) + 0	gives the address of the first element in the first 1-D array of a.	
* (a + 0) + 1	gives the address of the second element in the first 1-D array of a	
* (a + 0) + 2	gives the address of the third element in the first 1-D array of a, and so on.	
* (* (a + 0) + 0)	gives the first element in the first 1-D array	a [0] [0]
* (* (a + 0) + 1)	gives the second element in the first 1-D array	a [0] [1]
* (* (a + 0) + 2)	gives the third element in the first 1-D array	a [0] [2]

Similarly,

* (* (a + 1) + 0)	gives the first element in the second 1-D array	a [1] [0]
* (* (a + 1) + 1)	gives the second element in the second 1-D array	a [1] [1]
* (* (a + 1) + 2)	gives the third element in the second 1-D array	a [1] [2]

In general, a [i] [j] can be written as * (* (a + i) + j).

PROGRAM 12.7   To illustrate processing 2-D arrays using pointer notations

```c
#include <stdio.h>

int main(void)
{
        int a[10][10], m, n, i, j;

        printf("Enter the order of the matrix a \n");
        scanf("%d%d", &m, &n);

        printf("Enter elements of the matrix a of order %d * %d \n", m, n);
        for(i = 0; i < m; i++)
        for(j = 0; j < n; j++)
              scanf("%d", *(a + i) + j);

        printf("Matrix a \n");
        for(i = 0; i < m; i++)
        {
              for(j = 0; j < n; j++)
                     printf("%4d", *(*(a + i) + j));
              printf("\n");

        }

        return 0;
}
```

Input–Output:

```
Enter the order of the matrix a
2 2
Enter elements of the matrix a of order 2 * 2
1 2 3 4

Matrix a
1  2
3  4
```

Explanation:

a is declared to be an array of two dimensions and of size 10 * 10. m, n, i and j are declared to be variables of int type. The variables m and n are to collect the number of rows and the number of columns of the 2-D array. The variables i and j are to select rows and columns of the array respectively.

The segment of the program responsible for accepting the elements into the array a

```
for(i = 0; i < m; i++)
for(j = 0; j < n; j++)
        scanf("%d", *(a + i) + j);
```

Note that the second argument to scanf(), *(a+i)+j is same as &a[i][j].

The segment of the program responsible for displaying the elements of the array a

```
for(i = 0; i < m; i++)
{
        for(j = 0; j < n; j++)
                printf("%4d", *(*(a + i) + j));
        printf("\n");
}
```

Note that the second argument to printf(), *(*(a + i) + j) is same as a[i][j].

To find out whether a matrix is an identity matrix or not

A matrix is said to be an identity matrix if it is a square matrix and all the elements in the principal diagonal are 1s and all the other elements are 0s.

PROGRAM 12.8   To find out whether a matrix is an identity matrix or not

```
#include <stdio.h>

int main(void)
{
        int a[10][10], i, j, m, n, flag;

        printf("Enter the number of rows \n");
        scanf("%d", &m);
        printf("Enter the number of columns \n");
        scanf("%d", &n);

        if ( m != n)
        {
                printf("The matrix should be a square matrix \n");
                exit(0);
        }
        printf("Enter the elements of the matrix \n");
        for(i = 0; i < m; i++)
        {
                for(j = 0; j < n; j++)
                        scanf("%d", *(a + i) + j);
                printf("\n");
                }
        flag = 1;
        for(i = 0; i < m; i++)
```

```
for(j = 0; j < n; j++)
{
        if ((i == j) && (*(*(a + i) + j) != 1))
        {
                flag = 0;
                break;
        }
        if ((i != j) && (*(*(a + i) + j) != 0))
        {
        flag = 0;
        break;
        }
}
printf("The matrix \n");
for(i = 0; i < m; i++)
{
        for(j = 0; j < n; j++)
                printf("%4d", *(*(a + i) + j));
        printf("\n");
}
if (flag)
        printf("is an Identity Matrix");
else
        printf("is not an Identity Matrix");

        return 0;
}
```

Input–Output:

```
Enter the number of rows
3
Enter the number of columns
3
Enter the elements of the matrix
1 0 0 0 1 0 0 0 1

The matrix
  1  0  0
  0  1  0
  0  0  1
is an Identity Matrix
```

Explanation:

a is declared to be an array of two dimensions and of size 10 * 10. **m, n, i** and **j** are declared to be variables of **int** type. the variables **m** and **n** are to collect the number of rows and the number of columns of the 2-D array. The variables **i** and **j** are to select rows and columns of the array respectively.

After accepting the elements of the array of the given size, we find whether it is an identity matrix or not with the following segment:

```
flag = 1;
for(i = 0; i < m; i++)
for(j = 0; j < n; j++)
{
        if ((i == j) && (*(*(a + i) + j) != 1))
        {
                flag = 0;
                break;
        }
        if ((i != j) && (*(*(a + i) + j) != 0))
        {
                flag = 0;
                break;
        }
}
```

We start with the assumption that the matrix is an identity matrix by assigning 1 to the variable flag. Then we check whether the matrix satisfies the properties of an identity matrix. If it does not satisfy the variable flag is assigned 0. So ultimately, if the value of the variable flag retains 1, the matrix is displayed to be an identity matrix. Otherwise, it is displayed to be not an identity matrix. Note that the expression *(*(a + i) + j) is same as a[i][j] in the above segment.

12.5 POINTERS AND STRINGS

In the previous section, we learnt that pointers and arrays are close associates. They are so close to each other that arrays are processed using pointers internally. Strings also being arrays enjoy the same kind of relation with pointers. We know that a string is a sequence of characters terminated by a null character '\0'. The null character marks the end of the string. We also know that the name of an array gives the base address of the array. That is, the address of the first element of the array. This is true even in the case of strings. Consider the string variable char s[20]; here s gives the base address of the array. That is, the address of the first character in the string variable and hence can be regarded as a pointer to character. Since each string is terminated by a null character, it is enough for us to know the starting address of a string to be able to access the entire string. In view of these observations, we conclude that a string can be denoted by a pointer to character.

```
char s[20];
char *cp;
cp = s;
```

s is declared to be an array of **char** and it can accommodate a string. To be precise, **s** represents a string.

cp is declared to be a pointer to **char** type. assignment of **s** to **cp** is perfectly valid since **s** is also a pointer to **char** type. There is type compatibility. Now **cp** also represents the string in **s**.

Let us now consider a string constant "abcd". We know that a string constant is a sequence of characters enclosed within a pair of double quotes. The string constant is stored in some part of memory and it requires five bytes of space. Here also the address of the first character represents the entire string. The value of the string constant thus is the address of the first character 'a'. So it can be assigned to a pointer to **char** type.

If cp is a pointer to **char** type, cp = "abcd" is perfectly valid and cp now represents the entire string "abcd".

PROGRAM 12.9   To illustrate pointers to strings

```c
#include <stdio.h>

int main(void)
{
        char str[20], *cp;

        printf("Enter a string \n");
        scanf("%s", str);
        cp = str;
        printf("string in str = %s \n", cp);

        cp = "abcd";
        printf("%s \n", cp);

        return 0;
}
```

Input–Output:

```
Enter a string
Program
string in str = Program
abcd
```

Explanation:

In the above program; **str** is declared to be a string variable of size 20. Maximum 20 characters can be stored in it. **cp** is declared to be a pointer to **char** type. A string is accepted into the variable **str** using the statement scanf("%s", str); The pointer variable **cp**, being a pointer to **char** type is then assigned **str**, it is perfectly correct since **str**, the array name, gives the base address of the array and hence is a pointer to **char** type. Pointer assignment is permissible. After the assignment of **str** to **cp**, **cp** will also represent the string in **str**. It is confirmed by the statement printf("%s", cp), which displays the string in **str**. **cp** is then assigned a string constant "abcd" and the string constant is displayed by the statement printf("%s", cp);

Thus, a pointer to **char** type can represent a string and it can be made to represent different strings at different points of time. But an array of **char** type can represent only one string throughout the program. It is because of the fact that the name of a string variable is a constant pointer and it cannot be assigned any other address.

In the case of an array of **char** type, a string can be accepted into it through console. But in the case of a pointer to char type, we can only assign a string but cannot accept a string through the console.

Comparison between an array of char and a pointer to char

Array of char	Pointer to char
We can initialize a string during declaration `char str [20] = "abcd"`	We can initialize a string during a declaration `char* cp = "abcd"`
A string variable or a string constant cannot be assigned to an array of char type `char str [20];` `str = "abc"` is invalid	A string variable or a string constant can be assigned to a pointer to char type `char *p;` `p = "abcd";`
The number of bytes allocated for a string variable is determined by the size of the array	The number of bytes allocated for a string is determined by the number of characters within string.
An array of char refers to the same string (storage area)	A pointer to char can represent different strings (storage area) at different points of time
A string can be accepted through the console `char str [20];` `scanf("%s", str);` is valid	A string can not be accepted through the console `char *cp;` `scanf ("%s", cp);` is not valid since cp contains garbage value

12.5.1 Array of Pointers to Strings

We now know that a pointer variable to char type can represent a string. If we are to deal with more than one string, then we can use an array of pointers to char type to represent the strings. An example of the declaration of an array of pointers to char type is given below:

`char *ptr[10] ;`

Here, `ptr[0]`, `ptr[1]`.......`ptr[9]` are all pointers to char type and each of them can denote a string.

PROGRAM 12.10   To illustrate an array of pointers to strings

```
#include <stdio.h>

int main(void)
{
      char *names[5] = { "Nishu", "Harsha", "Shobha", "Devaraj", "Asha"
};
      int i;

      printf("The list of five Names \n");
      for(i = 0; i < 5; i++)
            printf("%s\n", names[i]);
      return 0;
}
```

Input–Output:

```
The list of five Names

Nishu
Harsha
Shobha
Devaraj
Asha
```

Explanation:

names is declared to be an array of pointers to **char** type and of size 5. The array of pointers is initialized with five strings. **names[0]** denotes the string "Nishu"; **names[1]** denotes the string "Harsha", and so on. **i** is declared to be a variable of **int** type. It is to select each string in the list of strings. A for loop is used to display the strings represented by the pointers of the array **names**.

PROGRAM 12.11   To sort a list of names using array of pointers to strings

```c
#include <stdio.h>
#include <string.h>

int main(void)
{
char *t, *names[5] = { "Nishu", "Harsha", "Shobha", "Devaraj", "Asha" };
      int i, j;

      printf("The unsorted list of five names \n");
      for(i = 0; i < 5; i++)
            printf("%s \n", names[i]);

      /* sorting begins */
      for(i = 0; i < 4; i++)
      for(j = i + 1; j < 5; j++)
            if (strcmp(names[i], names[j])>0)
            {
                  t = names[i];
                  names[i] = names[j];
                  names[j] = t;
            }
      /* sorting ends */
      printf("sorted list of names \n");
      for(i = 0; i < 5; i++)
            printf("%s \n", names[i]);
      return 0;
}
```

Input–Output:

```
The unsorted list of five Names

Nishu
Harsha
Shobha
Devaraj
Asha

sorted list of names

Asha
Devaraj
Harsha
Nishu
Shobha
```

Explanation:

names is declared to be an array of pointers to **char** type and of size 5. It is initialized with 5 strings. **t** is another pointer to **char** type and it is used as a temporary variable to represent a string during sorting process (swapping). The integer variables **i** and **j** are to be used to traverse the list of names. Initially, the unsorted list of strings is displayed. The following segment of the program accomplishes the task of sorting the list of strings.

```
for(i = 0; i < 4; i++)
for(j = i + 1; j < 5; j++)
      if (strcmp(names[i], names[j])>0)
      {
            t = names[i];
            names[i] = names[j];
            names[j] = t;
      }
```

Note that during the process of sorting, swapping of strings is done by just interchanging the pointers (without calling `strcpy()`).

12.6 POINTERS AND STRUCTURES

The concept of pointers can be used in combination with structures in two ways: One, since the address of a structure variable can be retrieved using & operator, we can think of pointers to structures; and two, having pointers to different data types as members of structures.

12.6.1 Pointers to Structures

Similar to pointers to basic type like **int**, **float** and **char**, etc., we can have pointers to structures also. The pointer variables should be declared to be the corresponding type. We use & operator to retrieve the address of a structure variable.

Example 12.5

```
struct temp
{
        int i;
        float f;
        char c;
};
```

```
struct temp t, *tp;
```

t is declared to be variable of **struct temp** type. **tp** is declared to be a pointer to **struct temp** type. The statement tp = &t ; assigns the address of **t** to **tp.** the pointer variable **tp** is now said to point to **t**. Pictorially, it can be shown as follows:

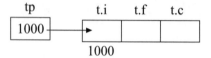

where 1000 is assumed to be the address of t.

The members of **t** are accessed through **tp** with the help of operator - > known as structure-pointer operator. - > expects the pointer variable to its left and member name to its right. **tp ->
i, tp -> f** and **tp -> c** represent **t.i, t.f** and **t.c** respectively.

PROGRAM 12.12   To illustrate pointers to structures

```
#include <stdio.h>

struct temp
{
        int i;
        float f;
        char c;
};

int main(void)
{
        struct temp t = {123, 34.56, 'p'}, *tp;
        tp = &t;
        printf("t.i = %d \n", tp->i);
        printf("t.f = %f \n", tp->f);
        printf("t.c = %c \n", tp->c);

        return 0;
}
```

Input–Output:

```
t.i = 123
t.f = 34.560000
t.c = p
```

Explanation:

The structure variable **t** is initialized with values 123, 34.56 and the character constant 'p'. The memory locations allocated for **t** will be filled with the given values as follows.

123	34.560000	p
t.i	t.f	t.c

The pointer variable **tp** is then assigned the address of **t**. The members of **t** are then accessed by means of **tp** with the use of the operator - >.

12.6.2 Structures Containing Pointers

We can even have pointers as members of structures. Consider the following structure definition.

```
struct temp
{
      int i;
      int *ip;

};
```

The structure definition includes ip, a pointer to int type as one of its members.

PROGRAM 12.13   To illustrate structure containing pointer

```
#include <stdio.h>

struct temp
{
      int i;
      int *ip;
};

int main(void)
{
      struct temp t;
      int a = 10;

      t.i = a;
      t.ip = &a;
      printf("Value of a = %d \n", t.i);
      printf("Address of a = %u \n", t.ip);

      return 0;
}
```

Input–Output:

```
Value of a = 10
Address of a = 65520
```

Explanation:

The definition of the structure **struct temp** includes two members **i** and **ip**. The member **i** is of type **int** and the member **ip** is a pointer to **int** type. In the main(), **t** is declared to be a variable of **struct temp** type. The storage for the variable t is as follows:

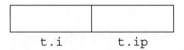

t.i is a variable of **int** type whereas t.ip is a pointer variable to **int** type. **a** is declared to be a variable of **int** type and it is initialized with the value 10. The value of **a** is assigned to t.i and the address of **a** is assigned to t.ip, a pointer to **int** type. The value of **a** and its address are displayed through t.i and t.ip respectively.

12.7 POINTERS AND UNIONS

The concept of pointers can be used in combination with unions in two ways: One, since the address of a union variable can be retrieved using & operator, we can think of pointers to unions; two, having pointers to different data types as members of unions.

12.7.1 Pointers to Unions

Similar to the concept of pointers to structures, we can think of pointers to unions as well. The address of (&) operator used with a union variable gives the address of the variable and it can be assigned to a pointer declared to be of the union type. The following program demonstrates this.

PROGRAM 12.14   To illustrate pointers to unions

```c
#include <stdio.h>
union temp
{
        int i;
        float f;
};

int main(void)
{
        union temp t, *tp;

        tp = &t;
        t.i = 10;
        printf("t.i = %d\n", tp -> i);
        t.f = 12.35;
        printf("t.f = %5.2f", tp -> f);
        return 0;
}
```

Input–Output:

```
t.i = 10
t.f = 12.35
```

12.7.2 Pointers as Members of Unions

Similar to the concept of pointers as members of structures, we can have pointers as members of unions as well. The following program illustrates this.

PROGRAM 12.15   To illustrate pointers as members of unions

```
#include <stdio.h>
union temp
{
      int i;
      int *ip;
};

int main(void)
{
      union temp t;
      int a = 20;

      t.i = a;
      printf("t.i = %d\n", t.i);
      t.ip = &a;
      printf("*(t.ip) = %d", *(t.ip));
      return 0;
}
```

Input–Output:

```
t.i = 20
*(t.ip) = 20
```

12.8   POINTERS AND FUNCTIONS

Here, we explore the possibility of the following:

- Passing pointers as arguments to functions,
- Returning a pointer from a function,
- Pointer to a function,
- Passing one function as an argument to another function.

12.8.1   Passing Pointers as Arguments to Functions

In our earlier programs which involve functions with arguments, we passed the values of actual arguments. The mechanism of calling a function by passing values is called **Call by Value**. We now discuss passing pointers as arguments to functions. The mechanism of calling a function by passing pointers is called **Call by Reference**. If a function is to be passed a pointer, it has to be reflected in the argument-list of the function prototype (if used) and the header of the function definition.

Example 12.6

```
void display(int*);
```

The function prototype indicates that the function `display()` requires a pointer to `int` as its argument.

```
void display(int *p)
{
    statements;
}
```

Note the type of the formal argument **p** in the definition of the `display()`. It is rightly declared to be a pointer to `int` type.

While calling the function `display()`, it needs to be passed the address of an integer variable as follows:

`display(&a);` where **a** is a variable of `int` type.

PROGRAM 12.16   To illustrate call by value and call by reference

---

```
#include <stdio.h>

void inc(int);
void incr(int*);

int main(void)
{
    int a = 10, b = 10;

    printf("Call By Value \n");
    printf("a = %d \n", a);
    inc(a);
    printf("After calling inc() \n");
    printf("a = %d \n", a);
    printf(" Call By Reference \n");
    printf("b = %d \n", b);
    incr(&b);
    printf("After calling incr() \n");
    printf("b = %d \n", b);

    return 0;
}

void inc(int x)
```

```
{
        x++;
        printf ("x = %d \n", x);
}

void incr (int *p)
{
        (*p)++;
}
```

Input–Output:

```
Call By Value
a = 10
x = 11
After calling inc ()
a = 10
Call By Reference
b = 10
After calling incr ()
b = 11
```

Explanation:

The function inc () is defined with a formal argument **x** of type **int**. The purpose of the function is to increment the value passed to it by 1. incr () is another function defined with one formal argument **p**, which is a pointer to **int** type. So the function incr () takes the address of a variable of **int** type and the purpose of the function is to increment the value pointed to by the address.

In the main (), **a** and **b** are declared to be variables of **int** type and are initialized with the value 10. To begin with, the value of **a** is displayed to be 10. The function inc () is invoked by passing **a** as the actual parameter. As a result, the value of **a** is copied to **x**, the formal parameter of the function and within the function, **x** is incremented by 1, it becomes 11 and is displayed. After the exit of the inc (), the control is transferred back to the main (). In the main (), the value of **a** is once again displayed. It turns out to be 10 only. The function inc () has not been able to change the value of **a**, which belongs to main (). It has acted on x, its formal parameter (a copy of a).

We now understand the working of incr () The initial value of **b** in **main ()** is displayed. Then a call is made to incr () by passing the address of the variable **b** to it as incr (&b). Now what happens is, the address of **b** is copied to **p**, the formal parameter of incr (). Within the function incr (), the value at address in **p** is incremented by 1, i.e. (*p)++, which turns out to be the variable **b** of main () itself. After the function is exited, the value of **b** is redisplayed and it is seen to be 11. So, the function incr () could change the value of the variable **b**, which belonged to main ().

PROGRAM 12.17   To illustrate passing call by value and call by reference

```
#include <stdio.h>

void swap (int, int);
```

```
void swapr(int*, int*);

int main(void)
{
        int a = 5, b = 6;
        int c = 7, d = 8;

        printf(" Call by value\n");
        printf("a = %d b = %d \n", a, b);
        swap(a, b);
        printf("After calling swap() \n");
        printf("a = %d b = %d \n", a, b);

        printf("Call by Reference \n");
        printf("c = %d d = %d \n", c, d);
        swapr(&c, &d);
        printf("After calling swapr() \n");
        printf("c = %d d = %d \n", c, d);

        return 0;
}

void swap(int x, int y)
{
        int t;

        t = x;
        x = y;
        y = t;

        printf("x = %d y = %d \n", x, y);
}

void swapr(int *p, int *q)
{
        int t;

        t = *p;
        *p = *q;
        *q = t;
}
```

Input–Output:

```
Call by value
a = 5 b = 6
x = 6 y = 5
```

```
After calling swap()
a = 5 b = 6

Call by Reference
c = 7 d = 8

After calling swapr()
c = 8 d = 7
```

Explanation:

The function swap() is defined with two formal arguments **x** and **y** of **int** type. The purpose of the function is to interchange the values taken by the formal arguments **x** and **y**. Within the function, the following statements accomplish interchanging of values of y and y.

```
t = x;
x = y;
y = t;
```

t is a local variable of the function, which acts as a temporary variable used to interchange the values.

The function swapr() is defined with two formal arguments **p** and **q** which are pointers to **int** type. The purpose of this function is to interchange the values of the variables pointed to by the pointers **p** and **q**. Within the function, the following statements accomplish interchanging of values of the locations pointed to by **p** and **q**.

   t = *p; The value at address in **p** is moved to **t**.
  *p = *q; The value at address in **q** is moved to the location whose address is in **p**.
  *q = t;   The value of **t** (the value at address in **p**) is moved to the location whose address is in **q**.

t is a local variable of the function, which acts as a temporary variable. It is used to interchange the values.

In the main(), the local variables of **int** type **a, b** and **c** and **d** are initialized with the values 5, 6, 7 and 8 respectively. The variables **a** and **b** are to be passed as arguments to swap(). Before calling swap(), the values of **a** and **b** are displayed to be 5 and 6 respectively. Then the function swap() is called by passing **a** and **b** as its arguments as swap(a, b);. The values of **a** and **b** are copied to **x** and **y**, the formal arguments of the function, respectively. the statements of the function interchange the values of **x** and **y** and they are displayed to be 6 and 5 respectively. after the exit of the function swap(), the main() function regains the control. The values of **a** and **b** are once again displayed in main() and they are seen to be 5 and 6 only, i.e. the values of **a** and **b** are not interchanged by swap(). The swap() has acted on **x** and **y**, the copies of **a** and **b** respectively not on **a** and **b** themselves.

Let us now understand the working of swapr(). The values of **c** and **d** of main() are displayed before calling swapr(). They are seen to be 7 and 8 respectively. the function swapr() is then called by passing the addresses of **c** and **d** as the arguments. the addresses of **c** and **d** are taken by the formal arguments of swapr(), **p** and **q** respectively. Within the function, the values at addresses in **p** and **q** are interchanged. Even within the swapr() also, locations of **c** and **d** are the targets. After the exit of the swapr(), control is gained by main(). In main(), the values of **c** and **d** are once again displayed. They are seen to be 8 and 7 respectively, i.e. the function swapr() has been able to interchange the values of **c** and **d** themselves.

PROGRAM 12.18   To illustrate passing both values and addresses as arguments

```c
#include <stdio.h>

void lar_seclar(int, int, int, int*, int*);

int main(void)
{
      int a, b, c, l, sl;

      printf("Enter three numbers \n");
      scanf("%d%d%d", &a, &b, &c);
      printf("Given Numbers: a = %d b = %d c = %d \n", a, b, c);
      lar_seclar(a, b, c, &l, &sl);
      printf(" Largest = %d \n", l);
      printf("Second largest = %d \n", sl);
      return 0;
}

void lar_seclar(int a, int b, int c, int *lp, int *slp)
{
      int l, s, sl;
      l = a;
      if (b > l)
            l = b;
      if (c > l)
            l = c;
      s = a;
      if (b < s)
            s = b;
      if (c < s)
            s = c;
      sl = (a + b + c) - (l + s);
      *lp = l;
      *slp = sl;
}
```

Input–Output:

```
Enter three numbers
4 5 6
Given Numbers: a = 4 b = 5 c = 6
Largest = 6
Second largest = 5
```

Explanation:

In the above program, the function `lar_seclar()` is defined with five formal arguments. The arguments **a**, **b** and **c** are the plain variables of **int** type, whereas **lp** and **slp** are pointers to **int** type. The purpose of the function is to find out the largest and the second largest of three numbers collected by the arguments **a**, **b** and **c** and assign them to the locations pointed to by the pointers **lp** and **slp** respectively. The important point being highlighted here is that the function is provided with both values as well as addresses when it is called.

On execution of the statement `lar_seclar(a, b, c, &l, &sl);` in the `main()`, the variables **s** and **sl** belonging to the `main()` would collect the largest and the second largest of the numbers in the variables **a**, **b** and **c** respectively.

Differences between call by value and call by reference

Call by value	Call by reference
The function operates on a copy of the actual arguments. Protects the integrity of the data passed since the original values remain intact. Inefficient when it comes to passing structured data types like arrays and structures as arguments.	Addresses are passed as arguments. Does not protect the integrity of the data of the calling program since the original data can be changed. Efficient when it comes to passing array and structures as arguments.
Constants can be passed as actual arguments.	Constants cannot be passed as reference arguments. Exception to this are string constants.
Functions cannot return more than one value.	The effect of changing the values of the variable belonging to the calling program is equivalent to returning more than one value.

12.8.2 Returning a Pointer from a Function

Under some circumstances, we require functions to return a pointer. The fact that a function returns a pointer should be indicated by its declaration and definition.

The syntax of declaration of a function returning a pointer is as follows:

```
data-type *function_name (arguments);
```

Note the presence of * before `function name`. It is to indicate that the function returns a pointer to data-type.

Example 12.7

```
int *sum(int, int);
```

The function `sum()` is declared to indicate that it requires two parameters of **int** type and it returns a pointer to **int** type.

___

PROGRAM 12.19   To illustrate a function returning a pointer

```
#include <stdio.h>

int *sum(int, int);
```

```
int main(void)
{
        int a, b, *s;


        printf("Enter two numbers \n");
        scanf("%d%d", &a, &b);
        printf("a = %d b = %d \n", a, b);
        s = sum(a, b);
        printf("sum = %d \n", *s);

        return 0;
}

int* sum(int a, int b)
{
        static int s;
        s = a + b;
        return (&s);
}
```

Input–Output:

```
Enter two numbers
4 5

a = 4 b = 5
s = 9
```

Explanation:

The function sum() is defined with two arguments of type **int** and it is made to return a pointer to **int** type. The purpose of the function is to find the sum of the values passed to it and return the address of the variable, which stores the sum of the values.

In the main(), values are accepted into the variables **a** and **b**. A call is then made to sum() by passing **a** and **b** as its actual arguments as s = sum(a, b); Note that **s** is declared to be a pointer to **int** type. The value pointed to by **s**, the sum of **a** and **b**, is then displayed.

12.8.3 Pointers, Strings and Functions

We know that a pointer to **char** type can represent a string. We will now write programs which incorporate our own functions to simulate the most commonly used string manipulation functions like strlen(), strcpy(), strcat() and strcmp(). All these functions are provided with pointers to **char** type as arguments.

PROGRAM 12.20　To find the length of a string using a user-defined function [simulator of `strlen()`]

```c
#include <stdio.h>

int str_len(char *p);

int main()
{
        char str[20];
        int length;
        printf("Enter a string \n");
        scanf("%s", str);
        length = str_len(str);
        printf("Length = %d\n", length);
        return 0;
}

int str_len(char *p)
{
        int l = 0;
        while ( *p != '\0')
        {
                l++;
                p++;
        }
        return (l);
}
```

Input–Output:

```
Enter a string
Bangalore
Length = 9
```

Explanation:

In the above program, the function `str_len()` is defined with a formal argument **p**, which is a pointer to **char** type and it is made to return a value of **int** type. The purpose of the function is to find the length of the string represented by the pointer **p** and return it to the calling program. The variable **l** in the function is to collect the length of the string. Initially, it is assigned 0. The segment of the function responsible for counting the number of characters in the string is:

```c
while ( *p != '\0')
{
        l++;
        p++;
}
```

As long as the null character in the string is not reached both **l** and **p** are incremented. The variable **p** is incremented to point to the next character location in the string. Once the null character is reached, the loop is exited and the variable **l** would collect the length of the string and it is returned to the `main()`.

PROGRAM 12.21   To copy one string to another string using a user-defined function [simulator of `strcpy()`]

```
#include <stdio.h>

char* str_cpy(char *t, char *s) ;

int main(void)
{
        char s[20] = "abcd", t[20];
        str_cpy(t, s);
        printf(" t = %s \n", t);
        return 0;
}

char* str_cpy(char *t, char *s)
{
        char *ts;
        ts = t;
        while ( *s != '\0')
        {
                *t = *s;
                s++;
                t++;
        }
        *t = '\0';
        return ts;
}
```

Input–Output:

---

t = abcd

Explanation:

In the above program, the function `strcpy()` is defined with two pointers to **char** type **t** and **s** as formal arguments and it is made to return a pointer to **char** type to the calling function. The purpose of the function is to copy the source string represented by **s** to the target string **t** and to return the address of the target string back to the calling function (`main()` in this case). Within the function as long as the end of the source string **s** is not reached, each character in **s** is assigned to the corresponding position of the target string **t** with the following segment:

```
        while ( *s != '\0')
        {
                *t = *s;
                s++;
                t++;
        }
}
```

Note that both **s** and **t** are incremented in each iteration. Once all the characters in **s** are copied to **t**, the null character `'\0'` is assigned to the last location of **t**. This is necessary to mark the end of the string in **t**. Ultimately, the starting address of the target string is returned back to the calling function. In the main (), the function call is like an independent statement. The return value is not used.

PROGRAM 12.22   To concatenate two strings using a user-defined function [simulator of strcat()]

```
#include <stdio.h>
#include <string.h>

char* str_cat(char *t, char *s);
int main(void)
{
        char s[20] = "abcd", t[20] = "xyz";
        printf("t = %s \n", t);
        printf("s = %s \n", s);
        str_cat(t, s);
        printf("After Concatenation \n");
        printf(" t = %s \n", t);
        return 0;
}

char* str_cat(char *t, char *s)
{
        char *ts;
        ts = t;
        int l;
        l = strlen(t);
        while ( *s != '\0')
        {
                *(t + l) = *s;
                s++;
                t++;
        }
        *(t + l) = '\0';
        return ts;
}
```

Input–Output:

```
t = xyz
s = abcd
After Concatenation
t = xyzabcd
```

Explanation:

In the above program, the function strcat() is defined with two pointers to **char** type **t** and **s** as formal arguments and it is made to return a pointer to **char** type to the calling function. The purpose of the function is to append the string in s to the end of the string in t and return the address of the target string back to the calling function (main() in this case). Within the function, the length of t is found out. As long as the end of the source string s is not reached, each character in s is assigned to the corresponding next position of the target string t with the following segment:

```
while ( *s != '\0')
{
        *(t + 1) = *s;
        s++;
        t++;
}
```

Note that both **s** and **t** are incremented in each iteration. Once all the characters in **s** are appended to **t**, the null character '\0' is assigned to the last location of **t** with the statement *(t+1) = '\0';. This is necessary to mark the end of the string in **t**. Ultimately, the starting address of the target string **ts** is returned back to the calling function. In the main(), the function call is like an independent statement. The return value is not used.

PROGRAM 12.23   To compare two strings using a user-defined function [simulator of strcmp()]

```
#include <stdio.h>
int str_cmp(char *s, char *t);

int main()
{
        char s[20], t[20];

        printf("Enter a string into s \n");
        gets(s);
        printf("Enter a string into t \n");
        gets(t);
        if (str_cmp(s, t) > 0)
                printf(" s is greater than t");
        else if (str_cmp(s, t) < 0)
                printf(" s is less than t");
        else
                printf("s and t are equal");
```

```
        return 0;
}
int str_cmp(char *s, char *t)
{
        while ((*s == *t) && (*s != '\0'))
        {
                s++;
                t++;
        }
        return (*s - *t);
}
```

Input–Output:

```
Enter a string into s
abc
Enter a string into t
abc
s and t are equal
```

Explanation:

In the above program, the function str_cmp() is defined with two pointers to char type t and s as formal arguments and it is made to return a value of **int** type. The purpose of the function is to compare the two strings represented by t and s and return the numerical difference between the ASCII values of the first non-matching pair of characters of the two strings if the strings are not equal and return 0 if the strings are equal.

12.8.4   Pointers to Functions

In the case of arrays, we know that name of an array gives its base address (address of the first location) and thus acts as a pointer to the first location of the array. This is true even in the case of functions. Name of a function also gives its starting address. Thus, we can use a pointer to invoke a function before which the pointer has to be declared appropriately and assigned the address of the function.

The syntax of declaring a pointer to a function is as follows:

```
data-type (*variable_name)(argument_types);
```

variable_name is declared to be a pointer to a function, which returns a value of type data-type.

Example 12.8

```
int (*fnp)(int, int);
```

fnp is declared to be a pointer to a function, which takes two arguments of **int** type and returns a value of type **int**. fnp can now be assigned the address of a function accepting two arguments of **int** type and returning a value of type **int**.

```
int sum(int, int);

fnp = sum;
```

fnp now points to the function sum().

PROGRAM 12.24   To illustrate pointers to functions

```
#include <stdio.h>

int sum(int, int);

int main(void)
{
       int a, b, s, (*fnp)(int, int);

       printf("Enter two numbers \n");
       scanf("%d%d", &a, &b);
       printf("a = %d b = %d \n", a, b);
       fnp = sum;
       s = *fnp)(a, b);
       printf("sum = %d \n", s);

       return 0;
}

int sum(int a, int b)
{
       int s;
       s = a + b;
       return s;
}
```

Input–Output:

```
Enter two numbers
4 6

a = 4 b = 6

sum = 10
```

Explanation:

The function sum() is defined with two arguments of type **int** and it is made to return a value of **int** type. The purpose of the function is to find the sum of the values passed to it and return the sum of the values.

In the main(), **a, b** and **s** are declared to be variables of **int** type. **fnp** is declared to be a pointer to a function which takes two arguments of **int** type and which returns a value of **int** type. Values are accepted into the variables **a** and **b**. The variable **fnp** is assigned the address of the function sum() with the statement fnp = sum; then, a call is made to sum() through the pointer **fnp** with the statement s = (*fnp) (a, b); The variable **s** collects the value returned by the function and it is displayed.

12.8.5 Passing One Function as an Argument to Another Function

We know that the name of a function always gives the starting address of the function and thus it is a pointer to the function. We also know that we can pass pointers to data types as arguments to functions. These facts lead us to think of the possibility of passing a pointer to a function to another function. This is certainly possible. The following program illustrates this.

PROGRAM 12.25 To illustrate passing one function as an argument to another function

```c
#include <stdio.h>

int lessthan(int, int);
int greaterthan(int, int);
void sort(int a[], int n, int (*fnp)(int, int));

int main(void)
{
        int a[10], i, n;

        printf("Enter the number of values \n");
        scanf("%d", &n);
        printf("Enter %d values \n", n);
        for(i = 0; i < n; i++)
                scanf("%d", &a[i]);

        printf("Unsorted List \n");
        for(i = 0; i < n; i++)
                printf("%d \n", a[i]);

        sort(a, n, lessthan);
        printf("sorted in decreasing order \n");
        for(i = 0; i < n; i++)
                printf("%d\n", a[i]);

        sort(a, n, greaterthan);
        printf("sorted in increasing order \n");
        for(i = 0; i < n; i++)
                printf("%d\n", a[i]);

        return 0;
}
```

```
int lessthan(int a, int b)
{
      return (a < b);
}

int greaterthan(int a, int b)
{
      return (a > b);
}

void sort(int a[], int n, int (*fnp)(int, int))
{
      int i, j, t;

      for(i = 0; i < n - 1; i++)
      for(j = i + 1; j < n; j++)
      if (fnp(a[i], a[j]))
      {
            t = a[i];
            a[i] = a[j];
            a[j] = t;
      }

}
```

Input–Output:

```
Enter the number of values
5
Enter 5 values
1 3 4 2 6

Unsorted List
1 3 4 2 6

sorted in decreasing order
6 4 3 2 1

sorted in increasing order
1 2 3 4 6
```

Explanation:

The function lessthan() is defined with two formal arguments **a** and **b** of **int** type and it is made to return a value of **int** type. The purpose of this function is to collect two numbers into **a** and **b** and return 1 if **a** is found to be less than **b** otherwise 0.

The function `greaterthan()` is also defined with two formal arguments **a** and **b** of **int** type and it is made to return a value of **int** type. The purpose of this function is to collect two numbers into **a** and **b** and return 1 if **a** is found to be greater than **b** otherwise 0.

The function `sort()` is defined with three formal arguments **a, n** and **fnp**. the argument **a** is a pointer to integer type; **n** is of **int** type and **fnp** is a pointer to a function which takes two arguments of **int** type and which returns an integer value. The purpose of the function is to take an array of integers and sort the elements of the array in the order determined by the function pointed to by **fnp**.

In the `main()`, **a** is declared to be an array of **int** type and of size 10. Maximum 10 elements can be accepted into the array. **i** and **n** are declared to be variables of **int** type. The variable **n** is to collect the number of elements to be accepted into the array **a** and the variable **i** is to select each location of the array.

After accepting a value for the variable **n**, **n** values are accepted into the array **a** and they are displayed. The list is then sorted in the decreasing order with the call `sort(a,n,lessthan)`. Within the function `sort()`, the function `lessthan()` is invoked to compare two numbers which returns true when the first number is less than the second number being compared. Thus, the list is sorted in the decreasing order. The sorted list is then displayed.

The list is then sorted in the increasing order with the call `sort(a, n, greaterthan)`. Within the function `sort()`, this time, the function `greaterthan()` is invoked to compare two numbers which returns true when the first number is greater than the second number being compared. Thus, the list is sorted in the increasing order. The sorted list is once again displayed.

A list of **n** numbers is accepted into the array **a**. the unsorted list is displayed. the function `sort()` is invoked by passing the array **a, n** and **lessthan** as the actual arguments (Note that `lessthan` is the address of the function `lessthan()`, which is mapped onto the third argument **fnp** of `sort()`) as `sort(a, n, lessthan)`; the function `call` sorts the elements in the array **a** in the decreasing order and then the function call `sort(a, n, greaterthan)`; sorts the elements in the array a in the increasing order. (Note that this time, **greaterthan**, the address of the function `greaterthan()` is passed and it is mapped onto **fnp**, the third parameter of the function `sort()`).

12.9 POINTERS TO POINTERS

We now know that a pointer is a special type of variable and it can collect the address of another variable. Once a pointer is assigned, the address of a plain variable, the value of the plain variable can then be accessed indirectly through the pointer with the help of * (value at address) operator. Since the pointer is also a variable, it is also allocated memory space of size two bytes and its address also is retrievable. The address of the pointer variable itself can also be stored in another appropriately declared variable. The variable which can store the address of a pointer variable itself is termed a **Pointer to Pointer**. Note that a pointer to pointer adds a further level of indirection. The syntax of declaring a pointer to pointer is as follows:

```
data-type **variable;
```

Note the usage of double * before the pointer variable name. They are to indicate that the variable is a pointer to a pointer to a variable of type `data-type`.

Consider the following declarations:

```
int a = 10, *ap, **app;
```

Here, **a** is a plain integer variable. The variable **ap** is a pointer to **int** type and the variable **app** is declared to be a pointer to pointer to **int** type (note that two * are used). Now **ap** can be assigned the address of the variable **a**. The variable **app** can be assigned the address of **ap**. The following statements accomplish these assignments.

```
ap = &a;
app = &ap;
```

To access the value of **a** through **ap** , we use ***ap**.
To access the value of **a** through **app** , we use ****ap**.

PROGRAM 12.26   To illustrate a pointer to a pointer

```
#include <stdio.h>

int main(void)
{
        int a = 10, *ap, **app;

        ap = &a;
        app = &ap;

        printf("Address of a = %u \n", ap);
        printf("Address of ap = %u \n", app);
        printf("value of a through ap = %d \n", *ap);
        printf("value of a through app = %d \n", **app);

        return 0;
}
```

Input–Output:

```
Address of a = 65524
Address of ap = 65522
value of a through ap = 10
value of a through app = 10
```

Explanation:

In the above program, we have seen that there are two levels of indirection to access the value of the variable **a**. This was accomplished through a pointer to pointer. Theoretically, the levels of indirection can be further extended. There is no constraint imposed on this. Further levels of indirection like three levels, four levels are rarely used because of the following fact: higher the level of indirection, lesser will be the degree of comprehensibility.

12.10   DYNAMIC MEMORY ALLOCATION

We know that the variables are named memory locations and they are to hold data to be manipulated by the programs. So far, in all our programs, memory locations for the variables were allocated during compilation time itself. For instance, the declarations `int a;` `float f;` and `char c;` direct the compiler to allocate two bytes, four bytes and one byte of memory to hold `integer value`, `float value` and `char value` respectively. So the quantum of memory is determined by the compiler itself depending on the type of variables. This type of memory allocation is termed **Static Memory Allocation**. Consider the declaration of arrays in C.

`int a[10];`

declares **a** to be an array of `int` type and size 10. The compiler thus allocates 10 contiguous memory locations as follows.

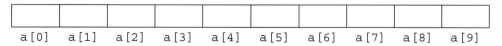

Memory locations are allocated for the array statically. Here we identify two shortcomings. Firstly, what if we need to deal with more than ten values of `int` type during runtime of the program, we cannot increase the size of the array during runtime. Secondly, many a time, not all the locations are used, when this is the case, we cannot decrease the size of the array. As a result, memory goes wasted. This is where the concept of **dynamic memory allocation** comes into picture. As the name itself indicates, memory can be allocated dynamically, i.e. during runtime of the programs. While allocating, we can specify the size of the memory block to be allocated and also we can release the unwanted memory blocks for later use.

12.10.1   Built-in Functions Supporting Dynamic Memory Allocation

The standard C library has the following built-in functions, which help in dealing with the dynamic memory allocation.

1. `malloc()`
2. `calloc()`
3. `realloc()`
4. `free()`

The declarations for the functions are available in the header file `alloc.h`.

1. `malloc()`

The `malloc()` allocates a block of memory of requested size and returns a pointer to the first byte of the block. The syntax of its usage is as follows:

`ptr = (data_type*) malloc(byte_size);`

where `byte_size` is the number of bytes to be allocated and `ptr` is a pointer of type data-type, which collects the address of the first byte of the memory block allocated. The memory block allocated will have garbage values. If the allocation is not successful, the function returns `NULL` value.

2. `free()`

The `free()` is to release a block of memory, which is previously allocated so that it can be reused for some other purpose. The syntax of its usage is as follows:

`free(ptr) ;`

where **ptr** is a pointer, which points to the first byte of the memory block to be released.

PROGRAM 12.27   To illustrate `malloc()` : Creation of an array dynamically

```
#include <stdio.h>
#include <malloc.h>

int main(void)
{
        int *a, n, i;

        printf("Enter the number of elements \n");
        scanf("%d", &n);
        a = malloc(n * sizeof(int)); /* allocate memory for n integers */

    printf("Enter %d elements \n", n);
    for(i = 0; i < n; i++)
    scanf("%d", a + i);
    printf("The list of elements \n");
    for(i = 0; i < n; i++)
    printf("%d\n", *(a + i));
    free(a); /* Release the allocated memory */

        return 0;
}
```

Input–Output:

```
Enter the number of elements
5

Enter 5 elements
1 2 3 4 5

The list of elements
1 2 3 4 5
```

Explanation:

In the above program, the variable **a** is declared to be a pointer to **int** type. **n** and **i** are declared to be plain variables of **int** type. The purpose of the program is to create an array dynamically by specifying the size of the array during runtime. The pointer variable **a** is to collect the address of the first byte of the memory block allocated by the `malloc()`. The variable **n** is to accept the size of the array during runtime. The variable **i** is used as the array index.

After accepting the size of the array, the required amount of memory space is allocated with the statement a = `malloc(n * sizeof(int));` On successful execution of the statement, a block of memory large enough to accommodate n integers is allocated in the memory heap and the starting address of the block is assigned to the pointer variable **a**. Now, the array is filled with integer values and they are displayed. Note that the constant pointer expression *(a + i) has been used to access each element of the array. Then the statement free (a) releases the block of memory pointed to by the variable **a**.

PROGRAM 12.28   To allocate memory for employee details dynamically

```
#include <stdio.h>
#include <malloc.h>

struct emp
{
        int empno;
        char name[20];
        float salary;
};
int main(void)
{
        struct emp *ep;
        int n, i;

        printf("Enter the number of employees \n");
        scanf("%d", &n);

        ep = (struct emp*) malloc(n * sizeof(struct emp));

        printf("Enter %d employees details \n", n);
        for(i = 0; i < n; i++)
                scanf("%d%s%f", &ep[i].empno, ep[i].name, &ep[i].salary);
        printf("Employees Details \n");
        for(i = 0; i < n; i++)
            printf("%6d%20s%8.2f\n",ep[i].empno, ep[i].name, ep[i].salary);
        free(ep);

        return 0;
}
```

Input–Output:

```
Enter the number of employees
2
Enter 2 employees details
121    Nishu    23000
124    Harsha   34500

Employees Details
121    Nishu    23000.00
124    Harsha   34500.00
```

Explanation:

The statement ep = (struct emp*) malloc (n * sizeof (struct emp)); allocates memory for storing n employees' details and the address of the first block is assigned to the variable ep. Using array notation, the data for the employees are accepted and they are displayed.

3. calloc()

The calloc() allocates multiple blocks of memory, all of which are of same size and returns a pointer to the first byte of the first block. The syntax of its usage is as follows:

ptr = (data_type*) calloc(n, block_size);

where **n** is the number of blocks of memory to be allocated. **block_size** is the number of bytes in each block and **ptr** is a pointer of type data-type, which collects the address of the first byte of the first memory block allocated. The memory block allocated will be filled with 0s. If the allocation is not successful, the function returns NULL value.

PROGRAM 12.29   To illustrate calloc(): Creation of an array dynamically

---

```c
#include <stdio.h>
#include <malloc.h>

int main(void)
{
        int *a, n, i;

        printf("Enter the number of elements \n");
        scanf("%d", &n);
        a = calloc(n, 2); /* allocate memory for n integers */
        printf("Enter %d elements \n", n);
        for(i = 0; i < n; i++)
                scanf("%d", a + i);
        printf("The list of elements \n");
        for(i = 0; i < n; i++)
                printf("%d\n", *(a + i));
        free(a); /* Release the allocated memory */

        return 0;
}
```

Input–Output:

```
Enter the number of elements
5
Enter 5 elements
4 5 6 7 8

The list of elements
4 5 6 7 8
```

Explanation:

In the above program, the variable **a** is declared to be a pointer to **int** type. **n** and **i** are declared to be plain variables of **int** type. The purpose of the program is to create an array dynamically by specifying the size of the array during runtime. The pointer variable **a** is to collect the starting address of the first block of the memory blocks allocated by the calloc(). The variable **n** is to accept the size of the array during runtime. The variable **i** is used as the array index.

After accepting the size of the array, the required amount of memory space is allocated with the statement a = calloc(n, sizeof(int)); On successful execution of the statement, n blocks of memory, all of equal size (sizeof(int) are allocated in the memory heap and the starting address of the first block is assigned to the pointer variable **a**. Now, the array is filled with integer values and they are displayed. Note that the constant pointer expression *(a + i) has been used to access each element of the array. Then the statement free(a) releases the block of memory pointed to by the variable **a**.

4. Realloc()

We now know that malloc() and calloc() are used to dynamically allocate memory space required to store data. Under some circumstances, we may need to alter the size of the memory block allocated by either malloc() or calloc(), during runtime itself. This is accomplished by realloc(). The syntax of its usage is as follows:

new_ptr = (data-type*) realloc(old_ptr, new_size);

where old_ptr points to the block of memory previously allocated by malloc() or calloc(). new_size is the size of the block to be reallocated. On successful execution, the function returns a pointer to the first byte of the reallocated memory block. If the function does not execute successfully, it returns NULL value.

Here, new_size may be smaller or larger than the earlier size of the memory block. The position of the old memory block and that of the reallocated block may be same or different. If they are different, the data in the old block will be safely shifted to the new block.

PROGRAM 12.30   To illustrate realloc() and free()

```
#include <stdio.h>
#include <alloc.h>
#include <string.h>

int main(void)
{
        char *str;

        /* allocate memory for string */
        str = (char *) malloc(7);
        /* copy "Mysore" into string */
        strcpy(str, "Mysore");
        printf("String %s is at address %p \n", str, str);
```

```
str = (char *) realloc(str, 10);
strcpy(str, "Bangalore");
printf("String %s is at address %p \n", str, str);

/* free memory */
free(str);

return 0;
}
```

Input–Output:

```
String Mysore is at address 07EC
String Bangalore is at address 07F8
```

Explanation:

ptr is declared to be pointer variable to char type. It can collect the address of a character. The statement ptr = malloc(7), on its successful execution, allocates a block of memory of size seven bytes in the memory heap and assigns the starting address of the block to the variable **ptr**. The string constant "Mysore" is then copied to the memory block. Since the length of the string constant "Mysore" is 6, the memory block allocated was of size 7 bytes (6 + Null Character). Later, in order to write the string "Bangalore" , the size of the block has been altered by the use of realloc() with the statement str = realloc(str, 10). Note that the new size is 10 bytes (length of "Bangalore" + Null Character). Then the string constant "Bangalore" has been copied to the new memory block.

SUMMARY

- A pointer is a variable which can collect the address of another variable or the address of a block of memory.
- The strength of C lies in the usage of pointers.
- The concept of pointers is extensively used in dealing with dynamic memory allocation.
- The operators which are used with pointers include & (address of) and * (value at).
- There is a close relationship between pointers and arrays.
- The elements of an array are accessed through pointers. String manipulations can be performed efficiently with the help of pointers.
- Structures and unions can be used in combination with pointers.
- By passing pointers as arguments to functions we implement call by reference.
- We can even pass one function as argument to another function.
- Allocation of memory during runtime of a program is termed dynamic memory allocation.
- The standard C library provides the functions, namely malloc(), malloc(), realloc() and free() to deal with dynamically allocate and deallocate memory during runtime of a program.

REVIEW QUESTIONS

12.1 What is a pointer?

12.2 What are the advantages offered by pointers?

12.3 Give the significance of & and * operators.

12.4 Give an account of pointer arithmetic.

12.5 Explain how one-dimensional array elements are accessed using pointer notation.

12.6 Explain how two-dimensional array elements are accessed using pointer notation.

12.7 a[i] and i[a] are equivalent. Justify.

12.8 What is call by value?

12.9 What is call by reference?

12.10 Differentiate between call by value and call by reference.

12.11 Explain the concept of passing one function as the argument to another function with an example.

12.12 Explain the concept of pointers to functions.

12.13 Give an account of string manipulation using pointers.

12.14 Differentiate between static memory allocation and dynamic memory allocation.

12.15 Mention the standard library functions supported by C to deal with dynamic memory allocation.

12.16 Differentiate between malloc() and calloc().

12.17 Explain the working of realloc().

12.18 What is a self-referential structure?

12.19 Explain the concept of pointers to structures.

State whether the following are true are false

12.1 Pointers facilitate static memory allocation.

12.2 int *p1;
float *p2;
p1 = p2; is a valid statement.

12.3 int *p;
p += 2; is a valid statement.

12.4 int *p1, *p2;
p1 < p2 is a valid test-expression.

12.5 We can have a pointer to a pointer to an integer.

12.6 Pointers enable us to write efficient programs.

12.7 We can access array elements using pointers.

12.8 We can use pointers as members of structures.

12.9 We can pass one function as argument to another function.

12.10 There is no difference between `malloc()` and `calloc()`.

12.11 We cannot reduce the amount of memory already allocated by `malloc()` or `calloc()`.

12.12 We can pass some arguments by value and some by reference to functions.

12.13 There is no way of protecting the variables from altering which are passed by reference.

Identify errors, if any, in the following

12.1
```c
int p;
float *fp;
fp = &p;
```

12.2
```c
int *ip, a;
ip = &a;
ip += 2;
```

12.3
```c
int a[] = {1,2, 3};
int i;
for(i = 0; i < 3; i++)
        printf("%d", *a+i);
```

12.4
```c
struct temp
{
     int a;
     float b;
};
struct temp t, *tp;
tp = &t;
scanf("%d%f:, &tp.a, &tp.b);
```

12.5
```c
int main(void)
{
     int a[] = {1, 2, 3,4 }, i;

     for(i = 0; i < 4; i++)
     {
          printf("%d", *a);
          a++;
     }
     return 0;
}
```

12.6
```c
int main(void)
{
     int a[][2] = {1, 2, 3, 4};
     int *ap;

     ap = a;
```

```
            return 0;
    }
12.7 int *sum(int*, int*);

    int main(void)
    {
        int a = 3, b = 5, s;

        s = sum(a, b);
        printf("sum= %d", s);
    }
    int sum(int a, it b)
    {
            return (a + b);
    }
12.8 #include<stdio.h>
    int main()
    {
    int X[5]={5,10,15,20,25};
    int i=3,Result
    Result=*X[--i]+2*X[--i]+3*X[--i];
    printf("%d %d\n",Result, i);
    return 0;
    }
```

PROGRAMMING EXERCISES

12.1 What is the output of the following programs

```
    int main(void)
    {
        int a[10], *ap, *bp;
        ap = a;
        bp = &a[0];
        printf("%d", ap-bp);
        return 0;
    }
```

12.2 What is the output of the following programs

```
    int main(void)
    {
        int a[10] = {1, 2, 5, 7}, *ap, *bp;
        ap = a;
        bp = &a[3];
```

```
        printf("%d%d", *ap, *bp));
        return 0;
}
```

12.3 Write a program to sort a list of numbers using pointers notation.

12.4 Write a program to create a list of students' details using a dynamic array.

12.5 Write a function to extract a part of a string using pointers.

12.6 Write a program to sort a matrix row-wise using pointer notation for the elements of the matrix.

12.7 Write a program to find the LCM and GCD of two numbers using a function.

The function call should be as follows: `lcm_gcd(a, b, &l, &g)`; where a and b are two numbers (inputs) and `l` and `g` are two variables collecting the LCM and the GCD of the two numbers.

12.8 Write a program using a function to accept an amount in figures and display the amount in words.

    Example: Amount in Figures: 478

                     Amount in Words: Four Hundred Seventy Eight Only

12.9 Write a program using a function to accept an amount and format it using commas for better readability.

    Example: Unformatted Amount   : 45678765

                     Formatted Amount   : 4,56,78,765

INTERVIEW QUESTIONS

12.1 What is the output of the following programs?

```
(a) int main(void)
    {
        int a[10], *ap, *bp;
        ap = a;
        bp = &a[0];
        printf("%d", ap-bp);
        return 0;
    }

(b) int main(void)
    {
        int a[10] = {1, 2, 5, 7}, *ap, *bp;
        ap = a;
        bp = &a[3];
        printf("%d%d", *ap, *bp));
        return 0;
    }
```

```
(c)#include <stdio.h>
   int main(void)

   {
         int C = 5, *ptr;
         ptr = &C;
         printf("%u%d\n", ptr, *ptr);
         ptr++;
         printf("%u%d\n ", ptr, C);
      return 0;
   }

(d)#include <stdio.h>
   int main(void)
   {
      int A[4] = {3, 6, 9, 12}, *p=A;
      printf("%d%d%d\n", *A, *(p++), *(p+1);
      return 0;
   }

(e)#include <stdio.h>
   int main(void)
   {
      int X[3] = {5, 10, 15};
      int *p = X;
      int *r = &p;
      printf("%d", ++(**r) + *p);
      return 0;
   }

(f)#include<stdio.h>
   int main(void)
   {
      int x=3, *y, **z;
      y=&x;
      x=&y;
      printf("%d\n", *y***y***z);
      return 0;
   }

(g)int main(void)
   {
      int a=10, b=20;
      change(&a,b);
      printf("%d%d\n", a, b);
      return 0;
   }
```

```
change(int *p, int q)
{
    *p=*p*3;
    Q=q*4;
}
```

(h) ```
#include<stdio.h>
int main(void)

{
    int a, *p1;
    char c, *p2;
    float f *p3;
    printf("%d%d%d\n", sizeof(p1), sizeof(p2), sizeof(p3));
    return 0;
}
```

**12.2** What are far, near and huge pointers?

**12.3** With an example, differentiate the expression *p++ and ++*p.

**12.4** If array name itself is a pointer, how do you access the $(i, j, k)^{th}$ element of a three dimension array X? (Where i, j and k are the index variables referring to table, row and column respectively.)

**12.5** Distinguish between `const char *p;` and `char const *p;`.

**12.6** What is the advantage of pointer to a character string compared to two-dimensional array of characters?

**12.7** What is a dangling pointer?

**12.8** If p is a pointer to a float array a with base address 1000, then what is the value of p after executing the statement p++;?

**12.9** Which operators are used to access structure members using pointer?
```

13

File Handling in C

13.1 INTRODUCTION

Each program revolves around some data. It requires some inputs; performs manipulations over them; and produces the required outputs. So far, in all our earlier programs, the inputs originated from the standard input device, keyboard, with the help of `scanf()`, `getchar()` and `gets()`. We displayed the outputs produced, through the standard output device, screen, by the use of library functions `printf()`, `putchar()` and `puts()`. This scheme of I/O operations suffers from the following drawbacks:

Firstly, the data involved in the I/O operations are lost when the program is exited or when the power goes off.

Secondly, this scheme is definitely not ideal for programs, which involve voluminous data.

But, many real life programming circumstances require to deal with large amount of data and require the data to be permanently available even when the program is exited or when the power goes off. This is where the concept of files comes into picture.

A file is defined to be a collection of related data stored on secondary storage device like disk. It is a named storage on secondary storage devices. The concept of files enables us to store large amount of data permanently on the secondary storage devices. The ability to store large amount of data and the ability to store them permanently are attributed to the physical characteristics of the devices.

13.2 OPERATIONS ON FILES

The commonly performed operations over files are the following:

1. Opening a file
2. Reading from a file

3. Writing to a file
4. Appending to a file (adding to the end of the file)
5. Updating a file
6. Deleting a file
7. Renaming a file
8. Closing a file

These operations are accomplished by means of standard library functions that are provided by C. Let us now get to know these functions.

13.3   OPENING AND CLOSING OF FILES

fopen()

The fopen() is to open a file. Opening a file basically establishes a link between a program and the file being opened. The syntax of its usage is as follows:

fp = fopen("filename", "mode of opening");

filename is the name of the file being opened (which is remembered by the operating system). Mode of opening can be any one of the following.

Mode of opening	Purpose
w	To create a text file. If the file already exists, its contents are destroyed, otherwise it is created, if possible.
r	To open a text file for reading; the file must exist.
a	To open a text file for appending (writing at the end); if the file does not exist, it is created, if possible.
w+	To create a text file for both reading and writing; if the file already exists, its contents are destroyed, otherwise it is created, if possible.
r+	To open a text file for both reading and writing; the file must exist.
a+	To open a text file for reading and appending; if the file already exists, its contents are retained; if the file does not exist, it is created if possible.
wb	To create a binary file. If the file already exists, its contents are destroyed, otherwise it is created, if possible.
rb	To open a binary file for reading; the file must exist.
ab	To open a binary file for appending (writing at the end); if the file does not exist, it is created, if possible.
wb+	To create a binary file for both reading and writing; if the file already exists, its contents are destroyed, otherwise it is created, if possible.
rb+	To open a binary file for both reading and writing; the file must exist.
ab+	To open a binary file for reading and appending; if the file already exists, its contents are retained; if the file does not exist, it is created if possible.

`fclose()`

the `fclose()` is the counterpart of `fopen()`. This is to close a file. Closing a file means delinking the file from the program and saving the contents of the file.

The syntax of its usage is as follows:

`fclose(fp);`

where `fp` is a pointer to FILE type and represents a file. The file represented by `fp` is closed.

13.4   FILE I/O FUNCTIONS

After a file is opened, we can read data stored in the file or write new data onto it depending on the mode of opening. C standard library supports a good number of functions which can be used for performing I/O operations. These functions are referred to as file I/O functions.

File I/O functions are broadly classified into two types.

1. High level file I/O functions
2. Low level file I/O functions

High level file I/O functions are basically C standard library functions and are easy to use. Most of the C programs handling files use these because of their simple nature. Low level file I/O functions are file related system calls of the underlying operating system. These are relatively more complex in nature when compared to high level file I/O functions but efficient in nature.

In this chapter, we shall deal with high level file I/O functions only. High level file I/O functions can be further classified into the following two types:

1. Unformatted file I/O functions
2. Formatted file I/O functions

1. Unformatted file I/O functions

- `fputc()` and `fgetc()`–character oriented file I/O functions
- `fputs()` and `fgets()`–string oriented file I/O functions

2. Formatted file I/O functions:
   `fprintf()` and `fscanf()` – mixed data oriented file I/O functions

13.4.1   Character Oriented Functions–`fputc()`, `fgetc()`

`fputc()` is to write a character onto a file. The syntax of its usage is as follows:

`fputc(c, fp);`

where `c` represents a character and `fp`, a pointer to FILE, represents a file. The function writes the content of `c` onto the file represented by `fp`.

`fgetc()` is to read a character from a file. The syntax of its usage is as follows:

`c = fgetc(fp);`

`c` is a variable of **char** type and `fp` is a pointer to **FILE** type. The function reads a character from the file denoted by `fp` and returns the character value, which is collected by the variable `c`.

PROGRAM 13.1   To create a file consisting of characters: Usage of `fputc()`

```c
#include <stdio.h>

int main(void)
{
        FILE *fp;
        char c;

        fp = fopen("text", "w");
        printf("Keep typing characters. Type 'q' to terminate \n");
        c = getchar();
        while (c != 'q')
        {
                fputc(c, fp);
                c = getchar();
        }
        fclose(fp);

        return 0;
}
```

Input–Output:

```
Keep typing characters. Type q to terminate.
Abnhhljkljkljq
```

Explanation:

fp is declared to be a pointer variable to **FILE** type and **c** is declared to be a variable of **char** type. The file pointer variable is to represent the file to be created by the program and the variable **c** of char type is to collect characters one at a time, entered through the standard input device, keyboard. Note that the external file "text" is opened in "w" mode. The program segment responsible for accepting characters and writing them onto the file is the following.

```c
c = getchar();
while (c != 'q')
    {
            fputc(c, fp);
            c = getchar();
    }
```

Till we type the letter 'q', all the characters are written into the external file "text" denoted by **fp** in the program. once the character 'q' is typed, the loop terminates. Note that the file is then closed by invoking `fclose()`.

PROGRAM 13.2   To read a file consisting of characters: Usage of `fgetc()`

```c
#include <stdio.h>

int main(void)
{
      FILE *fp;
      char c;

      printf("The contents of the file 'text' are: \n");
      fp = fopen("text", "r");
      while (!feof(fp))
      {
            c = fgetc(fp);
            putchar(c);
      }
      fclose(fp);

      return 0;
}
```

Input–Output:

```
The contents of the file 'text' are:
Abnhhljkljkljq
```

Explanation:

fp is declared to be a pointer variable to **FILE** type and **c** is declared to be a variable of **char** type. The file pointer variable is to represent the file ("text") to be read by the program and the variable **c** of char type is to collect characters one at a time, read from the file. Note that the external file "text" is now opened in "r" mode. The program segment responsible for reading each character from the file and displaying it on the screen is the following:

```c
while (!feof(fp))
{
      c = fgetc(fp);
      putchar(c);
}
```

The function `feof()` is to check for the end of a file being read. It takes the file pointer to the file as the argument and returns 1 if the end is reached. Otherwise, it returns 0. In the above looping segment, till the end of the file "text" is reached, all the characters are read and displayed. The file is then closed.

13.4.2   String Oriented Functions–`fputs()`, `fgets()`

The `fputs()` is to write a string onto a file. The syntax of its usage is as follows:

```c
fputs(buffer, fp);
```

buffer is the name of a character array and **fp** is a pointer to **FILE** type. The function writes the string represented by **buffer** to the file pointed to by **fp**.

```
fgets(buffer, size, fp);
```

buffer is the name of a character array, **size** is an integer value, **fp** is a pointer to **FILE** type. The function reads a string of maximum **size-1** characters from the file pointed to by **fp** and copies it to the memory area denoted by **buffer**.

PROGRAM 13.3   To create a file consisting of strings: Usage of puts()

```c
#include <stdio.h>

int main(void)
{
        char name[20];
        FILE *fp;
        int i, n;

        fp = fopen("names.dat", "w");
        printf("Enter the number of names \n");
        scanf("%d", &n);
        printf("Enter %d names \n", n);
        fflush(stdin);
        for(i = 1; i <= n; i++)
        {
                gets(name);
            fputs(name, fp);
        }
        fclose(fp);

        return 0;
}
```

Input–Output:

```
Enter no. of names
4

Enter 4 names
Asha
Nishu
Harsha
Devaraju
```

Explanation:

fp is declared to be a variable of type pointer to FILE type. name is declared to be an array of char type and of size 20. Variables i and n are declared to be of int type. The file variable fp is to denote the file names.dat to be created by the program; the string variable name is to collect a string entered through the keyboard, which is then written to the file. The variable n is to accept the number of names to be accepted and i acts as the control variable in the for loop used. The statement fp = fopen ("names.dat", "w"); opens the file names.dat in write mode and assigns a reference to the file to fp. After accepting the number of names into the variable n, n names are accepted and written to the file with the segment.

```
for(i = 1; i <= n; i++)
{
        gets(name);
        fputs(name, fp);
}
```

The file is then closed on execution of the statement fclose(fp);

PROGRAM 13.4   To read a file consisting of strings: Usage of fgets()

```
#include <stdio.h>

int main(void)
{
        FILE *fp;
        char name[20];

        printf("strings are \n");
        fp = fopen("names.dat", "r");
        while (!feof(fp))
        {
                fgets(name, 20, fp);
                puts(name);
                printf("\n");
        }
        fclose(fp);

        return 0;
}
```

Input–Output:

```
Strings are:
Asha
Nishu
Harsha
Devaraju
```

Explanation:

The variable **fp** is declared to be a pointer to **FILE** type. **name** is declared to be an array of **char** type and of size 20. The file variable **fp** is to denote the file names. dat to be read by the program; the string variable **name** is to collect a string read from the file. The statement fp = fopen ("names. dat", "r"); opens the file names.dat in read mode (names.dat should exist, otherwise fopen() returns NULL). The following loop set up reads each string in the file names.dat and displays it on the screen.

```
while (!feof(fp))
{
        fgets(name, 20, fp);
        puts(name);
        printf("\n");
}
```

As long as the end of file is not reached, the program continues to read strings and display them on the screen, the standard output device. On the exit of the loop, the file names.dat is closed.

13.4.3 Mixed Data Oriented Functions–fprintf(), fscanf()

fprintf() is to write multiple data items which may (or not) be of different types to a file. The syntax of its usage is as follows:

fprintf(fp, "control string", arguments-list);

It can be noticed that syntax of fprintf() is similar to that of printf() except the presence of an extra parameter fp, a pointer to **FILE** type. The parameter fp represents the file to which data are to be written. control string specifies the format specifiers. argument-list contains comma separated variables, the values of which are to be written to the file.

fscanf() is to read multiple data items which may be of different types from a file. The syntax of its usage is as follows:

fscanf(fp, "control string", argument-list);

It can be noticed that syntax of fscanf() is similar to that of scanf() except the presence of an extra parameter fp, a pointer to **FILE** type. The parameter fp represents the file from which data are to be read. control string specifies the format specifiers, argument-list contains comma separated variables preceded by address of operator & (except in the case of string type), into which data read from the file are to be copied.

PROGRAM 13.5   To create a file consisting of employees' details : Usage of fprintf()

```
#include <stdio.h>

struct emp
{
        int empno;
        char name[20];
        float salary;
};

int main(void)
{
```

```
        FILE *fp;
        struct emp e;
        int i, n;

        fp = fopen("emp.dat", "w");
        printf("Enter number of employees \n");
        scanf("%d", &n);
        printf("Enter %d Employees' Details \n", n);
        for(i = 1; i <= n; i++)
        {
                scanf("%d%s%f", &e.empno, e.name, &e.salary);
                fprintf(fp, "%d%s%f", e.empno, e.name, e.salary);
        }
        fclose(fp);

        return 0;
}
```

Input–Output:

```
Enter the number of employees
2
Enter 2 Employees Details
123     Nishu      12345
124     Harsha     12356
```

Explanation:

The structure **struct emp** is defined with the fields **empno**, **name** and **salary**. In the main(), variable **fp** is declared to be a pointer to **FILE** type and it is to denote the file emp.dat to be created by the program. **e** is declared to be a variable of **struct emp** type, which is to collect the employee details accepted through the keyboard. The statement fp = fopen("emp.dat", "w"); opens the file emp.dat in write mode and assigns reference to the file to the variable fp. The following segment enables us to accept n employees details and write them onto the file emp.dat

```
for(i = 1; i <= n; i++)
{
        scanf("%d%s%f", &e.empno, e.name, &e.salary);
        fprintf(fp, "%d%s%f", e.empno, e.name, e.salary);
}
```

PROGRAM 13.6   To read a file consisting of employees' details: Usage of fscanf()

```
#include <stdio.h>

struct emp
{
```

```
        int empno;
        char name[20];
        float salary;
};

int main(void)
{
        FILE *fp;
        struct emp e;

        fp = fopen("emp.dat", "r");

        while (!feof(fp))
        {
                fscanf(fp, "%d%s%f", &e.empno, e.name, &e.salary);
                printf("%6d%15s%7.2f\n", e.empno, e.name, e.salary);
        }
        fclose(fp);

        return 0;
}
```

Input–Output:

```
Contents of the file emp.dat
123    Nishu      12345
124    Harsha     12356
```

Explanation:

The structure **struct emp** is defined with the fields **empno**, **name** and **salary**. In the main(), variable **fp** is declared to be a pointer to **FILE** type and it is to denote the file emp.dat to be read by the program. **e** is declared to be a variable of **struct emp** type, which is to collect the employee details read from the file emp.dat the statement fp = fopen("emp.dat", "r"); opens the file in read mode and assigns reference to the file to the variable **fp**. The following segment enables us to read all the employees details and display them on the screen.

```
while (!feof(fp))
{
        fscanf(fp, "%d%s%f", &e.empno, e.name, &e.salary);
                printf("%6d%15s%7.2f\n", e.empno, e.name, e.salary);
}
```

On the exit of the loop, the file emp.dat denoted by **fp** is closed.

13.4.4 Unformatted Record I/O Functions–fwrite(), fread()

The fwrite() is used to write blocks of data (records) to a file. The contents which are written to the secondary storage devices are nothing but the exact copy of them in memory. The files of this kind are called **Binary Files**. But the `fprintf()`, another file output function, formats the memory contents according to the format specifiers passed to it and then writes them onto the secondary storage device.

The syntax of the usage of the `fwrite()` is as follows:

```
fwrite(buffer_address, size, count, file_pointer);
```

Here, `buffer_address` is the address of the memory area, the contents of which are to be written to the file denoted by the fourth argument `file_pointer`. The second argument `size` specifies the number of bytes of a block (record) and `count` specifies the number of blocks of data to be written to the file. If all goes well, the number of bytes written to the file would be equal to the product of size and count. The function returns the number of blocks of data written to the file. On successful execution, the value returned by the function would be the value of the third argument, `count`. Otherwise, the value would be less than the value of `count` (possibly 0).

Example 13.1

```
struct emp
{
        int empno;
        char name[20];
        float salary;
};

struct emp e;
FILE *fp;

fwrite(&e, sizeof(e), 1, fp);
```

The function call writes an employee record to the file denoted by `fp`.

The `fread()` is the counterpart of `fwrite()` and it is used to read blocks of data (records) from files. The syntax of the usage of `fread()` remains same as that of the `fwrite()`.

```
fread(buffer_address, size, count, file_pointer);
```

The first argument `buffer_address` is the address of the memory area, which the contents read from the file denoted by the fourth argument `file_pointer` are to be written into. The second argument `size` specifies the number of bytes of a block (record) and `count` specifies the number of blocks of data to be read from the file. If all goes well, the number of bytes read from the file would be equal to the product of size and count. The function returns the number of blocks of data read from the file. On successful execution, the value returned by the function would be the value of the third argument, `count`. Otherwise, the value would be less than the value of `count` (possibly 0).

Example 13.2

```
struct emp
{
        int empno;
        char name[20];
        float salary;
};
```

```
struct emp e;
FILE *fp;

fread(&e, sizeof(e), 1, fp);
```

The function call reads an employee record from the file denoted by **fp** into the variable **e**.

PROGRAM 13.7   To create a file consisting employee details: Usage of `fwrite()`

```c
#include <stdio.h>

struct emp
{
        int empno;
        char name[20];
        float salary;
};

int main(void)
{
        struct emp e;
        FILE *fp;
        int i, n;

        fp = fopen("emp.dat", "wb");
        printf("Enter the number of employees \n");
        scanf("%d", &n);
        printf("Enter empno, name and salary of %d employees \n", n);
        for(i = 1; i <= n; i++)
        {
                scanf("%d%s%f", &e.empno, e.name, &e.salary);
                fwrite(&e, sizeof(e), 1, fp);
        }
        fclose(fp);

        return 0;
}
```

Input–Output:

```
Enter the number of employees
2
Enter empno, name and salary of 2 employees

123     Nishu       12345
124     Harsha      12356
```

Explanation:

After accepting the number of employees into the variable **n**, details of them are accepted and written onto the file **emp.dat** with the following segment of code:

```
for(i = 1; i <= n; i++)
{
      scanf("%d%s%f", &e.empno, e.name, &e.salary);
      fwrite(&e, sizeof(e), 1, fp);
}
```

Note that the unformatted file output function **write()** has been used to write each record onto the file. As a result, the records are stored in binary form. Once the loop completes, writing n employees' details onto the file emp.dat. gets over and the file is then closed with the statement fclose(fp);

PROGRAM 13.8   To read from a file consisting employee details: Usage of fread()

```
#include <stdio.h>

struct emp
{
      int empno;
      char name[20];
      float salary;
};

int main(void)
{
      struct emp e;
      FILE *fp;
      int i, n;

      printf("Contents of the file emp.dat \n");
      fp = fopen("emp.dat", "rb");
      while (fread(&e, sizeof(e), 1, fp))
      {
            printf("%d%s%f\n", e.empno, e.name, e.salary);
      }
      fclose(fp);

      return 0;
}
```

Input–Output:

```
Contents of the file emp.dat

123    Nishu      12345
124    Harsha     12356
```

Explanation:

After opening the file **emp.dat** in read mode with the statement fp = fopen(emp.dat", "rb");, The records in the file are read and displayed on the screen with the following segment of code:

```
while (fread(&e, sizeof(e), 1, fp))
{
        printf("%d%s%f\n", e.empno, e.name, e.salary);
}
```

Note that the unformatted file input function **read()** has been used to read the records in the file. This is required because the file is a binary file, no formatting is associated with its contents. The function call fread(&e, sizeof(e), 1, fp) has been used as a test-expression. It is certainly valid since the function returns a non-zero value on successful read operation and 0 on failure, i.e. when the end of the file is reached. As long as the end of the file is not reached, each record is read into the variable **e** of **struct emp** type and it is displayed. Once the loop terminates, all the records have been read and displayed, the file **emp.dat** is closed with the statement fclose(fp);

To append records to a database file

Appending records to a file is one of the most commonly performed database operation. It is nothing but adding records to the end of the file by keeping the already existing records intact. The sequence of steps to be followed to append is the following:

1. Open the file in append mode, the mode of opening is "a".

    ```
    fp = fopen("Filename", "a");
    ```

2. Accept records to be appended and write them on to the file.

PROGRAM 13.9   To append records to the file emp.dat

```
#include <stdio.h>

struct emp
{
        int empno;
        char name[20];
        float salary;
};

int main(void)
{
        struct emp e;
        FILE *fp;
        int i, n;

        fp = fopen("emp.dat", "ab");
        printf("Enter the number of employees to be appended \n");
```

```
        scanf("%d", &n);
        printf("Enter empno, name and salary of %d employees \n", n);
        for(i = 1; i <= n; i++)
        {
                scanf("%d%s%f", &e.empno, e.name, &e.salary);
                fwrite(&e, sizeof(e), 1, fp);
        }

                fclose(fp);
            return 0;
}
```

Input–Output:

Enter the number of employees to be appended
1
Enter empno, name and salary of 1 employees

125 Asha 3456

[The contents of the file emp.dat will now be
        123   Nishu   12345
        124   Harsha   12356
        125   Asha   3456]

Explanation:

The structure **struct emp** is defined with the fields **empno**, **name** and **salary**. In the main(), variable **fp** is declared to be a pointer to **FILE** type and it is to denote the file emp.dat to which records are to be appended by the program. **e** is declared to be a variable of **struct emp** type, which is to collect the employee details entered through the keyboard. The statement fp = fopen("emp.dat", "ab"); opens the file in append mode and assigns reference to the file to the variable **fp**. Since the file emp.dat is opened in append mode, the previous contents of the file remain intact and the file pointer is positioned at the end of the file. The following segment enables us to accept n records of emp type and to append to the file emp.dat

```
for(i = 1; i <= n; i++)
{
        scanf("%d%s%f", &e.empno, e.name, &e.salary);
        fwrite(&e, sizeof(e), 1, fp);
}
```

To delete a record from a file

Deletion of unwanted records from a file is another most frequently used database operation. It can be accomplished by employing the following sequence of steps.

1. Open the file file1 (under consideration) in read mode
2. Open a new file file2 in write mode

3. Copy all the records of file1 to file2 except the record to be deleted
4. Remove the file file1.
5. Rename the file file2 as file1

PROGRAM 13.10   To delete records in employee file

```c
#include <stdio.h>

struct emp
{
        int empno;
        char name[20];
        float salary;
};

int main(void)
{
        FILE *fin, *fout;
        struct emp e;
        int eno;

        fin = fopen("emp.dat", "rb");
        fout = fopen("emp1.dat", "wb");
        printf("Enter empno of the employee to be deleted \n");
        scanf("%d", &eno);
        while (fread(&e, sizeof(e), 1, fin))
        {
                if (e.empno != eno)
                fwrite(&e, sizeof(e), 1, fout);
        }
        fclose(fin);
        fclose(fout);
        remove("emp.dat");
        rename("emp1.dat", "emp.dat");

        return 0;
}
```

Input–Output:

```
Enter empno of the employee to be deleted
125

[The contents of the file emp.dat will now be
        123    Nishu    12345
        124    Harsha    12356]
```

Explanation:

The structure struct emp is defined with the fields empno, name and salary. In the main(), variables fin and fout are declared to be pointers to FILE type. e is declared to be a variable of struct emp type, which is to collect an employee record read from the file emp.dat. the integer variable eno is to collect the empno of the employee to be deleted.

Deletion of a record from the file emp.dat proceeds as follows: the file emp.dat is opened in read mode with the statement fin = fopen("emp.dat", "rb"). The file pointer fin thus represents the file emp.dat One more temporary file by name emp1.dat is opened in write mode with the statement fout = fopen("emp1.dat", "wb"); The file pointer fout thus represents the file emp1.dat The empno of the employee to be deleted is accepted into the variable eno. Then the program starts reading the records of emp.dat and writing them onto the file emp1.dat except the record, empno of which matches with eno. The program segment responsible for this is as follows:

```
while (fread(&e, sizeof(e), 1, fin))
{
        if (e.empno != eno)
                fwrite(&e, sizeof(e), 1, fout);
}
```

After closing both the files, the original file emp.dat is deleted with the function call remove("emp.dat"); and the new file emp1.dat is renamed as emp.dat with the function call rename("emp1.dat", "emp.dat");

13.5   RANDOM ACCESSING OF FILES–fseek(), ftell(), rewind()

All the programs, which have been written so far, for reading the contents of files, employed sequential access mode. That is, the contents were read from the beginning of the files till their end is reached in a serial manner. Many a time, we need to access the contents at particular positions in the files not necessarily from the beginning till the end. This is referred to as random accessing of files. C standard library provides the following built-in functions to support this.

1. fseek()
2. ftell()
3. rewind()

1. fseek()

The function fseek() repositions the file pointer and the syntax of its usage is as follows:

fseek(fp, offset, Position);

where **fp** is a pointer to **FILE** type representing a file, **offset** is the number of bytes by which the file pointer is to be moved relative to the byte number identified by the third parameter **position**. The third parameter **position** can take one of the following three values 0, 1 and 2. The meanings of the values are given in the following table.

Position	Symbolic Constants	Meaning
0	SEEK_SET	Beginning of file
1	SEEK_CUR	Current position of file
2	SEEK_END	End of file

2. ftell()

The function **ftell()** returns the current position of the file pointer. The syntax of its usage is as follows:

```
position = ftell(fp);
```

where **fp** is a pointer to **FILE** type representing a file, the current position of the file pointer of the file is returned by the function.

3. rewind()

The rewind() repositions the file pointer to the beginning of a file. The syntax of its usage is as follows:

```
rewind(fp);
```

We will now write some programs which put the above discussed functions to use.

To count the number of records in a file

The following is the sequence of steps involved in counting the number of records in a file:

1. Open the file under consideration in read mode.
   (Mode of opening: "r" or "rb")
2. Move the file pointer to the last byte of the file.
   (fseek() is to be used)
3. Retrieve the last byte number of the file.
   (ftell() is to be used)
4. Divide the last byte number of the file by the size of a record. The quotient gives the number of records in the file.
5. Close the file.

PROGRAM 13.11   To count the number of records in employee file

---

```
#include <stdio.h>

struct emp
{
        int empno;
        char name[20];
        float salary;
};

int main(void)
```

```
{
        FILE *fp;
        int nor, last_byte;

        fp = fopen("emp.dat", "r");
        fseek(fp, 0L, SEEK_END);
        last_byte = ftell(fp);
        nor = last_byte/sizeof(struct emp);
        printf("The number of records = %d", nor);
        fclose(fp);

        return 0;

}
```

Input–Output:

```
The number of records = 2
```

Explanation:

The structure **struct emp** is defined with the fields **empno, name** and **salary**. In the main(), variables **fp** is declared to be a pointer to **FILE** type. The integer variables **nor** and **last_byte** are to collect the number of records in the file **emp.dat** and the last byte number of the file respectively. To be able to find the number of records in the file emp.dat, it is first opened in read mode with the statement fp = fopen("emp.dat", "r"); once the file is opened, the file pointer points to the first byte of the file. The file pointer is moved to the last byte with the statement fseek(fp, 0L, SEEK_END); The current position (the last byte number) of the file pointer is then retrieved and assigned to the variable last_byte with the statement last_byte = ftell(fp); Now, the variable **last_byte** has collected the size of the file **emp.dat** in terms of bytes. So, the expression last_byte/sizeof(struct emp) evaluates to the number of records in the file emp.dat and it is assigned to the variable **nor**, which is then displayed. Before the program terminates, the file **emp.dat** is closed.

To read *n*th record directly from a file

The following is the sequence of steps to be used to read *n*th record from a file:

1. Open the file in read mode.
    (Mode of opening: "r" or "rb")
2. Accept the record number of the record to be read.
3. Obtain the starting byte number of the record to be read.
4. Move the file pointer to the starting byte position of the record.
5. Read the record and display it.
6. Close the file.

PROGRAM 13.12   To read *n*th record directly in emp.dat file

```
#include <stdio.h>
#include <process.h>

struct emp
{
      int eno;
      char name[20];
      float salary;
};

int main(void)
{
      FILE *fp;
      int recno;
      struct emp e;

      fp = fopen("emp.dat", "rb");
      if (fp == NULL)
      {
            printf("emp.dat cannot be opened");
            exit(0);
      }
      printf("Enter recno of the record to be read directly \n");
      scanf("%d", &recno);
      fseek(fp, (recno-1)*sizeof(e), SEEK_SET);
      fread(&e, sizeof(e), 1, fp);
      printf("eno: %d\n", e.eno);
      printf("Name: %s \n", e.name);
      printf("Salary: %8.2f \n", e.salary);
      fclose(fp);

      return 0;
}
```

Input–Output:

```
Enter recno of the record to be read directly
2

eno: 124
Name: Harsha
Salary: 12356
```

Explanation:

The structure **struct emp** is defined with the fields **empno, name** and **salary**. In the main(), variable **fp** is declared to be a pointer to **FILE** type and it is to denote the file **emp.dat**, records of which are to be read directly. **e** is declared to be a variable of **struct emp** type, which is to collect the employee details read from the file **emp.dat** directly. The statement fp = fopen("emp.dat", "rb"); opens the file in read mode and assigns reference to the file to the pointer **fp**. The record number of the record to be read accepted into the variable recno. The file pointer of the file is moved to the beginning of the record to be read with the statement fseek(fp, (recno-1)*sizeof(e), SEEK_SET); . Note that the expression (recno-1) *sizeof(e) evaluates to the starting byte number of the record to be read. Once the file pointer is made to point to the record to be read, the record is read into the variable **e** with the following statement fread(&e, sizeof(e), 1, fp); The contents of the variable **e** are then displayed.

To update a record in a file

The following is the sequence of steps involved in updating a record in a file:

1. Open the file in update mode ("rb+").
2. Accept the record number of the record to be updated.
3. Move the file pointer to the starting byte position of the record to be updated.
4. Accept the new details of the record.
5. Write the new details into the record position.
6. Close the file.

PROGRAM 13.13   To update a record in emp.dat file

```c
#include <stdio.h>
#include <process.h>

struct emp
{
        int eno;
        char name[20];
        float salary;
};

int main(void)
{
        FILE *fp;
        int position, recno;
        struct emp e;

        fp = fopen("emp.dat", "rb+");
        if (fp == NULL)
        {
                printf("emp.dat cannot be opened");
                exit(0);
```

```
        }
        printf("Enter recno of the record to be updated \n");
        scanf("%d", &recno);
        fseek(fp, (recno-1)*sizeof(e), SEEK_SET);
        printf("Enter new details of the employee \n");
        scanf("%d%s%f", &e.eno, e.name, &e.salary);
        fwrite(&e, sizeof(e), 1, fp);
        fclose(fp);

        return 0;
}
```

Input–Output:

```
Enter recno of the record to be updated
2
Enter new details of the employee
125 Harsha 45000

[The contents of the file emp.dat will now be
123    Nishu     12345
125    Harsha    45000]
```

Explanation:

The structure **struct emp** is defined with the fields **empno**, **name** and **salary**. In the main(), variable **fp** is declared to be a pointer to **FILE** type and it is to denote the file **emp.dat**, records of which are to be updated. **e** is declared to be a variable of **struct emp** type, which is to collect an employee's new details entered through the keyboard. The statement fp = fopen("emp. dat", "rb+"); opens the file in update mode and assigns reference to the file to the file pointer **fp**. The record number of the record to be updated is accepted into the variable **recno**. The file pointer of the file is moved to the beginning of the record to be updated with the statement fseek (fp, (recno-1)*sizeof(e), SEEK_SET); Note that the expression (recno-1)*sizeof(e) evaluates to the starting byte number of the record to be updated. Once the file pointer is made to point to the record to be updated, new values for the record are accepted into the variable **e** and they are written back to the file with the statement fwrite(&e, sizeof(e), 1, fp); . The file is then closed.

To sort the records in a file

The following is the sequence of steps involved in sorting a database file:

1. Open the file to be sorted in read mode.
2. Count the number of records in the file.
3. Allocate the required amount of memory space dynamically to hold the records of the file.
4. Copy the records in the file to the memory area.
5. Close the input file.
6. Sort the records in the memory area on the specified field.

7. Open a new file in write mode.
8. Write the sorted records in the memory area into the file (sorted file).
9. Close the sorted file.

PROGRAM 13.14   To sort a file consisting of employee details in the increasing order of salary

```c
#include <stdio.h>
#include <alloc.h>

struct emp
{
        int empno;
        char name[20];
        float salary;
};

int main(void)
{
        FILE *fp, *fs;
        struct emp *ep, e, t;
        int position, i, j, nor;

        fp = fopen("emp.dat", "rb");
        printf("\n Unsorted List of Employees \n");
        while(fread(&e, sizeof(e), 1, fp))
        {
                printf("%6d%20s%8.2f\n", e.empno, e.name, e.salary);
        }

        fseek(fp, 0, 2);
        position = ftell(fp);
        nor = position / sizeof(struct emp);
        ep = (struct emp*) malloc(sizeof(struct emp) * nor);
        i = 0;
        fseek(fp, 0, 0);
        while (fread(&e, sizeof(e), 1, fp))
        {
                ep[i] = e;
                i++;
        }
        fclose(fp);

        /* sorting begins */

        for(i = 0; i < nor; i++)
        for(j = i + 1; j < nor; j++)
```

```
                    if (ep[i].salary > ep[j].salary)
                    {
                            t = ep[i];
                            ep[i] = ep[j];
                            ep[j] = t;
                    }

        /* sorting ends */

        fs = fopen("emps.dat", "wb");
        for(i = 0; i < nor; i++)
        fwrite(&ep[i], sizeof(ep[i]), 1, fs);
        fclose(fs);
        printf("\n Sorted List of Employees in the increasing order of salary
\n');
        fs = fopen("emps.dat", "rb");

        while(fread(&e, sizeof(e), 1, fs))
        {
                printf("%6d%20s%8.2f\n", e.empno, e.name, e.salary);
        }

        fclose(fs);
        return 0;
}
```

Input–Output:

```
Unsorted List of Employees
121         Raghav          23000.00
122         Ranjith         21000.00
123         Rakshith        34000.00
124         Ramesh          24000.00
125         Robin           23500.00

Sorted List of Employees in the increasing order of Salary
122         Ranjith         21000.00
121         Raghav          23000.00
125         Robin           23500.00
124         Ramesh          24000.00
123         Rakshith        34000.00
```

Explanation:

The structure emp is defined with three members **empno**, **name** and **salary** of **int**, array of **char** and float type respectively. A variable of struct emp type can thus accommodate the details (indicated by the member names) of an employee. The variables fp is to represent the input file emp.dat which is to be sorted. Note that the file emp.dat should be available for the program to work. The record structure of the file should be as per `struct emp`. Another variable `fs` of type `FILE` is to represent the output file (`emps.dat`)

After opening the input file `emp.dat` the number of records in it is found out. The amount of memory required to accommodate the records is then allocated. The records are read from the file and they are moved to the memory area. Once the records are placed in the memory they are sorted in the increasing order of salary. The sorted records are then written into the file `emps.dat` represented by the file pointer **fs**. The sorted records are then displayed from the file `emps.dat`.

To write to a printer

The following program writes to a printer:

```
#include <stdio.h>

int main(void)
{
        FILE *fprint, *fin;
        char ch;

        fin = fopen(text.dat", "r");
        fprint = fopen("PRN", "w");

        while (!feof(fin))
        {
        ch = fgetc(fin);
        fputc(ch, fprint);
        }
        fclose(fin);
        fclose(fprint);

        return 0;
}
```

13.6 ERROR HANDLING DURING FILE I/O OPERATIONS

The file I/O operations cannot always be expected to be smooth sailing. During the course of I/O operations, some errors may be encountered. As a consequence of the error conditions, the underlying program may prematurely terminate. Or it may produce erroneous results. Let us now try to enumerate the situations which lead to the error conditions and then understand how they can be countered.

The following are the circumstances under which the file I/O operations fail:

1. Trying to open a file, which does not exist, for reading purpose.
2. Trying to open a file for writing purpose when there is no disk space.
3. Trying to write to a read-only file.
4. Trying to perform an operation over a file when the file has been opened for some other purpose.
5. Trying to read a file beyond its end-of-file-mark.

When we try to open a file, which does not exist, for reading purpose, the fopen() returns NULL. This fact can be used to tackle the problem.

Example 13.3

```
fp = fopen("student.dat", "r");
```

In case, student.dat does not exist, the function fopen() returns NULL value, which is collected by the variable fp. The segment is used to handle this error situation.

```
if (fp == NULL)
{
        Printf("The file does not exist")
        Exit(1);
}
```

When an attempt to open a file for writing purpose fails (For want of sufficient disk space or When we try to open a read-only file for writing purpose), the fopen() returns NULL. This fact can be used to tackle the problem.

Example 13.4

```
fp = fopen("student.dat", "w");
```

The following segment is used to handle this error situation.

```
if (fp == NULL)
{
        Printf("The file cannot be created")
        Exit(1);
}
```

Suppose a file has been opened for reading purpose, any attempt to write to the file also gives rise to an error situation. Here, we can use the function ferror(). The ferror() takes the file pointer as its argument. It returns a non-zero value if an error is found. Otherwise, it returns 0.

Example 13.5

```
if(ferror(fp))
{
        printf("Error \n");
        exit(0);
}
```

To avoid reading a file beyond its end-of-file-mark, we can use feof().

Example 13.6

```
While(!feof(fp))
{
        reading statements
}
```

PROGRAM 13.15   To illustrate error handling during file I/O operations

```
#include <stdio.h>
#include <process.h>

int main(void)
{
        FILE *fp;

        fp = fopen("books.dat", "r");
        if (fp == NULL)
                printf("The file Books.dat does not exist");
        fp = fopen("students.dat", "w");
        if (fp == NULL)
                printf("The read-only file students.dat cannot be opened in
                        write mode");
        fp = fopen("text.dat", "r");
        fputc('a', fp);
        if (ferror(fp))
        {
                printf("The file text.dat has been opened in read mode");
                printf(" but you are writing to it. \n");
        }

        return 0;
}
```

Input–Output:

```
The file Books.dat does not exist
The read-only file students.dat cannot be opened in write mode
The file text.dat has been opened in read mode but you are writing to it.
```

Explanation:

In the above program, firstly, an attempt is made to open the file **books.dat**, which does not exist. As a result, when the statement fp = fopen("books.dat", "r"); is executed, the file variable **fp** collects the NULL value. The error is then trapped and the message "the file books. dat does not exist" is displayed.

Secondly, an attempt is made to open the file **students.dat**, a read-only file, in write mode, since opening of the file fails, once again when the statement fp = fopen("student.dat", "w"); is executed, the file variable **fp** would collect the NULL value. Since the expression fp == NULL evaluates to true, the message "The read-only file students.dat cannot be opened in write mode" is displayed.

Lastly, the file text.dat is opened in read mode and an attempt is made to write to the file, since the operation is not compatible with the mode in which the file is opened, the function ferror() traps the error and returns a non-zero value resulting in the display of the message "The file text.dat has been opened in read mode but you are writing to it".

The bottom line of the program is that the error situations which arise during file operations can be tackled by the programmers and the error messages that were displayed would help the programmers take corrective measures.

13.7 COMMAND LINE ARGUMENTS

We know that the arguments play a vital role of establishing data communication between a calling function and a called function. It is through arguments, a calling function passes inputs to a called function, which in turn performs required manipulations over them. So far, we have discussed passing arguments to functions other than main(). It is important to note that we can even pass arguments to main() also. If the main() is to be defined to accept arguments, the actual arguments should be provided at the command prompt itself along with the name of the executable file. Hence, these arguments are called **Command Line Arguments**. For example, consider TYPE command of DOS, which displays the contents of a file. To display the contents of emp.dat, we use the following command.

```
C:\> type emp.dat
```

Here **type** is the program file name (executable) and **emp.dat** is the input file, the contents of which are displayed.

To make main() of a program take command line arguments, the function header will have the following form.

```
int main(int argc, char *argv[])
```

Here, **argc** and **argv[]** are the formal arguments, which provide mechanism for collecting the arguments given at command line when the program is launched for execution. The **argc** is to collect the number of arguments passed and the array of pointers to char type **argv** is to collect the arguments themselves. **argv[0]** will always represent the program file name (executable) and **argv[1]**, **argv[2]** ...represent arguments passed to the main(). In the case of the DOS command **type emp.dat**, the command **type** is denoted by **argv[0]** and the file **emp.dat** is denoted by **argv[1]**.

PROGRAM 13.16   To illustrate command line arguments–Copying one file to another file

---

```
#include <stdio.h>
#include <process.h>

int main(int argc, char *argv[])
{
        FILE *fin, *fout;
        char c;

        if (argc != 3)
        {
                printf("Invalid number of arguments");
```

```
            exit(1);
    }
    fin = fopen(argv[1], "r");
    fout = fopen(argv[2], "w");
    while (!feof(fin))
    {
            c = fgetc(fin);
            fputc(c, fout);
    }
    fclose(fin);
    fclose(fout);

    return 0;
}
```

Input–Output:

The program is executed as follows:

`C:\>copy text.dat text1.dat`

As a result, the contents of text.dat are copied to text1.dat. We have thus simulated DOS copy command

Explanation:

The purpose of the program is to copy the contents of the file text.dat (source file) to the file text1.dat (target file). The source file and the target files are to be passed as the arguments to the main() itself. So, the main() is defined with two arguments **argc** (int) and **argv[]** (char*). The argument argc collects the number of arguments passed to the main() while it is launched for execution. In this case, the value of **argc** would be three. They are: the program file name (executable) (**argv[0]**), source file (**argv[1]**) and the target file (**argv[2]**).

On the entry into the program, initially, the value of argc is checked against 3. If it does not match, then the program terminates. If the number of arguments is found to be three, then the source file identified by **argv[1]** is opened in read mode and the target file identified by **argv[2]** is opened in write mode. The following segment of the program would then copy the contents of the source file to the target file.

```
while (!feof(fin))
{
        c = fgetc(fin);
        fputc(c, fout);
}
```

Before the program exits, both the files are closed.

SUMMARY

- The concept of files enables us to store large amount of data permanently on the secondary storage devices.

- A variable of type **FILE** is used to represent a file within a program. It acts as an internal file name for a file.
- The name remembered by the operating system is termed external filename. Before performing any operation over a file, it has to be opened.
- The operation of opening establishes the necessary linkage between the internal filename and the external file.
- Once the intended operation is over the file has to be closed. Closing a file ensures that the file is safely written to the disc.
- **fputc()** and **fgetc()** are the character-oriented file I/O functions;
- **fputs0()** and **fgets()** are the string oriented file I/O functions;
- **fprintf()** and **fscanf()** are the mixed data file I/O functions;
- **fwrite()** and **fread()** are the unformatted file I/O functions.
- Ability to move to a required record in a file irrespective of its position in the file is termed Random Accessing.
- The function **fseek()** is used to move the file pointer to the required byte in a file and the function **ftell()** is used to know the position of the file pointer in a file.
- We can pass arguments to main() also; argc (int) and argv (array of pointers to char) are the formal arguments which facilitate passing o command line arguments.

REVIEW QUESTIONS

13.1 What is a file? Why do we need the concept of files?

13.2 What are the most commonly performed operations over files?

13.3 Give the purpose and syntax of fopen() and fclose().

13.4 What are the different modes of opening a file?

13.5 What is the difference between the modes "w" and "a"?

13.6 What is the difference between "w" and "wb"?

13.7 What is the difference between "wb+" and "rb+"?

13.8 Mention the character oriented file I/O functions and syntax of their usage.

13.9 Mention the string oriented file I/O functions and their syntax.

13.10 Mention the mixed type oriented and formatted file I/O functions and their syntax.

13.11 Explain the syntax and usage of fwrite() and fread().

13.12 Differentiate between sequential and random accessing of files.

State whether the following are true or false

13.1 Secondary storage devices are volatile in nature.

13.2 File is a named storage on the secondary storage device.

13.3 Output of one program can be used as the input for some other program using files.

13.4 A file should be first opened before performing any operation.

13.5 Files representing standard I/O are opened and closed implicitly.

13.6 Input mode for text files is "rb".

13.7 There is no difference between "a" and "a+".

13.8 When a file is opened in "w" mode, the previous contents remain intact.

13.9 When a file is opened in "a" mode, the previous contents are lost.

13.10 When a file is opened in "a" mode, the file pointer is set to the first byte in the file.

13.11 To update a binary file, it has to be opened in "w+".

13.12 `fseek()` is to move the file pointer to any required byte in the file.

13.13 There is no difference between `fwrite()` and `fprintf()`.

Identify errors, if any, in the following:

13.1
```
FILE fp;
fp = fopen("text.dat", "w");
```

13.2
```
FILE *fin;
fin = fopen("text.dat", r);
```

13.3
```
FILE *fout;
fout = fopen("text.dat", "r");
while (fout)
{
    ch = fgetc(fout);
    printf("%c", ch);
}
```

13.4
```
rewind(fp);
position = ftell(fp);
the value of position is zero.
```

13.5
```
struct emp
{
    int empno;
    float salary;
} e;
FILE *fp;
Fp = fopen("emp.dat", "w");
fwrite(fp, &e, 1);
```

PROGRAMMING EXERCISES

13.1 Write a program to count the numbers of characters in a text file.

13.2 Write a program to copy the contents of one text file to another text file.

13.3 Write a program to sort a file consisting of names of students and display them.

13.4 Write a program to sort a file consisting of books' details in the alphabetical order of author names.

The details of books include book_id, Author_name, Price, No_of_pages, Publisher, Year_of_ Publishing

13.5 Write a menu driven program to perform the following operations over a student file. (a) Addition of records, (b) Deletion of records, (c) Updation of records, and (d) Displaying the records interactively. The details of students include roll_no, name, marks in five subjects.

13.6 Suppose there are two file **emp.dat** and **dept.dat** storing the details of employees and the departments respectively. The employee file has empno, name, salary and deptno as the fields with the empno being unique, and the dept file has the fields deptno, deptname with the deptno being unique. Write a program to display empno, name, deptname and salary of all the employees.

13.7 Incorporate error handling feature to all the programs in the chapter.

13.8 Write a program to insert a record into the sorted employee file (sorted on salary).

13.9 Write a program to merge two files.

(**Note:** The two files should have been sorted on the same field and the newly obtained file after merging should reflect the ordering on the same field).

13.10 Suppose **emp1.dat** and **emp2.dat** are two files having employees' details. Write a program to create a new file **newemp.dat** with records, which are either in emp1. dat or in emp2.dat or in both.

13.11 Suppose **emp1.dat** and **emp2.dat** are two files having employees' details. Write a program to create a new file **newemp.dat** with records, which are in both emp1. dat and emp2.dat.

13.12 Develop a program to search for a employee record in an employee file using binary search method.

INTERVIEW QUESTIONS

13.1 What is the purpose of text file?

13.2 In what way binary mode is different from text mode?

13.3 In which mode can we truncate the contents of the file?

13.4 What is the output of the following programs?

```
(a) #include<stdio.h>
    int main(int)
    {
        printf("%d",EOF);
        return 0;
    }
```

```
(b) #include<stdio.h>
    int main(void)
    {
        char c;
        FILE *fp;
        fp=fopen("sample.txt","w");

        while((c=fgetc(fp))!=EOF)
    {
        printf("%c",c);
    }
        fclose(fp);
        return 0;
    }
```

13.5 How do you determine the size of a file?

13.6 Can we close multiple files using single `fclose()` function in C?

13.7 What is the purpose of FILE pointer?

13.8 Which are the five standard streams in C?

13.9 What do you mean by file redirection?

13.10 How do you redirect the output of program to a file instead of standard output device (screen)?

13.11 Which is the file redirection operator in C?

14

The C Preprocessor

14.1 INTRODUCTION

The preprocessor is another distinctive feature of C. In other higher level languages, the source program is submitted directly to the corresponding language compiler, which in turn, produces object code. But in C, the source program is first passed to the program called preprocessor, the preprocessor acts on the source program according to the instructions specified to it in the source program and the output produced by the preprocessor is then submitted to C compiler. The instructions specified in the source program to the preprocessor are called the **Preprocessor Directives**. The preprocessor plays a very important role in enhancing the readability, modifiability, and portability of the C programs.

Source-program → Preprocessor → Expanded source program → C compiler

The following are the general rules governing the preprocessor directives:

1. All preprocessor directives should start with the symbol #. ANSI allows the symbol to be preceded by spaces or tabs.
2. Only one directive can appear in a line.
3. The directives are not terminated by semicolons.
4. The preprocessor directives can be placed anywhere in a source program. The directives apply to the source code, which follows them.

The preprocessor directives are broadly classified into three types based on the purposes for which they are used.

1. Files Inclusion Directives
2. Macros Definition Directives
3. Conditional Compilation Directives

14.2   FILES INCLUSION DIRECTIVE – [#include]

14.2.1   The #include Directive

The #include preprocessor directive has already been used in all our programs and we know that it is used to include a file as part of the source program file. For example, in response to the directive #include <stdio.h>, the preprocessor expands the source file by embedding the contents of the header file stdio.h, before the source program is submitted to the C compiler. In all our earlier programs, #include has been used to include the header files. As a matter of fact, contents of any text file can be included as part of a source program with the help of the directive. If the file name is enclosed within double quotes, then the file is expected to be available in the current working directory. Suppose a file by name functions.c in the current working directory, contains the definitions for the functions used by a program, the file functions.c can be included as part of the source program with the directive #include "functions.c".

```
#include <stdio.h>
#include "functions.c"

int main(void)
{
        return 0;
}
```

Here, the preprocessor embeds the contents of the header file **stdio.h** and contents of the file **functions.c** into the source program before the program is passed onto the compiler.

14.3   MACROS DEFINITION DIRECTIVES [#define, #indef]

A macro is defined to be a symbolic name assigned to a segment of text. The preprocessor directive #define is used for defining macros. The syntax of its usage is as follows:

```
#define MACRO_NAME segment_of_text
```

Here, MACRO_NAME is the name of a macro; it should conform to the rules, which are used to construct valid identifiers and normally it is written using upper case letters just to distinguish it from the identifiers. segment_of_text is actually the string referred to by the MACRO_NAME. Once a symbolic name (MACRO_NAME) is assigned to a segment of text, throughout the program, the symbolic name can be used in place of the segment of text. The preprocessor then replaces all the occurrences of the MACRO_NAME by the segment of text.

Example 14.1

(i) #define COUNT 10
     COUNT becomes the symbolic name for the constant **10**
(ii) #define NO_OF_STUDENTS 100
     NO_OF_STUDENTS becomes the symbolic name for the constant **100**
(iii) #define OR ||
     The symbolic name **OR** can be used in place of the logical operator ||

(iv) #define AND &&
The symbolic name **AND** can be used in place of the logical operator **&&**

(v) #define EQUAL_TO ==
The symbolic name **EQUAL_TO** can be used in place of the relational operator ==

(vi) #define MOD %
The symbolic name **MOD** can be used in place of the arithmetic operator **%**

(vii) #define NOT !
The symbolic name **NOT** can be used in place of the logical operator **!**

(viii) #define NOT_EQUAL_TO !=
The symbolic name **NOT_EQUAL_TO** can be used in place of the relational operator **!=**

PROGRAM 14.1 To illustrate macros definition

```
#define PI 3.14
#include <stdio.h>

int main(void)
{
        int r;
        float area, circum;

        printf("Enter radius of a circle \n");
        scanf("%d", &r);

        area = PI * r * r;
        circum = 2 * PI * r;
        printf("Area = %f \n", area);
        printf("Circumference = %f \n", circum);

        return 0;
}
```

The preprocessor acts on the source program produces the following output. Note that the macro PI has been replaced by the value 3.14 by the preprocessor. The process of replacement of macros by their corresponding segments of texts is termed **Macros Substitution**. The output produced by the preprocessor is then submitted to the compiler for compilation.

```
#include <stdio.h>

int main(void)
{
        int r;
        float area, circum;

        printf("Enter radius of a circle \n");
        scanf("%d", &r);
```

```
        area = 3.14 * r * r;
        circum = 2 * 3.14 * r;
        printf ("Area = %f \n", area);
        printf ("Circumference = %f \n", circum);

        return 0;
}
```

Input–Output:

```
Enter radius of a circle
4

Area = 50.240002
Circumference = 25.120001
```

In the above program, the segment of text happened to be a numeric value. In fact, it can be a string enclosed within double quotes or a C statement.

Example 14.2

#define ACCEPT printf ("Enter two numbers \n")

Here, the macro ACCEPT is assigned a C statement printf ("Enter two numbers").

PROGRAM 14.2   To illustrate a macro definition

```
#define ACCEPT printf ("Enter two numbers \n")
#include <stdio.h>

int main (void)
{
        int a, b;

        ACCEPT;

        /* Expanded to printf ("Enter two numbers \n"); by the preprocessor
        */ scanf ("%d%d", &a, &b);
    printf ("a = %d b = %d \n", a, b);

        return 0;
}
```

Input–Output:

```
Enter two numbers
4 5
a = 4 b = 5
```

14.3.1 Macros with Arguments

The preprocessor permits us to pass arguments to macros in much the same way as we pass arguments to functions. Let us now explore the possibility of passing arguments to macros and understand how macros with arguments are helpful.

Consider the following C statement

```
if (a > 0) a = a + 1
```

If we are to assign a symbolic name for this, we would define a macro `INCREMENT_A` as follows:

```
#define INCREMENT_A if ( a > 0) a = a + 1
```

Consider another C conditional statement

```
if (b > 0) b = b + 1
```

If we are to assign a symbolic name for the statement, we can define another macro `INCREMENT_B` as follows:

```
#define INCREMENT_B if ( b > 0) b = b + 1
```

As can be seen, both the statements have the same structure except the variable names. Here, we can define only one macro by name `INCREMENT` with an argument and it can represent both the conditional statements considered above. The macro is defined as follows:

```
#define INCREMENT(x) if ( x > 0 ) x = x + 1
```

Now,

`INCREMENT(a)` would be expanded to the statement	`if ( a > 0) a = a + 1`	
`INCREMENT(b)` would be expanded to the statement	`if ( b > 0) b = b + 1`	
`INCREMENT(c)` would be expanded to the statement	`if ( c > 0) c = c + 1`	
	and so on.	

PROGRAM 14.3   To illustrate a macro with arguments

```c
#include <stdio.h>
#define INCREMENT(x) if (x > 0) x = x + 1

int main(void)
{
    int a, b;

    printf("Enter the value of a \n");
    scanf("%d", &a);
    printf("Given value of a = %d \n", a);
    INCREMENT(a);        /* would expand to if ( a > 0) a = a + 1 */
    printf("New Value of a = %d \n", a);

    printf("Enter the value of b \n");
    scanf("%d", &b);
    printf("Given value of b = %d \n", b);
```

```
        INCREMENT(b);        /* would expand to if ( b > 0) b = b + 1 */
        printf("New Value of b = %d \n", b);

        return 0;
}
```

Input–Output:

```
Enter the value of a
4

Given value of a = 4
New value of a = 5

Enter the value of b
6

Given value of b = 6
New value of b = 7
```

PROGRAM 14.4   To find the area of a circle: macro with arguments

```
#define AREA(r) 3.14 * r * r
#include <stdio.h>

int main(void)
{
        int r1, r2;
        float area;

        printf("Enter the radius of the first circle \n");
        scanf("%d", &r1);
        area = AREA( r1 );
        printf("Area of the first circle = %f \n", area);

        printf("Enter the radius of the second circle \n");
        scanf("%d", &r2);
        area = AREA( r2 );
        printf("Area of the second circle = %f \n", area);

    return 0;
}
```

Input–Output:

```
Enter the radius of the first circle
3
```

```
Area of the first circle = 28.260000

Enter the radius of the second circle
4

Area of the second circle = 50.240002
```

Explanation:

In the above program, macro defined with argument is AREA(r). The purpose of the macro is to find the area of a circle when its radius r is given. It would be expanded to the expression 3.14 * r * r by the preprocessor. r1 and r2 are declared to be variables of int type. These variables are to collect the radii of two circles, the areas of which are to be found out. The variable r1 is passed to the macro AREA as its argument in the statement area = AREA(r1). The preprocessor expands it to the statement area = 3.14 * r1 * r1. Similarly, the variable r2 is passed to the macro AREA as its argument in the statement area = AREA(r2). The preprocessor expands it to the statement area = 3.14 * r2 * r2. After successful compilation, when the program is run, we would accept the values of r1 and r2, radii of two circles. The program in turn displays the areas of the two circles.

Consider the preprocessor directive

```
#define SQUARE(x) x * x
```

The macro SQUARE(x) is to find the square of the argument x. Now, the macro SQUARE(3) expands to 3 * 3. We would get the square of 3, which is 9. To find the square of the expression a + 2, we would use the macro SQUARE(a+2). The macro SQUARE(a+2) expands to a + 2 * a + 2, the value of the expression will not be the square of a + 2. This problem is eliminated by enclosing the argument within parentheses in the replacement string as (x) * (x). New definition of the macro would then be

```
#define SQUARE(x) (x) * (x).
```

Now, SQUARE(a+2) is expanded to (a + 2) * (a + 2), which evaluates correctly to the square of a + 2.

It is always better to enclose each occurrence of the argument in the replacement string within a pair of parentheses so that the corresponding macros are expanded to correct forms of expressions.

Now consider the expression 100/SQUARE(2). Here, the expression expands to 100/(2)*(2). According to the associativity rule the value of the expression would be 50 * 2 = 100. But actually square of 2, which is 4, should divide 100 and the result should be 25. We would be able to get the correct expression after expansion by the preprocessor if we enclose the entire replacement string within a pair of parentheses. The correct way of defining the macro would thus be:

```
#define SQUARE(x) ((x) * (x))
```

Now the expression 100 / SQUARE(2) is expanded to 100/((2) * (2)). This expression would evaluate correctly to 100 / 4 = 25. Thus, it is even better to enclose the replacement string itself within a pair of parentheses if the replacement string happens to be an expression.

PROGRAM 14.5   To find the square of a number: macro with argument

```
#include <stdio.h>
#define SQUARE(x) ((x) * (x))

int main(void)
{
        int a = 5, sqr, b;

        sqr = SQUARE(4);
        printf("Square of 4 = %d \n", sqr);
        sqr = SQUARE(a+2);
        printf("Square of a+2 = %d \n", sqr);
        b = 100 / SQUARE(2);
        printf("b = %d \n", b);

        return 0;
}
```

Input–Output:

```
Square of 4 = 16
Square of a+2 = 49
b = 25
```

Explanation:

In the above program, the macro SQUARE is defined with an argument x. It is important to note that the argument x is enclosed within a pair of parentheses in the substitution string. It is to ensure that the argument in the macro call is expanded correctly when the argument is an expression. During the preprocessing:

The statement sqr = SQUARE(4); is expanded to sqr = ((4) * (4))
The statement sqr = SQUARE(a+2); is expanded to sqr = ((a+2) * (a+2))
And the statement b = 100 / SQUARE(2); is expanded to b = 100 / ((2) * (2))

The expanded code is then passed on to the compiler to generate the appropriate code.

To find the roots of a quadratic equation

A quadratic equation is of the form $ax^2 + bx + c = 0$. The roots of the equation are given by:

```
x1 = -b + sqrt(b² - 4ac) / 2a
x2 = -b - sqrt(b² - 4ac) / 2a
```

Here the expression $b^2 - 4ac$ is called the discriminant. The value of the discriminant determines the type of the roots.

If $b^2 - 4ac > 0$ the roots are real and distinct
If $b^2 - 4ac = 0$ the roots are real and equal
If $b^2 - 4ac < 0$ the roots are complex numbers

We will now write a program to find the roots of a quadratic equation by using a macro with arguments for the discriminant.

PROGRAM 14.6   To find the roots of a quadratic equation

```c
#include <stdio.h>
#include <math.h>
#define DISC(a, b, c) ((b)*(b) - 4*(a)*(c))

int main()
{
        int a, b, c;
        float d, x1, x2, real, img;

        printf("Enter a, b & c \n");
        scanf("%d%d%d", &a, &b, &c);
        d = DISC(a, b, c);
   printf("d = %f\n", d);
        if (d > 0)
        {
                x1 = (-b + sqrt(d))/(2*a);
                x2 = (-b - sqrt(d))/(2*a);
                printf("Roots are real and distinct\n");
                printf("x1 = %5.2f\n", x1);
                printf("x2 = %5.2f\n", x2);
                }
        else if (d == 0)
        {
                x1 = x2 = (float) -b / (2 * a);
                printf(" Roots are real and equal \n");
                printf("x1 = %5.2f\n", x1);
                printf("x2 = %5.2f\n", x2);
        }
        else
        {
                real = (float) -b / (2 * a);
                img = sqrt(-d) / (2 * a);
                printf("Complex roots  \n");
                printf("x1 = %4.2f + %4.2fi\n",real,img);
                printf("x2 = %4.2f - %4.2fi\n",real,img);
        }

        return 0;
}
```

Input–Output:

```
Enter a, b & c
1 0 -25

Roots are real and distinct
x1 = 5.00
x2 = -5.00

Enter a, b & c
1 2 1
Roots are real and equal
x1 = -1.00
x2 = -1.00

Enter a, b & c
1 2 3

Complex roots
x1 = -1.00 + 1.41i
x2 = -1.00 - 1.41i
```

Explanation:

In the above program, the macro DISC is defined with three arguments a, b and c with the replacement string ((b) * (b) - 4 * (a) * (c)), the discriminant of a quadratic equation.

During preprocessing the statement d = DISC (a, b, c); is expanded to d = ((b) * (b) - 4 * (a) * (c)). The expanded code is then passed on to the compiler to generate the appropriate code. The variable d would thus collect the discriminant of the given quadratic equation. Depending on the value of d, branching takes place to calculate the roots of the equation.

Examples of macros with arguments

1. #define CUBE (x)   (x) * (x) * (x)
   Finds the cube of x.
2. #define MAX (x, y)   ((x) > (y)) ? (x) : (y)
   Finds the maximum of x and y.
3. #define SI (p, t, r)   ((p) * (t) * (r)) / 100
   Finds the simple interest given the principal, rate of interest and time period.
4. #define AREA (b, h)   0.5 * (b) * (h)
   Finds the area of a triangle whose base is b and height is h.
5. #define   AREA (l, b)   (l) * (b)
   Finds the area of a rectangle whose length is l and breadth is b.

14.3.2 Nesting of Macros

C preprocessor permits nesting of macros definitions, i.e. one macro can be expressed in terms of the other. If A is a macro already defined and B is another macro, which is to be defined and is expressible in terms of A then, the macro A can be embedded in the segment of text for B. When the macro B is used in the program, the preprocessor first expands B to its corresponding segment of text, which contains the macro A. In the second step, the macro A also is expanded to its segment of text. The nesting of the macros can be further extended.

We will now write a program which deals with nesting of macros.

PROGRAM 14.7   To illustrate nesting of macros

```
#include <stdio.h>

#define LARGEST_OF_TWO(a, b) ((a) > (b))? (a) : (b)
#define LARGEST_OF_THREE(a, b, c)  (LARGEST_OF_TWO((a), (b)) > (c))?
(LARGEST_OF_TWO((a), (b))): (c)
int main(void)
{
        int a, b, c, largest;

        printf("Enter Three Numbers \n");
        scanf("%d%d%d", &a, &b, &c);

        printf("Nesting of Macro Calls \n");
        largest = (LARGEST(a, (LARGEST(b, c));
        printf("Largest = %d \n", largest);

        printf("Nesting of Macro Definitions \n");
        largest = LARGEST_OF_THREE(a, b, c);
        printf("Largest = %d \n", largest);
        return 0;
}
```

Input–Output:

```
Enter Three Numbers
4 5 7

Nesting of Macro Calls
Largest = 7

Nesting of Macro Definitions
Largest = 7
```

Explanation:

In the above program, LARGEST_OF_TWO and LARGEST_OF_THREE are two macros defined with arguments. The purpose of the LARGEST_OF_TWO is to find the largest of two numbers and the purpose of the macro LARGEST_OF_THREE is to find the largest of three numbers.

Initially, the largest of the three numbers a, b and c is found out by nesting the calls to LARGEST_OF_TWO as in largest = (LARGEST(a, (LARGEST(b, c)); Here first, the macro call LARGEST(b, c) is expanded and then the outer macro call is expanded.

Secondly, the largest of the three numbers is found out using the macro LARGEST_OF_THREE. Note that the macro LARGEST_OF_TWO is used in the segment-of-text for the macro LARGEST_OF_THREE . The C preprocessor first expands LARGEST_OF_THREE(a,b,c) to LARGEST_OF_TWO((a),(b))>(c))? (LARGEST_OF_TWO((a),(b))): (c) And then the macro LARGEST_OF_TWO(a,b) is expanded to ((a)>(b))? (a) : (b) The expanded code is then passed onto the compiler which generates the code for finding the largest of three numbers.

Examples of nested macros

1. #define ONE_FOURTH(a)   HALF(HALF(a))
   Finds the one-fourth of the value of a where HALF(a) finds the half of the value of a.
2. #define CUBE(x)   (x) * SQUARE(x)
   Finds the cube of the value of x. where SQUARE(x) finds the square of the value of x. Macros can even be extended into multiple lines. In this case, each line except the last line must be terminated by a backslash \

Example 14.3

#define MSG   Learning C \
is quite interesting

Here the segment of text "Learning C is quite interesting" is a replacement string for the macro MSG. Note that there is a backslash \ at the end of the first line.

14.3.3 Macros vs. Functions

A macro is a symbolic name assigned to a segment of text. The segment of text can be merely a sequence of digits or it can be a string enclosed within double quotes or it can even be a C statement, whereas a function is a self-contained program by itself. As far as usage of the macros with arguments and functions in programs is concerned, they look alike. But there are significant differences between them. We will now try to figure out the differences between macros and functions with the help of the following program.

PROGRAM 14.8   To illustrate the differences between macros and functions

```
#include <stdio.h>
#define SQUARE(x) ((x) * (x))

int square(int x)
{
    return (x * x);
}

int main(void)
{
```

```
      int a = 6, sqr_of_a;

      printf ("a = %d \n", a);
      sqr_of_a = SQUARE(a);
      printf ("Square of a through the macro SQUARE(a) = %d \n", sqr_of_a);
      sqr_of_a = square(a);
      printf ("Square of a through the function square(a) = %d \n", sqr_of_a);

      return 0;
}
```

Input–Output:

```
a = 6

Square of a through the macro SQUARE(a) = 36
Square of a through the function square(a) = 36
```

Explanation:

In the above program, the preprocessor directive #define SQUARE(x) ((x) * (x)) defines the macro SQUARE with an argument **x** to represent the replacement string **((x) * (x))**. The purpose of the macro definition is to find the square of a number.

The function square() is defined with an argument **x** of type **int** and it is made to return a value of **int** type. The purpose of the function is also to find out the square of an integer passed to it and return it to the calling program.

In the main(), **a** and **sqr_of_a** are declared to be variables of **int** type. the variable **a** is to collect a number, square of which is to be found out and the variable **sqr_of_a** is to collect the square of **a**. The variable a is passed as an argument to the macro SQUARE in the statement sqr_of_a = SQUARE(a) and to the function square() in the statement sqr_of_a = square(a); During the preprocessing stage, the statement sqr_of_a = SQUARE(a) is expanded to sqr_of_a = ((a) * (a)). But no change is made to the statement sqr_of_a = square(a); by the preprocessor. The expanded source code is passed on to the compiler. The compiler generates the appropriate sequence of instructions for both the statements.

Differences between macros and functions

Macros	Functions
Macros are expanded to their replacement strings during preprocessing.	Function calls are not affected during preprocessing.
Arguments to macros are merely string tokens, no data type is associated with the arguments.	Arguments to functions should be declared to be of some data type (Built-in or User-defined).
During compilation, no type checking of arguments takes place.	During compilation, type checking of arguments takes place. If the actual arguments are not compatible with formal arguments, the compiler reports an error.

(Contd.)

Macros	Functions
More occurrences of a macro in a program lead to consumption of more memory space. This is because of the fact that each occurrence of the macro in the program is replaced by its replacement string by the preprocessor.	More calls to a function do not lead to consumption of more memory space. This is because of the fact that only one copy of the function will be available in the memory and whenever the function is called, the program control itself is transferred to the function; the instructions in the function are executed and after the execution of the function, the control is transferred back to the calling program.
A macro name does not evaluate to an address.	The function name evaluates to the address of the function and thus can be used in the contexts requiring a pointer.
Macro definitions can be nested.	Function definitions cannot be nested.
No CPU overhead involved.	Considerable amount of CPU time is consumed in tracking the transfer of control from a calling function to a called function and from the called function back to the calling function and also in establishing data communication between the functions like passing actual parameters to called function and returning a value from the called function.

14.3.4 Advantages of Macros

When macros are used as symbolic names for some replacement strings, which are used quite often in a program, following are the advantages offered by macros definition:

1. The macros definition increases the degree of readability of programs since the names selected for the macros are normally selected to be reflective of the meaning of the replacement strings.
2. The macros definition enhances easier modifiability since any change made in the replacement string in the macro definition will be effected in all its occurrences throughout the program.

Example 14.4

Consider the following macro definition

```
#define NO_OF_STUDENTS 100
```

Here, quite obviously, the symbolic name NO_OF_STUDENTS to the constant 100 is more readable than the constant itself. Suppose the macro NO OF STUDENTS has been used in our program in, say, 10 different places. Later, if the number of students changes, say, to 200, then only one change is to be made in the program. That is, in the macro definition, we replace 100 by 200 as:

```
#define NO_OF_STUDENTS 200
```

Thus, modification becomes simple. Once this is done, the preprocessor takes care of replacing all the occurrences of the macro by 200.

3. Sometimes, macros can be used in place of functions, thereby eliminating the CPU overhead involved in the execution of functions. Macros can be used in place of functions when the number of calls to macros is less.

The **#undef** directive

The #undef directive is used to remove a macro which has been previously defined using #define. The syntax of its usage is as follows:

```
#undef MACRO_NAME
```

Example 14.5

```
#undef COUNT
```

As a result of this directive, the macro COUNT loses its existence.

14.4   CONDITIONAL COMPILATION DIRECTIVES
[#ifdef, ifndef, #endif, #if, #else]

Conditional Compilation, as the name itself indicates, offers us a way for compiling only the required sections of code in a source program. Conditional Compilation of source programs is necessitated by the following reasons:

1. To make the programs portable so that they can be compiled according to the machines being used.
2. To make the programs suit different situations without the need for rewriting the programs from scratch.

Conditional Compilation is accomplished with the help of the following conditional compilation directives:

14.4.1   #ifdef - #endif Directives

The #ifdef - #endif directives check for the definition of a macro. The syntax of their usage is as follows:

```
#ifdef MACRO_NAME
statements
#endif
```

Here, the statements will be considered for compilation only when MACRO_NAME has been defined. Otherwise, the statements will be ignored by the compiler.

14.4.2   #ifdef - #else - #endif Directives

The syntax of the usages of the directives is as follows:

```
#ifdef MACRO_NAME
      statements-1
#else
      statements-2
#endif
```

Here, if MACRO_NAME has been defined previously, statements-1 will be compiled. Otherwise, statements-2 will be compiled.

PROGRAM 14.9 To illustrate conditional compilation: Usage of #ifdef-#else-#endif

```c
#include <stdio.h>
#define SUM

int main(void)
{
        int a = 1, b = 5, r;

        #ifdef SUM
                r = a + b;
                printf("Sum = %d", r);
        #else
                r = a - b;
                printf("Difference = %d \n", r);
        #endif

        return 0;
}
```

Input–Output:

```
Sum = 6
```

Explanation:

In the above program, a macro by name SUM has been defined with the directive #define SUM in the main(), since #ifdef SUM evaluates to true, the statements r = a + b; printf("sum = %d", r); are selected for compilation. The statements between #else and #endif are ignored by the compiler. As a result, when the program is run, the program finds the sum of the variables a and b, and displays it.

If we remove the definition of the macro SUM and compile and run the program, the program finds the difference between a and b, and displays it. This is because, in the absence of the macro SUM, the statements between #else and #endif are compiled.

14.4.3 #ifdef-#elif-#else-#endif **Directives**

The syntax of the usage of the directives is as follows:

```c
#ifdef macro1
        statements-1
#elif defined(macro2)
        statements-2
#elif defined(macro3)
        statements-3
```

```
#elif defined(macro4)
      statements-4
#else
      statements-5
endif
```

Here, only one out of many alternative blocks of code will be considered for compilation depending on what macro has been defined previously.

PROGRAM 14.10   To illustrate conditional compilation: Usage of `#ifdef` - `#elif defined()` - `#else` - `#endif`

```
#include <stdio.h>
#define MULT

int main(void)
{
      int a = 10, b = 5, r;

      #ifdef SUM
            r = a + b;
            printf(" Sum = %d", r);
      #elif defined(DIFF)
            r = a - b;
            printf("Difference = %d \n", r);
      #elif defined(MULT)
            r = a * b;
            printf("Product = %d \n", r);
      #elif defined(DIVIDE)
            r = a / b;
            printf("Quotient = %d \n", r);
      #else
            r = a % b;
            printf("Remainder = %d \n", r);
      #endif

      return 0;
}
```

Input–Output:

```
Product = 50
```

Explanation:

In the above program, since the macro defined is MULT, the statements:

```
r = a * b;
printf("Product = %d \n", r);
```

only will be compiled and other alternative blocks are skipped by the compiler. As a result, when the program is run, it displays the product of the values of the variables **a** and **b**.

#ifndef **directive**

The `#ifndef` directive is just the negative of the `#ifdef` directive. It is normally used to define a macro after ascertaining that the macro has not been defined previously. The syntax of the directive for the purpose is as follows:

```
#ifndef macro
        #define macro
#endif
```

Example 14.6

```
#ifndef SUM
    #define SUM
#endif
```

#if **directive**

The `#if` directive is to select a block of code for compilation when a test-expression (rather than a macro) evaluates to true. Otherwise, to ignore the block of code for compilation.

```
#if - #endif
#if - #else - #endif
#if - #elif defined() - #else - #endif
```

are similar to their `#ifdef` counterparts except the fact that, here macros are replaced by test-expressions.

The above example programs, which were written to illustrate conditional compilation, were just to highlight the fact that the compilation can be done selectively with respect to blocks of code. When we compiled and ran the programs, we understood this fact. In real life programming environments, we need to prepare programs in such a way that the programs run on different types of machines or the programs should cater to different clients. The facility of conditional compilation plays an important role since the same programs are made to suit to the differing environments by conditionally compiling the required sections of code for a particular environment.

Example 14.7

Suppose a program being written is targeted to two types of machines: 1. IBMPC and 2. VAX 8810. Since the word length, memory size and other architectural details vary between the two systems, the sections of code in the program, which are dependent on these, should be selectively compiled. The following code accomplishes this.

```
#ifdef IBMPC
        statements for IBMPC
#else
        statements for VAX 8810
#endif
```

Here, IBMPC and VAX8810 are macros.

14.5 ANSI ADDITIONS

The following are the new preprocessor facilities added by the ANSI Committee:

14.5.1 The Stringizing Operator

The `Stringizing` Operator serves the purpose of converting an argument in a macro to a string.

Example 14.8

```
#define macro(a) printf(#a)
```

Here the argument a to the macro is converted into the string "a", which in turn becomes the argument for the `printf()`.

PROGRAM 14.11   To illustrate stringizing operator #

```
#include <stdio.h>

#define prod(x) printf(#x "= %d", x);

int main(void)
{
        int a = 8, b = 7;
        prod(a * b);
        return 0;
}
```

Input–Output:

```
a * b = 56
```

Explanation:

In the above program, the statement `prod(a * b)` expands to `printf("a * b" "=%d", a * b)`, which in turn gets transformed to `printf("a * b=%d", a * b);`. Note that the strings "a * b" and "=%d" are concatenated to produce "a * b=%d".

As a result, the product of the values of **a** and **b** is calculated and displayed.

14.5.2 The Token Pasting Operator

The Token Pasting operator supported by ANSI standard enables us to merge two tokens into a single token.

Example 14.9

Suppose **t1** and **t2** are two tokens, which are to be merged together to form a single token **t1t2**, the following preprocessor directive can be used:

```
#define paste(t1, t2) t1##t2
```

Now all appearances of **paste(t1, t2)** in a program will be replaced by **t1t2** by the preprocessor.

PROGRAM 14.12   To illustrate the token pasting operator ##

```
#include <stdio.h>
#define DISPLAY(i) printf ("b" #i "= %d\n", b##i);

int main(void)
{
      int b1 = 10, b2 =20;

      DISPLAY(1);
      DISPLAY(2);

      return 0;
}
```

Input–Output:

```
b1 = 10
b2 = 20
```

Explanation:

In the above program, the macro DISPLAY has been defined with an argument. The replacement string contains a `printf` statement which in turn contains both the Stringizing operator # and the Token Pasting operator ## within the control string and the argument respectively. As a result, `DISPLAY(1)` is expanded to `printf ("b1 = %d\n", b1);` and similarly `DISPLAY(2)` also is expanded to `printf ("b2 = %d\n", b2);`.

14.5.3   The `#error` Directive

The `#error` Directive when it is encountered displays some error message and terminates the compilation process.

The syntax of its usage is as follows:

```
#error message
```

The following program demonstrates the usage of the directive.

PROGRAM 14.13   To illustrate `#error` directive

```
#if !defined(M)
#error M NOT DEFINED
#endif

#include <stdio.h>
int main(void)
{
      printf("Welcome");
      return 0;
}
```

Since the macro M has not been defined, !defined(M) evaluates to true and the control reaches the #error directive which when executed displays the message M NOT DEFINED and terminates the compilation process.

14.5.4   The #pragma Directive

The #pragma directive is an implementation specific directive and it allows us to specify various instructions to the compiler.

The syntax of its usage is as follows:

#pragma name

Where name refers to a kind of instruction to the compiler supported by the C implementation. The name can vary from one C implementation to another. If a particular name is not supported by a C implementation, it is simply ignored.

Some examples of #pragma directives include

#pragma startup <function name>

which indicates that the function identified by the function name is to be executed before the main()

#pragma exit <function name>

which indicates that the function identified by the function name is to be executed after the program terminates

#pragma argsused

which suppresses the error message "parameter not used" in case parameters are not used within the functions.

SUMMARY

- The preprocessor directives are the instructions to the C preprocessor to carry out operations like inclusion of header files (#include), definition of macros (#define).
- We can even define macros with arguments.
- Macros increase the degree of readability and the ease of modifiability of programs.
- Conditional compilation directives enable us to selectively compile sections of code depending on the requirement so that the programs become portable.
- The stringizing operator # converts an argument into a string.
- The token pasting operator ##, which merges two tokens into a single token.
- The #error directive, which terminates the compilation process itself on encountering an error (like unavailability of a macro).
- The #pragma directive, can be used for various purposes like executing a function before the main() or executing a function after the main() and suppressing the error message "Arguments not used" in case the arguments are not used in a function.

REVIEW QUESTIONS

14.1 What is the role of preprocessor during compilation?

14.2 What are preprocessor directives?

14.3 Mention the need for #define.

14.4 What is the need for #include?

14.5 Define a macro.

14.6 Why do we need macros with arguments?

14.7 Differentiate between functions and macros.

14.8 Explain the concept of nesting of macros.

14.9 What is the need for conditional compilation?

14.10 Explain conditional compilation-related directives.

State whether the following are true or false

14.1 Compilation precedes preprocessing.

14.2 Macro is a symbolic name assigned to a segment of text.

14.3 Macros can be defined with arguments.

14.4 There can be a space or tab space between # and define.

14.5 The symbol # can appear in any column.

14.6 Macros can be multiline.

14.7 A macro with arguments is just like a function with the same arguments.

Identify errors, if any, in the following

14.1
```c
#include stdio.h
int main(void)
{
    printf("File Inclusion Directive");
    return 0;
}
```

14.2
```c
# define LEAST(a, b) a < b ? a : b

int main(void)
{
    int x = 5, y = 7, l;

    l = LEAST(x, y);
    printf("Least = %d\n", l);
    l = LEAST(x+3, y-2);
    printf("least = %d\n", l);
```

```
        return 0;
    }
```

14.3
```
#define msg    printf ("Welcome to C Programming");
int main (void)
{
    msg;
    return 0;
}
```

14.4
```
#include <stdio.h>
    #define DISPLAY(j) printf ("b" #j" = %d\n", b#j);

    int main (void)
    {
        int b1 = 10, b2 =20;

        DISPLAY(1);
        DISPLAY(2);

    return 0;
    }
```

14.5
```
#pragma

    int main (void)
    {
        printf ("C is the mother of almost all the programming
Languages");
    return 0;
}
```

PROGRAMMING EXERCISES

14.1 Write a program to find the maximum of two numbers using a macro.

14.2 Write a program to find the smallest of three numbers using the concept of nesting of macro calls (Use the macro defined in the above program).

14.3 Define a macro by name RECT with two arguments length and breadth. Write a program to find the area of a rectangle for the given values length and breadth.

14.4 Define a macro by name SI with three parameters p, t and r (p-Principal Amount, t-Time Period, r-Rate). Write a program to find the simple interest for two sets of values of p, t and r using the macro.

14.5 Define a macro by name SWAP with two arguments a and b which swaps the arguments and write a program to use the macro.

14.6 Write a program to illustrate conditional compilation.

INTERVIEW QUESTIONS

14.1 What are the differences between a preprocessor directive and a compiler directive?

14.2 What is the advantage of a macro over a function call?

14.3 What is the output of the following programs?

```
(a) #define NEW(A+B+C)        A+B+C* A+B+C *A+B+C
    #include<stdio.h>
    int main(void)
    {

        int x;
        x = NEW(3+4+5);
        printf("%d", x);
        return 0;
    }
(b) #define CONCAT(S1, S2) strcat(S1, S2)
    #include<stdio.h>
    int main(int)
    {
        char s1[10] = "abcd";
        char s2[10] = "pqr";
        char s3[20] = "jkl";
        char s4[30];
        s4 = concat(conct(s1, s2), s3);
        printf("%s\n", s4);
        return 0;

    }

(c) #define TEST (A,B,C)   A*B+C
    #include<stdio.h>
    int main(void)
    {

        int x;
        result = TEST(2,3,4) * TEST(2,4,3) + TEST (4,3,2);
        printf("Result = %d\n", result);
          return 0;
    }
```

14.4 What is the difference between `#include<stdio.h>` and `"stdio.h"`?

14.5 How do you insert date and time into your program using macros?

14.6 How do you prevent a file from getting included twice into a program?

14.7 What is the scope of a macro in a program?

15

Programming at Bit Level

15.1   INTRODUCTION

One of the greatest strengths of the C language is that it empowers the programmers to deal with data at bit level by providing the special operators known as bitwise operators and the concept of bit-fields. The bitwise operators are employed to manipulate data at bit level. This property helps in performing arithmetic operations swiftly and efficiently, and controlling hardware devices by manipulating the bits in their control words. The bitwise operations find their application in simulating digital systems also. The bit-fields help in minimizing memory space usage by packing several data items in individual memory words. These facilities are of great help for system programmers as well as application programmers.

15.2   BITWISE OPERATORS [&, |, ^, ~, <<, >>]

The availability of bitwise operators is another distinctive feature of the C language. As the name itself indicates, these operators enable us to perform manipulations over data at bit level. The ability provided by the bitwise operators to deal with data items at bit level will in turn help us to perform low level functions. These operators will work on only integers. This category of operators were not available in the earlier higher level languages. The table given below shows the operators, which come under this category.

Operator symbol	Name of the operator
&	Bitwise AND
|	Bitwise OR
^	Bitwise Exclusive OR
~	Bitwise Complement
<<	Bitwise Left Shift
>>	Bitwise Right Shift

Bitwise AND (&), Bitwise OR (|) , Bitwise Exclusive OR (^), Bitwise Left Shift (<<) and Bitwise Right Shift (>>) are binary operators, whereas Bitwise complement (~) is unary operator.

Bitwise AND (&)

The general syntax of the usage of the Bitwise AND operator is as follows:
`op1 & op2`, where `op1` and `op2` are integer expressions. The value of the expression would also be an integer. If the corresponding bits of `op1` and `op2` are both 1s, then the bit in the corresponding position of the result would be 1, otherwise, it would be 0.

Bit1	Bit2	Bit1 & Bit2
0	0	0
0	1	0
1	0	0
1	1	1

Example 15.1

`int a = 4, b = 5;`

Binary equivalent of a 0000 0000 0000 0100
Binary equivalent of b 0000 0000 0000 0101
a & b 0000 0000 0000 0100

Bitwise OR (|)

The general syntax of the usage of the Bitwise OR operator is as follows:
`op1 | op2`, where `op1` and `op2` are integer expressions. The value of the expression would also be an integer. If the corresponding bits of `op1` and `op2` are both 0s, then the bit in the corresponding position of the result would be 0, otherwise, it would be 1.

Bit1	Bit2	Bit1	Bit2
0	0	0
0	1	1
1	0	1
1	1	1

Example 15.2

`int a = 4, b = 5;`

Binary equivalent of a 0000 0000 0000 0100
Binary equivalent of b 0000 0000 0000 0101
a | b 0000 0000 0000 0101

The Bitwise OR operator is used to set some specific bits ON in a value without affecting the other bits.

Consider the bit-pattern 1000 0100 0000 0010. To turn only the third bit ON without affecting other bits in the value, the value is bitwise ORed with the bit-pattern 0000 0000 0000 0100.

i.e.   0000 0000 0000 0010
        0000 0000 0000 0100

        0000 0000 0000 0110

Decimal equivalents of the above bit-patterns

   2
   4

   6

Bitwise Exclusive OR (^)

The general syntax of the usage of the Bitwise Exclusive OR operator is as follows:
op1 ^ op2, where op1 and op2 are integer expressions. The value of the expression would also be
an integer. If any one of the corresponding bits of op1 and op2 is 1, then the bit in the corresponding
position of the result would be 1, otherwise, it would be 0.

Bit1	Bit2	Bit1^Bit2
0	0	0
0	1	1
1	0	1
1	1	0

Example 15.3

int a = 4, b = 5;

```
Binary equivalent of a  0000 0000 0000 0100
Binary equivalent of b  0000 0000 0000 0101
                a^b     0000 0000 0000 0001
```

The Bitwise Exclusive OR operator is used to toggle bits.

Bitwise Left Shift (<<)

The Bitwise left shift operator is used to shift the bits of an integer towards left by the given number
of positions. The vacant positions on the right of the integer would be filled with 0s. The general
syntax of its usage is as follows:

operand << n

where operand is an integer or integer expression and **n** is the number of positions by which the
bits of operand are to be shifted towards left.

Example 15.4

int a = 5;

```
Binary equivalent of a  0000 0000 0000 0101
                a<<4    0000 0000 0101 0000
```

Note: Shifting an unsigned integer to left by n positions has the effect of multiplying the integer
by 2 to the power of n.

Bitwise Right Shift (>>)

The Bitwise Right Shift operator is used to shift the bits of an integer towards right by the given number of positions. The vacant positions on the left of the integer would be filled with 0s. The general syntax of its usage is as follows:

```
operand >> n
```

where operand is an integer or integer expression and **n** is the number of positions by which the bits of operand are to be shifted towards right.

Example 15.5

```
int a = 5;
```

Binary equivalent of a   0000 0000 0000 0101

           a >> 2   0000 0000 0000 0001

Note: Shifting an unsigned integer to right by n positions has the effect of dividing the integer by 2 to the power of n.

Bitwise Complement (~)

The Bitwise complement operator is used to invert the bits of an integer. That is, it replaces all 1s by 0s and all 0s by 1s of an integer.

Example 15.6

```
int a = 4;
```

Binary equivalent of a   0000 0000 0000 0100

           ~a   1111 1111 1111 1011

The bitwise complement operator ~ is used to find out the 1s complement of a number.

PROGRAM 15.1   To illustrate bitwise operators [&, |, ^, ~, <<, >>]

```c
#include <stdio.h>

void show_bits(int);

int main(void)
{
    int x, y, n, x_or_y, x_and_y, x_exor_y, x_lshift, x_rshift;

    printf("Enter x and y\n");
    scanf("%d%d", &x, &y);
    printf("x=");  show_bits(x);
    printf("y =");  show_bits(y);

    x_or_y = x | y;
    printf("x_or_y =");  show_bits(x_or_y);
```

```
        x_and_y = x & y;
        printf("x_and_y = "); show_bits(x_and_y);

        x_exor_y = x ^ y;
        printf("x_exor_y = "); show_bits(x_exor_y);

        printf("Enter the number of bits to be shifted by \n");
        scanf("%u", &n);
        x_lshift = x << n;
        printf("x_lshift = ");    show_bits(x_lshift);

        x_rshift = x >> n;
        printf("x_rshift = "); show_bits(x_rshift);

        return 0;
}

void show_bits(int n)
{
        int i, mask, result;

        for(i = 15; i >= 0; i—)
        {
              mask = 1 << i;    /* Application of << operator */
              result = mask & n;  /* Application of & operator */
              if (result != 0 )
                      printf("1");
              else
                      printf("0");
        }
        printf("\n");
}
```

Input–Output:

```
Enter x and y
4
5
Enter the number of bits to be shifted by
5
x             = 0000000000000100
y             = 0000000000000101
x_or_y        = 0000000000000101
x_and_y       = 0000000000000100
x_exor_y      = 0000000000000001
x_lshift      = 0000000001000000
x_rshift      = 0000000000000000
```

Explanation:

x and **y** are declared to be variables of **int** type. The values of these variables are subjected to the bitwise operations discussed above and hence they become the operands for the bitwise operators. The resultant value of each expression (constructed out of **x**, **y** and a bitwise operator) is assigned to a different variable. It is important to note that the operands **x** and **y**, and the resultant values of the bitwise operations are displayed in bit-patterns (in terms of 1s and 0s). This is to enhance better understanding of the working of the bitwise operations.

The user-defined function **show_bits()** accomplishes the task of displaying an integer value in bit-pattern, the width of the pattern is 16 bits, which is the number of bits in the size of an integer in C in 16 bit machines. Let us now understand how this function works. The function takes an integer value n as its input. It employs left-shift and bitwise AND operators to accomplish the assigned task.

The following segment in the function is responsible for the said task.

```c
for (i = 15; i >= 0; i—)
{
        mask = 1 << i;          /* Application of left-shift operator */
        result = n & mask;      /* Application of Bitwise AND operator */
        if (result != 0 )
                printf ("1");
        else
                printf ("0");
}
```

In the `for`-loop above, the loop variable **i** ranges from 15 to 0 downwards. Initially, i takes the value 15 and the loop is entered. Inside the loop, as a result of the execution of the statement `mask = 1 << i`, the integer constant 1 (Binary equivalent 0000000000000001) is subjected to left-shift operation by 15 bits. As a result, the variable `mask` will collect the binary equivalent 1000000000000000. Note that the most significant bit in mask is 1. The value of mask is then Bitwise ANDed with n in the statement `result = n & mask`, the result of the Bitwise AND operation is assigned to the variable `result`. The value of result would be non-zero if n also has 1 in its most significant position of its bit-pattern. Otherwise it would be 0. The following segment

```c
if (result != 0 )
        printf ("1");
else
        printf ("0");
```

Displays the numerical digit 1 if `result` is non-zero, otherwise it displays the numerical digit 0.

In the next iteration, the variable i, takes 14, the above procedure repeats displaying the numerical digit 1 if the bit in the fourteenth position in n is 1. Otherwise displaying the numerical digit 0. This continues till the least significant bit of n is considered.

15.2.1 Applications of Bitwise Operators

1. Turning bits OFF

The Bitwise AND (&) operator is used to turn specific bits of a value **OFF** without affecting the other bits. Consider an integer **a**, in order to turn the nth bit in it OFF, the integer has to be Bitwise ANDed with another integer whose n^{th} bit is 0 and all the other bits are 1s.

Example 15.7

Suppose the value in **a** is 5. The bit-pattern in 16-bits width is 0000 0000 0000 0101. To turn off the third bit of the number, it has to be bitwise ANDed with another integer, which has 0 in the third bit position and all the other bit positions have 1s. i.e. 1111 1111 1111 1011. The number which has this kind of bit-pattern is ~4 (complement of 4).

So, the following statement accomplishes the task of setting the third bit of the value in a OFF.

```
a = a & ~4;
```

```
  0000 0000 0000 0101
& 1111 1111 1111 1011
  _____
  0000 0000 0000 0001
```

2. Turning bits ON

The Bitwise OR (||) operator is used to turn ON specific bits of a value without affecting the other bits. Consider an integer a. In order to turn the nth bit in it ON, the integer has to be Bitwise ORed with another integer whose n^{th} bit is 1 and all the other bits are 0s.

Example 15.8

Let the value of **a** be 5. The bit-pattern in 16 bits width is 0000 0000 0000 0101. To turn ON the second bit of the number without affecting the other bits in it, it has to be bitwise ORed with another integer, which has 1 in the second bit position and all the other bit positions have 0s. The integer number which has this kind of bit-pattern is 2. (Bit-pattern of 2 = 0000 0000 0000 0010).

So, the following statement accomplishes the job of setting the second bit ON:

```
a = a | 2;
```

```
  0000 0000 0000 0101
| 0000 0000 0000 0010
  _____
  0000 0000 0000 0111
```

3. Toggling bits

The Bitwise Exclusive OR (^) operator is used to toggle bits in a value. Consider an integer **a**, In order to toggle the nth bit in it, the integer has to be Bitwise Exclusive ORed with another integer whose n^{th} bit is 1 and all the other bits are 0s.

Example 15.9

Let the value of **a** be 5. The bit-pattern in 16 bits width is 0000 0000 0000 0101. To toggle the second bit of the number without affecting the other bits in it, it has to be bitwise Exclusive ORed with another integer, which has 1 in the second bit position and all the other bit positions have 0s. The integer number which has this kind of bit-pattern is 2. (Bit –pattern of 2 = 0000 0000 0000 0010).

So, the following statement accomplishes the job of setting the second bit ON:

```
a = a ^ 2;
```

```
  0000 0000 0000 0101
^ 0000 0000 0000 0010
  _____
  0000 0000 0000 0111
```

4. To check whether a bit is ON or OFF

Suppose a is an integer. To check whether the **n**th bit of a is ON or OFF, we take another integer, say, b, which has 1 in its **n**th bit position and all the other bits are 0s and we bitwise AND a with b. If the result of the operation is b itself then we can say that the **n**th bit in a is ON. Otherwise, it is OFF.

Precisely, the nth bit in a is ON if the expression (a & b) == b) evaluates to true. Otherwise, it is OFF.

Example 15.10

The following segment of code checks whether the least significant bit in a is ON or OFF.

```
if ((a & 1) == 1)
      printf("The least significant bit is ON");
else
   printf("The least significant bit is OFF");
```

PROGRAM 15.2   To find whether a number is even or odd

```
#include <stdio.h>

int main(void)
{
      int number;

      printf("Enter a number \n");
      scanf("%d", &number);
      if (number & 1)
            printf("%d is odd", number);
      else
            printf("%d is even", number);

      return 0;
}
```

Input–Output:

```
Enter a number
5
5 is odd
```

Explanation:

The integer variable **number** is to collect an integer value from the terminal. We know that for a number to be even, the last bit in it should be 0 and for it to be an odd number the last bit in it should be a 1. This fact has been used to find out whether the number is even or odd. The expression number & 1 is checked. If it evaluates to a non-zero value, the number is displayed to be an odd number. On the other hand, if it evaluates to 0 then the number is displayed as even.

5. To convert a binary number into its decimal equivalent

Decimal equivalent of a binary number is given by the sum of the products of each bit in the number and its corresponding positional value. The positional values are powers of two. The positional value of the least significant digit is 2^0 and that of the second least significant digit is 2^1, and so on.

Example 15.11

Decimal equivalent of 110 is given by:

$$1 * 2^2 + 1 * 2^1 + 0 * 2^0$$
$$= 1 * 4 + 1 * 2 + 0$$
$$= 4 + 2 + 0$$
$$= 6$$

PROGRAM 15.3 To convert a binary number into its decimal equivalent

---

```c
#include <stdio.h>

int main(void)
{
        int bin, dec = 0, rem, k = 1, n;

        printf("Enter a binary number \n");
        scanf("%d", &bin);
        n = bin;
        while (bin > 0)
        {
                rem = bin % 10;
                dec += rem * k;
                k <<= 1;        /* same as k *= 2; */
                bin /= 10;
        }
        printf("Decimal equivalent of the binary number %d = %d", n, dec);

        return 0;
}
```

Input–Output:

```
Enter a binary number
1110
Decimal equivalent of the binary number 1110 = 14
```

Explanation:

In the above program, we have used the bitwise left shift operator to multiply the variable k by 2, each time through the loop, i.e. the statement k <<= 1 is equivalent to k *= 2. The variable k provides the positional value for each bit position for the given binary number.

15.3 BIT-FIELDS

Suppose a variable in a program takes a value, which is either 0 or 1. Since both 0 and 1 are integers, we may be inclined to declare a variable of `int` type. A variable of `int` type consumes two bytes of memory space. A careful look at the values to be taken by the variable reveals that only one bit is enough. When a variable of `int` type is used, only one bit out of 16 bits (2 bytes = 16 bits) would be used. The remaining 15 bits go waste! But we do not have a say in determining the number of bits to be allocated for a variable. Is there a way out, where the remaining 15 bits can be put to use? The concept of bit-fields answers this question.

A bit-field is basically a set of adjacent bits in a word of memory. Members of structures can include bit-fields. By making bit-fields as the members of a structure, we can pack several items of information into a single word. Thereby optimizing the memory usage. This is how the low level instructions consisting of opcode, addressing mode specifiers and operand addresses are packed into single words.

The syntax of defining structure template using bit-fields is as follows.

```
struct tag_name
{
        data-type m1 : size;
        data-type m2 : size;
        .
        .
        .
        data-type mn : size;
};
```

`data-type` can be either `int` or `unsigned int` only. Size can vary from 1 to 16, the word size of memory.

Points to Observe

1. Bit-fields cannot be arrayed.
2. We cannot retrieve the address of a bit-field. Consequently, the concept of pointer to a bit-field does not arise.
3. If a bit-field does not fit into a word, the bit-field is placed into the next word.
4. Some members in the structure can be of normal data type also.

PROGRAM 15.4   To illustrate the concept of bit-fields

```
#include <stdio.h>

struct temp
{
        int a : 3;
        int b : 3;
```

```
            unsigned int c :2;
};

int main(void)
{
        struct temp t;

        t.a = 3;
        t.b = 2;
        t.c = 3;
        printf("t.a = %d \n", t.a);
        printf("t.b = %d \n", t.b);
        printf("t.c = %d \n", t.c);

        printf("size = %d \n", sizeof(struct temp));

        return 0;
}
```

Input–Output:

```
t.a = 3
t.b = 2
t.c = 3
size = 2
```

Explanation:

The structure **struct temp** is defined with three bit-field members **a**, **b** and **c**. The members **a** and **b** are of **int** type and are of size three bits. The range of values represented by **a** and **b** thus is –4 to 3 (-2^2 to 2^2-1). The bit-field member **c** is of **unsigned int** type and is of size three bits. The range of values which can be stored in **c** is thus 0 to 3 (0 to 2^2-1). A variable of **struct temp** type requires one byte memory. As can be seen, three pieces of data can be stored in one byte of memory.

PROGRAM 15.5   To illustrate bit-fields

```
#include <stdio.h>

struct date
{
        unsigned int day : 5;
        unsigned int month : 4;
        unsigned int year : 7;
};

struct emp
{
```

```
        struct date doj;
        unsigned mar_status : 2;
        unsigned grade : 2;
        int empno;
        char name[20];
        float salary;
};

int main(void)
{
        struct emp e;
        unsigned int day, month, year, mar_status, grade;
        printf("Enter empno, name and salary \n");
        scanf("%d%s%f", &e.empno, e.name, &e.salary);

        printf("Enter date of joining \n");
        scanf("%u%u%u", &day, &month, &year);
        e.doj.day = day;
        e.doj.month = month;
        e.doj.year = year;

        printf("Enter marital status [1-3] \n");
        scanf("%u", &mar_status);
        e.mar_status = mar_status;

        printf("Enter grade [1-3] \n");
        scanf("%u", &grade);
        e.grade = grade;
        printf("%-4d%-15s%-8.2f", e.empno, e.name, e.salary);
        printf("%u/%u/%u %u %u \n", e.doj.day, e.doj.month, e.doj.year,
e.mar_status, e.grade);

        return 0;
}
```

Input–Output:

```
Enter empno, name and salary
121
Raghav
2345

Enter date of joining
12
3
1998
```

```
Enter marital status [1-3]
1
Enter grade [1-3]
2


121 Raghav   2345.00 12/3/78 1 2
```

Explanation:

The structure struct date is defined with three bit-field members day, month and year of unsigned int type with the sizes five, four and seven bits respectively. The member day can store a value in the range 0 to 31; the member month can store a value in the range 0 to 15 and the member year can store a value in the range 0 to 127. Thus, a variable of struct date type can represent a date [day 1–31, month 1–12, year 1 to 127 an offset value after the year 2000.

The structure **struct emp** is defined with a member **doj** of type **struct date** which represents the date of joining of an employee. Two bit-fields **mar_status** and **grade** are of size two bits, which are to collect the marital status and grade of an employee, each denoted by a value in the range 0 to 3. Empno, name and salary are the normal members. So a variable of type **struct emp** would thus pack several pieces of information.

SUMMARY

- The bitwise operators and the bit-fields enable us to deal with data at bit level.
- The bitwise OR operator denoted by the symbol | produces 1 when any or both the operand bits are 1's, otherwise, it produces 0.
- The bitwise AND operator denoted by the symbol & produces 1 when both the operand bits are 1's, otherwise, it produces 0.
- The bitwise complement operator denoted by the symbol ! produces 1 when the operand bit is 0, otherwise, it produces 1.
- The bitwise exclusive OR operator ^ produces 1 when any one of the operand bits is 1, otherwise, it produces 0. The bitwise left-shift and the bitwise right-shift operators are used to shift the specified number of bits towards left and right.
- All the bitwise operators are defined over integers only.
- The bit-fields provide facility for packing of multiple data into single memory word.

REVIEW QUESTIONS

15.1 What are bitwise operators? Enumerate all the bitwise operators.

15.2 Explain the working of bitwise OR operator. Mention an example of its usage.

15.3 Explain the working of bitwise AND operator. Mention an example of its usage.

15.4 Explain the working of bitwise Complement operator. Mention an example of its usage.

15.5 Explain the working of bitwise Exclusive OR operator. Mention an example of its usage.

15.6 Explain the working of bitwise left-shift operator. Mention an example of its usage.

15.7 Explain the working of bitwise right-shift operator. Mention an example of its usage.

15.8 What are bit-fields? Explain their significance.

State whether the following are true or false.

15.1 Bitwise operators can be applied over float values.

15.2 The result is a 1 when both the operand bits are a 1 in the case of | operator.

15.3 The result is a 1 when either of the two operand bits is a 1 in the case of & operator.

15.4 Shifting a signed integer by 1 bit to right is equivalent to multiplying it by two.

15.5 Shifting a signed integer by 1 bit to left is equivalent to dividing it by two.

15.6 Bit-fieldscan be arrayed.

PROGRAMMING EXERCISES

15.1 Write a program to convert a decimal number into its binary equivalent.

15.2 2's complement of a number is obtained by adding 1 to its 1's complement.

Example:

Given number :	1001
1's complement	0110
	+ 1
	0111

There is an alternative method of obtaining the 2's complement of number. That is, by scanning the bit-pattern of the number from right to left and complementing all bits after the first occurrence of a 1.

Write a program to find the 2's complement of a number using the alternative method.

15.3 Write a program to accept an integer as its input and display the number of 1's and the number of 0's in its bit-pattern.

15.4 Write a function which takes two integers as its arguments and return 1 if they are equal, 0 otherwise. (Use bitwise exclusive OR operator).

15.5 Write a function that rotates the bits of an unsigned integer by a specified number of bits to the right.

Example: Given number   1010100111001**101**

After rotating by four bits to the right

1101101010011100

Note that the bits moved out of the lower-order positions are placed in the higher-order positions.

INTERVIEW QUESTIONS

15.1 How do you mask specific bits in a number?

15.2 Which operator is useful to determine whether a given number is even or odd?

15.3 How do you exchange two numbers without using temporary variable using bitwise operator?

15.4 What is the output of the following programs?

(a)
```c
#include<stdio.h>
int main(void)
{
    int a = 7;
    printf("%d\n", a>>1);
    return 0;
}
```

(b)
```c
#include<stdio.h>
int main(void)
{
    int a = 4
    printf("%d\n", a<<2);
    return 0;
}
```

(c)
```c
#include <stdio.h>
int main(void)
{
    int x;
    x = 5 ^ 6;
    printf("%d\n", x);
    return 0;
}
```

(d)
```c
#include <stdio.h>
int main(void)
{
    int x = 10;
    y = ~x;
    printf("%d\n", y);
    return 0;
}
```

15.5 Which operator is suitable for turning on specific bit in a given number?

16

Graphics Using C

16.1 INTRODUCTION

Computer graphics is one of the fascinating areas of computer science. It includes hardware and software which allow the computer to display, manipulate and store pictures. We can see the application of computer graphics in diverse fields such as video games, simulation and modeling, engineering drawing, architecture, computer aided learning, animations, etc. The C language is one of the most suitable high level languages for graphics applications as it provides a number of features for developing graphical applications easily. It is possible to create sophisticated graphical applications using the library functions available in C.

In this chapter, we discuss about the basics of computer graphics using C, various built in functions available in the C library, drawing different shapes, working with colors and fonts and creating different types of charts using C.

16.2 INITIALIZE THE GRAPHICS MODE

Normally C programs run in text mode. In text mode, the information is displayed on the output devices in the form of characters or bytes. In this mode, the computer screen is interpreted as a matrix of rows and columns and each cell in the matrix can accommodate a single character. To work with graphics, we need to switch over from text mode to graphics mode. The C library contains a function namely `initgraph()` which does the job of initializing the graphics mode.

The `initgraph()` function performs the following tasks to initialize the graphics mode:

1. Detects a graphics driver
2. Allocates memory for the graphics driver and loads the driver
3. Resets all the graphic settings to their default values

The computer's mother-board comes with a slot for graphics card. The graphics card is also known as **display card** or **display adapter** or **video card.** This card is responsible for display of information on the computer's monitor. Different graphic components such as pictures, videos, animations, etc., are all controlled by the graphics card. Graphics driver is a piece of software which is responsible for the proper functioning of the graphics card.

The prototype `initgraph()` is as follows:

```
void initgraph(int *graphdriver, int *graphmode, char *pathtodriver);
```

This function takes three parameters and the purpose of each of these parameters is as follows.

16.2.1 `graphdriver`

The parameter `graphdriver` is an integer pointer which specifies the graphics driver to be used. We can indicate the particular driver to be used explicitly or tell `initgraph()` to automatically detect the suitable graphics driver. Different graphics drivers are defined with different integer constants in the header file `<graphics.h>`. The default constant value is 0 which is used when `initgraph()` automatically detects the graphics driver with the highest resolution. It makes use of `detectgraph()` function to automatically detect the best graphics driver. The following table gives the list of graphics drivers along with their symbolic constant names and corresponding integer values.

Symbolic graphics driver constant	Description	Value
DETECT	When `initgraph()` automatically detects the graphics driver at run time	0
CGA	Color graphics adapter	1
MCGA	Multi-colorgraphics array	2
EGA	Enhanced graphics adapter with 16 colors	3
EGA64	Enhanced graphics adapter with 64 colors	4
EGAMONO	Enhanced graphics adapter with black and white only	5
IBM8514	IBM graphics display standard with 256 colors	6
HERCMONO	Hercules graphics card for black and white	7
ATT400	AT&T personal computers	8
VGA	Visual graphics adapter	9
PC3270	IBM personnel computer XT	10

16.2.2 `graphmode`

The parameter `graphmode` tells the `initgraph()` as to which monitor we are using, its resolution, the number of video pages it supports and the list of colors that are available. Resolution of a monitor is an indicator of picture quality. It specifies the number of dots that can be displayed on the monitor without overlapping. For example, a monitor with resolution 640 × 480 means, we plot 640 dots horizontally in each row and 480 dots vertically in each column of the monitor without overlapping. Each dot that can be plotted on the monitor is also known as **picture element** or **pixel**. It is the smallest information that can be displayed on an output device (monitor).

16.2.3 `pathtodriver`

The parameter `pathtodriver` is a string which specifies the directory path where `initgraph()` looks for graphics drivers. Graphics driver has the file extension (*.BGI). The `initgraph()` first looks for the graphics driver in the path specified in `pathtodriver`. If the requested driver is not available in the specified path, then it searches for the driver in the current directory.

16.3 RESETTING THE GRAPHICS MODE

After the graphics application is completed, we can reset the system back to text mode. The `closegraph()` function does the job of resetting the system back to text mode.

The `closegraph()` deallocates the memory allocated by the graphics system and restores back to the mode existing before `initgraph()` was called. To switch over back to graphics mode again invoke `initgraph()` function.

The general format of this function is

```
closegraph();
```

As can be seen, it does not have any arguments.

PROGRAM 16.1   To illustrate the usage of initgraph() function in C

```
#include<stdio.h>
#include<graphics.h>
int main(void)
{
        intgd=DETECT,gm;
        initgraph(&gd,&gm,"c:\\tc\\bgi");
         /* c:\\tc\bgi is the path where the BGI file is available */
        getch();
        closegraph();
        return 0;
}
```

Explanation:

The above program is simply an illustration of how the graphics is initialized using `init-graph()` method. The above program just initializes the graphics mode and does not produce any output. The actual path for the BGI file depends on the computer on which the program is executed. In the subsequent section we discuss the different graphics functions available in the C library.

16.4 DISPLAYING TEXT

The C language supports two important functions namely outtextxy() and outtext() for displaying text in graphics mode. These two function are generally used along with the function settextstyle().

16.4.1 outtextxy()

The outtextxy() function displays text in the specified position on the display device. Its general format is

outtextxy(xcoordinate, ycoordinate, string);

where xcoordinate is the position of x-coordinate, ycoordinate is the position of y-coordinate and string is the text to be displayed. The xcoordinate and ycoordinate values depend on the resolution of the display device.

16.4.2 outtext()

The function outtext() is similar to outtextxy(). It also displays the specified string on the monitor. Unlike outtextxy() function where the position for display of string is specified explicitly, outtext() function simply displays the specified string on the monitor. The actual position for display is specified using moveto() function. Hence outtextxy() function is a combination of both moveto() and outtext() functions. The general syntax of outtext() function is

outtext(String);

16.4.3 settextstyle()

The settextstyle() is used to set the font of the text to be displayed, its size and the direction. The corresponding text to be displayed is specified either using outtext() or outtextxy() function. The general syntax of settextstyle() function is

settextstyl(fonttype, direction, fontsize);

where fonttype is the style of the text to be displayed, direction denotes whether the text is displayed horizontally or vertically. The fontsize specifies the size of the font of the desired text.

The header file <graphics.h> contains set of predefined styles for fonttype. These predefined styles are specified by means of their symbolic names or the corresponding integer constants. The following table shows the list of predefined styles for fonttype along with their integer constant values. Direction for the text to be displayed is specified using symbolic names HORIZ_DIR or VERTI_DIR. If the direction is HORIZ_DIR then the text is displayed horizontally. If the direction is VERTI_DIR, the text is displayed vertically.

Symbolic name	Integer value
DEFAULT_FONT	0
TRIPLEX_FONT	1
SMALL_FONT	2

SANS_SERIF_FONT	3
GOTHIC_FONT	4
SCRIPT_FONT	5
SIMPLEX_FONT	6
TRIPLEX_SCR_FONT	7
COMPLEX_FONT	8
EUROPEAN_FONT	9
BOLD_FONT	10

PROGRAM 16.2   To illustrate outtext() and outtextxy(), settextstyle() functions

```c
#include<graphics.h>
#include<stdio.h>
int main(void)
{
        intgd=DETECT,gm;
        int x = 200, y = 200;

        initgraph(&gd, &gm, "c:\\tc\\bgi");
        setcolor(WHITE);
        settextstyle(GOTHIC_FONT, HORIZ_DIR, 2);
        outtextxy(x, y, "COMPUTER");
        x = x + 100;
        y = y + 100;
        setcolor(YELLOW);
        settextstyle(TRIPLEX_FONT, HORIZ_DIR, 2);
        outtextxy(x, y, "GRAPHICS");
        x = x - 150;
        y = y - 120;
        setcolor(YELLOW);
        settextstyle(TRIPLEX_FONT, HORIZ_DIR, 2);
        outtextxy(x, y, "PROGRAMMING IN");
        moveto(300, 400);
        settextstyle(TRIPLEX_FONT, VERT_DIR, 3);
        getch();
        closegraph();
        return 0;
}
```

Output:

16.5   DETERMINING THE RESOLUTION OF A DISPLAY DEVICE

Resolution of a display device is the maximum number of pixels that can be displayed on it horizontally and vertically without overlapping of any pixel. These two values can be obtained using getmaxx() and getmaxy() respectively.

getmaxx() and getmaxy(): These two functions are used to get the maximum x and y values of pixel in the graphics screen respectively. Values returned by these functions depend on the monitor of the computer system in which the graphics programs are executed. These two functions do not accept any arguments. Their prototypes are given as follow:

int getmaxx()

int getmaxy()

PROGRAM 16.3   To illustrate getmaxx () and getmaxy () functions

---

```c
#include<graphics.h>
#include<stdio.h>
int main(void)
{
    int gd = DETECT, gmode;
    int x, y;
    initgraph(&gd, &gm, "c:\\tc\\bgi");
    x = getmaxx(); /* x is the maximum pixel value in x direction */
    y = getmaxy(); /* y is the maximum pixel value in y direction */
    printf("Resolution of your display device = %d pixels x %d
    pixels \n", x, y);

    getch();
    closegraph();
    return 0;
}
```

`Output:`

Resolution of your display device = 439 pixels x 479 pixels

16.6 DRAWING DIFFERENT SHAPES

In this section, we discuss various graphics functions available in the C library for drawing general shapes such as lines, circle, ellipse, rectangle, etc.

16.6.1 Drawing Line

The line() function in the C library is used to draw a line from the point with coordinates (x_1, y_1) to another point with the coordinates (x_2, y_2). Here (x_1, y_1) denote the coordinates of first end point of the line while (x_2, y_2) denote the second end point of the line. In the display device, x-coordinate values are measured from left to right and the y-coordinate values are measured from top to bottom. The general format of line() function is

$$\text{line}(x_1, y_1, x_2, y_2);$$

PROGRAM 16.4   To illustrate line () function

```
#include<stdio.h>
#include<conio.h>
#include<graphics.h>

int main(void)
{
        Int gd = DETECT, gm;
        initgraph(&gd, &gm, "c:\\tc\\bgi");
        setcolor(WHITE);
        line(300, 100, 200, 200);
        setcolor(YELLOW);
        line(300, 100, 400, 200);
        setcolor(MAGENTA);
        line(200, 200, 400, 200);
        getch();
        closegraph();
        return 0;
}
```

`Output:`

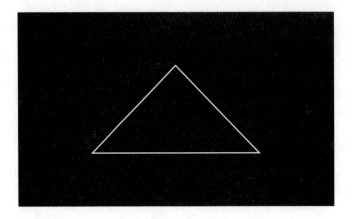

Explanation:

In the above program, the first call to the `line ()` function **line(300, 100, 200, 200);** displays the line with coordinates of the two end points (300, 100) and (200, 200) as

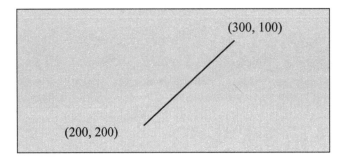

The second call to the line() **line(300, 100, 400, 200);** displays the line with coordinates of the two end points (300, 100) and (400, 200) as

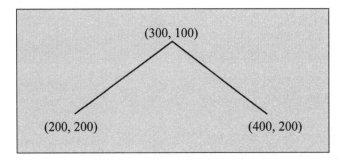

The third call to the `line ()` **line(200, 200, 400, 200);** displays the line with coordinates (200, 200) and (400, 200).

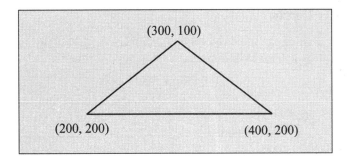

PROGRAM 16.5   To draw an equilateral triangle using line function

```
#include<stdio.h>
#include<conio.h>
#include<graphics.h>

int main(void)
{
        intgd = DETECT, gm;
        initgraph(&gd, &gm, "c:\\tc\\bgi");

        line(300, 200, 200, 300);
        line(200, 300, 400, 300);
        line(400, 300, 300, 200);
        getch();
        closegraph();
        return 0;
}
```

Output:

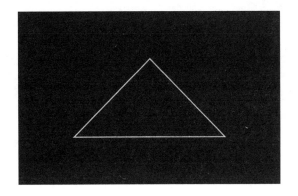

16.6.2 Drawing Circle

We can display a circle using specified color using `circle()` function available in the C library. The `circle()` function is used to draw a circle. Its general format is

$$\text{circle}(x,y, \text{radius})$$

where x and y are coordinates of the center of the circle and radius is the length of the radius. All these values are specified in pixels.

PROGRAM 16.6 To illustrate the usage of `circle()` function

```c
#include <graphics.h>
#include <conio.h>
int main(void)
{
intgd = DETECT, gm;
initgraph(&gd, &gm, "C:\\TC\\BGI");
 /* Display a circle with center at (25, 25) with 100 pixel radius */
circle(300, 200, 100);
getch();
closegraph();
    return 0;
}
```

Output:

PROGRAM 16.7   To draw a set of concentric circle with different colors

```
#include <graphics.h>
int void main()
{
int gd = DETECT, gm;
inti, x, y;
initgraph(&gd,&gm,"C:\\TC\\BGI");
 x=getmaxx()-300;
 y=getmaxy()-300;
for (i=1; i<=10; i++)
 {
    setcolor(i);
    circle(x,y, 50+10*i);
 }
getch();
closegraph();
return 0;
}
```

Output:

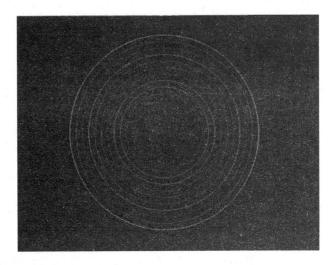

16.6.3 Drawing Polygon

Polygons are nothing but a sequence of connected line segments. Hence we can display a polygon by using a sequence of calls to `line()`. The C language also supports two additional functions for drawing a polygon namely `drawpoly()` and `fillpoly()` functions.

drawpoly():   This function draws a polygon using the line style and color specified using setlinestyle() and setcolor() function. The general syntax of this function is

void drawpoly(int numpoints, int *arrayname);

where,

numpoints specify the number of points in the polygon. For example, for pentagon it is 5, for hexagon, it is 6 and so on. In case of closed polygon, the number of points will be one more as the first and the last point is one and the same.

- arrayname is an array where the coordinates of all the points of the polygon is stored. For pentagon, the number of values in arrayname will be 10 as every point is specified by means of two coordinates. In the case of closed polygon, the number of values in the arrayname will be two more than the number of points in the polygon.

PROGRAM 16.8   To draw different polygons

```
#include<graphics.h>
#include<conio.h>
#include<stdio.h>
int main(void)
{

intgd=DETECT, gm;
/* Here the array Tri contains the coordinates of the triangle */
int tri[8]={100, 100, 50, 200, 150, 200, 100, 100};

/* The array Rect contains the coordinates of the rectangle */
intrect[10]={200, 100, 200, 200, 400, 200, 400, 100, 200, 100};

/* The array Pent contains the coordinates of the pentagon */
int pent [12]={100, 250, 50, 275, 125, 300, 175, 300, 135, 250, 100, 250};

intoct [18]={300, 300, 275, 325, 275, 350, 300, 375, 400, 375, 425,
             350, 425, 325, 400, 300, 300, 300};
               /* initialize the graphics */
               initgraph(&gd, &gm,NULL);

           outtextxy(195,15, "Drawing different Polygons");
        outtextxy(150,30, "Triangle, Rectangle, Pentagon and Octogan");
        drawpoly(4,tri);
```

```
        outtextxy(75,220, "Triangle");
        drawpoly(5,rect);
        outtextxy(270, 220, "Rectangle");
        drawpoly(6,pent);
        outtextxy(75, 320, "Pentagon");
        drawpoly(9,oct);
        outtextxy(325, 400, "Octagon");
        getch();
        closegraph();
        return 0;
}
```

Output:

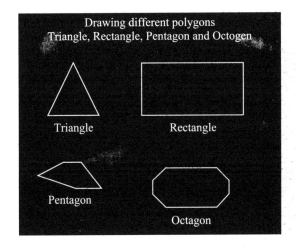

16.6.4 Drawing Rectangle

Rectangle can be drawn in graphics mode using `rectangle()` function. We can draw a rectangle as series of connected line segments using `line()` function also. The general syntax of `rectangle()` function is

$$\text{rectangle}(x_1, y_1, x_2, y_2)$$

where,
`rectangle()` function takes 4 arguments. First two arguments x_1, y_1 specify the coordinates of top left corner of the rectangle while the last two arguments x_2, y_2 specify the coordinates of bottom right corner of the rectangle as shown in the following figure. All the four arguments must be integers as they specify the pixel values.

PROGRAM 16.9   To draw rectangle using sequence of line segments and using rectangle function

```c
#include <graphics.h>
#include<conio.h>
#include<stdio.h>
int main(void)
{
        intgd = DETECT, gm;
        intx,y,i;
        initgraph(&gd, &gm, "C:\\TC\\BGI");
        setcolor(WHITE);

        /* Drawing Rectangle using line() function */
        setcolor(WHITE);
        outtextxy(350, 130, "Rectangle using line() functions");
        line (100, 100, 300, 100);
        line (300, 100, 300, 200);
        line (300, 200, 100, 200);
        line (100, 200, 100, 100);

        /* Drawing rectangle using rectangle() function */
        setcolor(YELLOW);
        outtextxy(350, 350, "Rectangle using rectangle() function");
        rectangle(100, 300, 300, 400);
        getch();
        closegraph();
        return 0;
}
```

Output:

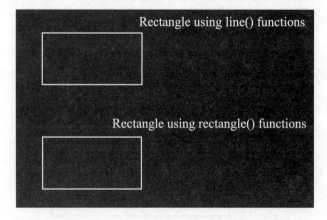

Explanation:

In the above example, the first line function line(100, 100, 300, 100); displays the top horizontal line of the rectangle

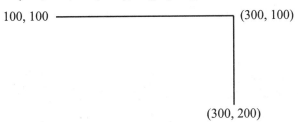

The second line function line (300, 100, 300, 200); displays right vertical line of the rectangle.

The third line function line (300,200, 100, 200); displays bottom horizontal line of the rectangle.

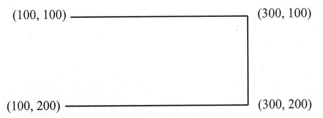

The last line function line (100, 200, 100, 100); displays the left vertical line of the rectangle.

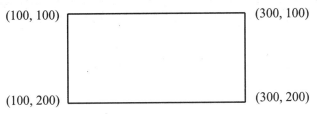

The rectangle function rectangle (100, 100, 300, 200); displays the same rectangle where only the coordinates of the top left corner and bottom right corners are specified.

(100, 100)

(300, 200)

setfillstyle():   This function fills the graphics shapes such as rectangle, bar with a pattern of particular style and color. Usually this function is used before calling `bar ()`, `circle ()` etc. The general format of this function is

setfillstyle(style, color)

The first parameter specifies the style of the pattern to be filled and the color specifies the color of the file pattern.

Different possible values for style and color are given in the following table. User can specify the style and color either by their symbolic names or by their integer constant values.

Style	Integer value	Color	Integer value
EMPTY_FILL	0	BLACK	0
SOLID_FILL	1	BLUE	1
LINE_FILL	2	GREEN	2
LTSLASH_FILL	3	CYAN	3
SLASH_FILL	4	RED	4
BKSLASH_FILL	5	MAGENTA	5
LTBKSLASH_FILL	6	BROWN	6
HATCH_FILL	7	LIGHTGRAY	7
XHATCH_FILL	8	DARKGRAY	8
INTERLEAVE_FILL	9	LIGHTBLUE	9
WIDE_DOT_FILL	10	LIGHTGREEN	10
CLOSE_DOT_FILL	11	LIGHTCYAN	11
USER_FILL	12	LIGHTRED	12
		LIGHTMAGENTA	13
		YELLOW	14
		WHITE	

PROGRAM 16.10   To illustrate the usage of setfillstyle function

---

```
#include<graphics.h>
#include<conio.h>
int main(void)
{
        intgd = DETECT, gm;
        intx,y, i;
        initgraph(&gd, &gm, "C:\\TC\\BGI");
        setcolor(WHITE);
        outtextxy(250, 50, "DIFFERENT FILL PATTERN");
        /* Drawing rectangle using bar() function */
        setfillstyle(LINE_FILL, YELLOW);
        bar(100, 100, 300, 200);
        outtextxy(180, 220, "LINE FILL");
```

```
setfillstyle(HATCH_FILL, WHITE);
bar(100, 300, 300, 400);
outtextxy(180, 420, "HATCH FILL");
setfillstyle(SOLID_FILL, YELLOW);
bar(350, 100, 550, 200);

outtextxy(400, 220, "SOLID_FILL");
setfillstyle(XHATCH_FILL, YELLOW);
bar(350, 300, 550, 400);
outtextxy(400, 420, "XHATCH_FILL");

getch();
closegraph();
return 0;
}
```

Output:

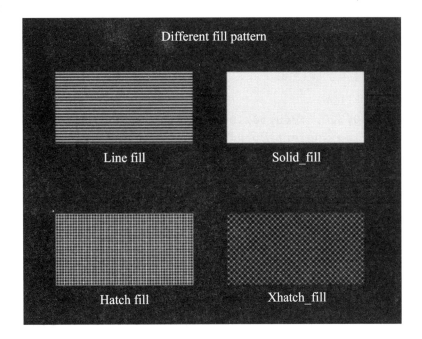

16.6.5 Drawing Ellipse

Ellipse can be drawn with current color using the graphics function `ellipse ()`. The general syntax of this function is

ellipse(x, y, start_angle, end_angle, x_radius, y_radius)

All the parameters are declared as int type. Here x and y specify the coordinates of the center, start_angle and end_angle specify the starting and ending angle of the ellipse. The values for the parameters start_angle and end_angle vary from 0 to 360. The x_radius and y_radius specify the horizontal and vertical radius respectively. If the start_angle = 0° and end_angle = 360°, x_radius and y_radius are equal then ellipse () function draws a circle.

PROGRAM 16.11 To draw ellipse

```c
#include<graphics.h>
#include<conio.h>
main()
{
        intgd=DETECT,gm;
        /* Initialize graphics */
        initgraph(&gd,&gm,"C:\\TC\\BGI");

        /* Setting the ellipse color */
        setcolor(WHITE);
        ellipse(200,100,0,360,100,75);
        outtextxy(160,100,"ELLIPSE-1");

        setcolor(YELLOW);
        ellipse(200,300,0,360,50,100);
        outtextxy(170,300,"ELLIPSE-2");

        setcolor(WHITE);
        ellipse(400,200,0,360,100,100);
        outtextxy(380,200,"CIRCLE");

        getch();
        closegraph();
        return 0;
}
```

Output:

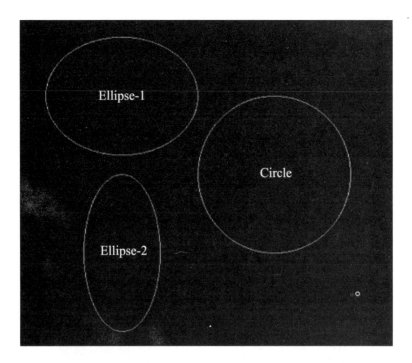

16.6.6 Pieslice ():

We know that by using `circle()` function, we can draw a circle. But the circle is displayed as a hollow circle. Sometimes, we need to draw a circle and fill different portions of the circle with different styles. The C language provides an additional function called `pieslice()` to draw a circle and to fill different portions of the circle with a suitable pattern and color by means of `setfillstyle()` function. Each portion of the circle filled with a particular pattern is called a **pie slice**. The `pieslice()` function takes two additional parameters, which specify the starting and ending angle of each slice of the circle. The general syntax of `pieslice()` function is

```
pieslice(int x, int y, intstart_angle, intend_angle, int radius);
```

PROGRAM 16.12   To illustrate `pieslice()` function

```
#include <conio.h>
#include <graphics.h>
#include <dos.h>
int main(void)
{
        intgd = DETECT, gm, x, y;
         /* initialize graphic mode */
        x=getmaxx()/2;
        y=getmaxy()/2;
```

```
initgraph(&gd,&gm,"C:\\TC\\BGI");
setcolor(WHITE);
setfillstyle(CLOSE_DOT_FILL, WHITE);
pieslice(300, 200, 0, 90, 100);
setcolor(YELLOW);
setfillstyle(BKSLASH_FILL, YELLOW);
pieslice(300,200, 90, 180, 100);
setcolor(CYAN);
setfillstyle(LINE_FILL, WHITE);
pieslice(300, 200, 180, 360, 100);
setcolor(WHITE);
outtextxy (270, 50, "PIE SLICE");
getch();
closegraph();
return 0;
}
```
Output:

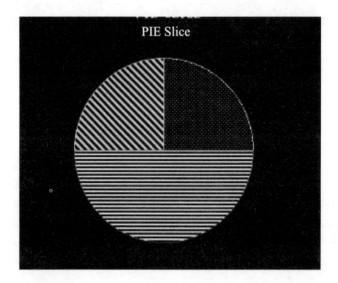

16.6.7 Drawing Bars

A bar is nothing but a filled rectangle and can be drawn using the bar() function in C. The bar () function is similar to rectangle () function to some extent. The difference between the rectangle() and the bar() function is that the rectangle() function draws a hollow rectangle without filling the rectangle with any pattern. Whereas the bar() function, in addition to drawing a rectangle, it also fills the rectangle with the style and color set using setfillstyle() function. The general syntax of bar() function is

$$\mathbf{bar(x_1, \ y_1, \ x_2, \ y_2)}$$

Where x_1 and y_1 denote the coordinates of top left corner of the rectangle and the parameters x_2 and y_2 denote the coordinates of bottom right corner of the rectangle. All the 4 values must be integers.

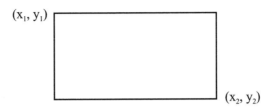

PROGRAM 16.13   To illustrate `bar()` function

```
#include <graphics.h>
#include <conio.h>
#include <math.h>
#include <dos.h>
#include <stdlib.h>

int main(void)
{
int i, gd, gm;
int x, y, w;

initgraph (&gd,&gm,"C:\\TC\\BGI");
setfillstyle (SOLID_FILL, WHITE);

bar(100, 100, 200, 200);
outtextxy(220, 140, "SOLID BAR");
setcolor (WHITE);
setfillstyle(CLOSE_DOT_FILL, YELLOW);
bar(100, 250, 200, 350);
outtextxy(220, 300, "CLOSE DOT");
setfillstyle(BKSLASH_FILL, BLUE);
bar(100, 400, 200, 450);
outtextxy(220, 430, "BACK SLASH");
      return 0;
}
```

`Output:`

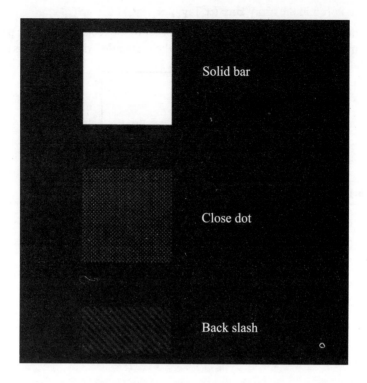

16.6.8 Some Simple Applications Using Graphics Functions

In this section we consider some simple general problems and illustrate how these problems can be solved using the graphics functions that we have discussed so far.

1. Following is the percentage of the budget allocation for various sectors:

Sector	Percentage of allocation
Defense	30%
Education	10%
Health	20%
Transport	40%

Create a pie chart to illustrate the allocation in the budget

Explanation:

Here we need to draw a pie chart illustrating the budget allocation. The pie chart is drawn using a series of `pieslice()` function.

First we need to calculate the percentage of the share of each sector in a circle with 360°.

For example

Defense = 30% of 360 = 108°
Education = 10% of 360 = 36°
Health = 20% of 360 = 72°
Transport = 40% of 360 = 144°

These values are stored in the array angle[]. In a pie chart, the starting angle and the ending angle for each pie slice will be

Defense = 0° to 108°
Education = 108° to 144°
Health = 144° to 216°
Transport = 216° to 360°

These values are stored in the array angle[].

PROGRAM 16.14   To create pie char

```c
#include <stdio.h>
#include <conio.h>
#include <graphics.h>
#include <dos.h>
void main(int)
{
        intgdriver = DETECT, gmode;
        int x, y, i;
        int data[4] = {25, 20, 20, 35};
        int angle[4], Tangle[5];
        static char Labels[4][50] = {"DEFENSE", "EDUCATION", "HEALTH",
                                     "TRANSPORT"};
        /* initialize graphic mode */
        initgraph(&gdriver, &gmode, "C:\\TURBOC3\\BGI");

        /* To obtain the coordinates of center of the screen */
        x = getmaxx() / 2;
        y = getmaxy() / 2;

/* First estimate the percentage of different sectors in the pie
chart */
for(i=0; i<=3; i++)
angle[i]=(data[i]/100.0) *360;

Tangle[0]=0;
for(i=0; i<=3; i++)
Tangle[i+1]=Tangle[i]+ angle[i];

  /* Display pie slice for Defense */
        setcolor(YELLOW);
        setfillstyle(CLOSE_DOT_FILL, YELLOW);
        pieslice(x, y, Tangle[0], Tangle[1], 100);

  /* Display pie slice for Education */
```

```
        setcolor(LIGHTRED);
        setfillstyle(LINE_FILL, LIGHTRED);
        pieslice(x, y, Tangle[1], Tangle[2], 100);

 /* Display pie slice for Health */
        setcolor(CYAN);
        setfillstyle(WIDE_DOT_FILL, CYAN);
        pieslice(x, y, Tangle[2], Tangle[3], 100);

/* Display pie slice for Transport */
        setcolor(LIGHTMAGENTA);
        setfillstyle(SLASH_FILL, LIGHTMAGENTA);
        pieslice(x, y, Tangle[3], Tangle[4], 100);

        /* naming pie slice with corresponding sector names */

        setcolor(WHITE);
        settextstyle(TRIPLEX_FONT, HORIZ_DIR, 2);
        settextjustify(CENTER_TEXT, CENTER_TEXT);
        sprintf(Labels, "%s", "Defense");
        moveto(x + 140, y - 40);
        outtext(Labels);

        sprintf(Labels, "%s", "Education");
        moveto(x-5, y - 130);
        outtext(Labels);

        sprintf(Labels, "%s", "Health");
        moveto(x - 140, y);
        outtext(Labels);

        sprintf(Labels, "%s", "Transport");
        moveto(x - 20, y + 110);
        outtext(Labels);

        /* Label for the graph */
        setcolor(WHITE);
        sprintf(Labels, "%s", "PIE CHART FOR BUDGET ALLOCATION");
        moveto(320, y+175);
        settextjustify(CENTER_TEXT, CENTER_TEXT);
        settextstyle(TRIPLEX_FONT, HORIZ_DIR, 2);
        outtext(Labels);
        getch();
```

```
/* deallocate memory allocated for graphic screen */
closegraph();
return 0;
 }
```

Output:

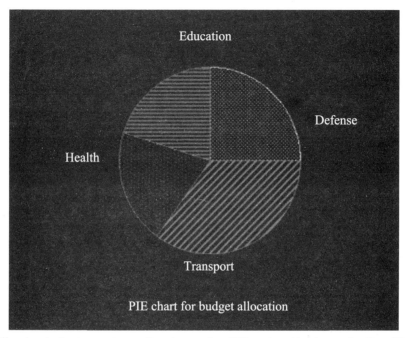

2. Following is the percentage of seats won by different parties in an election. Illustrate with the help of a bar chart.

Party name	Percentage of votes
INC	20%
BJP	45%
JDS	15%
DMK	10%
OTHERS	10%

In this program, we store the label of each party name in the array parties[], votes secured by each party are stored in the array votes[]. The bar () function is used to draw the bar chart whose length is proportional to the percentage of votes secured by different parties.

PROGRAM 16.15 To create bar chart

```
#include <stdio.h>
#include <conio.h>
#include <graphics.h>
```

```
int main(void)
{
int gd = DETECT, gm;
char parties[5][20] = {"INC", "BJP", "JDS", "DMK", "OTHERS"};
int votes[5] = {20, 45, 15, 10, 10};
initgraph(&gd, &gm, "C:\\TC\\BGI");
setcolor(YELLOW);
rectangle(0,30,639,450);

settextstyle(SANS_SERIF_FONT,HORIZ_DIR,2);
setcolor(WHITE);
outtextxy(275,0,"Bar Chart");

setlinestyle(SOLID_LINE,0,2);

 /* Bar for INC */
setfillstyle(LINE_FILL,YELLOW);
bar(1,50,100+votes[0]*10,75);

 /* Bar for BJP */
setfillstyle(HATCH_FILL,WHITE);
bar(1,125,100+votes[1]*10,150);

 /* Bar for JDS */
setfillstyle(WIDE_DOT_FILL,YELLOW);
bar(1,200,100+votes[2]*10,225);

 /* Bar for DMK */
setfillstyle(SOLID_FILL,MAGENTA);
bar(1,275, 100+votes[3]*10, 300);

 /* Bar for OTHER */
setfillstyle(XHATCH_FILL,YELLOW);
bar(1, 350, 100+votes[4]*10, 375);

/* Display labels infront of each bar */
/* Label for INC */
settextstyle(SANS_SERIF_FONT,HORIZ_DIR,2);
setcolor(WHITE);
outtextxy(320, 50, parties[0]);

/* Label for BJP */
settextstyle(SANS_SERIF_FONT,HORIZ_DIR,2);
setcolor(WHITE);
```

```
outtextxy(560, 125, parties[1]);

/* Label for JDS */
settextstyle(SANS_SERIF_FONT,HORIZ_DIR,2);
setcolor(WHITE);
outtextxy(260, 200, parties[2]);

/* Label for DMK */
settextstyle(SANS_SERIF_FONT,HORIZ_DIR,2);
setcolor(WHITE);
outtextxy(220, 275, parties[3]);

/* Label for OTHERS */
settextstyle(SANS_SERIF_FONT,HORIZ_DIR,2);
setcolor(WHITE);
outtextxy(220, 350, parties[4]);

getch();
return 0;
}
```

Output:

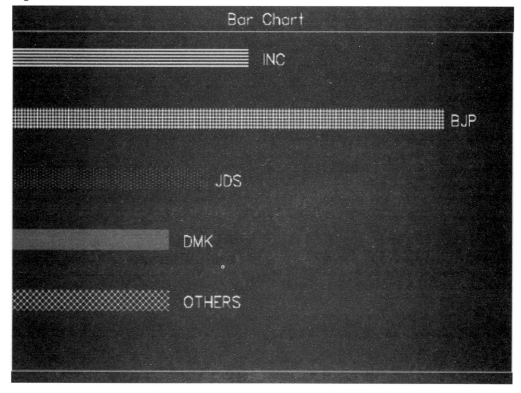

16.7 LINE AND CIRCLE DRAWING ALGORITHMS

In the previous sections, we discussed about drawing different shapes such as line, rectangle, circle and ellipse using the C library functions. In this section, we discuss about drawing line and circle using two famous algorithms in computer graphics namely Bresenham's and DDA.

16.7.1 Bresenham's Line Algorithm

Given the two end points of a line, the Bresenham's algorithm is based on computing the intermediate pixel that lies on the line path between the two end points. Each time the algorithm computes the coordinates of the intermediate points iteratively till the end point is reached. The intermediate pixel to be selected is based on a decision parameter.

Let (x_1, y_1) and (x_2, y_2) be the two end points of the line. The algorithm assumes that $(x_1 < x_2)$ and the slope of the line has a positive slope less than 1.

Algorithm

1. Input the two line endpoints and store the left endpoint in (x_0, y_0).
2. Load (x_0, y_0) into the frame buffer; that is, plot the first point.
3. Calculate constants Δx, Δy, $2\Delta y$, and $2\Delta y - 2\Delta x$, and obtain the starting value for the Decision parameter as

   $dx = x_2 - x_1$
   $dy = y_2 - y_1$
   $p_0 = 2\Delta y - \Delta x$

4. At each x_k along the line, starting at $k = 0$, perform the following test:
   If $p_k < 0$, the next point to plot is (x_{k+1}, y_k) and

   $$p_{k+1} = p_k + 2\Delta y$$

   Otherwise, the next point to plot is (x_{k+1}, y_{k+1}) and

   $$p_{k+1} = p_k + 2\Delta y - 2\Delta x$$

5. Repeat Step 4 Δx times.

PROGRAM 16.16   To draw a line using Bresenham's line drawing algorithm

---

```c
#include<stdio.h>
#include<conio.h>
#include<graphics.h>

int main(void)
{
intgd = DETECT, gm;
int dx, dy, p, end;
float x1, x2, y1, y2, x, y;

/* Initialize Graphics */
```

```
initgraph(&gd, &gm, "c:\tc\bgi");

 /* Input the coordinate of two end points of the line */

printf("Enter Value of X1: ");
scanf("%f", &x1);
printf("Enter Value of Y1: ");
scanf("%f", &y1);
printf("Enter Value of X2: ");
scanf("%f", &x2);
printf("Enter Value of Y2: ");
scanf("%f", &y2);


/* Calculate the initial parameters */

dx = abs(x1 - x2);
dy = abs(y1 - y2);

 /* Initial decision parameter */
 p = 2 * dy - dx;

/* Interchange the endpoints if the x1>x2 and y1>y2 */

if(x1 > x2)
 {
    x = x2;
    y = y2;
end = x1;
 }
else
 {
    x = x1;
    y = y1;
end = x2;
 }
    putpixel(x, y, 10);
    while(x < end)
 {
    x = x + 1;
if(p < 0)
 {
    p = p + 2 * dy;
 }
```

```
else
 {
    y = y + 1;
    p = p + 2 * (dy - dx);
 }
putpixel(x, y, 10);
 }
getch();
closegraph();
return 0;
}
```

Output:

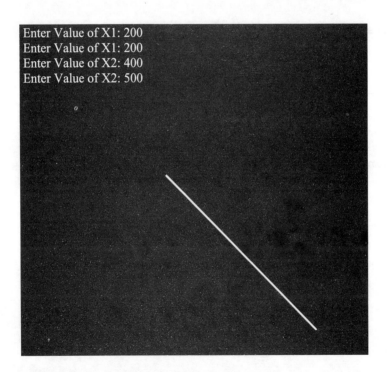

16.7.2 DDA Line Drawing Algorithm

The DDA line drawing algorithm another method for drawing a line. This algorithm is based on differential equations. Let (x_1, y_1) and (x_2, y_2) be the two end points of the line. The DDA line algorithm interpolates the intermediate points of the line in the interval (x_1, y_1) and (x_2, y_2). The intermediate points to be computed depend on the slope of the line. If the slope is positive and less than 1, then we sample x at unit intervals and the corresponding y value is computed as:

$$y_{k+1} = y_k + m, k = 1, 2, \ldots, .$$

On the other hand, if the slope is positive > 1, then we sample y at unit intervals, the corresponding x value is computed as:

$$x_{k+1} = x_k + \frac{1}{m}$$

where m is the slope of the line.

$$m = \frac{\Delta x}{\Delta y}$$

$$\Delta x = x_2 - x_1$$

$$\Delta y = y_2 - y_1$$

PROGRAM 16.17   To draw a line using DDA line drawing algorithm

```
#include<stdio.h>
#include<conio.h>
#include<graphics.h>
#include<math.h>
#include<stdlib.h>

int main(void)
{
      int x1,y1,x2,y2;
      voiddda (int x1, int y1, int x2, int y2);
      int gdriver = DETECT, gmode, gerror;
      initgraph(&gdriver,&gmode,"c:\\tc\\bgi:");
      printf("\n Enter the x and y value for starting point:\n");
      scanf("%d%d",&x1,&y1);
      printf("\n Enter the x and y value for ending point:\n");
      scanf("%d%d",&x2,&y2);
      printf("\n The Line is shown below: \n");
      DDA (x1,y1,x2,y2);
      getch();
      return 0;
}

void DDA (int x1,int y1,int x2,int y2)
{
      floatx,y,xinc,yinc,dx,dy;
      int k;
      int step;
      dx = x2 - x1;
      dy = y2 - y1;
      if(abs(dx)>abs(dy))
```

```
        step = abs(dx);
        else
        step = abs(dy);
        xinc = dx / step;
        yinc = dy / step;
        x = x1;
        y = y1;
        putpixel(x,y,WHITE);
        for(k = 1; k <= step; k++)
        {
            x = x + xinc;
            y = y + yinc;
            putpixel(x,y,WHITE);
        }
}
```

Output:

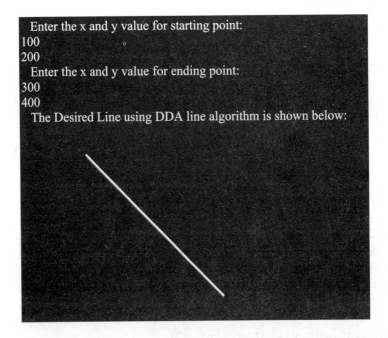

16.7.3 Bresenham's Circle Drawing Algorithm

The Bresenham's circle drawing algorithm is one of the most efficient algorithms for drawing a circle. The algorithm takes three parameters. The first two parameters correspond to the center of the circle and the last parameter is the radius of the circle. The algorithm iteratively computes the intermediate pixel to be plotted on the circumference that approximates a circle. The next point to be displayed is decided based on a decision parameter.

Algorithm: Bresenham's circle
Input: x_c, y_c and r
Output: Pixels along the circumference

1. Input radius r and circle center (x_c, y_c), then set the coordinates for the first point on the circumference of a circle centered on the origin as $(x_0, y_0) = (0, r)$.
2. Calculate the initial value of the decision parameter $p_0 = 1 - r$
3. At each x_k position, starting at k = 0, perform the following test.
   If $p_k < 0$, the next point along the circle centered on (0, 0) is (x_{k+1}, y_k) and $p_{k+1} = p_k + 2x_{k+1} + 1$
   Else
   The next point along the circle is $(x_k + 1, y_k - 1)$ and
   $p_{k+1} = p_k + 2x_{k+1} + 1 - 2y_{k+1}$ where $2x_{k+1} = 2x_k + 2$ and $2y_{k+1} = 2y_k$
4. Determine symmetry points in the other seven points.
5. Move each calculated pixel position (x, y) onto the circular path centered at (x_c, y_c) and plot the coordinate values:
   $$x = x + x_c$$
   $$y = y + y_c$$
6. Repeat Step 3 through 5 until $x \geq y$.

PROGRAM 16.18   To draw a circle using Bresenham's algorithm

```c
#include<stdio.h>
#include<conio.h>
#include<graphics.h>
#include<math.h>

int main()
{
    int gd = DETECT, gm;
    int r, x, y, p, xc = 320, yc = 240;

    initgraph(&gd,&gm,"C:\\TC\\BGI");
    cleardevice();

    printf("Enter the coordinates of the center of the circle\n");
    scanf("%d%d", &xc, &yc);

    printf("Enter the radius ");
    scanf("%d",&r);
    x = 0;
    y = r;
    putpixel(xc+x,yc-y,1);
    p = 3 - (2 * r);
```

```
for(x = 0; x <= y; x++)
{
   if (p < 0)
   {
        Y = y;
        P = (p + (4 * x) + 6);
   }
   else
   {
        Y = y - 1;
        P = p + ((4 *(x - y) + 10)));
   }
        putpixel(xc + x, yc - y, WHITE);
        putpixel(xc - x, yc - y, WHITE);
        putpixel(xc + x, yc + y, WHITE);
        putpixel(xc - x, yc + y, WHITE);
        putpixel(xc + y, yc - x, WHITE);
        putpixel(xc - y, yc - x, WHITE);
        putpixel(xc + y, yc + x, WHITE);
        putpixel(xc - y, yc + x, WHITE);
}
        getch();
        closegraph();
        return 0;
}
```

Output:

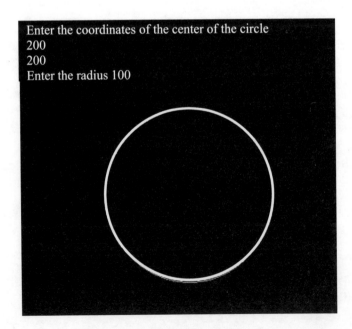

16.8 TWO-DIMENSIONAL TRANSFORMATION

In computer graphics, two-dimensional transformation on a point with coordinates (x, y) in a Euclidean space is an operation that maps the point with the coordinates (x, y) onto a new point with the coordinates (x′, y′). The three basic two-dimensional transformations on any point p with coordinates (x, y) are:

1. Translation
2. Scaling
3. Rotation

16.8.1 Translation

Translation is a basic two-dimensional transformation that changes the position of an object along the linear path. To translate an object to a new position, every point in the object should be shifted with equal distance. If p is a point in an object with coordinates (x, y), then to translate the point to a new position we should add the translation distance T_x to its x-coordinate value and translation distance T_y to its y-coordinate value. After translation, the point is shifted to a new position denoted as p′ and its new coordinate denoted as (x′, y′). The new coordinate values will be obtained as

$$x′ = x + T_x \text{ and } y′ = y + T_y$$

That means translation, a transformation applied on a point p(x, y) maps the point p onto a new position p′

$$T(p(x, y)) → p′(x′, y′)$$

Example: Let A(100, 100), B(50, 150) and C(150, 150) be the coordinates the triangle. Let $(T_x, T_y) = (30, 40)$. After translation, the coordinates of the triangle changes to
A(100, 100) becomes A′(100 + 30, 100 + 40) = A′(130, 140)
B(50, 150) becomes B′(50 + 30, 150 + 40) = A′(80, 190)
C(150, 150) becomes C′(150 + 30, 150 + 40) = C′(180, 190)

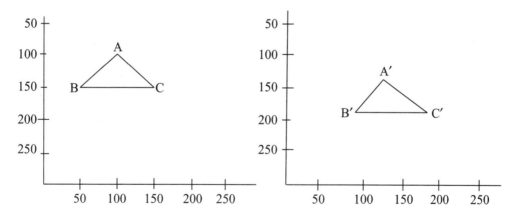

16.8.2 Scaling

Scaling is a transformation that changes the size of an object. To scale an object to a specific size, every point in the object should be multiplied by the same scaling factor. To scale a point p with coordinates (x, y) multiply the x-coordinate with a scaling factor S_x and multiply the y coordinate with the scaling factor S_y. After scaling, the coordinates of the point p change to (x′, y′) and the point is denoted as p′. For example, if $S_x = S_y = 2$, the size of the object doubles.

$$x' = x * S_x$$
$$y' = y * S_y$$
$$S(p(x, y)) = p'(x', y')$$

Example: Let A(100, 100), B(50, 150) and C(150, 150) be the coordinates of the triangle. Let $(S_x, S_y) = (2, 2)$. After scaling, the coordinates of the triangle changes to

A(100, 100) become A′(100*2, 100*2) = A′(200, 200)

B(50, 150) becomes B′(50*2, 150*2) = A′(100, 300)

C(150, 150) becomes C′(150*2, 150*2) = C′(300, 300)

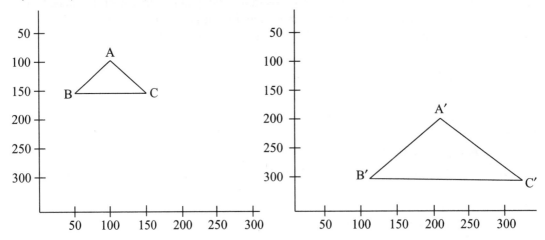

16.8.3 Rotation

Rotation is another two-dimensional transformation that rotates every point in the object by same angle. If the angle of rotation is positive then the point is rotated counter clockwise and if the angle of rotation is negative then the point is rotated clockwise. Let p be a point with the coordinates (x, y) and if p is rotated counter clockwise with an angle θ then after rotation, the new coordinates values will be

$$x' = x * \cos\theta - y * \sin\theta$$
$$y' = x * \sin\theta + y * \cos\theta$$

Consider the triangle with coordinates A(100, 100), B (50, 200) and C (150, 200) and rotation angle $\theta = 90°$.

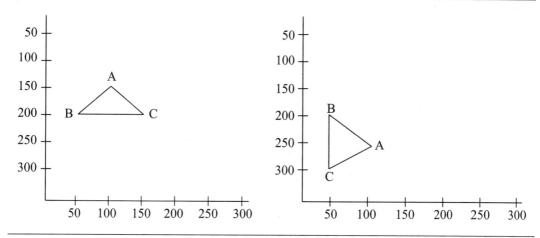

PROGRAM 16.19   To illustrate two-dimensional transformation

```
#include <graphics.h>
#include <stdlib.h>
#include <stdio.h>
#include <conio.h>
#include<math.h>
int main(void)
{
                int gm;
                intgd=DETECT;
                int x1, x2, x3, y1, y2, y3, x11, x21, x31, y11, y21, y31, c;
                int triangle[6];
                intsx, sy, tx, ty, theta;
                float t;
                initgraph(&gd,&gm,"c:\tc\bg:");
                printf("\n\t Enter the coordinates of the triangle");
                for (i=0; i<=5; i++)
                        scanf("%d", triangle[i]);

                printf("Before translation the triangle will be\n");
                Line (triangle[0], triangle[1], triangle[2], triangle[3]);
                Line (triangle[2], triangle[3], triangle[4], triangle[5]);
                Line (triangle[4], triangle[5], triangle[0], triangle[1]);

do
        {
                        printf("1. Translation\n");
                        Printf("2. Scaline\n");
                        Printf("3. Rotation\n");
```

```
Printf("Enter your choice\n");
Scanf("%d", &choice);

Switch(choice)
{
        Case 1: printf("Enter the translation
                distances\n");
                        Scanf("%d%d", &tx, &ty);
                For(i=0; i<6; i++)
                        {
                        If i%2 == 1
                        Triangle[i] = triangle[i]+tx;
                        Else
                        Triangle[i] = triangle[i]+ty;
                        }

printf("After translation the triangle will be\n");
Line (triangle[0], triangle[1], triangle[2], triangle[3]);
Line (triangle[2], triangle[3], triangle[4], triangle[5]);
Line (triangle[4], triangle[5], triangle[0], triangle[1]);
                Break;

        Case 1: printf("Enter the scaling factors\n");
                        Scanf("%d%d", &sx, &sy);
                For(i=0; i<6; i++)
                        {
                        If i%2 == 1
                        Triangle[i} = triangle[i]*sx;
                        Else
                        Triangle[i] = triangle[i]*sy;
                        }

        printf("After Scaling the triangle will be\n");
Line (triangle[0], triangle[1], triangle[2], triangle[3]);
Line (triangle[2], triangle[3], triangle[4], triangle[5]);
Line (triangle[4], triangle[5], triangle[0], triangle[1]);
                Break;

        case3:
                        printf("\n Enter the angle of
                        rotation");
                        scanf("%d",&theta);
                        radian=3.14*theta/180;
                For(i=0; i<3; i++)
```

```
                                    {
                                    Triangle[i] = triangle[i]*cos(radian) -
                                    triangle[i+1]*sin(radian)
                                    Triangle[i+1] = triangle[i]*
                                    sin(radian) + triangle[i+1]*cos(radian);
                                    }

                printf("After rotation the triangle will be\n");
                Line (triangle[0], triangle[1], triangle[2], triangle[3]);
                Line (triangle[2], triangle[3], triangle[4], triangle[5]);
                Line (triangle[4], triangle[5], triangle[0], triangle[1]);
                                    Break;

                        Case 4: break;
                default:
                                        printf("Enter the correct choice");
                                    }
                    }
                    while(choice!=4);
        }

            closegraph();
        return 0;
    }
```

Output:
First trial

Second trial

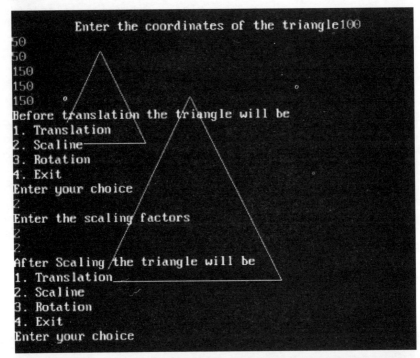

```
              Enter the coordinates of the triangle100
50
50
150
150
150
Before translation the triangle will be
1. Translation
2. Scaline
3. Rotation
4. Exit
Enter your choice
2
Enter the scaling factors
2
2
After Scaling the triangle will be
1. Translation
2. Scaline
3. Rotation
4. Exit
Enter your choice
```

Third trial

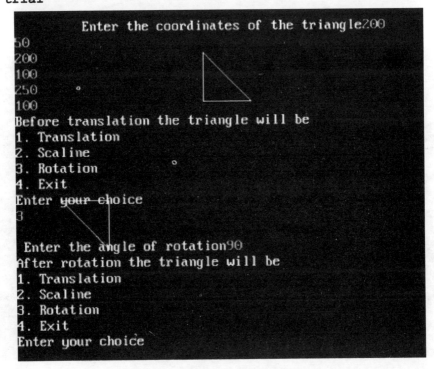

```
              Enter the coordinates of the triangle200
50
200
100
250
100
Before translation the triangle will be
1. Translation
2. Scaline
3. Rotation
4. Exit
Enter your choice
3

 Enter the angle of rotation90
After rotation the triangle will be
1. Translation
2. Scaline
3. Rotation
4. Exit
Enter your choice
```

SUMMARY

- C is one of the suitable languages for graphics applications due to the availability of a number of built-in functions for graphics operations
- To work with graphics, the mode should be switched over from the default text mode to graphics mode
- Graphics card in the computer's mother board is responsible for controlling graphics components namely text, audio, video
- initgraph() is the function which initializes the graphics mode
- The header file <graphics.h> provides the prototypes of the functions needed for graphics programming
- Library functions are available for drawing line, rectangle, circle, ellipse, polygon, barchart, piechart etc.
- We can draw lines and circles using standard algorithms namely DDA and Bresenham's methods

REVIEW QUESTIONS

16.1 What is computer graphics?

16.2 Mention the applications of computer graphics.

16.3 Define pixel and resolution.

16.4 What is the purpose of `initgraph()` in C?

16.5 Write the general syntax of:
```
Line()
Circle()
Bar()
Outtextxy()
```

16.6 What is the purpose of `closegraph()`?

16.7 Mention the different functions available for text display.

16.8 Present the algorithm for drawing line using Bresenham's method.

16.9 Present the algorithm for drawing circle using Bresenham's method.

16.10 How do you determine the resolution of your monitor?

16.11 What do you mean by transformation?

16.12 What is a translation?

16.13 What is a scaling?

16.14 What is a rotation?

PROGRAMMING EXERCISES

16.1 Write a program to display the solar system.

16.2 Write a program to draw a triangle and produce its mirror reflection.

16.3 Write a program to draw a bar chart to show the average temperature recorded in 5 cities.

16.4 Write a program to draw a rectangle and illustrate the basic two-dimensional transformation.

16.5 Write a program to animate a bouncing ball.

INTERVIEW QUESTIONS

16.1 What is the drawback of graphics mode compared to text mode?

16.2 What happens when a circle is scaled in one direction?

16.3 What is meant by presentation graphics?

16.4 Distinguish between pixel and voxel.

16.5 Distinguish between `outtext()` and `outtextxy()` functions.

17

Searching and Sorting

17.1 INTRODUCTION

Searching and sorting are the two major problem types the computers are used for. Here we will get to know about the basic searching and sorting methods and the development of pseudocodes and the C implementations.

17.2 SEARCHING

Often we need to search for a value in a list of values, for a record in a list of records and for a string in a list of strings. There are many searching methods. Here we discuss two important and most frequently encountered methods. They are linear search and binary search.

17.2.1 Linear Search

Suppose we have a list of five values consisting of 4, 7, 8, 10 and 12 and we need to search for a value say 8 in the list using linear search method. We compare the search value 8 with the first value 4 in the list. As 8 does not match with 4, we next compare 8 with the next value 7 in the list. As 8 does not match with 7, we then proceed to compare 8 with the next value 8 in the list. As the search value 8 matches with the value 8 in the list, we declare the search is successful. As noticed we continue to compare the search value with each value in the list till the search value is found or the list is exhausted. On the average, half of the list is traversed to search for a value in a list of values.

Input: A list of values in a one-dimensional array and a value to search for
Output: Whether the search value is found or not found

Pseudocode to search for a number in a list of numbers

```
// Read n values
for(i = 0; i < n; i++)
      read a[i]

// read the searching value
read s

// searching for s in a begins
f = 0;
for(i = 0; i < n; i++)
      if (a[i] == s)
            f = 1;
            break;
if f == 1
      display found
else
      display not found
```
End pseudocode

PROGRAM 17.1   To search for a number in a list of numbers using linear search

---

```c
#include <stdio.h>

int main(void)
{
      int a[10], n, i, f, s;


      printf("Enter the no. of numbers \n");
      scanf("%d", &n);

      printf("Enter %d numbers \n", n);
      for(i = 0; i < n; i++)
            scanf("%d", &a[i]);

      printf("Enter the number to be searched \n");
      scanf("%d", &s);

      /* searching for s in a begins */

      f = 0;
      for(i= 0; i < n; i++)
            if (a[i] == s)
```

```
        {
                f = 1;
                break;
        }

/* searching for s in a ends */

printf("\n List of elements \n");
for(i = 0; i < n; i++)
printf("%4d", a[i]);
printf("\n Element to be searched \n");
printf("\n s = %d \n", s);

if (f == 1)
        printf("%d is found", s);
else
        printf("%d is not found", s);

return 0;
}
```

Input–Output:

```
Enter the no. of numbers
5
Enter 5 numbers
1 2 3 4 5
Enter the number to be searched
3
List of elements
1 2 3 4 5
Element to be searched
3
3 is found
```

Explanation:

a is declared to be an array of **int** type of size 10. Maximum 10 values can be read into the array. **n**, **i**, **s** and **f** are declared to be variables of **int** type. n is to collect the number of values to be read into **a**, which lies within 1 and 10. **i** is to traverse all the elements of **a**. **s** is to collect a value which is to be searched. **f** is to determine whether **s** is found in **a** or not. It acts as a flag variable.

The procedure of searching for s in a is implemented in the following segment of the program.

```
f = 0;
for(i = 0; i < n; i++)
        if (a[i] == s)
```

```
        {
                f = 1;
                break;
        }
}
```

Before searching begins, **f** is set to zero with the assumption that **s** is not available in **a**. During the course of searching, that is, inside the body of the for loop, if **s** is found to match with any element in the array, **f** is set to 1 and the loop is exited. If **f** takes 1 then it means **s** is found in **a**. If f retains 0 we conclude that **s** is not found in **a**. The value of **f** would thus tell us whether **s** is found in **a** or not.

17.2.2 Binary Search

Binary search is another method to search for a value in a list of values. This method requires that the list be in order (increasing or decreasing) to work. Unlike sequential search where we search for a value in a list sequentially from the first value in the list till the value is found or the list is exhausted. Binary search method compares the searching value with the middle value in the list. If they match, search is successful. If they do not match either the first half of the list or the second half of the list will be used for further searching depending on whether the searching value is less than the middle element or greater than the middle element in the list and this is continued till the value is found or till the list is exhausted.

Suppose we have a list of six values consisting of 3, 5, 7, 8, 10 and 14 and we need to search for the value 5 in the list. Binary search procedure compares the search value 5 with the middle value in the list 7 (third value in the list of six values). Since 5 is less than the middle value 7, second half of the list consisting of 8, 10 and 14 is ignored in the next iteration (the search value cannot be in the second half as the list is in the increasing order). Searching is confined to the first half of the given list consisting of 3, 5 and 7. Binary search procedure will then compare the search value 5 with the middle value 5 in the new list and since they match, search is declared to be successful.

The procedure continues searching by halving the list under consideration each time till the value is found or the list is exhausted indicating unsuccessful search.

Input: A sorted list of values in a one-dimensional array and a value to search for

Output: Whether the search value is found or not found in the list

Pseudocode to search for a value in a list of values using binary search method

```
// Read the number of values in the list
Read n
// Read n values
for(i = 0; i < n; i++)
        read a[i]

// Read the searching value
Read s
```

```
/* searching for s in a begins */
f = 0;
l = 0;
u = n-1;
while(l <= u)
{
      mid = (l + u)/2; // find the middle position of the list
      if (s == a[mid])
      {
            f = 1
            Break;
      }
      else if (s < a[mid])
            u = mid -1      // ignore the second half
            else
                  l = mid + 1 // ignore the first half
      }

      /* searching for s in a ends */

if (f == 1)
      display found
else
      display not found
```
End pseudocode

PROGRAM 17.2   To search for a number in a list of numbers using binary search

---

```
#include <stdio.h>

int main(void)
{
      int a[10], n, i, f, s, l, u, mid;

      printf("Enter the no. of numbers \n");
      scanf("%d", &n);

      printf("Enter %d numbers \n", n);
      for(i = 0; i < n; i++)
            scanf("%d", &a[i]);

      printf("Enter the number to be searched \n");
      scanf("%d", &s);

      printf("\n List of elements \n");
      for(i = 0; i < n; i++)
```

```
        printf("%4d", a[i]);
        printf("\n Element to be searched \n");
        printf("\n s = %d \n", s);

        /* searching for s in a begins */
        f = 0;
        l = 0;
        u = n-1;
        while(l <= u)
        {
                mid = (l + u)/2;
                if (s == a[mid])
                {
                        f = 1;
                        break;
                }
                else if ( s < a[mid])
                        u = mid -1;
                else
                        l = mid + 1;
        }

        /* searching for s in a ends */

        if (f == 1)
                printf("%d is found", s);
        else
                printf("%d is not found", s);

        return 0;
}
```

Input–Output:

```
Enter the no. of numbers
5
Enter 5 numbers
1 2 3 4 5
Enter the number to be searched
3
List of elements
1 2 3 4 5
Element to be searched
3
3 is found
```

Explanation:

a is declared to be an array of int type of size 10. Maximum 10 values can be read into the array. The variables **n, i, s and f** are declared to be of **int** type. The variable n is to collect the number of values to be read into **a**, which has to lie within 1 and 10 since the size of the array a is 10. The variable **i** is to traverse all the elements of **a**; the variable **s** is to collect a value which is to be searched and f is to determine whether **s** is found in **a** or not. It acts as a flag variable.

After accepting the number of values into the variable n, n values are accepted into the array a. The value to search for is also accepted into the variable s.

The procedure of searching for **s** in the array **a** is implemented in the following segment of the program:

```
f = 0;
l = 0;
u = n-1;
while(l <= u)
{
        mid = (l + u)/2;
        if (s == a[mid])
        {
                f = 1;
                Break;
        }
        else if (s < a[mid])
                u = mid -1;
        else
                l = mid + 1;
}
```

Before searching begins, **f** is set to zero with the assumption that **s** is not available in **a**. The integer variables l and u are assigned the values 0 and n − 1 respectively. The variable l points to the first value in the list and the variable u points to the last value in the list. During the course of searching, that is, inside the body of the while loop, the middle position of the list is collected by the variable mid with the statement mid = (l + u)/2. We check whether the search value s matches with the middle value in the list. If they match the variable f is assigned 1 to indicate the search value is found and the loop is exited. If the search value does not match with the middle value and if it is less than the middle value the variable u is assigned mid − 1 and the loop continues for the next iteration. Note that the second half of the list is ignored in the next iteration. On the other hand, if the search value does not match with the middle value and if it is greater than the middle value the variable l is assigned mid + 1 and the loop continues for the next iteration. Note here that the first half of the list is ignored in the next iteration. This process of halving the list under consideration in each iteration and searching for the search value in one of the halves ignoring the other continues till the search value is found or the list is exhausted.

During the searching procedure if the variable **f** takes 1 then it means **s** is found in **a**. If it retains 0 we conclude that **s** is not found in **a**. The value of **f** would thus tell us whether **s** is found in the list **a** or not.

17.3   SORTING

Very often we will be required to arrange the values in a list either in the increasing order or in the decreasing order. The procedure of arranging the list of values in the specified order is called **sorting**. Sorting procedures involve repeated comparison of pairs of values in the list and swapping them if they are out of order till the values in the list are in order. There are a number of sorting methods. We will discuss some of them here.

17.3.1   Exchange Sort

Suppose we are given a list of five values consisting of 5, 4, 7, 10 and 9. Sorting the list in the increasing order using exchange sort method proceeds as follows:

The given list

5 4 7 10 9

First value 5 is compared with the second value 4 in the list.

5 4 7 10 9

Since 5 > 4, they are out of order and they are swapped.

The list now becomes

4 5 7 10 9

The first value 4 is compared with the third value 7 in the list.

4 5 7 10 9

Since 4 < 7, they are in order and hence no swapping is done. The list remains same

4 5 7 10 9

The first value 4 is compared with the fourth value 10 in the list.

4 5 7 10 9

Since 4 < 10, they are in order and hence no swapping is done. The list remains same

4 5 7 10 9

The first value 4 is compared with the fifth value 9 in the list.

4 5 7 10 9

Since 4 < 9, they are in order and hence no swapping is done. The list remains same

4 5 7 10 9

As noticed, the value in the first location is compared with each of the remaining values in the list. If the pairs of values being compared are out of order, they are swapped. This has resulted in the least value 4 occupying the first location in the list.

4 5 7 10 9

The list

4 5 7 10 9

Then second value 5 is compared with the third value 7 in the list.

4 5 7 10 9

Since 5 < 7 they are in order and no swapping is done. The list remains the same

4 5 7 10 9

The second value 5 is compared with the fourth value 10 in the list.

4 5 7 10 9

Since 5 < 10, they are in order and hence no swapping is done. The list remains same

4 5 7 10 9

The second value 5 is compared with the fifth value 9 in the list.

4 5 7 10 9

Since 5 < 9, they are in order and hence no swapping is done. The list remains same

4 5 7 10 9

As noticed, the value in the second location is compared with each of the remaining values in the list. If the pairs of values being compared are out of order, they are swapped. This has resulted in the second least value 5, occupying the second location in the list.

4 5 7 10 9

The list

4 5 7 10 9

Then the third value 7 is compared with the fourth value 10 in the list.

4 5 7 10 9

Since 7 < 10, they are in order and no swapping is done. The list remains the same

4 5 7 10 9

The third value 7 is compared with the fifth value 9 in the list.

4 5 7 10 9

Since 7 < 9, they are in order and hence no swapping is done. The list remains same

4 5 7 10 9

As noticed, the value in the third location is compared with each of the remaining values in the list. If the pairs of values being compared are out of order, they are swapped. This has resulted in the third least value 7, occupying the third location in the list.

4 5 7 10 9

The list

4 5 7 10 9

Then the fourth value 10 is compared with the fifth value 9 in the list.

4 5 7 10 9

Since 10 > 9, they are out of order and they are swapped. The list now becomes

4 5 7 9 10

As noticed, the value in the fourth location is compared with each of the remaining values in the list. If the pairs of values being compared are out of order, they are swapped. This has resulted in the fourth least value 9, occupying the fourth location in the list.

4 5 7 9 10

Since the list has five values, the value in the fifth location is naturally the fifth least value in the list occupying the fifth location and hence the list is sorted in the increasing order.

The sorted list

4 5 7 9 10

Input: A list of values

Output: The list of values in the sorted order

Pseudocode to sort a list of numbers using exchange sort method

```
// Read n values
for( i = 0; i < n; i++)
     read a[i]

// sorting begins
for( i = 0; i < n; i++)
for( j = i + 1; j < n; j++)
     if ( a[i] > a[j] )
          swap a[i] and a[j]

// sorting ends

// Sorted List
for( i = 0; i < n; i++)
     display a[i]
End pseudocode
```

PROGRAM 17.3   To sort a list of numbers using exchange sort method

```
#include <stdio.h>

int main(void)
```

```
{
    int a[10], n, i, j, t;

    printf("Enter the no. of numbers \n");
    scanf("%d", &n);

    printf("Enter %d numbers \n", n);
    for( i = 0; i < n; i++)
        scanf("%d", &a[i]);

    printf("Unsorted list \n");
    for( i = 0; i < n; i++)
        printf("%d\n", a[i]);

    /* sorting begins */

    for( i = 0; i < n; i++)
    for( j = i + 1; j < n; j++)
        if ( a[i] > a[j] )
        {
            t = a[i];
            a[i] = a[j];
            a[j] = t;
        }

    /* sorting ends */
    printf("Sorted list \n");
    for( i = 0; i < n; i++)
        printf("%d\n", a[i]);

    return 0;
}
```

Input–Output:

```
Enter the no. of numbers
5

Enter 5 numbers
1 3 2 5 4

Unsorted list
1 3 2 5 4

Sorted list
1 2 3 4 5
```

Explanation:

a is declared to be an array of type **int** and of size 10. **n**, **i**, **j** and **t** are declared to be variables of **int** type. **n** is to collect the number of values into the array **a**. The value of **n** has to lie between 1 and 10. **i** and **j** are to traverse the elements of the array **a**. **t** is to collect a value in the array temporarily during the course of sorting.

After accepting a value for **n**, **n** integer values are accepted into the array **a**. The given list (unsorted) is displayed. The list is then sorted by the following program segment.

```
for( i = 0; i < n; i++)
    for( j = i + 1; j < n; j++)
        if (a[i] > a[j])
        {
            t = a[i];
            a[i] = a[j];
            a[j] = t;
        }
```

Here, when **i** takes 0, the first value in the array is selected. It is compared with the remaining values of the array, which are selected by **j** (**j** ranges from 1 to n − 1). If necessary, two values being compared are interchanged. This produces the first least value. The first least value is placed in the location **a[i]**, that is, in **a[0]**.

When **i** takes 1, second value in the list is taken. It is compared with the remaining values of the list, which are taken by **j** (**j** now ranges from 2 to n−1). If necessary, two values being compared are interchanged. This produces the second least value. The second least value is placed in the location **a[i]**, that is, in a**[1]**. This process continues for all the values of the outer loop variable I and the entire array is sorted.

17.3.2 Selection Sort

Suppose we are given a list of five values consisting of 5, 4, 7, 10 and 9. Sorting the list in the increasing order using selection sort method proceeds as follows:

The given list

5 4 7 10 9

We assume that the first value in the list itself is the first least value by assigning the position value (0) of the first value 5 to a variable say, min (i.e. min = 0).
The value at the position min = 0, i.e. the value 5 is compared with the second value 4 in the list

5 4 7 10 9

Since 5 > 4, they are out of order and the position value (1) of the second value 4 is assigned to the variable min (i.e. min = 1).

The value at the position min = 1, i.e. the value 4 is compared with the third value 7 in the list
5 4 7 10 9

Since 4 < 7, they are in order and no change in the value of min is affected.

The value at the position min = 1, i.e. the value 4 is compared with the fourth value 10 in the list

5 4 7 <u>10</u> 9

Since 4 < 10, they are in order and no change in the value of min is affected.

The value at the position min = 1, i.e. the value 4 is compared with the fifth value 9 in the list

5 <u>4</u> 7 10 <u>9</u>

Since 4 < 9, they are in order and no change in the value of min is affected.

Since the entire list is traversed, the value of min = 1 gives the position of the first least value in the list. So the value at the position 0 and the value at position min = 1 are swapped

4 5 7 10 9

This produces the first least value 4 and is made to occupy the first location in the list.

4 5 7 10 9

The list

4 5 7 10 9

We now assume that the second value 5 in the list itself is the second least value by assigning the position value (1) of the second value 5 to the variable min (i.e. min = 1).
The value at the position min = 1, i.e. the value 5 is compared with the third value 7 in the list

4 <u>5</u> <u>7</u> 10 9

Since 5 < 7, they are in order and no change in the value of min is affected.

The value at the position min = 1, i.e. the value 5 is compared with the fourth value 10 in the list

4 <u>5</u> 7 <u>10</u> 9

Since 5 < 10, they are in order and no change in the value of min is affected.

The value at the position min = 1, i.e. the value 5 is compared with the fifth value 9 in the list

4 <u>5</u> 7 10 <u>9</u>

Since 5 < 9, they are in order and no change in the value of min is affected.

Since the entire list is traversed, the value of min = 1 gives the position of the second least value in the list and since the second least value is already in the correct position, no swapping is required.

4 5 7 10 9

This produces the second least value 5 and is made to occupy the second location in the list.

4 5 7 10 9

We now assume that the third value 7 in the list itself is the third least value by assigning the position value (2) of the second value 7 to the variable min (i.e. min = 2)

The value at the position min = 2, i.e. the value 7 is compared with the fourth value 10 in the list

4 5 7 10 9

Since 7 < 10, they are in order and no change in the value of min is affected.

The value at the position min = 2, i.e. the value 7 is compared with the fifth value 9 in the list

4 5 7 10 9

Since 7 < 9, they are in order and no change in the value of min is affected.

Since the entire list is traversed, the value of min = 2 gives the position of the third least value in the list and since the third least value is already in the correct position, no swapping is required.

4 5 7 10 9

This produces the third least value 7 and is made to occupy the third location in the list.

4 5 7 10 9

We now assume that the fourth value 10 in the list itself is the fourth least value by assigning the position value (3) of the fourth value 10 to the variable min (i.e. min = 3)

The value at the position min = 3, i.e. the value 10 is compared with the fifth value 9 in the list

4 5 7 10 9

Since 10 > 9, they are out of order, and the position value of 9, i.e. 4 is assigned to the variable min.

Since the entire list is traversed, the value of min = 4 gives the position of the fourth least value in the list. The value at position value 3 and the value at the position value min = 4 are swapped. This produces the fourth least value 9 and is made to occupy the fourth location in the list.

4 5 7 9 10

Since only one value 10 is left and is the fifth least value and it is in the fifth location of the list, the list is sorted.

The sorted list

4 5 7 9 10

Pseudocode to sort a list of numbers using Selection sort method
```
// Read n values
for( i = 0; i < n; i++)
      read a[i]

// sorting begins
      for( i = 0; i < n; i++)
      begin
            min = i;
```

```
                    for( j = i + 1; j < n; j++)
                          if (a[j] < a[min])
                                min = j;
                    if (i != min)
                          swap a[i] and a[min]
           end
// Sorting ends

// Sorted List
for( i = 0; i < n; i++)
       display a[i]
```
End pseudocode

PROGRAM 17.4   To sort a list of numbers using selection sort method

---

```c
#include <stdio.h>

int main(void)
{
       int a[10], n, i, j, t, min;

       printf("Enter the no. of numbers \n");
       scanf("%d", &n);

       printf("Enter %d numbers \n", n);
       for( i = 0; i < n; i++)
             scanf("%d", &a[i]);

       printf("Unsorted list \n");
       for( i = 0; i < n; i++)
             printf("%d\n", a[i]);

       /* sorting begins */

       for( i = 0; i < n; i++)
       {
             min = i;
             for( j = i + 1; j < n; j++)
                   if (a[j] < a[min])
                         min = j;
             if ( i != min)
             {
                   t = a[i];
                   a[i] = a[min];
                   a[min] = t;
             }
```

```
}.

/* sorting ends */
printf("Sorted list \n");
for( i = 0; i < n; i++)
        printf("%d\n", a[i]);

return 0;
}
```

Input–Output:

```
Enter the no. of numbers
5
Enter 5 numbers
1 3 2 5 4

Unsorted list
1 3 2 5 4

Sorted list
1 2 3 4 5
```

Explanation:

a is declared to be an array of type **int** and of size 10. **n, i, j** and **t** are declared to be variables of **int** type. **n** is to collect the number of values into the array **a**. The value of **n** has to lie between 1 and 10. **i** and **j** are to traverse the elements of the array **a**. **t** is to collect a value in the array temporarily during the course of sorting.

After accepting a value for **n, n** integer values are accepted into the array **a**. The given list (unsorted) is displayed. The list is then sorted by the following program segment.

```
for( i = 0; i < n; i++)
{
        min = i;
        for( j = i + 1; j < n; j++)
                if (a[j] < a[min])
                        min = j;
        if ( i != min)
        {
                t = a[i];
                a[i] = a[min];
                a[min] = t;
        }
}
```

Here, when i takes 0, the first value in the array is selected. We assume that it is the least value in the list and assign 0 (position of the first value in the list) to the variable min. It is compared with the remaining values of the array, which are selected by j (j ranges from 1 to n – 1). If any of the values is found to be less than a[0], the position of the value given by j is assigned to min. When the j loop completes, the variable min will have the position of the least value in the list. If the values of i and min differ then a[i] and a[min] are interchanged. Thus the actual first least value is placed in the location **a[0]**.

When i takes 1, the second value in the array is selected. We assume that it is the second least value in the list and assign 1 (position of the second value in the list) to the variable min. It is compared with the remaining values of the array, which are selected by j (j ranges from 2 to n – 1). If any of the values is found to be less than a[1], the position of the value given by j is assigned to min. When the j loop completes, the variable min will have the position of the second least value in the list. If the values of i and min differ then a[i] and a[min] are interchanged. Thus the actual second least value is placed in the location a[1]. This process continues for all the values of the outer loop variable i and the entire array is sorted.

17.3.3 Bubble Sort

Suppose we are given a list of five values consisting of 5, 4, 7, 10 and 9. Sorting the list in the increasing order using bubble sort method proceeds as follows:

The first largest is found and bubbled out as follows:

The list

4 5 7 9 10

The value in the first position 5 is compared with the value in the second position 4.
Since 5 > 4, they are out of order and they are swapped

4 5 7 10 9

The value in the second position 5 is compared with the value in the third position 7.

Since 5 < 7, they are in order and not swapped

4 5 7 10 9

The value in the third position 7 is compared with the value in the fourth position 10.

Since 7 < 10, they are in order and not swapped

4 5 7 10 9

The value in the fourth position 10 is compared with the value in the fifth position 9.

Since 10 > 9, they are out of order and they are swapped

4 5 7 9 10

This produces the largest value 10 and makes it to occupy the last position. So, 10 the largest value in the list is bubbled out and made to occupy its final position.

4 5 7 9 **10**

The second largest is found and bubbled out as follows:

The list

4 5 7 9 **10**

The value in the first position 4 is compared with the value in the second position 5.

<u>4</u> <u>5</u> 7 9 **10**

Since 4 < 5, they are in order and not swapped

4 5 7 9 **10**

The value in the second position 5 is compared with the value in the third position 7.

4 <u>5</u> <u>7</u> 9 **10**

Since 5 < 7, they are in order and not swapped

4 5 7 9 **10**

The value in the third position 7 is compared with the value in the fourth position 9.

4 5 <u>7</u> <u>9</u> **10**

Since 7 < 9, they are in order and not swapped

4 5 7 9 **10**

This produces the second largest value 9 and makes it to occupy the last but one position. So the value 9, the second largest value in the list, is bubbled out and made to occupy its final position.

4 5 7 **9 10**

The third largest is found and bubbled out as follows:

The list

4 5 7 **9 10**

The value in the first position 4 is compared with the value in the second position 5.

<u>4</u> <u>5</u> 7 **9 10**

Since 4 < 5, they are in order and not swapped

4 5 7 **9 10**

The value in the second position 5 is compared with the value in the third position 7.

4 <u>5</u> <u>7</u> **9 10**

Since 5 < 7, they are in order and not swapped

4 5 7 **9 10**

This produces the third largest value 7 and makes it to occupy the last but two positions. So the value 7, the third largest value in the list, is bubbled out and made to occupy its final position.

4 5 **7 9 10**

The fourth largest is found and bubbled out as follows:

The list

4 5 **7 9 10**

The value in the first position 4 is compared with the value in the second position 5.

<u>4</u> <u>5</u> **7 9 10**

Since 4 < 5, they are in order and not swapped

 4 5 **7 9 10**

This produces the fourth largest value 5 and makes it to occupy the last but three positions. So the value 5, the fourth largest value in the list, is bubbled out and made to occupy its final position.

4 **5 7 9 10**

Since there is only one value left that is the fifth largest value and it is in final place in the sorted order

4 **5 7 9 10**

The sorted list

4 **5 7 9 10**

Pseudocode to sort a list of numbers using bubble sort method

```
//Read n values
for( i = 0; i < n; i++)
     read a[i]

// sorting begins

for( i = 0; i <= n - 2; i++)
for(j = 0; j <= n - 2 - i; j++)
     if (a[j] > a[j+1])
          swap a[j] and a[j+1]
// sorting ends

// Sorted List
for( i = 0; i < n; i++)
     display a[i]
```
End pseudocode

PROGRAM 17.5   To sort a list of numbers using bubble sort method

```c
#include <stdio.h>

int main(void)
{
     int a[10], n, i, j, t;

     printf("Enter the no. of numbers \n");
     scanf("%d", &n);

     printf("Enter %d numbers \n", n);
     for( i = 0; i < n; i++)
          scanf("%d", &a[i]);

     printf("Unsorted list \n");
     for( i = 0; i < n; i++)
          printf("%d\n", a[i]);

     /* sorting begins */

     for( i = 0; i <= n - 2; i++)
     for(j = 0; j <= n - 2 - i; j++)
          if (a[j] > a[j+1])
          {
               t = a[j];
               a[j] = a[j+1];
               a[j+1] = t;
          }

     /* sorting ends */
     printf("Sorted list \n");
     for( i = 0; i < n; i++)
          printf("%d\n", a[i]);

     return 0;
}
```

Input–Output:

```
Enter the no. of numbers
5
Enter 5 numbers
1 3 2 5 4

Unsorted list
```

```
1 3 2 5 4

Sorted list
1 2 3 4 5
```

Explanation:

a is declared to be an array of type **int** and of size 10. **n, i, j** and **t** are declared to be variables of **int** type. **n** is to collect the number of values into the array **a**. The value of **n** has to lie between 1 and 10. **i** and **j** are to traverse the elements of the array **a**. The variable **t** is to collect a value in the array temporarily during the course of sorting.

After accepting a value for **n, n** integer values are accepted into the array **a**. The given list (unsorted) is displayed. The list is then sorted by the following program segment.

```
for( i = 0; i <= n - 2; i++)
for(j = 0; j <= n - 2 - i; j++)
        if (a[j] > a[j+1])
        {
                t = a[j];
                a[j] = a[j+1]
                a[j+1] = t;
        }
```

Here when the outer loop variable i = 0, the inner loop variable j ranges from 0 (index value of the first value to the index value of the last but one value in the array). When j = 0, the first two adjacent values of the array a[j] = a[0] and a[j+1] = a[1] are compared if they are out of order they are swapped. As a result, the larger of them is moved to the second position. Next j takes the value 1. Then the second value a[1] and the third value a[2] are compared. If they are out of order, they are swapped. As a result, the larger of them is moved to the third position. The comparison of the adjacent values and swapping if they are out of order continues for all the values of the outer loop variable j. When the j loop completes for i = 0, the largest value in the entire list is moved to the last location in the list.

Next the outer loop variable i takes the value 1 and the inner loop variable j ranges from 0 to n − 3 (= n − 2 − 1). Once again the pairs of the two adjacent values starting from the first value to the last but 2 values are compared. If they are out of order they are swapped. As a result, the second largest value is moved to the last but one location in the array.

Similarly, when the outer loop variable i takes the value 2 and the inner loop completes, the third largest value is moved to the last but two locations in the array. This process continues for all the values of the outer loop variable i and the entire array is sorted.

17.3.4 Insertion Sort

The basic idea behind this method involves inserting a value into an already sorted list at its proper position preserving the sorted order even after insertion of the new value. It requires us to scan the sorted list of values either from left to right or from right to left and shifting of the values in the sorted list appropriately to accommodate the new value.

If we opt to scan the sorted list from left to right to insert the new value at its proper position, we need to scan the list till we reach a value say, s, in the list which is greater than or equal to the value being inserted. Once we find it, we insert the new value right before the value s in the list. If the list is exhausted during the scan process, the new value is inserted at the end of the sorted list. (The new value is greater than all the values in the given sorted list.)

Suppose we have the following list:

3 5 7 8 10

To insert the value 6 into the list:

We scan the list from left to right till, we reach a value in the list which is greater than or equal to 6. Here we find that the value is 7 in the list

3 5 7 8 10

and we insert 6 right before it to get the new sorted list

3 5 **6** 7 8 10

Note that to be able to insert the new value in its proper position to get the new sorted list, all the values towards its left should have been shifted left by one position.

If we opt to scan the sorted list from right to left to insert the new value into the sorted list at its proper position, we need to scan the list from right to left till we reach a value say, s, in the list which is less than or equal to the value being inserted. Once we find it, we insert the new value right after the value s in the list. If we do not reach the value s and the list is exhausted, we insert the new value in the first position in the new list. (The new value is less than all the values in the given sorted list.)

Suppose we have the following list:

3 5 7 8 10

To insert the value 6 into the list:

We scan the list from right to left till we reach a value s in the list which is less than or equal to 6. Here we find that the value s is 5 in the list

3 5 7 8 10

and we insert 6 right after it to get the new sorted list

3 5 **6** 7 8 10

Note that to be able to insert the new value in its proper position to get the new sorted list, all the values towards its right should have been shifted right by one position.

Normally we use the second variation. We scan the list from right to left and shift the values in the list which are greater than the value being inserted towards right and on finding a value in the list which is less than or equal to the value being inserted, we insert the value right after the value in the list.

We have understood the basic principle of insertion sort procedure. Let us now get to know how the insertion sort method sorts an unordered list of values.

Suppose we are given a list of five values consisting of 5, 4, 7, 3 and 9. Sorting the list in the increasing order using insertion sort method proceeds as follows:

The list

5 4 7 6 9

To begin with, we confine our focus on the sublist consisting of the first value 5 in the list. The sublist is in the sorted order. (A list consisting of only one value is in sorted order.)

We now consider the sorted sublist

5 4 7 3 9

The second value 4 in the given list is now the value to be inserted into the sorted sublist. We adopt right to left scan on the sublist (there is only one value in the sublist 5). We move the value 5 (since it is greater than 4) in the sublist towards right by one position and insert 4 right before it to get the new sorted sublist consisting of two values

4 5 7 3 9

Now the sorted sublist has two values **4 5**

4 5 7 3 9

Consider the third value 7 in the list. We again adopt right to left scan of the sorted sublist to find the proper position for 7 in the sorted sublist. We find that the value 5 in the sorted sublist is less than 7 and insert 7 right after it in the new sorted sublist.

The new sorted sublist becomes **4 5 7**

4 5 7 3 9

Now consider the fourth value 3 in the list. We again adopt right to left scan of the sorted sublist to find the proper position for 3 in the sorted sublist. We find that the list is exhausted during the right to left scan and 3 inserted into the first position of the sorted sublist to produce

3 4 5 7 9

Now consider the fifth value 9 in the list. We again adopt right to left scan of the sorted sublist to find the proper position for 9 in the sorted sublist. During the scan process, we find that 7 is the first value which is less than the value 9. We insert 9 right after 7 in the new sorted sublist to produce the final sorted list of the given list of values

3 4 5 7 9

Pseudocode to sort a list of numbers using insertion sort method

```
//Read n values
for( i = 0; i < n; i++)
      read a[i]

// sorting begins
for( i = 1; i <= n - 1; i++)
begin
      v = a[i];
      j = i - 1;
      While ((j >= 0) && (a[j] > v))
      begin
            a[j+1] = a[j];
            j = j - 1
      end
      a[j + 1] = v;
end
// sorting ends

// Sorted list
for( i = 0; i < n; i++)
      display a[i]
```
End pseudocode

PROGRAM 17.6   To sort a list of numbers using insertion sort method

---

```c
#include <stdio.h>

int main(void)
{
      int a[10], n, i, j, temp;

      printf("Enter the no. of numbers \n");
      scanf("%d", &n);

      printf("Enter %d numbers \n", n);
      for( i = 0; i < n; i++)
            scanf("%d", &a[i]);

      printf("Unsorted list \n");
      for( i = 0; i < n; i++)
            printf("%d\n", a[i]);

      /* sorting begins */

      for( i = 1; i <= n - 1; i++)
```

```
        {
                temp = a[i];
                j = i - 1;
                while ((j >= 0) && (a[j] > temp))
                {
                        a[j+1] = a[j];
                        j = j - 1;
                }
                a[j + 1] = temp;
        }

        /* sorting ends */

        printf("Sorted list \n");
        for( i = 0; i < n; i++)
                printf("%d\n", a[i]);

        return 0;
}
```

Input–Output:

```
Enter the no. of numbers
5
Enter 5 numbers
1 3 2 5 4

Unsorted list
1 3 2 5 4

Sorted list
1 2 3 4 5
```

Explanation:

a is declared to be an array of type **int** and of size 10. **n, i, j** and **temp** are declared to be variables of **int** type. The variable **n** is to collect the number of values into the array **a** and its value has to lie between 1 and 10. The variables **i** and **j** are to traverse the elements of the array **a**. The variable **temp** is to collect a value in the array temporarily during the course of sorting.

After accepting a value for **n**, **n** integer values are accepted into the array **a**. The given list (unsorted) is displayed. The list is then sorted by the following program segment.

```
        for( i = 1; i <= n - 1; i++)
        {
                temp = a[i];
                j = i - 1;
```

```
While ((j >= 0) && (a[j] > temp))
{
        a[j+1] = a[j];
        j = j - 1
}
a[j + 1] = temp;
}
```

The outer loop variable i ranges from 1 to n - 1 (i.e. from the index value of the second value to the index value of the last value in the array). When the loop variable takes the value 1, the second value in the array is placed in the temporary variable temp and the variable j is set to i - 1 (i.e. 0). The body of the while loop is entered if the expression (j >= 0) && (a[j] > v) evaluates to true. Otherwise, the body of the loop is not entered into at all. It evaluates to true when both the conditions j >= 0 (the array index has not gone beyond the first value in the array) and a[j] > temp are true. Here j >= 0 is true since j = 0. If a[j] > temp is also true, i.e. if a[0] > temp, the first value in the list is found to be greater than the value in temp (the second value of the list a[1]). Then a[1] is moved to a[0] (because of the statement a[j+1] = a[j]) and j is decremented by one and it becomes -1. The control goes back to the beginning of the while loop. Now since j < 0, the while loop is exited. The value of temp (a[1]) is moved to a[0] (because of the statement a[j+1] = temp. So the second value in the list is inserted into its proper place into the sublist consisting of the first value. As a result we have now a sorted sublist having the first two values of the list.

Then the outer loop variable I takes the value 2, the index value of the third value in the list. It is also inserted into its proper position into the sorted sublist having two values giving rise to an extended sorted sublist having three values. This procedure continues for all the values of the outer loop variable I and the entire list is sorted.

17.3.5 Quick Sort

Quick sort is based on the idea of selecting a value in the list called as the **pivot value** (normally it is the first value in the list) and placing it in its correct place in the sorted list. Placing it in its final position involves two scans of the list. The first one, left to right scan starting from the second value onwards; skipping over the values which are less than the pivot value and stopping at a value which is greater than equal to the pivot value. The second one, right to left scan starting from the last value; skipping over the values which are greater than the pivot value and stopping at a value which is less than or equal to the pivot value. Here three situations may occur. The first one, the scans may stop at two values and there may be some other values between them. In this case, the values are swapped and the scans will continue.

The second one, both the left to right scan and the right to left scan may stop at the same value. In this case, the value at which the scans have stopped and the pivot value are swapped resulting in the formation of two partitions. The third one, the left to right scan and the right to left scan may cross over. In this case, the value at which the right to left scan has stopped and the pivot value are swapped resulting in the formation of two partitions. The same procedure is applied to each partition recursively till we get down to partitions with single values and stop the procedure as the partitions with single values are already sorted.

Suppose we have a list of values consisting of five values 4, 3, 7, 5 and 9.

Quick sort proceeds as follows:

4 3 7 5 9

The first value 4 is taken as the pivot value. We perform left to right scan and right to left scan of the list.

The left scan starts from the second value 3 of the list and skips it since 3 < 4 and move to the third value 7 and it stops at 7 since 7 > 4. The right to left scan starts from the last value (fifth value) 9 skips it since 9 > 4; moves to the fourth value 5 and skips it since 5 > 4 and then moves to the third value 7 and skips it also since 7 > 4 and stops at the second value 3. So the left to right scan and the right to left scan have crossed as the left to right scan has stopped at the value 7 and the right to left scan has stopped at the value 3. In this situation, the pivot value 4 and the value 3 at which right to left scan has stopped are swapped resulting in the list

3 **4** 7 5 9

So the pivot value 4 has got into its final position and resulted in splitting of the list into two partitions. One partition to the left of it and the other to the right of it. The left partition has the sublist consisting of only one value {3 }.

And the right partition has the sublist { 7 5 9}

{3} **4** {7 5 9}

Since the left partition has only one value 3, it is already in sorted order. The procedure of quick sort is repeated for the right partition where the pivot value 7 is placed in its final position by performing left to right and right to left scan and swapping the pivot value with the value at which the right to left scan stops resulting the sublist 5 **7** 9 . Thereby dividing the sublist into two further sublists consisting of 5 and 9 separately {5} **7** {9}.

Since both the left and the right partitions have single values. They are already in sorted order.

The final list in the sorted order would thus be

3 4 5 7 9

Pseudocode quickSort(a[l..r])

```
// a[l..r] is a subarray of a[0..n-1]
if ( l < r)
Begin
      s = partition(a[l..r])
      quicksort(a[l..s-1])
      quicksort(a[s=1..r])
end
```
End pseudocode

Pseudocode partition(a[l..r])

```
//Partitions the subarray by using its first value as pivot
//Input: A subarray a[l..r] of the array a[0..n-1]
```

```
//Output: a partition of a[l..r] with the split position as the output

p = a[l]
i = l
j = r + 1
While (i <= j)
Begin
        While (a[i] < p)
        begin
              i = i + 1
        End
        While (a[j] > p)
        begin
              j = j - 1
        end
        if ( i <= j)
        swap a[i], a[j]
end
swap a[l] and a[j]
return j
```
End pseudocode

Pseudocode to sort a list of values using quick sort
```
// Read the number of values
Read n
// Read n values
for(i = 0; i < n; i++)
      Read a[i]

// unsorted list
for(i = 0; i < n; i++)
      display a[i]

// sort the list
Quicksort(a[0..n-1])

// Sorted list
for(i = 0; i < n; i++)
      display a[i]
```

End pseudocode

PROGRAM 17.7   To sort a list of values using quick sort

```c
#include <stdio.h>
void quicksort(int[], int, int);
int partition(int[], int, int);

int main(void)
{
      int a[10], i, n;

      printf("Enter the number of values [1-10]\n");
      scanf("%d", &n);

      printf("Enter %d vaues\n", n);
       for(i = 0; i < n; i++)
       scanf("%d", &a[i]);

      printf("Unsorted list\n");
       for(i = 0; i < n; i++)
       printf("%4d", a[i]);
       printf("\n");

      quicksort(a, 0, n-1);

      printf("Sorted list\n");
       for(i = 0; i < n; i++)
       printf("%4d", a[i]);

      return 0;
}

void quicksort(int a[], int l, int r)
   {    int s;
       if ( l < r)
       {
             s = partition(a, l, r);
             quicksort(a, l, s-1);
             quicksort(a, s+1, r);
       }
   }

int partition(int a[], int l, int r)
{
      int p, i, j, t;
       p = a[l];
       i = l+1;
```

```
        j = r;
        while (i <= j)
{
                while (a[i] < p)
                        i++;

                while (a[j] > p)
                        j--;

                if (i <= j)
                {
                        int t = a[i];
                        a[i] = a[j];
                        a[j] = t;

                }
}

t = a[l];
a[l] = a[j];
a[j] = t;

return j;
}
```

Input–Output:

```
Enter the number of values [1-10]
5
Enter 5 values
1 5 3 4 2

Unsorted list
1 5 3 4 2

Sorted list
1 2 3 4 5
```

Explanation:

a is declared to be an array of type **int** and of size 10. **n** and **i** are declared to be variables of **int** type. The variable **n** is to collect the number of values into the array **a** and its value has to lie between 1 and 10. The variables **i** is to traverse the elements of the array **a**.

After accepting a value for **n**, **n** integer values are accepted into the array **a**. The given list (unsorted) is displayed. The list is then sorted by the following statement.

```
quicksort(a, 0, n-1);
```

As can be seen, the function takes three arguments. They are the array name, the index of the first value and the index of the last value of the array. The function `quicksort()` in turn calls the function `partition()` and itself recursively twice as long as the array is not exhausted. The responsibility of the function `partition()` is to split the list under consideration (specified by the arguments of `quicksort()`) into two partitions by placing the pivot value in its proper place in the sorted order.

17.3.6 Merge Sort

The merge sort method basically involves merging two sorted lists of values preserving the sorted order even in the new list. Suppose we have two sorted lists of values consisting of two values each. Let the two sorted lists be

L1 = {2, 4}

L2 = {3, 8}

The process of merging the two lists proceeds as follows:
We consider the first value 2 in L1 and compare it with the first value 3 in L2. Since 2 < 3, we assign 2 to the first position a new list L3.

L3 = {2}

Then we move to the second value 4 in L1 and compare it with the first value 3 in L2. Since 3 < 4, we move 3 to the second position in the new list L3. Now L3 becomes

L3 = { 2, 3}

Then we compare the second value 4 in L1 with the second value 8 in L2. Since 4 < 8, we move 4, to the third position in L3. Now L3 becomes

L3 = {2, 3, 4}

As the list L1 is exhausted, we move the remaining values in L2 to the next positions in L3. Because 8 is the only value left in L2, we move 8 to the fourth position in L3.
Now L3 becomes {2, 3, 4, 8}, the new sorted list.

Now let us look at how merge sort works on an unordered list of values.
Suppose we are given the following list of values

2, 5, 3, 8, 6, 10, 9

The list gets divided about its middle position into two lists recursively as follows till we arrive at sublists consisting of single values

{2 5 3 8 6 10 9} Given list

Division of the list and sublists thereafter about the middle position recursively till we get sublists with single values

{2 5 3 8 | 6 10 9}

↓   ↓

{ 2 5 3 8} { 6 10 9}

{ 2 5 | 3 8} { 6 | 10 9}

↓   ↓   ↓   ↓

{2 5} { 3 8} { 6} {10 9}

{2 | 5}   {3 | 8}   { 6}   { 10 | 9}

↓ ↓   ↓   ↓   ↓   ↓   ↓

{2} { 5} { 3} { 8 } { 6}   {10} { 9}

As noted recursive division of the list till we arrive at the sublists consisting of single values is a top down process. There are 7 sublists consisting of single values. Each sublist is in sorted order.

Now the merging of the sorted lists proceeds as follows:
The first two sublists consisting of 2 and 5 are merged preserving the sorted order to give the new sublist {2 5}. The third and fourth sublists consisting of 3 and 8 respectively are merged together to give the new list {3, 8}. Similarly the fifth sublist and sixth and seventh sublists giving {6} and {9, 10}.

{2 5} {3 8} { 6} { 9 10}

Now the first two sublists consisting of {2 5} and {3 8} respectively are merged to produce the new list {2 3 5 8}.

The third and the fourth sublists consisting of {6} and {9, 10} respectively are also merged to produce {6 9 10}.

{2 3 5 8} {6 9 10}

Now we have two sublists {2 3 5 8} and {6 9 10}. They are also merged to produce the final sorted list

{2 3 5 6 8 9 10 } Sorted list

As noted merging the sorted sublists at each stage till we get the final sorted list is a bottom up process.
Following are the pseudocodes for the mergesort method:

Pseudocode mergesort(a[l..r])
```
if (l < r)
begin
```

```
      mid = (l + r)/2
      mergesort(a[l..mid])
      mergesort(a[mid+1]..r)
      Merge(a[l..r], mid)
end
```
End pseudocode

Pseudocode merge(a[l..r], mid)
```
i = l
j = mid + 1
h = l
while ((i <= mid)and (j <= r))
begin
      if (a[i] < a[j])
      begin
            b[h] = a[i]
            i = i + 1
      else
            b[h] = a[j]
            j = j + 1
      end
      h = h + 1
end
if ( i > mid)
      for(k = j; k <= r ; j++)
            b[h] = a[k]
            h = h + 1

if ( j > r)
      for(k = i; k <= mid; k++)
            b[h] = a[k]
            h = h + 1
for(i = l; i <= r; i++)
      a[i] = b[i]
```
End pseudocode

Pseudocode to sort a list of values using merge sort
```
// Read the number of values
Read n
// Read n values
for(i = 0; i < n; i++)
      Read a[i]

// unsorted list
for(i = 0; i < n; i++)
      display a[i]
```

```
// sort the list
mergesort(a[0..n-1])

// Sorted list
for(i = 0; i < n; i++)
    display a[i]
```

End pseudocode

PROGRAM 17.8   To sort a list of numbers using merge sort method

```c
#include <stdio.h>
void mergesort(int[], int, int);
void merge(int[], int, int, int);
int b[20];

int main(void)
{
    int a[10], i, n;

    printf("Enter the number of values\n");
    scanf("%d", &n);
    printf("Enter %d values\n");
    for(i=0; i<n;i++)
    scanf("%d", &a[i]);

    printf("Unsorted list\n");
    for(i=0; i<n;i++)
    printf("%4d", a[i]);
    printf("\n");


    mergesort(a, 0, n - 1);

    printf("Sorted list\n");
    for(i=0; i<n;i++)
    printf("%4d", a[i]);
    return 0;
}

void mergesort(int a[], int low, int high)
{
    int mid;
     if (low < high)
```

```
        {
                mid = (low + high)/2;
                mergesort(a, low, mid);
                mergesort(a, mid+1, high);
                merge(a, low, mid, high);
        }
}

void merge(int a[], int low, int mid, int high)
{
        int h, i, j, k;
        h = low;
        i = low;
        j = mid + 1;

        while ((i <= mid)&& (j <= high))
        {
                if (a[i] < a[j])
                {
                        b[h] = a[i];
                        i++;
                }
                else
                {
                        b[h] = a[j];
                        j++;
                }
                h++;
        }
        if ( i > mid)
                for(k = j; k <= high ; k++)
                {
                        b[h] = a[k];
                        h++;
                }


        if ( j > high)
                for(k = i; k <= mid; k++)
                {
                        b[h] = a[k];
                        h++;
                }
        for(i = low; i <= high; i++)
                a[i] = b[i];
}
```

Input–Output:

```
Enter the number of values
5
Enter 5 values
 5 6 4 8 1

Unsorted list
 5 6 4 8 1
Sorted list
 1 4 5 6 8
```

Explanation:

a is declared to be an array of type **int** and of size 10. The variables **n and i** are declared to be of **int** type. The variable n is to collect the number of values into the array **a** and its value has to lie between 1 and 10. The variables **i** is to traverse the elements of the array **a**.

After accepting a value for **n, n** integer values are accepted into the array **a**. The given list (unsorted) is displayed. The list is then sorted by the following statement

```
mergesort(a, 0, n-1);
```

As can be seen the function takes three arguments. They are the array name, the index of the first value and the index of the last value of the array. The function mergesort() in turn calls itself recursively twice and the function merge() as long as the array is not exhausted. The responsibility of the function merge() is to merge the two sorted lists under consideration (specified by its arguments) into one sorted list.

SUMMARY

- Searching is the most common problem type in computing.
- Linear search and binary search are the two most commonly used search algorithms.
- Linear search as the name itself indicates searches for a value in a list of values linearly till the value is found or till the list is exhausted. On the average, it traverses half the list during the searching process.
- Binary search works on sorted lists only. This is faster than linear search as half of the subsequent list's search space is ignored in each iteration.
- Sorting is a process of arrangement of values in a list in either ascending or in the descending order.
- Exchange sort, selection sort and the bubble sort algorithms are based on the straight forward approach for sorting.
- Merge sort and quick sort algorithms are based on divide and conquer approach. These are faster than exchange sort, selection sort and bubble sort algorithms.

REVIEW QUESTIONS

17.1 Explain linear search procedure and produce its pseudocode.

17.2 Explain binary search procedure and produce its pseudocode.

17.3 Explain exchange sort procedure and produce its pseudocode.

17.4 Explain selection sort procedure and produce its pseudocode.

17.5 Explain bubble sort procedure and produce its pseudocode.

17.6 Explain insertion sort procedure and produce its pseudocode.

17.7 Explain merge sort procedure and produce its pseudocode.

17.8 Explain quick sort procedure with its pseudocode. How does it differ from merge sort? Explain.

PROGRAMMING EXERCISES

17.1 Write C functions to perform the following:
   (a) To search for a value in a list of values using linear search.
   (b) To search for a value in a list of values using binary search.
   (c) To sort a list of values using exchange sort.
   (d) To sort a list of values using selection sort.
   (e) To sort a list of values using bubble sort.
   (f) To sort a list of values using insertion sort.

17.2 Write C functions to perform the following:
   (a) To search for a string in a list of strings using linear search.
   (b) To search for a string in a list of strings using binary search.
   (c) To sort a list of strings using exchange sort.
   (d) To sort a list of strings using selection sort.
   (e) To sort a list of strings using bubble sort.
   (f) To sort a list of strings using insertion sort.
   (g) To sort a list of strings using merge sort.
   (h) To sort a list of strings using quick sort.

17.3 Write a program to create a list of employees with the details of employees including empno, name, dept, designation and salary and provide functions to perform the following:
   (a) To search for an employee in the list of employees using linear search.
   (b) To search for an employee in the list of employees using binary search.
   (c) To sort the list of employees using exchange sort on name.
   (d) To sort the list of employees using selection sort on dept.

(e) To sort the list of employees using bubble sort on designation.

(f) To sort the list of employees using insertion sort on salary.

(g) To sort the list of employees using merge sort on name.

(h) To sort the list of employees using quick sort on salary.

17.4 Write a recursive function to implement linear search.

17.5 Write a recursive function to implement binary search.

17.6 Develop a procedure for finding whether the elements in a sorted array are unique or not and write C functions implementing the procedure:

(a) To find the uniqueness of the values in a list of values.

(b) To find the uniqueness of the strings in a list of strings.

(c) To find the uniqueness of the records in a list of records.

INTERVIEW QUESTIONS

17.1 Can binary search method be applied to all the lists of values?

17.2 Binary search scores over linear search always. Is the statement true?

17.3 Mention any one difference between exchange sort and selection sort.

17.4 Mention any one difference between merge sort and quick sort methods.

18

Miscellaneous Topics

18.1 CREATION OF A TWO-DIMENSIONAL ARRAY DYNAMICALLY

We know that a two-dimensional array is an array of one-dimensional arrays and we also know how to create a one-dimensional array dynamically. In order to create a one-dimensional array dynamically, we use `malloc()` or `calloc()` to allocate the required amount of memory to store the elements the address of the location for the first element is assigned to a pointer of the corresponding type. The pointer then represents the array and we access the elements of the array by performing pointer arithmetic.

Example 18.1

Suppose we need to create an array of `int` type dynamically to store, say, 5 integers.

The following segment of code can be used

```
int *p;
p = (int*) malloc(sizeof(int) * 5);
```

As a result of the execution of the statements, a block of memory of size 10 bytes gets allocated (each integer requires two bytes) and the address of the first location is assigned to the pointer variable a.

```
100   102   104   106   108
```

p = 100

So, the pointer variable **p** is pointing to the first location. The elements of the array are then accessed with the variable names p[0], p[1], etc. So, a pointer to the corresponding type represents a one-dimensional array. Having said that a two-dimensional array is an array of one-dimensional arrays, to allocate a two-dimensional array of **m** rows and **n** columns dynamically, First, we should allocate memory for **m** pointers to the corresponding type, and then **m** one-dimensional arrays can be allocated as discussed above and the starting address of each one-dimensional array can be assigned to the corresponding pointer.

Allocation of space for **m** pointers is done by the statements

```
int **p;
p = (int**)malloc(sizeof(int*) * m);
```

Note that **p** is declared to be a pointer to a pointer to **int** type. This is required since **p** is expected to collect the address of a pointer itself.

To allocate memory for **m** rows each row consisting of **n** columns, the following segment of code is ued.

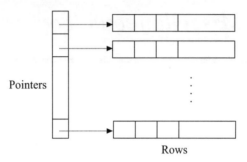

```
for(i = 0; i < m; i++)
    p[i] = (int*) malloc(n * sizeof(int));
```

Note that each p[i] is now a pointer to **int** type and represent a row.

The elements in the 2-D array are then accessed with two subscripts with **p**.

p[i][j] indicates the element in the **i**th row and **j**th column.

PROGRAM 18.1   To create a 2-D array dynamically

```
#include <stdio.h>
#include <malloc.h>

int main(void)
{
        int **p, no_of_rows, no_of_columns, i, j;

        printf("Enter the number of rows \n");
        scanf("%d", &no_of_rows);
        printf("Enter the number of columns \n");
        scanf("%d", & no_of_columns);
        p = (int**)malloc(no_of_rows * sizeof(int*));

        for(i = 0; i < no_of_rows; i++)
        {

                p[i]= (int*)malloc(no_of_columns * sizeof(int));
```

```
        }
        printf("Enter the elements of the matrix \n");
        for(i = 0; i < no_of_rows; i++)
        {
                for(j = 0; j < no_of_columns; j++)
                        scanf("%d", &p[i][j]);
        }

        printf("The matrix is \n");
        for(i = 0; i < no_of_rows; i++)
        {
                for(j = 0; j < no_of_columns; j++)
                        printf("%4d", p[i][j]);
                printf("\n");
        }

        for(i = 0; i < m; i++)
                free(p[i]);
        free(p);

        return 0;
}
```

Input–Output:

```
Enter the number of rows
2
Enter the number of columns
3
Enter the elements of the matrix
1 2 3 4 5 6

The matrix is
1  2  3
4  5  6
```

Explanation:

p is declared to be a pointer to pointer to **int** type (two levels of indirection). **no_of_rows**, **no_of_columns**, i and j are declared to be variables of **int** type. The pointer to pointer variable p represents the two-dimensional array being created dynamically. The variables no_of_rows and no_of_columns are to collect the number of rows and the number of columns for the array, and the variables i and j are to be used to traverse the individual locations of the array.

After accepting the number of rows into the variable **no_of_rows**, memory for **no_of_rows** pointers to **int** type is allocated with the statement

```
p = (int**)malloc(no_of_rows * sizeof(int*));
```

Now each **p[i]** i ranging from 0 to **no_of_rows** – 1 is a pointer to **int** type and thus can represent a row. Now the memory space for each row is allocated with the statements

```
for(i = 0; i < no_of_rows; i++)
{

        p[i] = (int*)malloc(no_of_columns * sizeof(int));

}
```

Now the memory for a 2-D array with the given number of rows and the given number of columns has been allocated. The array elements are then accepted and displayed.

PROGRAM 18.2   To allocate memory for a 2-D array of char type dynamically
---

```
#include <stdio.h>
#include <malloc.h>

int main(void)
{
        char **p;
        int n, i;
        printf("Enter the number of names \n");
        scanf("%d", &n);

        p = (char**)malloc(n * sizeof(char*));

        for(i = 0; i < n; i++)
                p[i] = (char*) malloc(20 * sizeof(char));
        printf("Enter %d Names \n", n);

        for(i = 0; i < n; i++)
                scanf("%s", p[i]);

        for(i = 0; i < n; i++)
                printf("%s \n", p[i]);

        return 0;
}
```

Input–Output:

```
Enter the number of names
3
Enter 3 Names
Nishu
Harshith
Shobha
```

The names are
Nishu
Harshith
Shobha

Explanation:

p is declared to be a pointer to pointer to `char` type n and i are declared to be variables of `int` type. The pointer to pointer variable p is to represent the two-dimensional array of `char` type being created. The variables n and i are to collect the number of names to be stored in the array and traverse the names respectively.

After accepting the number of names into the variable n, the memory for n pointers is allocated with the statement

```
p = (char**)malloc(n * sizeof(char*));
```

Now each p[i], i ranging from 0 to n–1 is a pointer to `char` type and thus can represent a string. Memory for n names each name containing maximum 20 characters is allocated with the statement.

```
for(i = 0; i < n; i++)
        p[i] = (char*) malloc(20 * sizeof(char));
```

Now n names are accepted into the memory space and they are displayed. Note that here the size of each row can differ since the number of characters in the names may not be same.

18.2 CREATION OF A THREE-DIMENSIONAL ARRAY DYNAMICALLY

We know that a 3-D array is an array of 2-D arrays. If the number of 2-D arrays in the 3-D array is say, **k**, then we need to allocate memory for **k** two-dimensional arrays. We have discussed allocation of memory for a 2-D array previously. The procedure has to be repeated **k** times.

We also know that a pointer to pointer represents a 2-D array. To be able to create k 2-D arrays, we need to dynamically allocate space for k pointers to pointer type. If l is the number of rows in each 2-D array, since each row is identified by a pointer, memory space for l pointers to the given type is to be allocated for each 2-D array. The starting address of the memory block is assigned to each pointer to pointer to the specified type which was allocated earlier. This is repeated for all the 2-D arrays. This is further extended even for each row elements for each table.

PROGRAM 18.3   To allocate memory for a 3-D array of `int` type dynamically

---

```
#include <stdio.h>
#include <malloc.h>

int main(void)
{
        int ***p, no_of_tables, no_of_rows, no_of_columns, i, j, k;

        printf("Enter tables, rows and columns \n");
        scanf("%d%d%d", &no_of_tables, &no_of_rows, &no_of_columns);
```

```
p = (int***) malloc(no_of_tables * sizeof(int**));
for(i = 0; i < no_of_tables; i++)
{
        p[i] = (int**) malloc(no_of_rows * sizeof(int*));
        for(j = 0; j < no_of_rows; j++)
                p[i][j] = (int *)malloc(no_of_columns * sizeof(int));
}

printf("Enter the elements of the three-dimensional array\n");

for(i = 0; i < no_of_tables; i++)
for(j = 0; j < no_of_rows; j++)
for(k = 0; k < no_of_columns; k++)
        scanf("%d", &p[i][j][k]);

printf("The Tables are \n");
for(i = 0; i < no_of_tables; i++)
{
        for(j = 0; j < no_of_rows; j++)
        {
                for(k = 0; k < no_of_columns; k++)
                        printf("%4d", p[i][j][k]);
                printf("\n");
        }
        printf("\n");
}

for(i = 0; i < no_of_tables; i++)
for(j = 0; j < no_of_rows; j++)
        free(p[i][j]);
for(i = 0; i < no_of_tables; i++)
        free(p[i]);
free(p);

return 0;
}
```

Input–Output:

```
Enter tables, rows and columns
2 2 2

Enter the elements of the three-dimensional array
1 2 3 4 5 6 7 8
The tables are
```

```
1 2
3 4

5 6
7 8
```

Explanation:

p is declared to be a pointer to pointer to pointer to **int** type (three levels of indirection) and it is to represent the 3-D array being created dynamically.

The statement `p = (int***) malloc(no_of_tables * sizeof(int**));` allocates Memory for `no_of_tables` number of pointers to pointers to `int` type. Now each `p[i]` being a pointer to pointer to `int` type, `i` ranging from 0 to `no_of_tables - 1` can represent a two-dimensional array of `int` type.

Now within the following segment of the program

```
for(i = 0; i < no_of_tables; i++)
{
        p[i] = (int**) malloc(no_of_rows * sizeof(int*));
        for(j = 0; j < no_of_rows; j++)
                p[i][j] = (int *)malloc(no_of_columns * sizeof(int));
}
```

The statement `p[i] = (int**) malloc(no_of_rows * sizeof(int*));` allocates space for **no_of_rows** pointers to int type for each 2-D array. Note that i ranges from 0 to no_of_tables−1.

The statements

```
for(j = 0; j < no_of_rows; j++)
        p[i][j] = (int *)malloc(no_of_columns * sizeof(int));
```

allocates space for **no_of_columns** values of int type for each row. Note that j ranges from 0 to no_of_rows−1.

Now memory for the 3-D array has been allocated. The elements are accepted and they are displayed.

18.3 VARIABLE LENGTH ARGUMENTS TO FUNCTIONS

So far, in all the functions which we defined we specified fixed number of arguments. We will now understand how we can pass a variable number of arguments to functions. The `scanf()` and `printf()` work this way. The following program illustrates the concept.

PROGRAM 18.4   To illustrate variable length arguments to functions

```
#include <stdarg.h>
#include <stdio.h>

int sum(int count, ...);
int main(void)
```

```
{
      int s;

      s = sum(2, 10, 20);
      printf("sum = %d\n", s);

      s = sum(3, 10, 20, 30);
      printf("sum = %d\n", s);

      return 0;
}

int sum(int count, ...)
{
      var_list parameters;
      int i, s = 0, num;

      va_start(parameters, count);

      for(i = 1; i <= count; i++)
      {
            num = va_arg(parameters, int);
            s += num;
      }

      va_end(parameters);
      return s;
}
```

Input–Output:

```
sum = 30
sum = 60
```

Explanation:

The function sum() is defined to take variable number of arguments. The first argument **count** is to tell the sum() how many arguments are being passed and the three dots are to specify that the variable number of arguments are being passed. The purpose of the function is to find the sum of the given number of integer values and return it to the calling program.

Within the function four macros var_list, var_start, var_arg and var_end are used to deal with the variable number of arguments. Since these macros are defined within the header file stdarg.h, it has been included as part of the program.

In each function dealing with variable-length arguments there should be a variable of type var_list. In the above function, the variable parameters is of type var_list. The variable maintains an array required by the macros var_start, var_arg and var_end.

The macro `var_start` sets its argument of type `var_list` to the first of the arguments being passed. In the above function, the statement `var_start(parameters, count);` sets the first argument to the variable parameters.

The macro `var_arg` is to fetch each argument one by one and the macro `var_end` helps the function perform a normal return to the calling program.

18.4 CONST AND VOLATILE

The keyword **const** is used to declare variables which are read-only. The syntax of its usage is as follows:

```
const data-type variable = value;
```

`const int a = 10;`	declares a to be a constant integer
`const float f = 12.56;`	declares f to be constant float
`const char s[] = "abcd";`	declares s to be a constant array of `char` type.

Any attempt to modify these gives rise to compile time error.

The keyword `const` can also be used while declaring formal arguments of functions. This is particularly useful when we need to pass arrays and structures to functions and we do not want them to be modified within the function.

Example 18.2

```
void display(const int a[], int n)
{

}

void display(const struct emp* e)
{

}
```

The keyword **volatile** is used to indicate that a variable can be changed even by some external agency (some other program or even the operating system) in addition to the program in which it is enclosed. The syntax of declaring volatile variables is similar to that of `const` variables.

```
volatile int a = 10;
```

The keywords `volatile` and `const` can be used in combination as:

```
volatile const int a=10;
```

in which case the value of **a** can be changed by some external agency but not by the program in which it is enclosed.

18.5 GENERIC POINTERS

A pointer variable of type **void** is called a generic pointer. A generic pointer can collect the address of any type of variable.

Example 18.3
```
void *vp;

int a;

vp = &a;
```
Here the pointer vp collects the address of the variable **a** of int type.
```
float f;

vp = &f;
```
Here the pointer vp collects the address of the variable f of float type.
```
double d;

vp = &d;
```
Here the pointer vp collects the address of the variable d of double type.

Even though void pointer can be assigned the address of any type of variable it cannot be used to de-reference the value, i.e. after vp = &a, where vp is the generic pointer and a is a variable of int type *vp does not give the value of a. Even though void pointer can be assigned to any other pointer, the converse is not true (without explicit type casting).
```
void* vp;
int *ip;

vp = ip; is valid

ip = vp; is not valid
```
But, ip = (int*) vp; is valid.

18.6   SELF-REFERENTIAL STRUCTURES

A structure containing a pointer to the same type is referred to as self-referential structure.
```
struct list
{
        int n;
        struct list *p;
};
```
Self-referential structures are used to create and manipulate what are called linked lists. A linked list is defined to be a collection of nodes scattered all over the memory (when the nodes are allocated dynamically) but tied together with the pointer assignments. Each node in a linked list

will have a data part and an address part, the address part being able to collect the address of another node. Pictorially, a linked list appears as follows:

Note that the address part of the last node is filled with the value NULL. It is to indicate that the pointer does not point to any node.

PROGRAM 18.5 To illustrate self-referential structure

```c
#include <stdio.h>

struct list
{
        int n;
        struct list *next;
};

int main(void)
{
        struct list l, m, *p;

        p = &l;

        l.n = 123;
        l.next = &m;

        m.n = 124;
        m.next = NULL;

        while (p != NULL)
        {
                printf("%d -> ", p -> n);
                p = p ->next;
        }
        printf("NULL");
        return 0;
}
```

Input–Output:

```
123 -> 124 -> NULL
```

Explanation:

The structure **struct list** is defined with an integer member n and a pointer **next** to itself. Each variable of **struct list** would thus can store a value of integer type and the address of another variable of struct list type and as a result each variable can represent a node.

In the main(), **l** and **m** are declared to be variables of **struct** list type and **p** is declared to be a pointer to struct list type. The data part of the variables **l** and **m** are assigned the values 123 and 124 respectively with the statements l.n = 123; and m.n = 124.

The pointer variable **p** is assigned the address of **l** and the address part of **l**, i.e. **l.next** is assigned the address of the variable **m**. and lastly the address part of **m**, i.e. m.next is assigned NULL.

The data values in each of the nodes are displayed by the following segment of the program.

```
while (p != NULL)
{
       printf ("%d -> ", p -> n);
       p = p ->next;
}
```

Here, the important point to be noted is that through the pointer p, which collects the address of the first node in the linked list, the entire list can be traversed by setting up a loop.

PROGRAM 18.6   To create a linked list dynamically

```
#include <stdio.h>
#include <malloc.h>

struct list
{
       int n;
       struct list *next;
};
int main (void)
{
    struct list *p = NULL, *tp, *t;
       char ch = 'y';
       int m;


       while (ch == 'y')
       {
          if (p == NULL )
          {
             tp = (struct list*) malloc (sizeof (struct list));
             printf ("Enter data \n");
             scanf ("%d", &m);
             tp ->n = m;
             tp ->next = NULL;
             p = tp;
          }
          else
          {
                t = p;
                while (t->next != NULL)
                       t = t->next;
             tp = (struct list*) malloc (sizeof (struct list));
             printf ("Enter data \n");
             scanf ("%d", &m);
             tp ->n = m;
```

```
                tp ->next = NULL;
                t ->next = tp;


            }
            printf ("Do you want to continue ? y/n \n");
            fflush (stdin);
            ch = getchar ();
    }

    while (p != NULL)
    {
        printf ("%d -> ", p->n);
        p = p->next;
    }
        printf ("NULL");

        return 0;
}
```

Input–Output:

```
Enter data
10
Do you want to continue ? y/n
y
Enter data
20
Do you want to continue ? y/n
y
Enter data
30
Do you want to continue ? y/n
y
Enter data
40
Do you want to continue ? y/n
n

The Linked List created is:

10 -> 20 -> 30 -> 40 -> NULL
```

18.7   TRIGRAPH SEQUENCES

Trigraph sequences offer an alternative way of supporting some characters even though some keyboards do not support them. These are a new ANSI addition. Each trigraph sequence consists of two question marks followed by another character supported by the keyboard. The following table shows the trigraph sequences and their corresponding characters.

Trigraph sequence	Character
??)	]
??(	[
??>	}
??<	{
??/	\
??=	#
??!	|
?-	~
??'	^

18.8   HOW TO MEASURE TIME TAKEN BY A FUNCTION IN C?

To calculate time taken by a process, we can use `clock()` function, the prototype of which is available in the header file *time.h*. We can call the clock function at the beginning and end of the code for which we need to measure time, subtract the values, and then divide by clocks_per_sec (the number of clock ticks per second) to get processor time. The following program segment illustrates this.

```
#include <time.h>

clock_t start, end;
double cpu_time_used;

start = clock();
... /* Do the work. */
end = clock();
cpu_time_used = ((double) (end - start)) / CLOCKS_PER_SEC;
```

The following is a sample C program where we measure time taken by a function by name `fun()`. The function `fun()` waits for enter key press to terminate.

PROGRAM 18.7   To demonstrate time taken by function `fun()`

```
#include <stdio.h>
#include <time.h>

/* The function fun()terminates when enter key is pressed */

void fun()
```

```
{
    printf("fun() starts \n");
    printf("Press enter to stop fun \n");
    while(1)
    {
        if (getchar())
            break;
    }
    printf("fun() ends \n");
}

int main(void)
{
    /* Calculate the time taken by fun()*/

    clock_t t;
    t = clock();
    fun();
    t = clock() - t;
    double time_taken = ((double)t)/CLOCKS_PER_SEC; /* in seconds */

    printf("fun() took %f seconds to execute \n", time_taken);
    return 0;
}
```

Input–Output:

```
fun() starts
Press enter to stop fun

fun() ends
fun() took 5.017000 seconds to execute
```

The above output is obtained after waiting for around 5 seconds and then hitting enter key.

SUMMARY

- We can create a one-dimensional array dynamically using `malloc()` and `calloc()`
- We can create a two-dimensional array dynamically also using `malloc()` and `calloc()` as each two-dimensional array is an array of one-dimensional arrays.
- We can create a three-dimensional array dynamically also using `malloc()` and `calloc()` as each three-dimensional array is an array of two-dimensional arrays.
- We can define a function to take variable number of arguments.
- A pointer variable of type void is called a **generic pointer**. A generic pointer can collect the address of any type of variable.

- A structure containing a pointer to the same type is referred to as **self-referential structure.** Each node in a linked list is a self-referential structure.
- The keyword **const** is used to declare variables which are read only. Any attempt to modify these gives rise to compile time error.
- The keyword **const** can also be used while declaring formal arguments of functions. This is particularly useful when we need to pass arrays and structures to functions and we do not want them to be modified within the function.
- The keyword **volatile** is used to indicate that a variable can be changed even by some external agency (some other program or even the operating system) in addition to the program in which it is enclosed.
- Trigraph sequences offer an alternative way of supporting some characters even though some keyboards do not support them. These are a new ANSI addition. Each trigraph sequence consists of two question marks followed by another character supported by the keyboard.
- The clock() can be used to measure the time taken by a program or a function.

REVIEW QUESTIONS

18.1 Explain the procedure of dynamically creating a two-dimensional array.

18.2 Dynamically creating of a two-dimensional array of char type to store strings saves memory space usage. Justify.

18.3 How do you allocate memory for a three-dimensional array? Explain.

18.4 Explain the significance of variable length arguments to functions. Write a program to illustrate the concept.

18.5 Explain VA_LIST, VA_START, VA_ARG and VA_END.

18.6 Give an account of **const** and **volatile** keywords.

18.7 What is a generic pointer?

18.8 What is a self-referential structure?

18.9 What is a linked list?

18.10 What is the significance of trigraph sequences? List out all the trigraph sequences.

State whether the following are true or false

18.1 When a two-dimensional array is created dynamically, all the rows will be contiguous.

18.2 A function in C can take fixed number of arguments only.

18.3 scanf() and printf() are examples of functions which take variable number of arguments.

18.4 The Header file **stdarg.h** should be included while dealing with variable number of arguments.

18.5 Variables declared using the keyword **const** cannot be changed at all.

18.6 The variables declared with volatile can be changed even by external agencies.

18.7 The trigraph sequences are supported by on all keyboards.

INTERVIEW QUESTIONS

18.1 Can you dynamically create an array?

18.2 Can you create a 2-D array with different number of elements in each row?

18.3 Can we define functions to take variable number of arguments?

18.4 What is the use of a self-referential structure?

Appendix A

Mathematical Functions

Header file: **math.h**

Since the prototypes of the mathematical functions are made available in the header file math.h, the header file math.h has to be included as part of the source programs, which use these functions. The preprocessor directive #include <math.h> is used for this purpose.

Function prototype	Purpose
double cos(double x);	Takes an angle x (in radians) as the argument and returns the cosine value for the angle (in the range −1 to 1).
double sin(double x);	Takes an angle x (in radians) as the argument and returns the sine value for the angle (in the range −1 to 1).
double tan(double x);	Takes an angle x (in radians) as the argument and returns the tangent value for the angle.
double cosh(double x);	Takes an angle x (in radians) as the argument and returns the hyperbolic cosine value for the angle.
double sinh(double x);	Takes an angle x (in radians) as the argument and returns the hyperbolic sine value for the angle.
double tanh(double x);	Takes an angle x (in radians) as the argument and returns the hyperbolic tangent value for the angle.
double exp(double x);	Takes a value x of type double as its argument and returns its exponential function value e^x.

(Contd.)

(Contd.)

Function prototype	Purpose
`double log(double x);`	Takes a value x of type double as its argument and returns the natural logarithmic of the value.
`double log10(double x);`	Takes a value x of type double as its argument and returns the base 10 logarithm of the value.
`double pow(double x, double y);`	Takes two values x and y of type double as its arguments and returns the value of x raised to the power of y.
`double sqrt(double x);`	Takes a value x of type double as its argument and returns the square root of the value.
`double ceil(double x);`	Takes a value x of type double as its argument and returns the smallest integral value not less than x.
`double floor(double x);`	Takes a value x of type double as its argument and returns the largest integral value not greater than x.
`double fabs(double x);`	Takes a value x of type double as its argument and returns the absolute value of x.
`double acos(double x);`	Takes a cosine value x of type double as its argument and returns equivalent angle (in radians in the range 0 to π).
`double asin(double x);`	Takes a sine value x of type double as its argument and returns equivalent angle (in radians in the range $-\pi/2$ to $\pi/2$).
`double atan(double x);`	Takes a tangent value x of type double as its argument and returns equivalent angle (in radians in the range $-\pi/2$ to $\pi/2$).
`double fabs(double x);`	Takes a value x of type double as its argument and returns the absolute value of x.

Appendix B

Character Test Functions

Header file: **ctype.h**

Since the prototypes of the character test functions are made available in the header file ctype.h, the header file ctype.h has to be included as part of the source programs, which use these functions. The preprocessor directive #include <ctype.h> is used for this purpose.

Function prototype	Purpose
int isalpha(int c)	Takes a character as its argument and returns true if the character is an alphabetic letter (A to Z or a to z). Otherwise, false.
int isalnum(int c)	Takes a character as its argument and returns true if the character is an alphabetic letter or a digit (A to Z, a to z, 0 to 9). Otherwise, false.
int isdigit(int c)	Takes a character as its argument and returns true if the character is a digit (0 to 9). Otherwise, false.
int isxdigit(int c)	Takes a character as its argument and returns true if the character is an hexadecimal digit (0 to 9, A to F). Otherwise, false.
int islower(int c)	Takes a character as its argument and returns true if the character is a lower case letter (a to z). Otherwise, false.
int isupper(int c)	Takes a character as its argument and returns true if the character is an upper case letter (A to Z). Otherwise, false.
int isspace(int c)	Takes a character as its argument and returns true if the character is a space, form feed, newline, horizontal tab or vertical tab. Otherwise, false.

(Contd.)

(Contd.)

Function prototype	Purpose
`int ispunct(int c)`	Takes a character as its argument and returns true if the character is any punctuation character like ! " # % & ' ( ) ; < = >> ? [\ ] * + , - . / : ^ _ { | } ~ etc. Otherwise, false.
`int isctrl(int c)`	Takes a character as its argument and returns true if the character is a control character. Otherwise, false.
`int isprint(int c)`	Takes a character as its argument and returns true if the character is a printable character including space. Otherwise, false.
`int isgraph(int c)`	Takes a character as its argument and returns true if the character is a printable character excluding space. Otherwise, false.
`int toupper(int c)`	Takes a character as its argument and converts it to upper case if it was a lower case letter and returns the upper case letter. If the character was not a lower case letter, the character is returned unchanged.
`int tolower(int c)`	Takes a character as its argument and converts it to lower case if it was an upper case letter and returns the lower case letter. If the character was not an upper case letter, the character is returned unchanged.

Appendix C

String Manipulation Functions

Header file: **string.h**

Since the prototypes of the string manipulation functions are made available in the header file string.h, the header file string.h has to be included as part of the source programs, which use these functions. The preprocessor directive #include <string.h> is used for this purpose.

Function prototype	Purpose
`int strlen(char* s);`	Takes a string s as an argument and returns its length
`char* strcpy(char* trg, char* src);`	Takes two strings trg and src as its arguments, copies src to trg and returns trg. The size of trg is expected to be large enough to collect the string in src.
`char* strcat(char* trg, char* src);`	Takes two strings trg and src as its arguments, adds src to the end of trg and returns trg. The size of trg is expected to be large enough to collect the string in src in addition to its own.
`int strcmp(char* s1, char* s2);`	Takes two strings s1 and s2 as its arguments, compares them and returns the numerical value of the difference between the ASCII values of the first non-matching

(Contd.)

(Contd.)

Function prototype	Purpose
	pair of characters of the two strings. The value returned is +ve if s1 is lexicographically greater than s2. It is –ve if s1 is lexicographically less than s2. And the value returned is zero if s1 and s2 are same.
char* strncpy (char* trg, char* src, int n) ;	Takes two strings trg and src, and an integer n as its arguments, copies n characters of src to trg and returns trg. The size of trg is expected to be large enough to collect n chara-cters in src.
char* strncat (char* trg, char* src, int n) ;	Takes two strings trg and src, and an integer n as its arguments, adds n characters of src to the end of trg and returns trg. The size of trg is expected to be large enough to collect n characters in src in addition to its own contents.
int strcmpi (char* s1, char* s2) ;	Similar to strcmp (). But ignores case while comparing s1 and s2. That is, the strings "ABC" and "abc" are treated as same.
int strchr (char* s1, char c) ;	Takes a string s1 and a character c as its arguments, returns the pointer position of the first occurrence of c in the string s1. If the character is not found, the function returns NULL value.
char* strstr (char* s1, char* s2) ;	Takes two strings s1 and s2, and returns the pointer position of the first occurrence of the entire string s2 in s1. If s2 is not found in s1, it returns NULL.

Appendix D

File Manipulation Functions

Header file: **stdio.h**

Since the prototypes of the file manipulation functions and the definitions of NULL, stdin, stdout, stderr and FILE are made available in the header file stdio.h, the header file stdio.h has to be included as part of the source programs, which use these functions. The preprocessor directive #include<stdio.h> is used for this purpose.

Function prototype	Purpose
FILE* fopen (char file_name [] , char *mode) ;	Takes name of a file and mode of opening as its arguments and opens the file in the mode specified. Different modes of opening files are given below. The function returns a pointer to the file.
Mode of opening	**Purpose**
w	To create a text file. If the file already exists, its contents are destroyed, otherwise it is created, if possible.
r	To open a text file for reading, the file must exist.
a	To open a text file for appending (writing at the end); if the file does not exist, it is created, if possible.
w+	To create a text file for both reading and writing: if the file already exists, its contents are destroyed, otherwise it is created, if possible.
r+	To open a text file for both reading and writing, the file must exist.
a+	To open a text file for reading and appending: if the file already exists, its

(Contd.)

(Contd.)

Mode of opening	Purpose
	contents are retained; if the file does not exist, it is created if possible.
wb	To create a binary file: if the file already exists, its contents are destroyed, otherwise, it is created, if possible.
rb	To open a binary file for reading: the file must exist.
ab	To open a binary file for appending (writing at the end); if the file does not exist, it is created, if possible.
wb+	To create a binary file for both reading and writing; if the file already exists, its contents are destroyed, otherwise it is created, if possible.
rb+	To open a binary file for both reading and writing; the file must exist.
ab+	To open a binary file for reading and appending; if the file already exists, its contents are retained; if the file does not exist, it is created if possible.

Function prototype	Purpose
`int fclose(FILE *fp);`	Takes a file pointer `fp` as its argument and closes the file pointed to by it. The function returns 0 on success, EOF on its failure.
`int fgetc(FILE *fp);`	Takes a file pointer `fp` as its argument and returns a character read from the file pointed to by `fp`. The function returns the character after converting it to an integer.
`int fputc(char c, FILE *fp);`	Takes a character `c` and a file pointer `fp` as its arguments, and writes the character `c` onto the file pointed to by `fp`. On success, the function returns the character and on error, it returns EOF.
`int fputs(char *s, FILE *fp);`	Takes a string `s` and a file pointer `fp` as its arguments; writes the string `s` to the file pointed to by `fp`.

(Contd.)

(Contd.)

Function prototype	Purpose
`int fgets(char *s, int size, FILE *fp);`	Takes a string `s`, an integer `size` and a file pointer `fp` as its arguments; the function reads `size-1` characters or up to new line character, whichever comes first, from the file pointed to by `fp` and stores it in the string `s`.
`int fscanf(FILE *fp, "control string", arguments);`	Similar to `scanf()`, but reads mixed types of data from the file pointed to by `fp` into the arguments specified. The function returns the number of fields successfully read, converted according to the corresponding format specifier and stored in the arguments.
`int fprintf(FILE *fp, "control string", arguments);`	Similar to `printf()`, but writes mixed types of data stored in the `arguments` to the file pointed to by `fp`. On success, the function returns the number of bytes written to the file and on failure, it returns `EOF`.
`int fwrite(char *buffer, int size, int count, FILE *fp);`	Writes equal-sized data items stored in the `buffer` to the file pointed to by `fp`. On success, the function returns the value of `count` and on failure, a short count.
`int fread(char *buffer, int size, int count, FILE *fp);`	Reads equal-sized data items stored into the `buffer` from the file pointed to by `fp`.

(Contd.)

(Contd.)

Function prototype	Purpose
	On success, the function returns the value of count and on failure, a short count.
`int fseek (FILE *fp, int offset, int Position);`	Moves file pointer to the byte number offset from the given position in the file pointed to by fp. The third parameter position can take one of the following three values 0, 1 and 2. The meanings of the values are given in the following table.

Position	Symbolic constants	Meaning
0	SEEK_SET	Beginning of file
1	SEEK_CUR	Current position of file
2	SEEK_END	End of file

Function prototype	Purpose
`void rewind (FILE *fp);`	Takes a pointer to FILE type fp as its argument and repositions the file pointer to the beginning of the file pointed to by fp.
`long ftell (FILE *fp);`	Takes a pointer to FILE type fp as its argument and returns the current position of file pointer in the file pointed to by fp.
`int fflush (FILE *fp);`	Flushes the buffered data to the file pointed to by fp.

Appendix E

Utility Functions

Header file: **stdlib.h**

Since the prototypes of the utility functions are made available in the header file stdlib.h. The header file stdlib.h has to be included as part of the source programs, which use these functions. The preprocessor directive #include <stdlib.h> is used for this purpose.

Function prototype	Purpose
`void abort();`	Terminates a process abnormally.
`int abs(int x);`	Takes an integer value x and return its absolute value.
`long labs(long x);`	Takes a long value x and return its absolute value.
`double atof(char *s);`	Takes a string s as its argument and return its double equivalent. If the conversion is not possible, it returns 0.
`int atoi(char *s);`	Takes a string s as its argument and return its integer equivalent. If the conversion is not possible, it returns 0.

(Contd.)

(Cont.)

Function prototype	Purpose
`long atol (char*s);`	Takes a string s as its argument and returns its long integer equivalent. If the conversion is not possible, it returns 0.
`char* itoa (int i, char* s, int radix);`	Takes an integer i, a string s and an integer radix as its arguments; converts the integer i into a string collected by s radix specifies the base being used while converting.
`void*calloc (unsigned no_of_items, unsigned size);`	Allocates size * no_of_items bytes in the memory heap and returns a pointer to the block of memory.
`void*malloc (unsigned size);`	Allocates size bytes in the memory heap and returns a pointer to the block of memory.
`void* realloc (void*ptr, unsigned size);`	Adjusts the previously allocated block pointed to by ptr to size bytes and moves the data to new location, if necessary.
`void free (void*ptr);`	Takes a pointer to a block of memory as its argument and releases the memory block.

Multiple Choice Questions

1. The inventor of C language is _____.
   - (a) Blaise Pascal
   - (b) Dennis M Ritchie
   - (c) Kernighan
   - (d) Charles Babbage

2. The operating system with which C language has close association is_____.
   - (a) DOS
   - (b) Windows
   - (c) UNIX
   - (d) None of these

3. C is a successor of _____ language.
   - (a) BCPL
   - (b) Fortran
   - (c) Pascal
   - (d) None of these

4. Which of the following best describes C language?
   - (a) It is a general purpose programming language
   - (b) Portability
   - (c) Rich with its library functions
   - (d) All of the above

5. _____ statement is used declare constants in C.
   - (a) `#include`
   - (b) `#define`
   - (c) Declaration
   - (d) Assignment

6. Which of the following is not a basic data type in C?
   - (a) `float`
   - (b) `int`
   - (c) `char`
   - (d) `string`

7. The float data types have _____ digits of precision.
   - (a) 6
   - (b) 8
   - (c) 14
   - (d) 4

8. The `short int` takes _____ bytes of memory.
   (a) 2 or 4   (b) Exactly 2
   (c) Exactly 4   (d) 1

9. Which of the following is not a modifier for `int`?
   (a) `short`   (b) `unsigned`
   (c) `long`   (d) `double`

10. The double data type takes _____ bytes of memory.
    (a) 4   (b) 6
    (c) 8   (d) 10

11. Range of unsigned `char` is _____.
    (a) −128 to +127   (b) 0 to 255
    (c) −255 to 255   (d) None of these

12. The `short int` data can be displayed using _____ format character.
    (a) `%d`   (b) `%sd`
    (c) `%ld`   (d) None of these

13. #define is a _____.
    (a) Preprocessor directive   (b) Compiler directive
    (c) Both (a) and (b)   (d) Neither (a) nor (b)

14. Range of signed `char` is _____.
    (a) −128 to +127   (b) 0 to 255
    (c) −255 to 255   (d) None of these

15. Which of the following is a modifier of `char` type?
    (a) Unsigned   (b) Short
    (c) Long   (d) None of these

16. If a = 10 and b = 20 then the value of c in the expression `c = ++a + b++ + 10` is
    (a) 41   (b) 42
    (c) 40   (d) 43

17. The `int` data type takes _____ bytes.
    (a) 2 or 4   (b) Exactly 2
    (c) Exactly 4   (d) Unpredictable

18. The prototype of round() is available in _____.
    (a) `<stdio.h>`   (b) `<string.h>`
    (c) `<math.h>`   (d) `<conio.h>`

19. The double data type takes _____ bytes of memory with precision of _____ digits.
    (a) 8 and 6   (b) 8 and 14
    (c) 4 and 14   (d) 4 and 6

20. The operator with least priority is _____.
    (a) Assignment   (b) Comma
    (c) Bitwise   (d) Indirection

21. The value of 10% 16 is _____.
- (a) 10
- (b) 16
- (c) Cannot be determined
- (d) 6

22. The operator used to evaluate related expression is _____.
- (a) Comma
- (b) Relational
- (c) Bitwise
- (d) Assignment

23. The highest precedence relational operator is
- (a) ==
- (b) >=
- (c) !=
- (d) None of these

24. The value of –10% –3 is
- (a) –1
- (b) 1
- (c) % operator does not work with –ve numbers
- (d) % unpredictable

25. The lowest precedence arithmetic operator is _____.
- (a) Binary +
- (b) %
- (c) *
- (d) /

26. Which of the following is a unary operator?
- (a) ++
- (b) !
- (c) =
- (d) Both (a) and (b)

27. The operator to find a^b is
- (a) ^
- (b) **
- (c) No such operator
- (d) None of these

28. The highest precedence logical operator is _____.
- (a) &
- (b) !
- (c) ||
- (d) All are equal

29. The printf() is a _____.
- (a) Output statement
- (b) Output function
- (c) Input statement
- (d) Input function

30. Multi-word string reading function in C is
- (a) gets()
- (b) get()
- (c) scanf()
- (d) scan()

31. What is the value of A in the expression if x = 10, y = 20? A = (x<y) || (++x < y)
- (a) 10
- (b) 11
- (c) 1
- (d) Cannot be determined

32. What is the value of z in the expression if x = 10, y = 20? z = (x<y) && (++x < y)?
- (a) 10
- (b) 11
- (c) 1
- (d) Cannot be determined

33. The range of int in the 16-bit word length machine is
    (a) –32767 to +32767   (b) –32768 to +32767
    (c) –32768 to +32768   (d) –32765 to +32765

34. The format character for printing long integer variable's value is
    (a) %ld   (b) %d
    (c) %Ld   (d) None of these

35. The value of x in the expression (a = 10, b = 5); x = a++ * ++b%7 is
    (a) 4   (b) 3
    (c) 60   (d) None of these

36. In the expression x = (++a > --b)?(10): (20), the value of x if a = 3, b = 5 is
    (a) 10   (b) 20
    (c) Cannot be predicted   (d) None of these

37. How many times the body of the loop is executed?

```
for(i = 1;  i < 5;  i++)
{
    for( j = 5;  j >= 1;  j--)
{
    x = I + j;
}
}
```

    (a) 20   (b) 25
    (c) 15   (d) 24

38. Which of the following is a pretested loop?
    (a) do while   (b) for
    (c) while   (d) Both (b) and (c)

39. If a is an array declared as long int with base address = 1000 then the address of a[3] is
    (a) 1004   (b) 1008
    (c) 1012   (d) 1003

40. Which of the following is a structured data type in C?
    (a) Array   (b) Double
    (c) Long int   (d) Int

41. If a = 32767 then a++ prints
    (a) –32767   (b) 32768
    (c) Junk number   (d) None of these

42. If a =–32767 then –a prints
    (a) –32768   (b) –32766
    (c) 32767   (d) None of these

43. Bitwise operator to turn on a specific bit is
    (a) OR (|)   (b) AND (&)
    (c) Exclusive OR (^)   (d) Shift left (<<)

44. Shift left by one bit is equal to

(a) Multiplication by 2   (b) Division by 2
(c) Multiplication by 1   (d) None of these

45. The operator whose associativity is right to left is

(a) +   (b) ++
(c) &   (d) |

46. The final value of i in the following statement is

```
for (i = -5;  i <= 6;  i++)
{
Statement-1;

}
```

(a) 6   (b) 7
(c) 5   (d) None of these

47. The macro NULL is defined in the header file

(a) <stdio.h>   (b) <stdlib.h>
(c) <stdio.h> and <stddef.h>   (d) None of these

48. Structure member can be accessed using _____ operator with pointer.

(a) &   (b) Arrow (->)
(c) Period (.)   (d) None of these

49. The library function used to find the last occurrence of a character in a string is

(a) strstr();   (b) strnstr();
(c) lastchr();   (d) strlastchr();

50. The printf() function to print \n character is

(a) printf("\\n");   (b) printf("\n");
(c) printf(""\n"");   (d) None of these

51. The library function to allocate memory dynamically is

(a) malloc()   (b) calloc()
(c) free()   (d) Both (a) and (b)

52. An invalid identifier in C is

(a) Float   (b) Int
(c) int_float   (d) None of these

53. Which of the following operator does not work with float operands?

(a) +   (b) %
(c) *   (d) None of these

54. The library functions are linked to _____ program.

(a) Source program   (b) Object program
(c) Header file   (d) None of these

55. Which of the following is not a token?
    (a) Identifier
    (b) Constants
    (c) Operators
    (d) Control structure

56. The output of the statement 10<20>5 is
    (a) Non-zero
    (b) Zero
    (c) Invalid usage
    (d) None of these

57. The output of

```
#define x 3+2
int main()
{
        int i;
        i = x * x * x;
        printf("%d",i);
    return 0;
}
```
    (a) 3 + 2 * 3 + 2 * 3 + 2
    (b) 125
    (c) Compile error
    (d) None of these

58. In automatic type conversion, short and char are converted to
    (a) int
    (b) float
    (c) unsigned int
    (d) No such conversion

59. In C, explicit type conversion is also known as
    (a) Casting
    (b) Type modification
    (c) Type change
    (d) None of these

60. Which of the following could be a legal operation on pointers?
    (a) Adding two pointers
    (b) Substracting one pointer from another pointer
    (c) Multiplication of two pointers
    (d) Division of one pointer by another pointer.

61. The function to read a single character from a file is
    (a) getchar()
    (b) getc()
    (c) scanf()
    (d) getch()

62. The function to read a single integer from a file is
    (a) getw()
    (b) scanf()
    (c) geti()
    (d) None of these

63. The main advantage of structured programming is
    (a) Easy testing
    (b) Modification is easy
    (c) Sharing of functions
    (d) All of these

64. The file related function to determine the file pointer position is
    (a) rewind()
    (b) fseek()
    (c) ftell()
    (d) fget()

65. Which of the following is not true about logical OR operator?
(a) It is a binary operator
(b) The second expression is not evaluated if the first expression is true
(c) The expression is evaluated if the first expression is true
(d) All are true

66. The file access mode w+
(a) Erases the content of the file if it exists
(b) Writes operation continues from the previous position
(c) Truncates the file size to 0
(d) Both (a) and (c)

67. The output of the following macro is

```
#define MULT(a,b) a*b
int main()
{
    int x = 5,y = 8;
    printf("%d", MULT (x + 4, y - 3));
    return 0;
}
```
(a) 45   (b) 34
(c) None of these   (d) Run time error

68. Output of the printf() statement is

```
int main()
{

    int a[5]={2, 4, 6, 8, 10};

    printf("%d", (&a[3]-&a[1]));
    return 0;
}
```
(a) Garbage value   (b) 3
(c) 2   (d) 4

69. The statement *p++
(a) Increments the content of the memory location pointed by p
(b) Increments the pointer and prints the content of the location
(c) Invalid operation on pointer
(d) None of these

70. The output of the following program is (Assume a = 2, b =1)
switch(a+b)

```
{
    case 1: printf("one\n");
    case 2: printf("Two\n");
    case 3: printf("Three\n");
```

```
case 4: printf ("Four\n");
case 5: printf ("Five\n");
}
```
(a) Three   (b) Four
(c) Three and four   (d) Three, four and five

71. The output of the following program is

```
#include<stdio.h>
int main()
{
    extern int x;
    x=10;
    printf("%d %d",x, sizeof(x));
    return 0;
}
```
(a) 10 2   (b) 10 1
(c) Error as x is undeclared   (d) Cannot predict

72. Which of the following categories of operators have the higher precedence?
(a) Arithmetic   (b) Logical
(c) Relational   (d) All are equal

73. The main drawback of union is
(a) All the members cannot be accessed simultaneously
(b) Increases the wastage of memory
(c) Members of a union cannot be another union
(d) None of these

74. If a union with three fields a, b and c of float, char and double type then the memory allocated to any union variable is
(a) 8   (b) 4
(c) 13   (d) None of these

75. In a structure with three fields a, b and c of float, char and double type then the memory allocated to any union variable is
(a) 8   (b) 4
(c) 13   (d) None of these

76. Which of the following is not true about #define statement?
(a) It is a macro   (b) It is a preprocessor directive
(c) It should not end with semicolon (d) None of these

77. The value of final will be

```
#include<stdio.h>
int main()
{
    inti=-5, j=10, k=0, Final;
        Final = ++i + ++j || ++k;
```

```
    printf("%d, %d, %d, %d\n", i, j, k, Final);
    return 0;
}
```
(a) 6 11 0 17   (b) 6 11 1 17
(c) 6 11 0 1   (d) None of these

78. The output of the following program will be

```
#include<stdio.h>
int main()
{
    int i = -5,  j = 10,   k = 0, final;
    final = ++I && ++j || ++k;
    printf("%d, %d, %d, %d\n", i,  j,  k, final);
    return 0;
}
```
(a) 6 11 1 1   (b) 6 11 0 1
(c) Cannot be predicted   (d) None of these

79. Number of significant characters in an identifier is
(a) 8   (b) 15
(c) 18   (d) 31

80. The backslash character constant for producing audible alert is
(a) `'\b'`   (b) `'\s'`
(c) `'\a'`   (d) `'\v'`

81. The backslash character constant vertical tab is
(a) `'\vt'`   (b) `'\Vt'`
(c) `'\v'`   (d) `'\f'`

82. Which one of the following is an invalid constant?
(a) "19.26"   (b) +100
(c) 'W'   (d) None of these

83. If A = 12, B = 15, then the value of X in the following expression
X = (A%5!=0)?(++A++ + b++) : (--A + --B); is
(a) 28   (b) 29
(c) 26   (d) None of these

84. The default precision for real number is
(a) 4   (b) 6
(c) 14   (d) 8

85. Switch statement can be realized in terms of
(a) `nested if`   (b) `if else ladder`
(c) `break` and `continue`   (d) None of these

86. We can print a string without any format specification character using _____ function.
(a) `scanf()`   (b) `gets()`
(c) `fscanf()`   (d) Both (b) and (c)

87. The duration in which a particular variable remains in memory during execution is called
_____.
(a) Scope   (b) Visibility
(c) Persistence   (d) Lifetime

88. Which of the following is not true about bit fields?
(a) It is not possible to take their address   (b) They cannot be arrayed
(c) We can use pointer to access bit fields   (d) Both (b) and (c)

89. If p1 and p2 are two properly initialized pointer for the variables x and y (Assume x = 5, y = 5) then the value of ++(*p1) - *p2 is
(a) 1   (b) 2
(c) 0   (d) None of these

90. To update a file we must open the file in _____ mode.
(a) r   (b) w
(c) a   (d) None of these

91. Bitwise operators are not applicable for
(a) char   (b) float
(c) short int   (d) None of these

92. The function to determine the position of file pointer is
(a) size(f)   (b) ftell()
(c) fseek()   (d) fpos()

93. Scope of macro is always
(a) Global   (b) Local
(c) Can be either local or global   (d) Depends on the storage class

94. Header file which contains the details of malloc() and free() function is
(a) stdio.h   (b) dynamic.h
(c) stdlib.h   (d) alloc.h

95. Operator which helps in determining whether a given number is even or odd is
(a) Bitwise OR   (b) Bitwise EX-OR
(c) Bitwise AND   (d) Complement

96. The output of the following program is
```
int main()
{
    int a = 50, b = 3;
    if (a < 10)
        a = a + 5;
        b = b - 5;
    printf("%d %d", a, b);
    return 0;
}
```
(a) 50 –2   (b) 55 –2
(c) 50 3   (d) None of these

97. The way of calling a function by passing the address of a variable is
    (a) Call by value
    (b) Call by address
    (c) Call by reference
    (d) Call by pointer

98. The way of calling a function by passing the name of the actual argument is
    (a) Call by value
    (b) Call by reference
    (c) Call by name
    (d) Call by pointer

99. Default data type of the value returned by a C function is
    (a) `int`
    (b) `float`
    (c) `char`
    (d) `void`

100. Storage class where the variable is initialized only once is
    (a) Auto
    (b) Extern
    (c) Static
    (d) Register

101. Storage class with least longetivity is
    (a) Extern
    (b) Auto
    (c) Register
    (d) None of these

102. Prototyping is a type of
    (a) Declaration
    (b) Initialization
    (c) Definition
    (d) Calling a function

103. A variable which is initialized when a function is called and destroyed when the function is quit is
    (a) Register
    (b) Static
    (c) Extern
    (d) Auto

104. Function has the following advantages except
    (a) Re-usability
    (b) Minimizing testing time
    (c) Minimizing programming time
    (d) Minimizing programming errors

105. A technique of calling a function repeatedly by itself is called
    (a) Recursion
    (b) Nesting of function
    (c) Prototyping
    (d) None of these

106. If p is a pointer to an `int` array a with base address = 4000 then *(p + 3) gives
    (a) Address of a[3];
    (b) Content of a[3];
    (c) p holds the address 4003
    (d) None of these

107. If p is a pointer to an `int` array a with base address = 400 then increment pointer
    (a) Increases the address by 1
    (b) Increases the address by 2
    (c) New address cannot be determined
    (d) None of these

108. If a function is called by value then change to the formal argument
    (a) Changes the actual argument
    (b) Has no effect on actual argument
    (c) Creates new actual argument
    (d) Neither (a) nor (b)

109. Reading and writing from standard I/O device is
    (a) Console I/O
    (b) File I/O
    (c) Standard I/O
    (d) Formatted I/O

110. Recursive function's main drawback is
   (a) Increased over head
   (b) Increased complexity
   (c) Reduced portability
   (d) None of these

111. Consider the following program.
```
int   main(void)
{
    int a, *b=a;
    printf("%d%d", sizeof(a), sizeof(p));
    return 0;
}
```
The output will be
   (a) 2 2
   (b) 4 2
   (c) 4 4
   (d) 2 4

112. The ASCII value for "space" is
   (a) 65
   (b) 48
   (c) 32
   (d) 97

113. Semicolon in C programming language is called _____.
   (a) Line separator
   (b) Statement separator
   (c) Operator
   (d) None of these

114. _____ are used as single line comment and multiple line comments in C programming language respectively.
   (a) # and %...%
   (b) /*...*/
   (c) @ and /.../
   (d) & and $...$

115. What is the value of A, after the execution of statement A*=A+A; in C programming language? (Hint: A = 5)
   (a) 15
   (b) 30
   (c) 50
   (d) 25

116. The string function used to find the substring from a main string is
   (a) substr( )
   (b) strsub( )
   (c) string( )
   (d) strstr( )

117. The parameters passed in a function call in a main C program are called_____.
   (a) Actual parameters
   (b) Formal parameters
   (c) Parameters
   (d) None of these

118. Eliminate the odd one out from the following.
   (a) auto
   (b) register
   (c) var
   (d) static

119. Which one of the following is not a decision making statement?
   (a) continue
   (b) if
   (c) if-then-else
   (d) switch

120. The format specifier for the "double" data type is
   (a) %f
   (b) %lf
   (c) %d
   (d) %ld

121. What is the output of the following statements?

```
{
    int a = 10, b = 5;
    c = a + b;
    printf("Sum=%d", c);
}
```

    (a) 15   (b) 10
    (c) Syntax error   (d) Sum=%d

122. The function `open( )` in C programming comes under _____ header file.
    (a) `io.h`   (b) `stdio.h`
    (c) `console.h`   (d) `string.h`

123. The C function which copies text from memory to output screen is
    (a) `display()`   (b) `print()`
    (c) `puttext()`   (d) `gettext()`

124. Which of the following is a user defined data type in C programming language?
    (a) `enum`   (b) `int`
    (c) `float`   (d) `char`

125. The n-dimensional array can be represented in memory as
    (a) 1 n-dimensional array   (b) n 1-dimensional array
    (c) (n − 1) 1-dimensional array   (d) 2 n-dimensional array

126. While saving a file in C program, the maximum number of characters accommodated in a filename is
    (a) 8   (b) 16
    (c) 2   (d) 0

127. The character set of a C programming language is from _____ code.
    (a) EBCDIC   (b) Unicode
    (c) ASCII   (d) BCD

128. The function used to copy a string from source to destination is
    (a) `copy()`   (b) `strcpy()`
    (c) `stringcopy()`   (d) `cpystr()`

129. The format specifier used to display the address of a variable is
    (a) `%d`   (b) `%s`
    (c) `%a`   (d) `%u`

130. Which of the following statement is not true?
    (a) All the arithmatic operators have the same precedence
    (b) Arithmetic operators have higher precedence than relational operators
    (c) Associativity of + operator is left to right
    (d) C does not have any operator for computing a^b

131. Defining a new data type which is equivalent to an existing type can be done using
    (a) Type casting   (b) `typedef`
    (c) `enum`   (d) Either (a) or (b)

132. Signed decimal integer can be displayed using _____ conversion character.
    (a) %sd   (b) %d
    (c) %i   (d) %c

133. When an existing file is opened in w mode,
    (a) Content of the file will be deleted
    (b) Error occurs in opening a file
    (c) The content of the file will be retained and the file pointer points to the beginning of the file
    (d) The content of the file will be retained and the file pointer points to the end of the file

134. Which of the following is true?
    (i) It is erroneous to use sizeof(constant)
    (ii) free() is used to release the memory allocated dynamically
        (a) Only (i)   (b) Only (ii)
        (c) Both (i) and (ii)   (d) Neither (i) nor (ii)

135. In memory allocation, local variables are stored in
    (a) Stack   (b) Heap
    (c) Either stack or heap   (d) None of these

136. Which of the following is an incorrect variable name?
    (a) Emp.Name   (b) Emp_Name
    (c) EmpName1   (d) Emp1Name

137. Output of the following program is
```
int main(void)
{
    float m = 65.1234567;
    double n = 5.543235343;
    printf("m = %f\t,   n = %lf\t",   m, n);
    return 0;
}
```
    (a) m = 65.123456   n = 5.543235   (b) m = 65.1234567   n = 5.543235343
    (c) m = 65.123457   n = 5.543235   (d) m = 65.123456   n = 5.543235

138. Output of the following statement is int x = 10 printf ("%d", ++x%22)
    (a) 10   (b) 9
    (c) 11   (d) 5

139. Output of the following program is
```
int main(void)
{
    int i = 10;
    for(;;)
    {
            if( (++I * 2 ) % 7 == 0)
                break;
```

```
    }
    printf("%d", i);
    return 0;
}
```

(a) 12   (b) 10
(c) 14   (d) 6

140. Output of the following program is

```
int main(void)
{
    Int i = 0, count = 0;
    while(i <= 10)
    {
            if(i % 2 == 0)
                continue;
            else
                count = count + 1;
            i++;
    }
    printf("%d", count);
    return 0;
}
```

(a) 10   (b) 5
(c) 9   (d) 11

141. Which of the following is correct for a variable 'stringabc' of type string?
   (a) scanf("% s", stringabc);   (b) scanf("% c", &stringabc);
   (c) scanf("% s", &stringabc);   (d) scanf("% c", stringabc);

142. Which of the following header files should be included while using character handling functions?
   (a) <stdio.h>   (b) <string.h>
   (c) <ctype.h>   (d) <character.h>

143. Which of the following statements is not true with respect to functions in C?
   (a) The list of parameters should be separated by commas in the function header
   (b) The parameter names used in function definition should be same as that of the function prototype declaration
   (c) The void should be used as return type when the function is not returning any value
   (d) The returning value should match against the return type specified in the function definition

144. The variables whose scope extends to entire program, are called
   (a) Global   (b) Local
   (c) Internal   (d) Floating

145. Default return type of functions is
   (a) float   (b) char
   (c) int   (d) void

146. Default value initialized for integer variables inside structure definition is
(a) 1   (b) NULL
(c) −1   (d) 0

147. Consider the following extract of a C program.
```
int *p,  x;
p = &x;
p++;
```
What is the value of p, if p =100 before execution?
(a) 102   (b) 100
(c) 104   (d) 101

148. What is the output of the following program?
```
int main(void)
{
    int a[5] = { 1,2,3,4,5}, *p, *q;
    p = &a; q = &a; q++;
    printf("%d", *q+*(p++));
    return 0;
}
```
(a) 4   (b) 3
(c) 2   (d) 5

149. The statement fopen("mydata", "r+") opens the file 'mydata' for
(a) Only reading   (b) Only writing
(c) Both reading and writing   (d) None of the above

150. Which of the following is not a file related function
(a) ftell()   (b) rewind
(c) seek()   (d) fseek()

Answers to Multiple Choice Questions

S. No.	Answer	S. No.	Answer	S. No.	Answer
1	b	11	b	21	a
2	c	12	a	22	a
3	a	13	a	23	b
4	d	14	a	24	a
5	b	15	a	25	a
6	d	16	a	26	d
7	a	17	a	27	c
8	b	18	c	28	b
9	d	19	b	29	b
10	c	20	b	30	a

S. No.	Answer	S. No.	Answer	S. No.	Answer
31	c	64	c	97	c
32	b	65	c	98	a
33	b	66	b	99	a
34	a	67	b	100	c
35	c	68	b	101	b
36	b	69	b	102	a
37	a	70	d	103	d
38	d	71	d	104	d
39	c	72	a	105	a
40	a	73	a	106	b
41	a	74	a	107	b
42	a	75	c	108	b
43	a	76	d	109	a
44	a	77	a	110	a
45	b	78	a	111	a
46	b	79	d	112	c
47	c	80	c	113	b
48	b	81	c	114	b
49	d	82	b	115	b
50	a	83	c	116	a
51	d	84	b	117	a
52	d	85	b	118	c
53	b	86	b	119	a
54	b	87	d	120	b
55	d	88	c	121	c
56	a	89	a	122	b
57	d	90	c	123	c
58	a	91	b	124	a
59	a	92	b	125	b
60	b	93	a	126	a
61	b	94	c	127	c
62	a	95	c	128	b
63	d	96	a	129	d

S. No.	Answer	S. No.	Answer	S. No.	Answer
130	a	137	a	144	a
131	b	138	c	145	c
132	b	139	c	146	d
133	a	140	b	147	a
134	c	141	a	148	d
135	a	142	c	149	c
136	a	143	b	150	c

Solution to Interview Questions

Chapter 1

1.1 One or more inputs, at least one output, Unambiguity of each step, Finite number of steps, Each step taking finite amount of time are the characteristics of an algorithm

1.2 Sequence, selection and repetition are the characteristics of structured programming methodology

1.3 Pseudocode to find the largest and the second largest of three integers

```
Algorithm LarSecLar(a, b, c)
l = a
if ( b>l)
l = b
if ( c > l)
l = c

s = a
if ( b>s)
s = b
if ( c > s)
s = c

sl = (a + b + c) - (l + s)
return (l, sl)
End Algorithm
```

1.4 Pseudocode to find whether an integer is an Armstrong number or not (An integer is said to be an Armstrong number if the sum of the cubes of the individual digits is equal to the integer itself. Example. $153 = 1^3 + 5^3 + 3^3$)

```
Algorithm Armstrong(n)
n1 = n
s = 0
while (n > 0)
        r = n % 10
        s = s + r * r * r
        n = n / 10
EndWhile

if ( s == n1)
        return true
else
        return false
End Algorithm
```

Pseudocode to find whether an integer is palindrome or not

```
Algorithm Palindrome(n)
n1 = n
rev = 0
While(n > 0)
    r = n % 10
    rev = rev * 10 + r
    n = n / 10
EndWhile
if ( n1 == rev)
    return true
else
    return false
End Algorithm
```

Chapter 2

2.1 Advantages of machine level language are:
(a) Execution is fast as it is in machine understandable form
(b) No need for any translators

2.2 Once the program is translated into machine language, the program can be executed any number of times with different inputs without translation.

2.3 Syntax errors are detected by the compiler while the logical errors have to be detected by the programmer himself. Syntax errors occur if the instructions in a program are not correct as per the grammar of the language.

2.4 An algorithm is an ordered sequence of instructions written by a user illustrating the procedure for solving a particular problem. It can not be directly executed by the computer. A program is nothing but an algorithm with the required data structures suitable for the computer to solve a problem expressed in a programming language.

2.5 Both compilers and interpreters are translators for converting high level language programs into machine language equivalents. In the case of interpreters, the programs are translated into machine language equivalents line by line and executed as well. While a compiler first translates the source programs into machine language equivalents completely and then the execution begins. In case of compiler, once the program is completely translated into machine code, program can be executed any number of times without translation. In case of interpreter, each time during execution translation of the program takes place on a line by line basis.

2.6 A compiler that runs on one computer and produces the machine code for some other machine.

2.7 Fast execution and no need for translation every time a program is executed.

2.8 C, PASCAL, C++ are compiler-based high level languages.

2.9 The memory requirement is less for interpreter and since the translation of source program to machine language takes place instruction; by instruction, debugging of the program is easy in case of an interpreter.

2.10 Visual Basic, Basic, MATLAB.

2.11 Definitely yes and such a compiler is known as a cross-compiler.

2.12 Logical errors are more difficult to detect than the syntax errors and have to be detected by the programmer himself.

2.13 Dbase, FoxPro, Perl, Python, etc.

2.14 Natural languages are the communication links between two human beings, while computer languages are the links between a human being and a computer.

Chapter 3

3.1 This is due to the fact that the code for UNIX operating system has been written almost entirely in C language.

3.2 Yes, because C language is suitable for both scientific and commercial applications. Language like COBOL was designed exclusively for commercial applications and FORTRAN for scientific applications.

3.3 Once a source program is compiled into machine code, the compiler is no longer required and the object code can be executed any number of times without the source program.

3.4 C language contains the features of high level language such as operators, looping statements and also low level features such as bitwise operators for manipulating data at bit or binary level. Due to the availability of features of both high level language and machine language, C is considered as a middle level language.

3.5 Some of the major characteristics of structured programming are:
   (a) Non-usage of goto statement
   (b) Single entry and exit construct
   (c) Modularity
Since C language supports all the above characteristics, it is a structured oriented language.

3.6 If an `int` variable takes 16 bits, then binary equivalent of 5 in 16-bit representation is 0000000000000101. First eight bits of data from right side, i.e. 00000101 will be stored in the leftmost byte from right to left side and rest seven bit of data bit, i.e. 0000000 will be stored in rightmost byte from right to left side. The middle bit represents the sign bit as shown below.

0	0	0	0	0	1	0	1	0	0	0	0	0	0	0	0
Lower order bits								Sign bit	Higher order bits						

3.7 In a 16-bit representation of a binary number, the first 8 bits from the right are called higher order byte and the last 8 bits from the right are called lower order byte.

3.8 Assignment of `double` variable to `float` variable results in rounding of digits as `float` support 6 digits of precision and double can support 14 digits of precision.

3.9 Assignment of `long int` variable to int variable results in truncation of higher order digits in the number. Example: If a is a `long int` variable with value 123456789 and b is an `int` variable then the statement b = a results in b = 6789

3.10 Using `%o` and `%x` format specifier in the `printf()` function.

3.11 Error: Multiple declaration for a.

3.12 (c) `double` (As double is a keyword)

3.13 (a) 16 20

(b) 97 a

(c) 98 b

(d) 49 1

3.14 6 (It display the length of the string "printf")

3.15 (a) Since a is declared with `const` qualifier, a cannot be assigned a value using the assignment operator.

(b) Since a is declared with const qualifier its value cannot be changed using assignment operator

3.16 In `printf()` function, the control string must be enclosed with double quotes not with single quotes. Semicolon is missing at the end of `printf()` function.

3.17 No syntax error.

3.18 Using format specifier `%d` only.

Chapter 4

4.1 (a) 0 (Here an integer number is displayed using `%f` format specifier)

2.35 (If the width specified is less than the number of digits in the number, width specified is ignored)

2.3 (Integer part of the number is displayed within a width of 5 places right justified)

2.35

2.3456000 (If the number of digits in the fractional part is less than the specified width unused places are filled with 0's)

(b) 6790 (Since the specified width is less than the number of digits in the number, specified width is ignored)

006790 (Since the specified width is more than the number of digits in the number, extra places are filled with zeros and the number is displayed right justified)

6790 (Same as %6d but the number is displayed left justified and unused places are filled with blanks)

(c) 67.91(Number is displayed within a field width of 7 positions with 2 digits in the fractional part and it is rounded off)

67.906700 (Default display format with 6 digits of precision)

67.9

(d) 10 (Since the first digit in the number is 0, the number is treated as octal constant)

(e) 0.00000 (An integer number is displayed with float format)

0

45.240002

4.2 (a)

4.3 (d)

4.4 No. %c is used to print a single character, and due to the non-termination of the NULL character, some junk characters may print.

4.5 The compiler prints the error 'multiple declaration for a'.

4.6 Since both function name and variable name are considered as identifiers, the compiler prints the message duplicate identifier.

Chapter 5

5.1 (a) 13 12 11. This is due to the associativity of operator. ++ operator has right to left associativity. Hence the rightmost a++ is executed first, then the last but one and finally the first statement is executed

(b) 10 5 8 1. Here the two relational expressions are connected by means of logical OR operator. In an OR operator, if the first relational expression is true (non-zero) then the second expression is not evaluated.

(c) 10 5 8 0. Here the first relational expression is false (zero).

(d) 5 10. Here the two variables are swapped using comma operator.

(e) 11 5 9 1. Here the two relational expression are connected by means of logical OR operator. Since the first relational expression is false (zero), the second expression is also evaluated.

(f) 0. Here the variables are connected by mean of relational operator. The expression looks like $1 < 2 > 3$. This is equivalent to $(1 < 2) > 3$. Since the first expression is true the equation becomes $1 > 3$ which is false and hence 0 is assigned to x.

(g) 2 2 3 0. Here the two relational operators are connected by logical AND operator. In case of AND operator, if the first relational expression is false (zero) then the second relational expression is not evaluated.

(h) 1 2 3 0.

(i) Here in the expression x = a &5 | 7, first bitwise AND of 10 and 5 is evaluated which is equal to 0 followed by bitwise OR of 0 and 7 is performed.

```
int a = 8, b = 4, c = 5, x
    x = b*c + a*b +(a > b? a:b);
```

(j) Here the expression is evaluated as follows x = 4*5 + 8*4 + (8 > 4? 8:4). In case of ternary operator, if the value of the expression is true then the value of the first expression is assigned otherwise, the value of the second expression is assigned. Hence, the equation become x = 4*5 + 8*4 + 8 = 60.

(k) Here the expression become b = 4 + 6 + 3 * (4 > 3? 8:3) = 4 + 6 + 3*8 as the value of the conditional expression is 8. Hence, the output will 34.

(l) 1. In C, character constant is converted to its integer code before evaluation. Hence, the expression is evaluated as c = 116 && 115 || 70 = 1 && 115 = 1. In case of && operator, if the two operands are non-zero, then the result is 1. In case of || operator, if one of the operand is non-zero, the result is 1.

(m) 9 –1 5 9

(n) 46

(o) 0. In C, if both the numerator and denominator are integers, then the fractional part in the quotient is truncated.

(p) 1. Here first, the arithmetic operators are applied before the relational operators as the precedence of arithmetic operators is higher than the relational operators. Hence the expression is evaluated as c = 4 < 16 since 4 < 16 is true, 1 is assigned to c.

(q) 0. Here the first relational expression is zero and the second one is non-zero and the conditional operator used is logical AND the final result is 0.

(r) 16 18

(s) 26 20. Here in the first expression, a is incremented twice and hence a = 12. In the second expression, the variable a is pre-incremented and hence it becomes 13 and value of c in the second expression is 20.

(t) 7 6 5. This is due to right to left associativity of ++ operator and the usage of ++ as a postfix operator. After the first `printf()` is evaluated a's value will be 8.
10 9 9 output of second `printf()` is

(u) 6 7 8

(v) 5 10
10 5. This is another way of swapping two numbers using bitwise exclusive OR operator.

(w) 20. Shift right a number by two bits is equivalent to multiplication by 4.
1. (Shift right a number of two bits is equivalent to integer division by 4.

5.2 >, >=, <, <=
5.3 Comma operator.
5.4 Bitwise AND (&).
5.5 Bitwise OR (|).
5.6 For manipulation of data at bit level makes C language suitable for low level programming.
5.7 By shifting right the number by 1 bit.
5.8 By shifting left the number by 2 bits.

Chapter 6

6.1 (a) False. Here x < 0.5 is false as the value of the x is equal to 0.5 and hence the statement after else is executed.

(b) Good Evening. Since `t==0` is true, the statement `printf("Good")` while there are two statements after else statement. Unless the statements are enclosed within a pair of parentheses only, the first statement after else is skipped while the second statement `printf("Evening")` is executed irrespective of the whether the if condition is true or false.

(c) C is confusing. In C, the statement if (x) means if (x is non-zero). Since the value of x is equal to 0, the statement after else is executed.

(d) Since x = 4 and y = 2, the statement x % y results in 0 (Remainder of 4 % 2). Since the value of the expression x % y matches with 0, case 0 is true. Due to the absence of break statement at the end of each of block of case statements, the statements associated with remaining case is also executed and hence the output will be

Zero One Two More Than Two

6.2
```
printf("Enter three numbers : ") ;
scanf("%d %d %d", &x, &y, &z) ;
large = a > b ? (a > c ? a : c) : (b > c ? b : c) ;
printf("\nThe biggest number is : %d", large) ;
```

6.3 `a++, a = a + 1, a += 1;`

6.4
```
#include<stdio.h>
int main(void)
{
        int i, j, n;

        printf("Enter the limit\n");
        scanf("%d", &n);

        for (i = 1; i <= n; i++)
          {
                if (i % 2 == 1)
                        j = i;
        else
                j = -i;
        printf("%d\t", j);
        }
        return 0;
}
```

6.5
```
#include<stdio.h>
#include<math.h>
int main(void)
{
        int i, y, n;

        printf("Enter the limit\n");
        scanf("%d", &n);
```

```
for (i = 1; i <= n; i++)
{
        y = pow(i, i);
        printf("%d\t", y);
}
return 0;
}
```

6.6 Type-1(Bitwise)   Type-2 (Comma)   Type-3(Arithmetic)

```
a = a ^ b;          t = a, a = b, b = t;       a = a + b;
b = a ^ b;                                     b = a - b;
a = a ^ b;                                     a = a - b;
```

Chapter 7

7.1 (a) Here in the first `while` loop starting with an initial value of 0, each time a condition is checked and then x is incremented and hence the while loop is executed 6 times. When the first while loop is exited, x value will be 6 and in the second while loop, each time it checks the condition and then x is incremented. The second `while` loop is executed only 3 times and hence the output will be

c programming
c programming
c programming
c programming
c programming
c programming
programming in c
programming in c
programming in c

(b) Here the initial value of x = 0 and each time in `while` loop, the condition x==0 is checked. Since the condition is always true, the first `while` loop is executed infinite number of times. The second `while` loop is not at all executed. Hence, the string

"c programming" is printed infinite number of times

(c) Here x = 012 which is in octal system and hence its decimal equivalent is 10. The `for` loop is executed from 0 to 10 in step 3 and hence different values i are 0, 3, 6 and 9. The output will be

0   3   9

(d) 3   1
    4   0

(e) Here, since the `for` loop is terminated with a semicolon, the statement following the `for` loop is not executed each time through the loop. The loop is simply executed by incrementing the loop control variable I each time till the condition for the termination of the loop is satisfied. Here the `for` loop is terminated once I value become 6. Hence, the `printf()` function following the `for` loop is executed only once.

The output will be 6

(f) This program prints the integer from 125 to 0 along with the ASCII code associated with the integer.

(g) Here the loop is executed infinitely till the stack overflows.

(h) Here the initial value of i and j is equal to 2. In the while loop, the condition while (--i&&j++) is checked with the values 1 and 2 as I is pre-incremented and j is post incremented. After checking the condition, the first printf() function is executed and print the values 1 and 3. After this, the condition in the while loop is checked with the values 0 for i. Since the value of I is zero (false), the value of j is not incremented at all. Hence, the while loop is skipped and the second printf() is executed with the values

0 3

(i) Here the while loop is executed till t1 and t2 both become 10. Hence, the output will be

10 10

7.2 A pre-tested loop is one in which the minimum number of times the loop is executed is 0. That means the body of the loop is not executed even once if the condition is false for the first time itself.

Example:

```
for (i = 10; i >= 0; i++)
    {
            printf("For loop\n");
    }
    printf("%d\n", i);
```

Here the string "for loop" is not printed even once as the condition is false in the beginning itself.

Chapter 8

8.1 main() is a user defined function. The reason why main() is considered as a user defined function is that every programmer needs to define the main() function in his program and the prototype of the main() function is not available in any header file.

(a) 10
   10

Here the function is called by value and whenever a function is called by value, any changes to formal arguments insider the function definition have no effect on the actual arguments. Hence, the value of actual argument x in the main() function remains unaltered.

(b) 10 20
   10 20

Here the values of the formal arguments are swapped inside the function but has no effect on the actual arguments (call by value).

(c) 1   2
    2   3
    3   4
    4   5
    5   6

In this program, the function Funct () is called with the value of actual argument i. The value of the actual argument is copied to the formal argument j in the function Funct (). But since j is declared with the storage class static, j is initialized only once.

(d) 6

(e) 6

(f) Here each time the function is called, the same value is returned as the formal argument is pre-incremented.

8.3 The function is called infinitely or till the stack memory overflows. The size of the stack memory varies from machine to a machine.

8.4 No such restriction.

Chapter 9

9.1 (a) This program finds the cumulative sum of array elements starting from the last element of the array, i.e. first a [4] is added to the variable s so that the value of s will be 5, next time it add a [3], i.e. 4 to s so that the value of s will be 9 and so on till a [0] is added to s. Hence the output will be

        4   5
        3   9
        2   12
        1   14
        0   15

(b) In this program, an array a of size 5 is initialized with the values 1 and 2. Hence, a [0] = 1, a [1] = 2, all the remaining elements are automatically initialized to 0 so that elements of the array will be {1, 2, 0, 0, 0}. The program determines the sum of all the elements in the array by adding the elements one by one to the variable s. The output will be

        0   1
        1   3
        2   3
        3   3
        4   3

(c) In this program, the body of the for loop contains only the statement s = s + a [i] while the printf () function is executed after the termination of the for loop. Here the condition is false in the beginning itself and hence the statement s = s + a [i] is not executed even once and hence the output will be

        0   0

(d) Here the declaration statement a [4] [4] initialized all the elements of the first row to 1, all the elements of the second row to 2 and all the elements of the third row to 3 while all the elements of the fourth row is by default initialized to 0 and hence the matrix becomes

1	1	1	1
2	2	2	2
3	3	3	3
0	0	0	0

The program adds all the elements of the array and the sum is stored in the variable s. Output will be

24

(e) In C, array name itself acts as a pointer. The program prints the array elements starting from s [1] as ++s takes the pointer to the second element of the array and hence the output will be

4

5

6

(f) Here the statement s [2] ++ takes the value of s [2] which is equal to 5 as it is post incremented and similarly --s [3] decrements the pointer so that it points to s [2] again is equal to 5 and add them together and hence the output will be

10

9.2 Some garbage value will be printed.

9.3 Here in the first statement i = ++a [0] becomes i = 4 as a [0] is equal to 3. In the statement j = a [4] ++ first the value of a [4], i.e. 15 is assigned to j after that a [4] becomes 16. In the third statement k = a [i++] since the present value of i, is equal to 4 the content of a [4], i.e. 16 is assigned to k and i is incremented to 5. Hence, the output will be

5   15   16

9.4 Address of a [0] in case of one-dimensional array and the address of a [0] [0] in case of two-dimensional array is called base address. In general, the address of first element of the array is called base address.

9.5 Suppose a is an array then base address and the corresponding value in the base address can be printed as:

```
printf("%u %d\n", a, a);
```

9.6 No, C language does not have the flexibility for changing the array size dynamically.

9.7 In this example, we are printing the value of first row-zero the column of the second dimension where each dimension of order 2 × 3. Hence, element of second dimension will be

6   4   13

15   50   100

The value of a [1] [0] [2] will be 15.

9.8 Here the array named `Test` of size 10 is initialized as `Test[10]` = {10}. Here only `Test[0]` is initialized with 10 while the remaining nine locations are initialized to 0 by default. Hence the output will be

       0   0

9.9 Provides a way of storing logically of related data items by a single name.

9.10 The following example show different ways of initializing two-dimensional array.

```
int a[3][3] = {0, 0, 0, 1, 1, 1, 2, 2, 2}
int a[3][3] = {{0}, {1}. {2}};
int a[3][3] = {{0, 0, 0}, {1, 1, 1}, {2, 2, 2}};
```

Chapter 10

10.1 (a) `Output:` **GOD**

Here the output will be the string "GOD" followed by a set of junk characters. The reason being, NULL character is not explicitly appended as the last character of the string.

(b) `Output:` 1 2

Here x is declared as a character variable and hence in case of `sizeof(x)`, size of the character variable is printed which is equal to 1 byte. In case of `sizeof('A')`, the character constant `'A'` is converted into integer type and returns the size of `int` data type which is equal to 2 bytes.

(c) `Output:` `Computer`

Here the fifth character of the string variable is assigned the value ' (' without altering the remaining content of the variable.

(d) `Output:` `ScienceDepartment`

In the above example, first the innermost `strcpy(s,t)` is executed so that the string "Science" available in the variable t is copied to the string variable t resulting in overwriting of the original content of the string variable s. Now the string s contains "Science". Next the function `strcat()` function is executed so that the content of the string variable p which is "Department" is concatenated to the string variable s resulting in s = "ScienceDepartment"

10.2 Here in the declaration char s[5] = { 'A', 'B', 'C', 'D','\0' }, the character array s is initialized with individual characters which require the NULL character to be specified explicitly and hence the string variable s becomes "ABCD".

In the second declaration char s[5] = "ABCD", NULL character is automatically appended as the last character of the string

10.3 A character array is an array of character while a string is an array of character terminated with a NULL character

10.4
```
#include<stdio.h>
int main(void)
{
   char s[10];
   printf("Enter a string\n");
```

```
    gets(s);
    n=strlen(s);
    for (i=n-1; i>=0; i--)
    s1[n-i-1]=s[i];

    s1[n]='\0';
    printf("%s", s1);
    return 0;
}
```

10.5 If a string is printed with `%c` format specifier, it prints a NULL character `while` a string printed with `%s` prints the actual string and hence the output will be

`@Computer Science`

10.6 `strcmp()` compares two strings and returns 0 if the two strings given as argument are same. It returns –1 if the second string appears alphabetically first than the first string. It returns +1 if the first string appears alphabetically first than the second string. The function `strncomp()` compares the first n characters of the two strings to be compared.

Chapter 11

11.1 Yes. It is possible to define a union inside a structure.
11.2 C does not provide any relational operator to compare two structure variables. But two structures can be compared by comparing their members individually.
11.3 A structure can be passed as a function argument just like any other variable. When a structure is passed as an argument, each member of the structure is copied.
11.4 To initialize a union, initialize the first member only.
11.5 (a) 10   0.00000   10
   (b) 2   4   4   4
       In a union, the size of the union variable will be equal to size of the largest member.
   (c) Here each union variable takes 4 bytes as the size of the member with largest size is 4 bytes and there are four such union variables.
   (d) 40 bytes. In a structure, the size of the structure variable is equal to the sum of the sizes of the data type of individual members. In this case, the size of the structure variable is the sum of 3 members whose size is 2 bytes, 4 bytes and 4 bytes respectively. Hence the total size of each structures variable is 10 bytes and there are 4 such structure variables.
11.6 It is used to create another name to an existing data `type`.

Chapter 12

12.1 (a) `Output:   0`

   Here both the pointers ap and bp point to the first element of the array. The expression ap-bp gives the value zero.

(b) Output: 1 7
Here the pointer ap points to a[0] = 1 and bp points to a[3] = 7

(c) Output:
65524   5
65526   5
Here in the first printf() function, ptr and *ptr print the address of the memory location pointed to by ptr and the content of the memory location pointed to by ptr. Since ptr is a pointer to the variable C, *ptr prints the value of C. In the statement ptr++, the pointer is incremented depending on the data type of the variable for which ptr is a pointer. Since ptr is a pointer to an int variable, ptr++ increments the value of ptr by 2 bytes.

(d) Output: 3   3   6
Here p is a pointer to the array A. In the printf() function, *A prints the value of A[0] which is equal to 3. *(p++) prints the value of the memory location pointed by and the pointer is incremented. Hence *(p++) prints the value of A[0] only. *(p+1) takes p to the next element from the beginning and prints the value which is 6.

(e) Output: 12
Here ++(**r) increments the content of the memory location pointed by r. Initially r points to a[0] = 5. Hence ++(**r) results in 6. r is pointer to p which is a pointer to a. Hence, the statement ++(**r) + (*p) gives 6 + 6 = 12.

(f) Output: 27
Here y is a pointer to the variable x whose value is equal to 3. Z is a pointer to y. Hence to access the value of x, we can either use *y or **z. *y and **z holds the content of the memory location reserved for the variable x and hence the statement x**y***z is nothing but x*x*x = 27.

(g) Output: 30   20
This example is to illustrate call by reference and call by value. Here during the function call of change(), we are passing two arguments, &a and b. Whenever a function is called with the address of the variable, the formal argument in the function definition must be a pointer (call by reference). In call by reference, any changes to formal argument actually change the value of actual argument also. In the function definition, the content of the pointer variable is multiplied by 3 hence it becomes 30. In call by value, any change to the value of formal argument has no effect on the actual argument. Hence, any change to the variable q has no effect on the variable b.

(h) Output: 2   2   2   2
Here we are printing the size of the pointer variable. All the pointer variables take same amount of the memory.

12.2 Far, near and huge pointers are the different variations of a pointer variable available on 16-bit compilers like Turbo C++ 3.0 or Borland C++ 3.0. They depend on the memory model of compilation and linking.

A near pointer is of 2 bytes wide and it holds only the address of the offset.

A far pointer is of 32-bits wide and hold both 16-bit segment and 16-bit offset addresses. It can point to any segment and can point to any offset within the segment.

Huge pointers are similar to far pointer in the sense that they are also 4 bytes long. The difference between far pointer and huge pointer is that in case of far pointer, the compiler rounds off the offset to zero after the offset reaches the value 0Xffff and in case of huge pointer, it increments the segment value after reaching 0Xffff. Huge pointer are more flexible compared to far pointer.

12.3 `*p++` takes the content of the pointer `p` and then the pointer is incremented to the next memory location while `++*P` increments the content of the pointer variable `p`.

Example: If `p` is a pointer variable to array A with base address 1000 and values 0, 8, 9 and 10 then `*p++` takes `p` to the memory location 1002. `++*p` gives 1.

12.4 `(*(*(X+i)+j)+k)`

12.5 `const char *p` – means `p` is a pointer to a constant character. That means it is not possible to change the value pointed by `p`, but you can change the pointer `p` itself.

`char const *p` means `p` is pointer to a constant char, i.e. you cannot change the content of the location pointed by `p` but we can change the pointer itself to point to some other `char` variable.

12.6 It results in better utilization of memory. In a two-dimensional array of characters for every string, same amount of memory is allocated irrespective of length of the string. In case of pointer to a characters string, the memory allocated to a string depends on the number of characters in the string.

12.7 Void pointer is a special type of pointer. It is a generic pointer which can be made to point to data of any type.

12.8 Whenever an object is deleted, without appropriately modifying the pointer, then the pointer still points to the memory location previously it was pointing to. Such a pointer is generally referred to as a dangling pointer.

12.9 1004. Because whenever a pointer is incremented, its value is incremented by the number of bytes depending on the data type of the variable it is pointing to.

12.10 Arrow operator or * operator

(*Example:* If `p` is a pointer to a structure variable `x` with two members `x` and `y`, we can access `x` and `y` either `p->x, p->y` or `(*p).x, (*p).y`

Chapter 13

13.1 A text file contains sequences of ASCII characters organized into lines. Each line in a text file is terminated with new line character. It is easy to edit a text file.

13.2 Binary files are more efficient in terms of memory usage and faster access compared to text files.

13.3 A file can be truncated if it is opened in output mode.

13.4 (a) `Output: -1 because EOF is predefined with an integer constant -1.`

(b) Nothing is printed because to read the content of the file, it must be opened in read mode. But here the file is opened in write mode.

13.5 To determine the size of the file in terms of number of bytes, first take the file pointer to the end of the file using `fseek()` function as

`fseek(fp, 0L, SEEK_END);`

and then use the function `ftell()` to determine the file pointer position which in turn gives the file size

`n = ftell(fp);`

13.6 No. It is not possible to close all multiple files using single `fclose()` function

13.7 FILE pointer is a special pointer defined in the standard library `<stdio.h>`. It has been defined as `struct` type.

13.8 The five standard streams in C are:
(a) Standard input (`stdin`)
(b) Standard output (`stdout`)
(c) Standard error (`stderr`)
(d) Standard auxiliary (`stdaux`)
(e) Standard printer (`stdprn`)

13.9 Redirection is the process of accepting output from a file and send it as input to another file or a program.

13.10 The output of a program can be redirected to a file instead of console output as shown below.

`Programfile>newfile`

13.11 `*pointername`

Chapter 14

14.1 Preprocessor directives are processed by preprocessor before it is passed onto the compiler while compiler directives are directly translated by the compiler. To differentiate these two type of directives, compiler directives are terminated with a semicolon while the pre-processor directives are not terminated with semicolon.

14.2 Increase in the execution speed and overhead time of calling a function is avoided.

14.3 (a) 50. Here the macro is translated as $3 + 4 + 5 * 3 + 4 + 5 * 3 + 4 + 5 = 3 + 4 + 15 + 4 + 15 + 4 + 5 = 50$
(b) `abcepqrjkl`
(c) 55

14.4 In case of `"stdio.h"`, desired header file is searched in the current working directory and in case of `<stdio.h>`, it looks for the desired header file in all the default locations.

14.5 Using the macro _DATE_ and _TIME_ e.g., `printf("Today's date = 5s\n", _DATE_)L printf("Time = %s\n", _TIME_);`

14.6 To stop header file from being included multiple times, `<include>` guards are used. Detail regarding the usage of header guards can be found by opening the file `stdio.h`.

14.7 Scope of the macro is the whole source program starting from the definition of a macro

Chapter 15

15.1 To mask the specific bit in a number perform bit AND of the number with specific bit to be masked. This operation sets off the corresponding bit.

Example: To mask the last bit of the number 1001 perform

$$1001\&1000 = 1000$$

Similarly, we mask the specific bit by performing bitwise OR of the number with specific bit to be masked. This operation turns on the specific bit.

Example: $1001|1001 = 1001$

15.2 Bitwise AND (&) can be used to check whether a given number is even or not

15.3 Using bitwise Ex-OR operator as shown below.

```
a = a ^ b;
b = a ^ b;
a = a ^ b;
```

15.4 (a) 3. Because shift right a number by 1-bit is equivalent to integer division by 2.

(b) 16. Because shift left a number by 2-bit is equivalent to multiplication by 2.

(c) 3. Here a = 5 = 0101 and b = 6 = 0110

$$0101^\wedge 0110 = 0011 = 3$$

In case of bitwise exclusive OR operator if both the bits in the two numbers are same, it gives 0 and gives 1 if the two bits are different.

(d) −11.

15.5 `int` and `char`;

Chapter 16

16.1 Higher memory requirement and slower rate of data manipulation.

16.2 When a circle is scaled in only one direction then its shape is deformed. It will not be the magnified version of the original circle.

16.3 It is a type of application software that helps in creating customized sequence of text and pictures for presenting information to the target audience attractively.

16.4 Every point in a two-dimensional image is called pixel while every point in a three-dimensional image is called voxel.

16.5 `outtext()` function displays text at current position using current font, color and direction. `outtextxy()` displays text at specified position using current font, color and direction.

Chapter 17

17.1 No. The binary search works on only sorted lists.

17.2 No. Since linear search does not require the input list to be in the sorted order, for an unsorted list linear search can be preferred. If the search operation is to be repeated, the list can be sorted and binary search can be used.

17.3 In the case of exchange sort, the number of times of the swapping operation is more when compared to selection sort. However, the number of comparison operations will remain the same.

17.4 Merge sort requires extra memory space to keep a copy of the input list. Whereas quick sort does not require to maintain the extra copy of the input list.

Chapter 18

18.1 Yes. We can create arrays dynamically.

18.2 Yes. We can create a 2-D array with different number of elements in each row.

18.3 Yes. We can define our own functions also to take variable number of arguments.

18.4 A self-referential structure is used to describe the structure of a node in linked lists.

Glossary

Actual arguments: Actual arguments are those which are specified in the function call.

Algorithm: An algorithm is a step by step procedure to solve a given problem. It is characterized by the properties of unambiguity and finite number of steps.

Alphabet: The set of all permissible symbols in a language is referred to as its alphabet.

Application software: An application software is one which is written for the purpose of accomplishing some user-defined jobs like pay calculation, students' details maintenance, etc.

Array: It is a group of finite number of data items of similar type, stored in contiguous locations sharing a common name but distinguished by subscript values.

Assembler: It is system software, which converts assembly level language programs into the machine level language programs equivalent.

Associativity: It is a rule, which determines the order of evaluation if an arithmetic expression has more than one operator, which are at the same level.

Binary operator: A binary operator is one which is defined over two operands.

> *Example:* +, -, *, /, ||

Bit-field: It is a set of adjacent bits in a memory word.

Call by reference: It is the mechanism of calling a function by passing references (addresses) of variables belonging to its calling program.

Call by value: It is the mechanism of calling a function by passing merely the values.

Command line arguments: Command line arguments are the arguments provided by the command line and these arguments are taken by the main() of the C programs.

Compiler/Interpreter: It is a system program, which converts a higher level language program into its machine level language equivalent.

Constant: A constant is one the value of which does not change during the execution of the program enclosing it.

Dynamic memory allocation: It is the allocation of memory during runtime with the amount of memory to be allocated decidable while the program is being executed.

Enumerated data type: It enables us to assign symbolic names to integer constants.

Expression: An expression in C is a combination of variables or constants and operators conforming to the syntax rules of the language.

File: It is a named storage on the secondary storage devices. It represents a collection of related data.
>   *Example:* *Text file:* Text file consists of formatted data.
>   *Binary file:* Binary file consists of exact copies of contents in memory.

Formal arguments: Formal arguments are those which are specified in the function header while a function is defined.

`function:` It is a self-contained program written for the purpose of accomplishing some task. It is a named section of code.

Function call: It is the invocation of a function.

Function definition: It is the function header plus function body.

Function prototype: It is nothing but the declaration of a function for its return type and its arguments.

Global variable: A global variable is one, which is accessible by more than one function.

`goto statement:` It is an unconditional branching statement, which is used to transfer control from one part of a program to another.

Identifier: An identifier is one, which is used to designate program elements like variables, constants, array names, function names, etc.

Instruction: An instruction is a command to a computer to perform some operation. The operation can be arithmetic, logical or data movement operation.

Instruction set: The instruction set is a collective term, which refers to the collection of all the instructions supported by a computer. Each family of computers will have its own instruction set.

Keyword: A keyword is one, which has a predefined meaning assigned by the C language.

Lifetime: Lifetime of a variable is the duration for which the variable exists.

Local variable: A local variable is one, which is accessible by the function only in which it is declared.

`loop or iteration:` It refers to repeated execution of statements as long as some condition is true.

Memory leak: It is the phenomenon of allocating memory dynamically but not releasing it with the help of `free()`.

Object program: The machine code generated by a compiler is called object program.

Operator precedence: It is the relative priority of the operators, which determines the order of evaluation of an arithmetic expression and ensures that the expression produces only one value.

Pointer: It is a variable, which can collect the address of another variable or address of a block of memory.

Preprocessor: It is a program, which processes the source program (macro expansion, file inclusion, etc.) before it is compiled.

Program: A program is defined to be a set of instructions (statements) constructed in accordance with the grammatical rules of the underlying language.

Recursion: It is the phenomenon of a function calling itself. The function involved is called recursive function.

Scope: Scope of a variable is the area of the program in which it is accessible.

Self-referential structure: It is a structure containing pointer to itself as one of its members.

sizeof() operator: It is used to find the size of a variable or the size of a data type in terms of the number of bytes.

Source program: A program written in a higher level language is called a source program.

Static memory allocation: It is the allocation of memory during compile time with the amount of memory being fixed.

Structure: It is a group of finite number of data items, which may be of different types, stored in contiguous locations sharing a common name but distinguished by member names.

Structure template: It is a way of grouping logically related data items.

Structured design: Structured design is a design technique, the basic idea behind which is to divide a big program into number of relatively smaller programs so that managing the program becomes fairly easy.

switch statement: It is used to select one block of statements out of many blocks of statements, which are mutually exclusive.

Syntax: It is the set of grammatical rules of a language.

System software: A system software is one which is aware of the architectural details of the hardware components and can directly interact with the hardware components of computer systems.

Ternary operator: It is one which is defined over three operands.
   Example: ?:

Trigraph sequences: Trigraph sequences are groups of three characters first two of which are question mark (?) symbols which are followed by another character.

typedef: It is used to rename an existing data type.

Unary operator: It is one, which is defined over a single operand.
   Example: ++, — , !

Union: It is a collection of data items, which may be of different types and at any point of time, only one data item can be stored in it.

Variable: A variable is a named memory location, the value of which can change during the execution of the program enclosing it.

Index

1-D array, 214
3-D array, 241
#define, 445
#else, 458
#endif, 458
#error, 463
#ifdef, 458
#ifdef – #elif - #else - #endif, 459
#include, 445
#indef, 445
#pragma, 464
#undef, 458

Address, 358
Address of, 360
Advantages and disadvantages of algorithms, 6
Advantages and disadvantages of flow charts, 10
Advantages and disadvantages of pseudocode, 14
Advantages of functions, 173
Advantages of macros, 457
Alert character, 34
Algorithm, 1, 3, 17
   design, 2
Alloc.h, 399
Alphabet, 33
American National Standard Institute (ANSI), 26
Application software, 25
Arithmetic and relational operations on characters, 276
Arithmetic expression, 65, 67

Arithmetic operators, 65, 67
Array of bytes, 358
Array of pointers to strings, 375
Array of structures, 317
Arrays and functions, 246
Arrays and structures, 317
Arrays within structures, 325
Arrays within unions, 345
Assembler, 19, 22
Assembly level languages, 19
Assignment operator, 65, 66
Assignment statement, 30, 66
Associativity, 71
Attributes, 310
Automatic, 200
   conversion, 88
   storage class, 200
   type conversion, 87

Backspace, 34
Backward jumping, 129, 137
Basic Combined Programming Language, 25
Binary files, 421
Binary languages, 18
Binary operators, 65
Binary search, 528
Bit-fields, 468, 477
Bitwise AND (&), 469
Bitwise complement (~), 469, 471

Bitwise exclusive OR (^), 469, 470
Bitwise left shift (<<), 469, 470
Bitwise operators, 66, 468
Bitwise OR (|), 469
Bitwise right shift (>>), 469, 471
Boolean expression, 73
Break, 155
Bubble sort, 541, 543
Built-in functions, 174
Byte, 358

Call by reference, 382, 387
Call by value, 381, 387
Calling function, 175, 189
Calloc(), 399, 402, 563
Carriage return, 34
Char, 39
Character constants, 35, 38
Character set, 33
Circle symbol, 7
Classification of functions, 174
Coding, 2
Collective manipulation, 213
Command line arguments, 438
Comma operator, 85
Comments, 27
Compartmentalization, 174
Compiler, 20, 22
Compile-time errors, 33
Compiling the source program, 30
Composite objects, 27
Compound conditional expressions, 75
Compound statement, 100
Concatenation, 289
Conditional compilation directives, 444, 458
Conditional expression, 73, 99
Conditional operator, 66, 81, 82
Console I/O, 50
Const, 571
Constant, 35
Continue, 155, 157, 164
Control characters, 34
Control string, 51
Control variable, 138
Creating the source program, 30
Cross-assembler, 22

Dangling pointer, 408
Database languages, 21

Data processor, 49
Data types, 39
DBase, 21
Debugging, 2
Decimal integer constant, 36
Declaration of structure variables, 311
Declaration of three-dimensional arrays, 241
Declaration of two-dimensional arrays, 224
Decrement operator, 66, 79
Discriminant, 451, 452
Disk I/O, 50
Division by zero, 33
Documentation, 2
Double, 41
Do-while loop, 138, 150
Dynamic memory allocation, 398, 399

Else-block, 104
Else–if ladder, 103, 111, 119
Entity, 310
Entry-controlled, 139, 145
Enumerated data type, 345
Error handling, 435
Escape sequence characters, 52
Even or odd, 4
Evolution of programming languages, 17
Exchange sort, 532, 534
    method, 299
Executing the program to get the expected outputs, 30
Execution of AC program, 30
Exit(), 189
Exit-controlled, 150, 151
Exponential notation, 37
Expression, 65
Extensible, 26
Extern, 200
    storage class, 202
External variables, 199, 200

Factorial, 191
Fclose(), 413
Fgetc(), 413
Fgets(), 413, 415
Fibonacci series, 143, 195
File, 411
    I/O functions, 413
Files inclusion directives, 444, 445
First generation languages, 18
Float, 41

Flow charts, 1, 6
Flowlines, 7
Fopen(), 412
For, 12
Forcible conversion, 87
For loop, 138, 145
Formatting, 56
Form feed, 34
Forward jumping, 128
Fourth generation languages, 21
FoxPro, 21
Fprintf(), 413, 418
Fputc(), 413
Fputs(), 413, 415
Fractional notation, 37
Fread, 421
Fread(), 420, 421
Free(), 399
Fscanf(), 413, 418
Fseek(), 427
Ftell(), 427, 428
Function, 173
    body, 175
    header, 175
Functions returning a non-integer value, 186
Functions with arguments and no return value, 177
Functions with arguments and return value, 181
Functions with no arguments and no return value, 175
Functions with no arguments but with return value, 185
Fwrite, 421
Fwrite(), 420

Generic pointers, 571
Getchar(), 50, 271
Gets(), 272
Global variables, 28, 200, 202
Goto, 128, 138
Grammatical rules, 20
Graphics packages, 21

Header files, 27
Hexadecimal integer constant, 36
Higher degree of readability, 20
Higher level languages, 20
Horizontal tab, 34

Identifier, 35
Identity matrix, 371

If-block, 100, 104
If-else, 103, 104
Increment [++, —], 66, 79
Indexing, 291
Initialization of arrays of structures, 319
Initialization of a structure containing another s, 330
Initialization of one-dimensional arrays, 216
Initialization of structure variables, 313
Initialization of three-dimensional arrays, 243
Initialization of two-dimensional arrays, 225
Initializer-list, 216
Inner-if, 108
Inner-loop, 159
Input-output operations, 49
Insertion sort, 545, 548
Instruction executor, 201
Instruction set, 17
Int, 40
Integer constants, 35
Integer mode expression, 69
Internal variables, 199, 200
Interpreter, 20, 22
I/O functions, 413
Iteration, 10, 12, 136

Keywords, 34

Lack of readability, 18
Language, 17
Language of functions, 173
Largest of three numbers, 4
Leap year, 106
Lifetime of the variable, 199
Linear search, 525
Linear search method, 297
Linker errors, 33
Linking the program with the functions in the stan, 30
Local variables, 200
Logical AND, 75
Logical errors, 33
Logical expressions, 65
Logical NOT, 76
Logical operators, 66, 75
Logical OR, 75
Long double, 41
Long int, 40
Looping, 136
Lvalue, 364

Machine dependence, 18
Machine independence, 20, 21
Machine level languages, 18
Macros definition directives, 444, 445
Macros substitution, 446
Macros vs. functions, 455
Macros with arguments, 448
Maintenance, 2
Malloc(), 399, 563
Matrix, 223
Mean, 250
Member operator, 311
Memory, 358
Merge sort, 555, 557
Middle level language, 26
Mixed mode expression, 69, 70
Mnemonics, 19
Modularization, 174
Multidimensional arrays, 223
Multifile programs, 204

Natural numbers, 4, 146, 151
Nested if–else, 103, 108
Nested loops, 162
Nested switch statement, 127
Nesting of conditional operators, 82
Nesting of functions, 188
Nesting of loops, 158, 159
Nesting of macros, 453
New line, 34
New line character, 30
Non-procedural, 21
Null character, 268, 373
Numeric constants, 35

Object program, 20
Octal integer constant, 36
One-dimensional arrays, 214, 219, 563
One-dimensional arrays as arguments to functions, 246
Operands, 65
Operations on files, 411
Operations on structures, 315
Operator, 65
    precedence, 71
Outer-if, 108
Outer-loop, 159

Padding with 0s, 56
Palindrome, 281
Parallelogram symbol, 6
Passing 2-D arrays of char to functions, 303
Passing address of a structure variable, 335
Passing arrays of structures to functions, 337
Passing entire structure at once, 334
Passing members of a structure individually, 332
Passing structures to functions as arguments, 332
Passing three-dimensional arrays to functions, 257
Passing two-dimensional arrays to functions, 253
Pointer, 360
    arithmetic, 361, 563
    expressions, 363
    operators, 360
Pointers, 358
    and arrays, 364
    and functions, 381
    and strings, 373
    and two-dimensional arrays, 368
    as members of unions, 381
    to functions, 393
    to pointers, 397
    to structures, 377
    to unions, 380
    to pointer, 397
Portable, 26
Port I/O, 50
Post-tested, 150, 151
Power(), 198
Precedence of arithmetic operators and associativity, 70
Predefined functions, 26
Preprocessor directives, 444
Pre-tested, 139, 145
Prime, 183
Prime number, 5, 141
Printer out of paper, 33
Printf(), 29, 269
Problem analysis, 2
Problem definition, 1
Problem solving, 1, 17
Procedural, 21
    solution, 3
Processing one-dimensional arrays, 219
Processing two-dimensional arrays, 230
Product of two matrices, 237
Program, 17

Pseudocode, 1, 10
Putchar(), 50, 271
Puts(), 272

Quadratic equation, 451
Quick sort, 550, 552

Random accessing of files, 427
Real constants, 37
Realloc(), 399
Real mode expression, 69, 70
Rectangle, 3
Rectangle symbol, 6
Recursion, 191
Recursive function, 191
Register, 200
    storage class, 201
Relational expressions, 65, 73
Relational operators, 66, 73
Repeat-until, 12
Report generators, 21
Reserved words, 34
Resident assembler, 22
Returning a structure from a function, 338
Rewind(), 427, 428
Rhombus symbol, 6
Running out of memory, 33
Runtime errors, 33

Scanf(), 29, 51, 269
Scope of the variable, 199
Searching, 525
Second generation languages, 19
Selection, 10, 11, 99, 136
Selection sort, 536, 538
Self-referential structures, 572
Sequence, 10, 136
Sequential execution, 99
Shorthand arithmetic assignment operator, 66, 78
Short int, 40
Simple-if, 100, 103
Simple interest, 3
Simple statement, 100
Single-precision numbers, 41
Sizeof(), 84
Sorting, 532
Source program, 20

Sprintf(), 273
Sscanf(), 273
Stack overflow, 33
Standard deviation, 250
Standard library, 26
Static, 200
Static memory allocation, 399
Static storage class, 201, 314
Step-by-step procedure, 3
Stepwise refinement, 2
Storage classes, 199
Strcat(), 289, 388
Strcmp(), 286, 287, 388
Strcpy(), 390
Strcpy(), 285, 388
String, 268
String constant, 38, 268, 269
String.h, 283
Stringizing operator, 462
String manipulations, 282
Strings and functions, 302
String variable, 269
Strlen(), 283, 388
Strstr(), 291
Struct, 311
Structured design, 26, 173
Structured programming, 10
Structured query language, 21
Structure-pointer operator, 378
Structures and functions, 332
Structures within unions, 345
Structure template definition, 311
Structure within structure, 328
Sum of the digits of a number, 5
Sum of the first n natural numbers, 4
Sum of two matrices, 233
Swapping, 377
Switch statement, 119
Symbolic constants, 28
Symbolic names, 19
Symbolic words, 19
Symbols used in flow charts, 6
Syntactical errors, 33
System software, 25

Table of values, 223
Technical documentation, 2
Terminating condition, 191
Ternary operator, 65, 81

Testing, 2
Third generation languages, 20
Three-dimensional array, 241, 567
Toggling bits, 474
Token pasting operator ##, 462
Top-down approach, 173
Top-down design, 2
Trigraph Sequences, 575
Turbo C++/ borland C++ integrated development
    environment, 31
Turning bits off, 473
Turning bits on, 474
Two-dimensional array, 223, 563
Two-dimensional array of char type, 294
Type casting, 87
Type conversion, 86
Typedef, 349

Unary operators, 65
Under MS-DOS environment, 31
Under unix environment, 31

Union, 340
    within structures, 342
    template, 340
Unsigned char, 40
Unsigned int, 40
User-defined data type, 311
User-defined functions, 29, 174
User documentation, 2

Value at address, 360
Variable, 39
Variable length arguments to functions, 569
Variance, 250
Vertical tab, 34
Void, 41
Volatile, 571

While loop, 138
White spaces, 34
Wild pointers, 360